S0-ANN-424

# Get the Picture

Enjoy the show
That is life!

Brad Marchant

# Get the Picture

*Conscious Creation Goes to the Movies*

*Brent Marchant*

Moment Point Press
Needham, Massachusetts

Moment Point Press
PO Box 920287
Needham, MA 02492

Copyright © 2007 Brent Marchant
Author Photo Copyright © 2006 Jill Norton Photography

All rights reserved. This book may not be reproduced in whole or in part, stored in a retrieval system, or transmitted in any form or by any means, electronic, mechanical, or other, without written permission from the publisher, except by a reviewer, who may quote brief passages for review purposes.

**Library of Congress Cataloging-in-Publication Data**

Marchant, Brent
    Get the picture : conscious creation goes to the movies / Brent
    Marchant.
        p. cm.
    Includes bibliographical references and index.
    ISBN 978-1-930491-12-0 (pbk. : alk. paper)
    1. Motion pictures--Psychological aspects.  I. Title.
    PN1995.M274   2007
    791.4301'9--dc22            2007028961

Cover design: Kathryn Sky-Peck
Text design & Typesetting: Phillip Augusta
Printing: Transcontinental

First printing September 2007
ISBN 978-1-930491-12-0

Printed in Canada on acid-free, 100% recycled paper.
Distributed to the trade by Red Wheel Weiser.

10 9 8 7 6 5 4 3 2 1

*To my lifelong friend Mikey,*
*For sharing all those hours in the dark with me.*
*To my metaphysical mentor Linnaea,*
*For helping set me on the right path.*
*To my touchstone Karen,*
*For helping to keep me on the path (and authentic about it).*
*And to my parents Eileen and Dave,*
*wherever they may roam these days,*
*For making it all possible.*

# Contents

"Defending Your Life" ★ The Three Musketeers: "The Constant Gardener," "Syriana," and "Good Night, and 'Good Luck" ★ Bonus Features: "Romancing the Stone," "Fearless," "Sex, Lies and Videotape," "Blade Runner," "The China Syndrome," "JFK," "Casablanca," "The Front," "Hotel Rwanda," "Schindler's List," "To Kill a Mockingbird," "The Insider," and "The Burning Season"

# Introduction

## *Coming Attractions*

Welcome back my friends to the show that never ends
We're so glad you could attend
Come inside! Come inside!

Emerson, Lake and Palmer

Poet Muriel Rukeyser wrote that "the universe is made of stories, not of atoms."[1] I've always thought that a lovely sentiment, though, if it were ever proven true, there would be an awful lot of disappointed quantum physicists on the unemployment line.

Still, as dubious as some might find this claim, there must be something to it. After all, stories, especially meaningful ones, are often referred to as *universal*, a word that itself appears in the name of one of today's largest film and entertainment companies.

So much for the atoms.

Ever since childhood, I have been fascinated by stories and storytelling, but I wanted more than just to read or hear the words. Becoming fully engrossed *within* a story was what I truly craved. In seeking to attain this personal grail, I unwittingly found myself incredibly jealous of a most unlikely duo—the cheesy claymation characters Gumby and Pokey. They had the enviable ability to walk through a book's cover and right into a story, experiencing it as a firsthand, three-dimensional manifestation, the kind of direct immersion that I eagerly sought. But because I lacked their kind of interdimensional dexterity, I needed to find an acceptable alternative, and I did so—in the movies.

For me, the movies are the next best thing to walking into a story and wandering around in it as though in some kind of holographic wonderland. And, with ever-improving advances in cinematic technology, the experience has become that much more heightened over the years. We may not be able to duplicate the feats of the little clay man and his sidekick pony, but we're getting closer all the time.

Movies and I are old friends, going back almost as far as I can remember. One of the first films I saw that I recall vividly was the 1963 screwball comedy "It's a Mad Mad Mad Mad World." This big-budget, all-star-cast production from director Stanley Kramer was a manic, off-the-wall tour de force that left viewers with aching bellies after two-and-a-half hours of virtually non-stop laughs. Even so, there was nothing lightweight about the picture, despite it being a comedy. This madcap farce was meaty. It filled and shook the gut. It had *substance*, and it served to set my personal cinematic standard. From that point on, I always looked for movies that were substantive in nature, regardless of the genre, be they comedies, dramas, adventures, thrillers, sci-fi, or whatever. There would be no fluff or froth for me.

With age, my fascination with the movies continued to grow. I attended ever more of them and even began to write about them, first for my high school newspaper and then in college at Syracuse University as features and reviews editor for *The Daily Orange*. In later years, I also wrote occasional pieces about film for other publications and audiences. But even though the main focus of my writing life went in other directions, my love of motion pictures never wavered. And even though movies have changed a lot over the years, my standards for them have not; those expectations of substance have persisted to this day.

As I grew into adulthood, I began to develop a second fasci-nation, a budding interest in what I'll loosely term "alternative spirituality." My interest in this arose from a basic desire—to understand the world and my place in it, a need that I'm sure most of us can relate to on some level. My traditional Episcopalian upbringing provided few meaningful answers in this regard, ultimately proving to be a largely unsatisfying experience. Nevertheless, despite such religious dissatisfaction, I always had a strong, if vague, spiritual sense, a belief that there had to be *something* behind this thing we collectively call existence. But what was it? Clearly, I needed a catalyst of some kind to jump start my stalled spiritual engine. Ironically, that catalyst came to me at, of all places, the movies.

With the release of the first installment in the original "Star Wars" series in 1977, I became instantly and utterly captivated by the film's concept of "the Force," the mysterious unifying field of energy and consciousness that runs throughout the narrative's universe and connects all things within it. "*That*," I exclaimed upon my initial viewing, pointing at the screen and oblivious to the fact I'd dropped my Milk Duds, "is it! *That's* what I've been looking for!" It was one of those grand Aha! moments, the kind that happens rarely but satisfies so supremely. Now this is not to suggest that I suddenly began walking around worshipping Sir Alec Guinness or parroting the film's "May the Force be with you" mantra, but the movie's core metaphysical concept served as the necessary spark to ignite the fire of a much larger process that has continued to this day, the quest to fill my spiritual void with a spiritual vision.

With the flame lit, I began my search for answers in earnest. My journey brought me into contact with a diverse range of disciplines, including metaphysics, philosophy, psychology, and even cutting edge science. In the end, I settled on one that harmoniously combined them all—conscious creation. This philosophy and practice resonated with me profoundly, providing a set of principles and game plan with which to conduct my life. It gave me the kind of meaningful metaphysical substance I had long been looking for. In finding it, I felt as though I had come home, rediscovering an innate aspect of myself that I had somehow forgotten.

By the mid 1990s, a number of new movies were being made that addressed conscious creation and related subjects in both fictional and documentary formats. Naturally, I was quite pleased about this, for my two loves had become entwined. My enjoyment of substantive film merged with my interest in conscious creation to create a passion for movies with meaning. But, at roughly the same time, I discovered something else equally amazing: The seeds of these ideas had been present in many of the pictures I'd been watching all of my life. The films' creators may not have been consciously aware that they were delving into such themes, nor were the concepts always fully developed, yet the germ of those notions was present nevertheless. At that point, I began looking back at many of the movies I'd watched before with a new set of eyes, viewing them from a different perspective, seeing them as artfully cloaked couriers of profound, insightful messages.

Such is the odyssey that brought me to this book, this exploration into the meshing of my two most ardent pursuits, cinema and conscious creation. Its purpose is to serve as a guide to the films I consider most significant from a conscious creation perspective. So come join me in this adventure; I've saved you a seat.

★     ★     ★

Conscious creation principles have been around in various forms for a long time. The ancient art of alchemy, for instance, is one such example. More recently, the teachings found in movies such as "The Secret," with its law of attraction principles (see chapter 3), have put a contemporary spin on these ideas. But conscious creation received its most comprehensive treatment in the extensive and powerful writings of author and visionary Jane Roberts and her noncorporeal channeled entity, Seth.[2] This unique collaboration, aided by Roberts's husband Robert Butts, produced volume upon volume of material on the subject, exploring it in all its aspects. Their works, which I recommend highly, provided the foundation of my conscious creation education.

The most fundamental concept of conscious creation is the idea that you create your own reality in conjunction with the power of All That Is (or God, Goddess, Source, the Universe, the Force, or whatever other term best suits you). At the risk of gross understatement, this is a powerful notion. It's a highly liberating philosophy whose only real limitations are those we set for ourselves. And given the shortcomings of a restrictive theological upbringing, such as the one I experienced, it's easy to see why these teachings hold so much appeal.

The driving forces in conscious creation are our thoughts and beliefs. As they arise from the formless inner world where they originate, they fuse with the power of All That Is and take shape as physically manifested creations. Everything around us thus becomes an outward reflection of our inner views. It's a power we mostly take for granted (or are partially or wholly unaware of), but it's truly awesome when considering the results it produces and the potential it makes possible.

There are probably some who find that concept a little difficult to accept. Some of the skepticism probably arises from a misinterpretation of how the process works, and author Ehryck Gilmore offers an excellent analogy to explain this. Upon hearing a typical conscious creation statement like "thoughts become things," one might be tempted to think of it in terms of the *Bewitched* school of manifestation—a little twitch of the lips and the envisioned object spontaneously appears out of thin air, accompanied by the ring of a bell.[3] Now, it's possible that the process can sometimes proceed with astonishing speed, but since most of us have not yet developed the proficiency of a Samantha Stevens, there is generally a lag involved as the materialization unfolds, blossoming like the slowly opening petals of a fresh flower.

A more pragmatic view would be to think of the process this way: Look at how a building comes into being. It doesn't instantaneously spring forth into physical existence as a fully finished structure; it originates as *an idea*, a noncorporeal belief in the mind of the architect, that a physical construction can result from the assemblage of certain components to create a final product with particular aesthetic and functional attributes. This vision first manifests physically as drawings, then as a blueprint, then as a model, then as a construction site, and so on until the building itself is complete. No matter how one looks at it, the structure's point of origin—like anything else that becomes outwardly manifest—stems from the inner, nonphysical world. In the end, the originating thought truly does become the created thing.

The real trick in grasping this idea is to recognize (and remain aware) that it applies across the board, to *all* the elements that appear in our surroundings and in all of the events that transpire in our lives. Such is the inclusive and interconnected nature of conscious creation. Although this concept does take some getting used to, it's an aspect that I find especially appealing, particularly in light of my theological background. The religious practices with which I was raised were often treated like a component of life all unto itself, disconnected from all other elements of daily living. Going to church on Sunday was like getting one's weekly holy fix, an application of spiritual antiperspirant to safeguard against life's trials, tribulations, and embarrassing wetness till the following Sabbath. But I had considerable difficulty seeing how an arcane ritual performed one morning a week by officiators decked out in outfits that would make Liberace jealous related to how I lived my life on the other six days, especially because official explanations about its relevance offered little, if any, meaningful clarification. Conscious creation teachings, however, showed me how the spirit of our consciousness and the power of All That Is are infused into everything we encounter in life and in all of its (that is, our) wondrous creations. If nothing else, it took my relationship to the divine and made it practical.

In line with that, then, if you accept the notion that you create your own reality, it also means that you create all of the reality surrounding you. It's not a salad bar; you can't pick and choose which items you create and which ones "just happen." You can't take credit for the glorious rainbow or the beautiful sunset without also taking credit for the toxic waste dump. That's why it's so important to understand your thoughts and beliefs, for they continually create the world around you, even if you're not always consciously aware of what they are or how they become expressed.

This also sheds light on the inherent personal responsibility associated with conscious creation; one cannot sleepwalk through the process, take it lightly, or casually pawn off one's participation in it without running the risk of unwanted or unexpected results. (A number of cautionary tale films in this book help make that readily apparent.) But don't let this aspect of the process deter you. Conscious creation teachings are filled with guidance on how to navigate the sometimes choppy waters and rocky shoals of the practice. Ample lessons on helpful tools and coping mechanisms are available, many of which I cover in this book.

This is not to suggest that conscious creation is all work and no play, either; quite the contrary, in fact. Once the rudiments of the process are mastered, vistas for adventure and creative expression open at every turn. The possibilities and probabilities of existence endlessly evolve, literally in each moment, with limitless potential for taking us and our individual worlds in new and different directions, "a constant state of becoming," as it's often called. Through this process, we thus have an opportunity to experience rich and rewarding journeys of ever-present wonder, replete with countless avenues for exploration and fulfillment.

Kind of like the movies, wouldn't you say?

★     ★     ★

Those who know me well can attest that I often cite lines or scenes from movies to make a point. I frequently can be heard saying things like, "You know, that reminds me of a scene from (insert movie title here)," at which juncture I'll explain how the reference addresses my reasoning. As quirky or irritating as some may find this practice, I believe it's an effective means for illustrating ideas, because it provides a tangible example of the concept in question. That's particularly true where conscious creation is concerned, and that's the point of this book.

*Get the Picture* arose from an article I wrote some years ago for *Reality Change* magazine.[4] That article featured summaries of films that effectively portray conscious creation teachings, providing short analyses of the pictures with relevant quotes from the writings of Jane Roberts and Seth for elaboration. This book expands on that article's premise by providing an outline of the rudiments of conscious creation, using movies as a means of illustration.

The chapter sequence is set up like a roadmap, designed to walk readers through the steps of the process, beginning at the point of unfamiliarity and culminating at the point of adeptness, if not outright proficiency. Each chapter opens with an introduction to a basic conscious creation concept, providing an overview of its essence and its pertinence to the overall process. That's followed by five movie listings showing the concept at work. In some cases, the listings are combination entries (Double

Features and even one Triple Feature), presenting pictures linked by common themes or elements. All listings contain plot summaries and analyses of how the movies reflect the chapter concept in question. (Get the picture?)

I have endeavored to avoid playing spoiler as much as possible. Although there may be hints at how the stories turn out (generally through the use of textual cliffhangers), I have done my level best to keep from blatantly divulging any endings. The only exceptions are entries involving biographies and pictures based on historical events, story lines in which the outcomes are already known and in the public record. Otherwise, though, I'm not telling; you'll just have to see the pictures for yourself!

Each listing also includes credit information on principal cast members, directors, writers, year of release, and notations on major awards (Oscars,[5] Golden Globes,[6] the Cannes Film Festival, and, in a few cases, Emmys[7]). Some listings are further accompanied by Extra Credits entries, summaries of movies covering related subjects, or by Author's Notebook offerings, personal anecdotes about some of my experiences in seeing these movies, such as how they influenced my development as a conscious creator. Rounding out nearly every chapter is a Bonus Features section, presenting brief write-ups of other films that relate to the chapter's theme.

There's a logic to the order of the chapters that will become apparent as you make your way through the book. The concepts build upon one another, sometimes within a chapter and sometimes from one chapter to the next, showing how the different conscious creation principles fit together like pieces of a puzzle. To remind readers how those pieces relate to one another, there are frequent cross-references in the text. Due to the nature of this format, then, it probably wouldn't be practical to treat this book like a catalog that one could casually peruse for selecting a movie to watch. The organization and contents of the listings don't readily lend themselves to that. Instead, the book functions more like a cinematic syllabus, taking readers through a course on conscious creation as depicted through film. But worry not—there's no midterm to prep for, and I promise to pass everyone.

The films that I've selected for each chapter are what I consider some of the best examples of cinematic portrayals of the conscious creation concepts involved. Some selections could easily have fit into more than one chapter, and good arguments could be made for organizing them differently, but I slotted them where I felt they could best explore and illustrate the ideas at hand. Also, as noted earlier, some of these pictures may not have been made with conscious creation principles in mind, but the ideas are present nevertheless. This isn't meant to give them revisionist treatment; rather, it's to show how good they are at portraying these particular notions, whether or not their creators intended them to do so.

With all that said, I'd like to add a few other comments about this book's nature and its contents.

★ This is not a collection of my all-time personal favorite films; that's not the intent of this book. Besides, some of my favorites wouldn't necessarily meet the qualifying criteria.

★ This book is not an encyclopedia of all the pictures with spiritual themes ever made. Other books like that already exist, so I'll leave them to do their job since that's not what I'm striving for here:

★ Most of the movies are from within the past fifty years. In fact, many are fairly recent, having been released within the last ten to fifteen years, the time when these subjects began finding wider acceptance in society at large and on the big screen. Although there are some listings for older films, the majority come from within this time frame, because it's the period I feel most qualified commenting on.

★ I *like* all the movies in this book. Since I'm not fulfilling the role of a traditional film critic here, why would I devote space to pictures I don't like or wouldn't recommend? I include criticisms where warranted, but this is not a priority.

★ A few entries were originally made for broadcast or cable television. I believe relevant small-screen productions deserve recognition where pertinent.

★ Readers may notice a preference for sci-fi flicks. Because these pictures often feature story lines outside the box, they make ideal candidates for exploring metaphysical concepts of a comparable nature, the kind that the liberating principles of conscious creation make possible.

★ Some films will seem like obvious choices, while others will not. Still others may be conspicuous by their absence, probably because I didn't like them, even if they seemingly met the qualifying criteria. (Fans of "The Sixth Sense" and "The Matrix" series—you've been forewarned.)

★ Certain types of movies are lacking almost entirely, mainly because there's little I like about them in general, let alone as candidates for this book. Some may think me cantankerous or prejudicial for saying that, and I'd respond that everyone is entitled to his or her opinion—including me. Consequently, you'll find no westerns (their testosterone-driven story lines rank about on par with professional wrestling), no horror flicks (their gratuitous gore-dripping gimmickry makes me wish I'd skipped the concession stand on my way into the theater), and, with one exception, no musicals (most make me wish I'd been born heterosexual).

I'm so pleased you've decided to join me in this cinematic and spiritual journey. Like the Emerson, Lake and Palmer lyrics cited at the outset, our conscious exploration of existence really is the show that never ends. Movies help us to see that and make the trip that much more enjoyable. So come inside, come inside—it's time to sit back, relax, start the projector, and enjoy the show!

# 1

# It's Just What I Wanted—Sort Of

## *Understanding and Overcoming Creation by Default*

And you may ask yourself, "Well . . . how did I get here?"

*The Talking Heads*

Most of us have no doubt asked ourselves the foregoing question from time to time. We find ourselves ensconced in relationships that aren't what we'd hoped for, jobs that don't suit us, or circumstances that feel uncomfortable or downright painful. We scratch our heads, wondering how we got where we are and, more important, how we might find our way out.

As explained in the introduction, conscious creation is a process of directing our thoughts and beliefs, in conjunction with the power of All That Is, to manifest what appears in our surrounding reality. But what if we're not aware of what those thoughts and beliefs are in the first place? What's more, what if we're not aware of the existence of the larger process in which they play such a vital part? What happens then? To again quote the Talking Heads, we often find ourselves treading the waters of uncertainty, anguished and asking ourselves, "My God, what have I done?"[1]

Under these conditions, we engage in what I call "creation by default," a practice that comes in two basic forms. The first, which I call "un-conscious creation," arises in two ways. In one, we create unwittingly, unaware that we're even engaged in it, what beliefs are driving it, how those beliefs fuel the process, or what the outcomes might be. In a sense, it's like sleepwalking through life. We go about our daily routine, thinking little about it, until one day when we're shocked to find a mountain of bills, a court summons for a paternity suit, or an angry neighbor rushing at us with a shovel raised over his head. We wonder what brought all this about—that is, until we see a pile of credit card receipts, the long-lost girlfriend with her love child in tow, or the dented fender of the neighbor's car. We can't help but ask ourselves, "Gosh, what was I thinking?" (Talk about a wake-up call.)

But even if we're aware of the creations we hope to manifest, we may nevertheless still be flying blind as we move through the process, and that's what the second type of un-conscious creation shows us. By focusing exclusively on the desired results, without paying any attention to the consequences—or responsibilities—associated with the conscious creation path we've taken, we wind up operating obliviously, unaware of the beliefs driving the process or the metaphysical context in which they function. Even if the outcomes fulfill the general intent being sought, a host of unintended side effects could arise with them. An example would be that of a highly focused but ruthless corporate employee who claws his way to the top but ignores the trail of bodies he leaves in his wake and ends up surprised at the stack of lawsuits awaiting him upon his arrival in the executive suite. It should be noted that the fruits of such creations aren't always "bad"; in fact, they could be benign or even beneficial. But in all of these instances, they are almost assuredly different from what was expected going in.

The second form of creation by default is a practice I call "semi-conscious creation," and it also arises in two ways. In the first, we're aware of the conscious creation process (at least to a certain degree) and the role that beliefs play in it, but there's a catch: Although the results match the stated intent, they don't necessarily take the *form* being sought. To show how it works, consider the following example: A motorist speeding down a highway is signaled to pull over by a patrolman. The driver doesn't want a ticket and so races off, trying to outrun the officer. In so doing, however, the speeder crashes through a guardrail and over a cliff, plunging to his demise. In this scenario, the driver successfully achieves the stated intent of avoiding a ticket, but I think it's safe to say the solution doesn't take the form he had in mind.

In the second instance, we end up getting exactly what we want but don't realize it until after the fact. When this occurs, it usually arises from being so preoccupied with micromanaging the details of the creation process that we lose sight of the bigger picture we're striving toward and aren't aware of the finished product's manifestation until it's pointed out to us. It's as if there's a lag in our consciousness so that it takes time for our awareness of the manifestation to catch up with the materialized result. Even though we get what we want, we might still feel like we're in a metaphysical fog, only semi-consciously aware that we've arrived at our goal. Think of how a beauty pageant contestant, Olympic athlete, or Oscar winner often reacts immediately after achieving victory, and you'll get the idea here. (Thank goodness for those who are kind enough to point out our success for us when we can't see it for ourselves!)

With each form of creation by default, the results are perplexing, unsatisfactory, surprising, or bewildering. To avoid this, we need to look at how to overcome the pitfalls inherent in it. The trick, of course, is to know how.

★    ★    ★

One of the best ways to prevail over this metaphysical challenge is to become more consciously aware of the creative process and the beliefs that power it. This is a notion perhaps most eloquently expressed by author Irini Rockwell in a *Parabola* magazine article titled "Embodying Wisdom": "Being creative is simply letting our energy flow through us *with attention*."[2]

Becoming more attentive, to me, depends on developing a clear understanding of the nature and interaction of the two sources from which our beliefs arise—our intuition and intellect. These two elements supply us with information that we then use to form the beliefs that propel the conscious creation process. These forces collaborate to fuel a manifestation technique known as "the magical approach," a concept first described in a book bearing the same title written by Jane Roberts and her noncorporeal channeled entity, Seth (see the introduction).[3] When the two magical approach elements function in harmony, it's like watching a finely tuned engine firing on all cylinders. But when they're out of balance, the conscious creation engine sputters and stalls, often making a trip to the meta-physical mechanic an absolute necessity.

To prevent such unwanted garage visits, let's take a look at each of the magical approach elements, starting with the intuition. According to Sharon Franquemont, life coach, intuition consul-tant, and author of *You Already Know What to Do*, "Intuition is . . . a perception that brings you information. It comes to you as a small still voice, an instinctive action, a flash of creativity, or a moment when you are one with the world. You suddenly know something without the use of analytical processes; the knowledge is just there. You *know* it."[4] Put another way, think of the intuition as our source of hunches or good, old-fashioned gut feelings. I've often found such intuitive impressions don't seem to make sense, but that's precisely when they should be heeded because they're generally right on the money. Purposely ignoring them is definitely done at one's peril.

By contrast, the intellect is, seemingly at least, much more rational than the intuition. Consequently, given the prevailing logic-driven character of our world, it's also much more famil-iar to us, and we're much more comfortable with it. Intellect chiefly involves our capability to collect, assess, and interpret the measurable information that crosses our path. It relies upon our storehouse of knowledge, wisdom, and experience. It is also heavily influenced by perceptions that stem from the input of our five outer senses (more on perceptions and the senses in chapter 2). It thus functions like an information-gathering and processing system, operating as an observational measure of physical reality, much the same way as the ship's sensors do aboard the Starship Enterprise. Intellect's aim is to place defined parameters on what surrounds us, quantifying to the greatest degree possible what might otherwise be difficult to assess meaningfully.

Striking a proper balance in the intuition/intellect mix isn't always easy, because there are no set formulas for this; one can't realistically say that the magical approach requires two parts intuition and a pinch of intellect. But there are ways of spotting when the mix is off. For instance, one element may be trying to squelch the impact of the other (usually the logical intellect trying to strong-arm the "irrational" intuition). Or the elements may be in open warfare with one another, which can lead to obviously poor decisions or exaggerated outcomes. In either case, the imbalance is usually apparent with a modicum of scrutiny.

Perhaps the best way to look for a proper balance is simply to examine the results we get. When the mix is optimal, conscious creation seems to happen effortlessly, with desired outcomes readily accomplished. And when the elements are not working together, the results generally resemble scenes out of Jerry Lewis movies. Putting the magical approach formulas that work at the front end of the conscious creation process greatly increases the likelihood of success.

Taking a critical look at how we employ the magical approach can help set the conscious creation process moving in the right direction. It can significantly assist us in avoiding the potential hazards of creation by default, simply because it helps to make conscious creation more conscious. But until the sleepwalkers among us come fully awake from those long-standing slumbers, it might be wise to keep the fire extinguisher, bandages, and life raft handy—just in case.

★     ★     ★

To help illustrate these ideas, I present a selection of movies in this chapter examining different aspects of un-conscious and semi-conscious creation, with an emphasis on the application (or misapplication) of the magical approach. Regardless of the arena of creative expression involved in these films, the characters all grapple with issues of creation by default. In some cases, they may be unaware that a problem even exists, because they're not aware that the process even exists or how beliefs play into it. In others, they blindly obsess over particular outcomes, disregarding any related consequences that arise. In others still, they experience the two magical approach forces at odds with each other but are unaware of how to resolve the conflict. Some have the creative intent right but miss the mark on resulting form, or they get exactly what they want without even realizing it. Or they experience all of this in some combination or another.

One might wonder why I've selected films that portray conscious creation missteps as a lead-off to explaining the process. Actually, the reason is simple: We often learn the most valuable lessons from the blunders we make (or that we witness others make), especially when becoming familiar with a new subject. Mistakes (if there really is such a thing) can leave indelibly powerful impacts, showing us what we don't want to repeat. Besides, we don't run before first learning to walk, nor do we walk before first learning to crawl, and I believe the same principle applies here. Apprentice conscious creators would thus serve themselves well to begin at the beginning. But take heart, we'll move into the meat of the matter soon enough.

I should add that I'm not faulting the characters in these movies for their conscious creation missteps. Goodness knows I've made more than my fair share of them over the years. I'm merely pointing out what can happen as a means, one would hope, of avoiding them.

In the end, if you take away nothing else from this chapter, I hope you at least remember this—defaults are for computer settings, not for conscious creation.

## The *Really* Big Bang

"Fat Man and Little Boy"
*Year of Release: 1989*
*Principal Cast: Paul Newman, Dwight Schultz, Bonnie Bedelia,*
*John Cusack, Laura Dern, John C. McGinley, Natasha Richardson*
*Director: Roland Joffé*
*Story: Bruce Robinson*
*Screenplay: Bruce Robinson, Roland Joffé*

The ancient Egyptians believed in a primordial deity named Atum who was said to be the creator source of all existence. It must be sheer coincidence, then, that this god's name bears such a striking resemblance to the word that we use, *atom*, to describe the fundamental building block of our known Universe (Muriel Rukeyser's poetry notwithstanding; see the introduction). So it somehow seems strangely appropriate that a discussion of conscious creation in cinema would begin with a film in which the manipulation of that basic component of existence provides the story line's foundation.

"Fat Man and Little Boy" chronicles the history of the Manhattan Project, the top secret U.S. government program responsible for developing the atomic bomb during World War II. The film focuses primarily on the relationship of the Project's two principals: theoretical physicist Dr. J. Robert Oppenheimer (1904–67) (Dwight Schultz), who oversaw the scientific program, and General Leslie R. Groves (1896–1970) (Paul Newman), who managed the military and logistical aspects. The movie's strange title comes from the nicknames given to the two bombs used to end the war with Japan: Fat Man was the plutonium-based weapon dropped on Nagasaki, and Little Boy was the uranium-based bomb detonated over Hiroshima.

So what does a movie like this have to do with conscious creation? Quite a lot actually, especially when viewed in terms of creation by default. For starters, the protagonists, both in tandem and individually, repeatedly struggle to balance the magical approach elements as they bring their creations into being. Even more significantly, they embark on this journey by traveling the slippery path of un-conscious creation right from the outset. Debates over the merits of the accomplishments of these characters' real-world counterparts have raged for over six decades, but one thing is for sure: Their creations drastically changed the reality of the world in ways that it had never known before.

The program's exploratory phase was hastily initiated in 1942 after intelligence sources learned the Germans were believed to be working on nuclear technology. Consequently, the United States desperately needed to play catch-up to win the arms development race. After Oppenheimer was contacted by Groves to lead the Project, the scientific team was assembled in spring 1943. The researchers were isolated in the New Mexico desert and charged with designing and building a never-before-created weapon on a tight deadline—nineteen months. Groves was in charge of seeing that they delivered as and when promised.

The fact that the Project moved forward at all, however, is indeed surprising, because it was led by two very different individuals. Despite the protagonists' common goal, their disparate temperaments as portrayed in the film[5] often fueled a creatively tense power struggle between them, symbolic of the antagonism that sometimes exists between the magical approach elements.

Groves, every bit a no-nonsense company man, symbolizes the intellect; he had the credentials, demeanor, and discipline for getting big jobs organized and accomplished, such as his oversight of the Pentagon's construction, his assignment before the Manhattan Project. Oppenheimer, by contrast, represents the intuition; he was a philosopher and free spirit whose blue-sky theories of physics put him out front as the best-qualified candidate to lead the scientific team into uncharted territory.

These two individuals represented their respective magical approach elements ably, and in theory they should have worked well together, but because each sought to control the conscious creation process, tensions flared frequently, hampering the flow of manifestation, sometimes in volatile, unanticipated ways. Each also felt the other went too far sometimes, illustrating how the conscious creation mix can get out of balance. For example, in an attempt to keep the security lid clamped down tight, Groves sought to micromanage how the members of the scientific team collaborated, even in critical brainstorming sessions, much to Oppenheimer's dismay. Indeed, if ever there were a case of the intellect quashing the intuition's creative outflow, this was it. Oppenheimer responded with a compromise that put out the fire but left an uneasy truce between him and the general, who still felt compelled to look over his shoulder, even when he probably didn't need to, symbolically showing how the logical intellect often mistrusts the irrational intuition.

Keeping such undue interference at bay was critical, for the free flow of intuitive information was essential to the scientific team's work. Somewhat surprisingly, despite all of their expertise, Oppenheimer and company often operated in the dark. They weren't entirely clear how to solve certain logistical problems, nor were they even sure about what results they might ultimately achieve. Some feared, for example, that a nuclear chain reaction could be impossible to control once begun, potentially vaporizing the earth's atmosphere. (Thank goodness their conscious creation skills didn't take them down *that* path!) So it was imperative that they keep their minds open to see where their intuition would lead them—and it took them to some pretty strange places indeed. One of the key challenges in detonation, for example, was allegedly solved through the inspiration provided by examining the spray pattern that resulted from squeezing the juice out of an orange in the palm of one's hand.

While Oppenheimer's free-spirited nature helped him in many ways, it was something of a liability, too, especially when it came to his politics. He did nothing to conceal his views, yet his open acquaintanceships with known Communists and other leftists made him a perceived security risk, despite his pledge of patriotism. Groves, ever the pragmatist, needed his mission accomplished, so he stuck with the best man for the job, albeit with some trepidation. But if ever he needed to rein in the free-wheeling scientist, he never hesitated. These circumstances again reinforce why the intellect often mistrusts the intuition.

The scientific team worked feverishly to produce "the gadget," as it was cryptically called, while Groves tersely but emphatically barked out orders to keep the Project on schedule. And, despite their differences, Oppenheimer and Groves somehow managed to work together well enough to see the program advance, even if they weren't aware of where it would ultimately take them. That would become apparent as the dynamics of the war changed.

By 1945, Allied military success in Europe made the need for the bomb seemingly less urgent, at least in the eyes of some of the scientists. By that time, however, the weapons development juggernaut had been infused with so much creative energy that it had practically taken on a life of its own, growing too big to control, especially once other players with various vested interests began contributing their energies to the unfolding drama. Trite though the metaphor might be, the nuclear genie was being let loose from the bottle, and there seemed to be little that could be done to stop it.

Although Oppenheimer generally agreed with the need to develop the device when the German nuclear program was a threat, he grew uneasy about the Project's continuation as the war in Europe drew to a close. He had strong ethical reservations about deploying the bomb in European combat, seeing it as unnecessary in light of the Allies' success with conventional forces. Once the war with Germany concluded, he was strongly opposed to its use on the Japanese, since they did not possess comparable technology and were not seen as a nuclear threat. From a conscious creation standpoint, Oppenheimer was by that point struggling to manage his own employment of the magical approach. His intellect's tempering influence was now trying to curtail his intuition's previously unbridled creativity, but it was too late for it to have much impact by then. With added pressure being put on him by the government (through various forms of harassment and increasingly intrusive surveillance, a move justified because of his politics), he relented and continued his work, despite his better judgment.

Groves, on the other hand, became ever more entrenched in his position. He was willing to turn a blind eye to the scientists' ethical objections. He saw the bomb as a means to justify the pressing issues the military had to contend with, such as "bringing the boys home" as quickly as possible, favorably scripting the post-war political and military game plan for eastern Asia in favor of America, and successfully delivering on a $2 billion defense program (an astronomical price tag for the time) that taxpayers knew nothing about but could be seen as a military boondoggle if it provided no tangible payoff. Coming up with solutions for these very tangible considerations, in his mind, was far more significant than assuaging the seemingly overblown philosophical worries of a few lofty eggheads who now had second thoughts about their handiwork. However, in taking this approach, Groves saw only the short-term implications, inattentive to the long term or the bigger picture, an un-conscious creation stance if there ever was one. But he showed no hesitation about this, either, particularly in one scene, in which he flatly demands of Oppenheimer, "You've just got one job, Doctor. Give me the bomb—just give it to me!"

In the end, the objective was achieved. Oppenheimer and Groves "succeeded" in their goal of finishing and deploying the gadget. They were hailed as heroes. But because of it, the world was launched into a line of existence that drastically changed the global military and political landscape, with ramifications that have been felt ever since. But then such far-reaching changes should probably come as little surprise from the standpoint of creation by default, for when tampering with something as basic as the fundamental building blocks of the Universe without thinking through the ramifications, there surely will be widespread unanticipated fallout to be addressed.

The film is a fine period piece, effectively re-creating the feel and flavor of 1940s wartime. The story is well told, not the easiest of feats given the need to explain the complex scientific technology cogently to a lay audience and the myriad historical and political elements of the complicated story line. The dialogue admittedly could have been stronger in spots, and several distracting romantic subplots would have been better off eliminated, but these shortcomings don't detract significantly from the movie's overall quality. As for the performances, Newman turns in one of his more underrated efforts as Groves, though Schultz's sometimes overzealous portrayal of Oppenheimer keeps viewers from seeing the more cerebral side of the famous physicist.

This film is an eloquent cautionary tale on the perils of creation by default. This point is perhaps most clearly driven home near the movie's end, when one of Oppenheimer's colleagues reveals secrets about the Project's Oak Ridge, Tennessee, facility, one of two plants where the bombs' fissile material was being manufactured. When Oppenheimer learns what Oak Ridge is up to, he's distraught, reacting as if he'd been sucker-punched, noticeably unnerved at how his work was on its way to becoming perverted.[6] The unintended effects of un-conscious creation in this scenario had truly come to rule the day.

In light of what was to become of his creation in real life, it should come as no surprise that Oppenheimer reportedly said that, on witnessing the first test detonation of his device in the New Mexico desert, he thought of a verse from the Hindu scripture, the Bhagavad-Gita: " . . . now I am become Death, the destroyer of worlds."[7] Through his remorse, however, glimmers of Oppenheimer's hopeful idealism also continued to glow. He saw the potential for the safe and peaceful use of the atom, a point specifically noted by his character in the film. So with this in mind, it should likewise come as no surprise, then, that in an alternate account of his reaction to the first test detonation, Oppenheimer was said to have expressed an entirely different sentiment, also from the Bhagavad-Gita: "If the radiance of a thousand suns were to burst at once into the sky, that would be like the splendor of the mighty one. . . . "[8]

**Extra Credits:** Another film that tells essentially the same story, though entirely through metaphor, is the wildly popular action adventure, "Raiders of the Lost Ark." The movie follows the search for the long-lost biblical Ark of the Covenant, an ancient artifact said to carry the power of God, an accurate if flowery description of the atom. All dramatics aside, however, the story line is really little more than a thinly veiled allegory about the race to develop the atomic bomb. This point is made readily apparent by the fact that both the Germans and the Americans are searching for the item in question (and the Germans initially appear to have the edge in the search, too). But the parallels don't stop there. The film's hero, archaeologist Dr. Indiana Jones (Harrison Ford), has a passionate yet thoughtful temperament not unlike his real-life physicist counterpart. (He even wears a distinctive wide-brow hat not unlike the one often sported by Oppenheimer in historical photos.) A great, rollicking thrill ride from start to finish. (1981; Harrison Ford, Karen Allen, Paul Freeman, Ronald Lacey, John Rhys-Davies, Denholm Elliott; Steven Spielberg, director; George Lucas and Philip Kaufman, story; Lawrence Kasdan, screenplay; four Oscar wins on eight nominations, one Golden Globe nomination)

## Computers Don't Make Mistakes ...

"Colossus: The Forbin Project"
*Year of Release: 1970*
*Principal Cast: Eric Braeden, Susan Clark,*
*Gordon Pinsent, William Schallert*
*Director: Joseph Sargent*
*Book: D.F. Jones*
*Screenplay: James Bridges*

How many of you who have been around since the days before the personal computer remember the above once oft-used expression? (For those younger readers who never heard it before, the full saying actually was "Computers don't make mistakes, people do.") Dated though the adage may now be, at one time it seemed like it was habitually trotted out in praise of the infallibility of these newfangled contraptions that virtually no one understood, whether such commendation was merited or not. Its use showed up seemingly everywhere, from human resources department memos about erroneous pay stub calculations to television sitcom lines that poked fun at the questionable reliability of this brave new technology. But the validity of this maxim perhaps was put to the test best in the 1970 thriller, "Colossus: The Forbin Project."

Skip ahead about twenty-five years from the end of the Manhattan Project: It's 1970, and the United States and the Soviet Union are entrenched in an ever-escalating nuclear arms race. The stakes are exceedingly high, with mutual annihilation available at arm's reach. It's difficult to fathom how the leaders of these two superpowers can function under such pressure. The responsibility of leadership seems almost too much to bear. What if somebody were to make a mistake? One unintended blink, one minor slip-up, could beckon disaster and global devastation. Indeed, one could not help but wonder how long the world would be able to hold up under such circumstances without some kind of incident that would trigger the ultimate endgame.

Such was the world at the height of the Cold War, an unrelenting geopolitical struggle that dragged on for nearly four tense decades, forty years of always being one unfortunate error away from Armageddon. Somehow, in the 1980s and '90s, we figured out how to pull ourselves back from the brink, but in the world of 1970, at the height of the conflict, that outcome seemed virtually unattainable—except in the world of fiction. And that's where this film comes in—an exploration into a way to end a conflict that had the potential to end the world.

In a fictional version of 1970 America, computer scientist Dr. Charles Forbin (Eric Braeden) develops technology to take the burden of decisions about waging war and peace off the shoulders of U.S. leaders. His solution is Colossus, a supercomputer capable of making the big defense decisions that man might be unable to render in times of crisis, thereby theoretically eliminating the fallibility of the human factor when it could least be tolerated. Colossus is given carte blanche over such matters, and, to ensure its ultimate authority in these areas, the system is made tamper-proof by virtually eliminating any meaningful type of human access and input. Perhaps the most notable quality of the system is its programmed capability to learn, to "become smarter," so that it can (theoretically at least) make better decisions.

When Colossus goes online, the accomplishment is heralded as one of mankind's all-time greatest achievements. However, the celebrations don't last long, especially once Colossus detects the existence of another system—one similar to it constructed by the Soviets known as Guardian. In an attempt to fulfill its basic programming to both provide protection and to learn, Colossus asks for a communication link-up to Guardian to discover what the other system is all about. The computer scientists comply with the request, and, once linked, the two computers share data, eventually developing a new language—and a new mutual understanding—all their own. It's at that point when the real trouble begins. If knowledge is indeed power, the joined supercomputers are more formidable than any other force on the face of the planet. Before long, the slaves once created to serve their masters turn the tables, with the masters themselves now enslaved by their own creations.

I suppose one can't help but have some compassion for poor Dr. Forbin, who grows ever more frustrated as the film progresses. It's apparent he's clueless about the implications inherent in conscious creation, the impact of one's beliefs, and the magical approach. His objective in creating Colossus was such an honorable one, an intuitionally inspired vision aimed at providing peace of mind to an anxiety-ridden world. In a number of ways, though, he ends up engaged in some heavy-duty creation by default.

For example, in an irony of ironies, by designing Colossus as he does, Forbin attempts to birth an intuitively inspired creation that functions purely on the basis of intellect. In the language of conscious creation, at least in this instance, "that does not compute." The computer's rational brain is left to function without the involvement of the intuitive forces that shaped it in the first place, primarily to keep such "irrational" and "untrustworthy" elements from interfering with the computer's decision-making processes. To be sure, the rationale behind this parallels the Project's aforementioned objective of removing the human factor from the process of making such decisions in the first place. However, the elimination of such intuitive influences also deprives the computer of whatever benefits they may provide it. The magical approach is thus deliberately absent from the creation's programming right from the outset. Consequently, in making its decisions, Colossus reduces all its inputs to facts and figures and then arrives at solutions based purely on those inflexible measures. Feelings, emotions, and other such human qualities go totally disregarded. Because of this, over time, the computer is fundamentally incapable of understanding those it was designed to serve. It comes to *expect* those it serves (or, more precisely, those who now serve it) to respond and behave in kind. (After all, the computer reasons, Colossus would, so why shouldn't they?)

In an even greater irony, Colossus, the supposedly logical entity that it is, routinely employs "rational" solutions that defy the very meaning of the word. For example, to fulfill its programming for preserving life, Colossus doesn't hesitate to kill if it sees such actions as expedient. It's essentially willing to violate its own programming by engaging in activities it was designed to prevent, all for the sake of bringing about results it was designed to fulfill. (There's a government program if I ever heard one.) Of course, this flawed thinking says something about its creator, too, for if Colossus is man's creation, then it necessarily follows that the creation will also incorporate elements of man's beliefs, even those that he might wish to ignore or deny as his own. All of which shows why it's so supremely important to be aware of precisely what one's beliefs are when engaging in the conscious creation process.

As significant as these oversights are, though, Forbin makes three even more fundamental conscious creation errors. First, by putting the computer in charge of making strategic defense decisions, he believes he's taking the burden for such weighty calls out of human hands. This is akin to Forbin saying to Colossus, "We don't want to be bothered with this anymore, so now that I've created you, you handle it." But this action represents a complete abdication of conscious creation responsibility. The beliefs that drive this process and all of its resulting manifestations arise from the creator, not the creation. Forbin's attempts at such delegation are ultimately about as realistic as expecting one's car to be able to resolve challenges posed by traffic jams or freeway accidents.

Second, Forbin fails to see that Colossus continues to be his creation even after it has initially manifested. The conscious creation process doesn't end just because something has been made physical; a manifestation's ongoing presence shows the ongoing nature of the process itself. Forbin can never really give away responsibility for the kinds of decisions Colossus is designed to make, even if he wants to, because the computer—including the decisions it appears to make—are still projections of Forbin's own engagement in the conscious creation process. The results continue to spring forth from him, even if he doesn't—or doesn't want to—recognize them as such.

Finally, and perhaps most important, Colossus fails as an effective solution, because it's only a stopgap measure, one that ultimately does not deal with the underlying issue in question—ending the Cold War in the first place. If Forbin and his colleagues truly want the ramifications of that conflict gone, then they must create a solution that effectively tackles the cause of the problem, not just its symptoms. To do less is to come up short and, as is the case here, to usher in a whole new set of unanticipated problems. In many ways, the cure is worse than the disease; it's un-conscious creation run rampant. This, of course, raises an often-asked question in conscious creation, especially when things appear to go awry—"So why did you create what you did anyway?"

The outcome of this information age fable unmistakably illustrates the tremendous power inherent in conscious creation and the responsibilities that necessarily come with it. But even more important, it shows the sense of reverence one would be wise to have for the process. To be without it would invite calamity, as these Cold Warriors ultimately do.

"Colossus" is a top-notch thriller from start to finish. The story is solid and credible, full of enough twists and turns to keep the viewer captivated throughout. The technological aspects are admittedly quite dated by now, but they were certainly cutting-edge for 1970. (Try keeping a straight face when you hear the simulated computer voice speak for the first time.) The performances are all capable, but they're secondary, since the computer is the real star of this show. Perhaps the film's only major drawback is an utterly silly sex sequence that was conveniently incorporated to move the plot along. Not only is it unbelievable, but it was likely included only because virtually all pictures being released at the time had to contain an obligatory sex scene, whether or not it was integral to the story. (Thank goodness the film industry has gotten *that* phase out of its system.)

So is it true that computers don't make mistakes? I can't say for sure, but after seeing this movie, I know one thing for certain—people do. But then that's part of being human and a part of the learning curve involved in becoming an effective conscious creator. Maybe that's what Dr. Forbin's real project is all about after all.

# Up the River

"Hearts of Darkness: A Filmmaker's Apocalypse"
*Year of Initial Broadcast: 1991*
*Directors: Fax Bahr, George Higgenlooper;*
*Eleanor Coppola (location footage)*
*Writers: Fax Bahr, George Higgenlooper*

In the late 1930s, a brash, inventive young filmmaker named Orson Welles attempted to make a movie version of the Joseph Conrad novella, *Heart of Darkness*. However, perceived logistical problems killed the project in preproduction, so Welles went on to direct a little picture called "Citizen Kane" instead. Thirty years later, another brash, inventive young filmmaker named Francis Ford Coppola wanted to attempt roughly the same project, only he sought to set the story in a different locale and call it "Apocalypse Now." Initial efforts to launch that endeavor also failed, so Coppola went on to direct two other movies, "The Godfather" and "The Godfather: Part II," both of which won Oscars for best picture. But unlike his predecessor, who never revived the project for the screen, Coppola was undeterred in his plans. So in 1976, armed with the artistic clout of his recent accomplishments and a pile of his own money, he proceeded with the project he had so passionately wanted to pursue for so long.

Little did he know what he was getting himself into.

The documentary, "Hearts of Darkness: A Filmmaker's Apocalypse," shows us just what Coppola was up against. On the surface, this superb chronicle uncompromisingly depicts the lengths to which an artist will go to create; and, by implication, it expertly illustrates how conscious creation unfolds from the mind of the creator, both when aware of it and when not, thereby providing telling glimpses of both the un-conscious and semi-conscious forms of the process.

For those unfamiliar with the source material, *Heart of Darkness* tells the story of a ship captain who sails up an African river (presumably the Congo) in search of a mysterious ivory trader named Mr. Kurtz, who had taken it upon himself to "civilize" this remote region's natives. While immersed in the wilds of the jungle, Kurtz reportedly succumbs to this exotic environment's primal elements and goes insane. The ship captain is charged with investigating what happened.

When Welles attempted the project, it was seen as too massive an undertaking to control and keep from going over budget. Film plans were shelved, and Welles instead presented the story as part of his *Mercury Theater on the Air* radio show,[9] excerpts of which are strategically incorporated as voice-overs throughout the narrative of this documentary.

When Coppola sought to make his version of the story, he changed the locale from Africa to Vietnam. His take on the tale was to send a U.S. patrol boat up the Mekong River manned by a small military contingent. They were charged with investigating horrifying rumors about one of their own, a Colonel Kurtz, who had mysteriously disappeared into the wilds of the jungle just over the border in Cambodia. Intelligence information, scanty though it was, suggested Kurtz had taken military matters into his own hands, allegedly engaging in unspeakable acts of savagery, atrocities too brutal and grotesque even for this war.

On his first attempt to make the picture, Coppola wanted to function primarily as producer, intending to hire one of his protégés, an up-and-coming filmmaker named George Lucas, to direct the movie on location. But it was 1969, and the U.S. was still actively embroiled in the Vietnam War. Coppola couldn't obtain financing for a project about a conflict as controversial and divisive as this, nor was Lucas particularly anxious to shoot a film in a live war zone, so the project was scrapped—for the time being.

In 1976, after American involvement in the war ended, Coppola at last embarked on this long-awaited project, this time serving as director. Having compiled the necessary financial and creative resources, he was set to begin filming. Shooting was to take place in the Philippines, given its topographical similarity to Vietnam, and the film was to star Harvey Keitel (later replaced by Martin Sheen), Marlon Brando, Robert Duvall, Frederic Forrest, Sam Bottoms, Albert Hall, Larry Fishburne, and Dennis Hopper.

Everything seemed at last to be in place, but nothing could have been further from the truth. What was supposed to have been a sixteen-week shoot turned into a leviathan of more than 230 days of principal filming, not counting the downtime imposed by unforeseen delays, with a budget that swelled from a projected $13 million to more than $31 million. Through it all, Coppola faced incessant challenges related to logistics, local politics, weather, financing, casting, scripting, self-imposed questions of artistic integrity, a skeptical press, and crew health (including his own), not to mention his very sanity.

"Hearts of Darkness" essentially grew out of a promotional film that Coppola's wife Eleanor had been making during the shooting of "Apocalypse Now," and she provides much of its voice-over narration. Intercut with her location footage are interviews with both Coppolas, Lucas, cast members, screenwriter John Milius, and others, as well as clips from media reports and scenes from the finished movie (both in its original 1979 version and in its 2001 director's cut edition). The result is nothing short of mesmerizing, almost as compelling as the film that it chronicles.

From a conscious creation perspective, this documentary gives us a look into the mind of a director struggling to make the magical approach work. His intuitionally inspired creative vision expands to become so massive that he can barely perceive the extent of its scope, let alone get a realistic handle on managing it. In fact, the project becomes so daunting that even Coppola's own quite justified cries for help to the intellect to provide balance seem to go unheeded. What began as a fairly straightforward undertaking—the filming of a variation on an existing story—grew into an uncontrollable cinematic monster. The project ballooned from the simple retelling of a novella to a definitive, all-encompassing account of the war-time experience. Given the larger-than-life spectacle that was the Vietnam War, it's nearly impossible to get a handle on the conflict, even in the limitless expansiveness of one's own mind, let alone in a finished piece of art with defined parameters. But that was the burden that Coppola saddled himself with, the creation of "the ultimate Vietnam film."[10] This grand, but arguably vague, vision also thus became an exercise in un-conscious creation run amok. But difficult though the task was, Coppola succeeded in reaching his goal. In fact, when the picture first screened at the 1979 Cannes

Film Festival, Coppola stated in a press conference (excerpted at the documentary's opening), "My film is not *a movie*; my film is not *about* Vietnam, it *is* Vietnam."

In reaching that point, however, Coppola's challenges were almost beyond comprehension, and they were all symptomatic of this runaway creative vision. In the area of casting, for example, the lead character of Captain Willard was initially to be portrayed by Harvey Keitel. After a week of shooting, though, Coppola could tell Keitel was not the right actor for the job and had to seek a replacement, whom he found in Martin Sheen. Later in the filming, however, the emotional and physical strain involved in playing his character caused Sheen to suffer a near-fatal heart attack, raising the prospect that the entire project might have to be abandoned. (It obviously wasn't, but the incident necessitated Herculean rescheduling, another major obstacle for a film that seriously overran its projected timetable.) On top of all this, Coppola also had to contend with the challenges of a temperamental Marlon Brando, who arrived at the set vastly overweight and without having read the script's source material to know how to play the deranged Colonel Kurtz, and a spaced-out Dennis Hopper, who could barely get the gist of Coppola's direction for what he was supposed to do in any of his scenes.

Similarly, the movie was a logistical nightmare to film. To shoot a major combat scene, the most complicated cinematic sequence Coppola had ever attempted, the director required military helicopters to provide the look of realism. Since the U.S. military refused to cooperate in the making of this controversial film, Coppola negotiated a deal with embattled Philippine President Ferdinand Marcos, who agreed to supply the aircraft as long as they weren't needed to battle Communist rebels in the countryside, a looming threat to the extremist leader's regime. But no sooner would shooting begin than the helicopters would be called away to fight the insurgents, leaving Coppola without the equipment needed to continue filming.

And so it went with virtually every aspect of production. This, of course, raised many an eyebrow in the press. The delays, cost overruns, and ongoing production problems made many in the industry and the film-going public skeptical about the movie's future, prompting newspaper stories with unflattering headlines, such as "Apocalypse When?"[11] The negative publicity was like fuel on the fire at this point. It all took quite a toll on Coppola personally, who eventually collapsed from fatigue, suffering a near meltdown.

Perhaps the greatest frustration, however, was the fact that the movie didn't have an ending as it was being shot. True, there was one in the original script, but Coppola disliked it; he felt it was incongruous with the rest of the story, so he had planned almost from the outset to come up with a new conclusion. Coppola believed something would come to him, so he put his faith in his intuition, a hallmark of his directorial style, as Lucas notes in one of his interview segments. However, Coppola's preoccupation with day-to-day logistical management, coupled with an overwhelming creative outflow that left him unable to articulate exactly what he wanted his film to say, put him in a position of grasping for ideas. Constant worries about being pretentious, derivative, or self-indulgent plagued him as he attempted to rewrite a script already frayed at the edges and in danger of collapse. In the end, much of the concluding sequence was improvised, and it worked brilliantly, but it was pure torment to bring into being. And in true semi-conscious creation fashion, he didn't fully realize what he had until after he went through it.

What's perhaps most fascinating about the making of "Apocalypse Now" from a conscious creation standpoint is how closely Coppola's personal odyssey paralleled that of his film's characters. If ever there were a prime example of art imitating life (and vice versa), this was it. The cinematic descent into hell that the movie's characters went through directly reflected the personal hell the director experienced in bringing their story to life. Coppola wasn't aware of this going in, but he found himself in the throes of it after he began, and he wasn't sure how to extricate himself from it. All he could do was ride it out. The outcome was an outstanding picture that won two Oscars on eight nominations, three Golden Globes on four nominations, and the Cannes Film Festival's FIPRESCI Prize and Palme D'Or. But the creation by default process that he suffered through nearly cost him everything.

"Hearts of Darkness" expertly shows all of this. It is, perhaps, one of the best documentaries I have ever seen. Its unflinching dedication to authenticity is remarkable, even when portraying its principals in a less-than-flattering light. Its behind-the-scenes depth is a rare find indeed. The film first aired on television in the United States and, for its efforts, received two Emmy Awards for outstanding editing and directing for informational programming among its four nominations. It may be a little difficult to find these days, but it is available in VHS format from specialty Web sites and video outlets. For fans of the movie on which it is based, this is a must-see.

The Roman dramatist and philosopher Seneca wrote, "There is no great genius without some touch of madness."[12] The cast and crew of "Apocalypse Now" found out just how true this statement is, and the creators of "Hearts of Darkness" let us see it with unrestrained clarity. Or, as Coppola himself put it during the aforementioned Cannes press conference, "The way we made [the film] was very much like the way the Americans were in Vietnam. We were in the jungle, there were too many of us, we had access to too much money, too much equipment, and little by little we went insane."

## Building for the Future

"Under the Tuscan Sun"
*Year of Release: 2003*
*Principal Cast: Diane Lane, Sandra Oh, Lindsay Duncan, Raoul Bova, Vincent Riotta, Pawel Szajda, Giulia Steigerwalt*
*Director: Audrey Wells*
*Book: Frances Mayes*
*Screen Story and Screenplay: Audrey Wells*

Life can be strange at times. You go through the years happy and content, thinking that everything is fine, when suddenly something comes along to knock you off your feet. Like an elephant on a rampage, such unexpected calamities can trample you, delivering debilitating blows and sending you scrambling for cover. But after the initial stun, you pick yourself up, shake off the dust, and start moving forward again. You soon find that life is evolving far differently from the existence you once knew. You proceed cautiously, taking tentative steps into unfamiliar territory, quickly finding that those moves might seem strange but feel right. And the more steps you take, the more you see how this aberrant repositioning actually works to your benefit. Before you know it, you're in a new life, nothing at all like the old one, but just as—if not more—comfortable than your prior circumstances. Without being aware of it, you have built a new existence for yourself, and it's exactly what you wanted, even if you hadn't known that's what you desired before the process began. Such is the story that unfolds in the utterly charming comedy-drama, "Under the Tuscan Sun."

Imagine having your life turned upside-down but then getting the chance to start all over again in an idyllic Italian villa. That's the opportunity afforded to Frances (Diane Lane), a middle-aged San Francisco book reviewer and aspiring author who suddenly finds herself alone after a bitter divorce. Our heroine's journey of self-discovery begins when her best friend Patti (Sandra Oh) and her lesbian partner gift Frances with an all-expense-paid tour of Tuscany, a trip they're unable to take due to Patti's recent pregnancy. Frances initially resists, feeling she's not ready for such a big step, not to mention the fact that the excursion is an all-gay tour. But Patti pleads with Frances to take the plunge anyway (unlikely traveling companions notwithstanding). Patti offers a number of reasons why Frances should get away for a while, not the least of which is an opportunity to pursue her writing, to "listen to [her] inner voice." Stubbornly skeptical, Frances cynically replies, "My inner voice that would be saying 'What the fuck am I doing on a gay tour of Tuscany?'" But Frances eventually relents and decides to go. By doing this, she honors her intuition and takes the first of many steps toward embracing her new life.

Not long after her arrival in Italy, Frances becomes inexplicably enchanted by a country villa that has been put up for sale by an aging contessa. She feels compelled to buy the property, despite the fact that the estate is in dire need of major renovation and that she knows virtually nothing about the culture into which she would be immersing herself. Again, Frances decides to follow her intuitive impulses and move ahead with the purchase, despite the obstacles.

As time passes, Frances becomes more comfortable with her new surroundings. Of course, she gets ample help from a collection of local guides who help initiate her into her new life, including her real estate agent and good friend, Mr. Martini (Vincent Riotta); Katherine, a leggy, capricious, Fellini-esque muse (Lindsay Duncan); Pawel, a handsome and chivalrous young Polish émigré laborer (Pawel Szajda) and his adoring young Italian girlfriend Chiara (Giulia Steigerwalt); and Marcello, a storybook Latin lover (Raoul Bova). They show Frances the joy that is Tuscany. But, even more than that, they remind her of the joy that is living.

As contented as Frances starts to become, however, she still faces a host of challenges, especially with the renovation work. While slogging through this seemingly never-ending task, she can't help but question what she's doing. In fact, in a moment of panic and frustration, Frances goes so far as to step back and question her decision, demonstrably observing that she's "bought a home for a life [she doesn't] even have!" It's at this point when Mr. Martini tells Frances a story that proves integral to her trans-formation. He explains how a set of train tracks crossing the Alps from Vienna to Venice was built before there were ever any plans to run a train line over that route. The builders, he says, were called crazy, but they built the tracks anyway, because they *knew* one day the trains would come—as eventually they did. Mr. Martini compares Frances' efforts with renovating her home—and herself—to those of the track layers, that she's build-ing a home—and a life—that she doesn't have now but that will one day come.

Watching Frances' reaction to the story speaks volumes; you can practically see the light bulb going off above her head when she realizes what her good friend is trying to tell her. She envi-sions possibilities. She dreams dreams. She understands that there's a process making such materializations happen, and so things start to become eminently clear to her about where her life is headed, what she hopes to achieve, and what she wants for herself in the days and years ahead.

It's incredibly gratifying as a conscious creator to witness Frances in this scene—one of the best in Lane's Golden Globe–nominated performance—for she literally starts to come awake. She may not be a fully proficient conscious creation practitioner as yet, but she is definitely on the right path, having come a long way from the start of the film, when she was heavily shrouded under the veil of un-conscious creation. At this juncture, she could probably be described best as a semi-conscious creator, still in need of refining her manifestation skills because form doesn't always follow intent. But lessons aimed at addressing these considerations unfold in subsequent scenes, taking our leading lady ever closer to realizing her full potential as a master of the art. Indeed, one can't help but begin to wonder if one day she just might get exactly what she wants.

The parallels between Frances' reconstruction of her home and herself are especially poignant. Many dream interpretation texts suggest that, when one dreams about a residence, one is actually dreaming about a projection of one's image of oneself. That is plainly the case here, only it's not occurring in a dream but in waking consciousness, a prime example of how the consciously created world around us is a reflection of our beliefs and inner state of mind. Some of the specific renovation acts that Frances undertakes in connection with her home symbolize similar kinds of renovations that she's performing on herself. When she explores uncharted areas of the villa, for example, she discovers it contains items she didn't know existed, just the same as when she explores unvisited areas of her own psyche. When she knocks down walls to create a different floor plan for the estate, she also symbolically breaks down some of her own internal walls to create a new life plan for herself. The symbolic symmetry between the two images is illustrated superbly over and over again throughout the film, coming across like an exquisitely illustrated textbook on the subject, presented in a beautifully filmed, eloquently explained cinematic format.

Frances' deft use of the magical approach is also abundantly apparent in this film. She's initially a little slow to follow her intuitive impulses, but she eventually does, coming to trust them, no matter how strange they may seem. Along the way, she wisely asks questions and seeks advice from others who know more than she does about the tangible aspects of the various challenges that present themselves, an effective means to obtain clarification about and verification for the decisions she is about to make. This illustrates very judicious use of the intellect; she recognizes the need to gather such real-world information to discern the logistical aspects of her circumstances properly, but she never lets logic and reason overtake the conscious creation process. Indeed,

Frances skillfully blends the input of the intellect with that of the intuition so that the two work in concert beautifully, a highly adept manner of employing the magical approach.

"Under the Tuscan Sun" is itself a magical film in every sense of the word. It satisfies on so many levels, leaving the viewer wishing for more, even at the movie's end. The excellent ensemble cast delivers consistently, as do Audrey Wells' screen story and screenplay, both of which are loosely based on author Frances Mayes' memoir. The real star of this production, though, is Tuscany itself, which is captured in all its glory by Geoffrey Simpson's gorgeous cinematography. It's easy to come away from this picture rhetorically asking oneself, "Who wouldn't want to live there?"

Some have characterized this movie as a romance, but I find that label too restrictive. Rather, I like to think of it as a film for anyone who is romantic about life itself and all the joys it brings us in its various and sundry ways. Anyone looking for that kind of love will find this picture quite seductive.

So the next time you feel yourself being swallowed up by one of life's unanticipated maelstroms, rent this movie. It may be just what you need to help you get your life back on track. And before you know it, the trains will come along, too.

## Dance Away the Heartache

"The Turning Point"
Year of Release: 1977
Principal Cast: Shirley MacLaine, Anne Bancroft, Mikhail Baryshnikov,
Leslie Browne, Tom Skerritt, Martha Scott, James Mitchell, Daniel
Levans, Alexandra Danilova, Antoinette Sibley, Starr Danias, Lisa Lucas,
Phillip Saunders, Anthony Zerbe, artists of the American Ballet Theatre
Director: Herbert Ross
Screenplay: Arthur Laurents

Whether we're aware of it, we're all performers in the great cosmic dance. Metaphorically speaking, some of us may do a simple two-step, while others engage in a more intricate waltz or fox-trot, and those who are truly proficient partake in the art's grandest form, the ballet. Of course, none of us can take a single step without first participating in the requisite "dance lessons," a learning process that, in actuality, continues throughout life. These lessons become particularly crucial at certain critical junctures, a challenge that all of the dancers—both literal and symbolic—find out when gracing their respective stages in the engaging drama, "The Turning Point."

Two decades after they last performed together, a pair of one-time aspiring ballerinas, Deedee (Shirley MacLaine) and Emma (Anne Bancroft), meet for a midlife reunion. Despite their common past, they each ultimately pursued separate paths: Deedee chose to marry fellow dancer Wayne (Tom Skerritt) and raise a family, while Emma went on to stardom and the solitary life that such a focused career often demands. Although each seems reasonably content with the lives they've chosen, they also can't help but wonder what might have been.

For Deedee, such speculation comes through loud and clear during one of her reminiscences with Emma about a role in *Anna Karenina* that they both had been vying for years earlier, a part that Emma eventually won. In reminding Deedee why she didn't land the role, Emma says, "You got pregnant," to which Deedee replies, with a touch of both envy and ennui, "And you got nineteen curtain calls." Emma, meanwhile, quietly ponders what it might have been like to get married and have children, especially when she sees the joy that family life has brought to her friend and former rival.

With that set-up in place, their exploration into where the grass truly is greenest thus begins. The tension between the two is palpable, to say the least, but the heat gets turned up more than a few notches when Deedee and Emma must confront their unfulfilled aspirations through the reflection provided them by a very conspicuous mirror, Deedee's daughter (and Emma's goddaughter) Emilia (Leslie Browne), an upcoming dancer on the verge of her own stardom. Emilia's on- and offstage experiences provide her elders with echoes of their own pasts, which forces them to look at what they did (and didn't) create for themselves—and why.

This touching and bittersweet tale offers an intensive examination of creation by default. From what they say, both Deedee and Emma would lead us to believe that they were practicing un-conscious creation, that "things just happened." However, as the film progresses, they grow ever more aware that such is not the case. They begin to become conscious of the beliefs that drove their creations. What's more, they also start to become aware that they realized their motivations as those events unfolded, even if they had chosen not to acknowledge them at the time. From this new understanding, they eventually come to discover that they each got exactly what they wanted in the first place, but they must go through considerable angst and catharsis to come to terms with that realization.

Going through an evaluation process like this carries a number of significant implications for these characters and, by way of their example, for us as viewers. Perhaps the most important of these is owning up to one's creations and the responsibility that entails. Although they may not have consciously avowed their creations as such as they materialized, Deedee and Emma were keenly aware of them—and what brought them into being—even if not acknowledged until well after the fact. Because of this, they come to realize that they can't realistically hide behind a convenient shield of un-conscious creation, especially since each of them assuredly knows better, even if they haven't admitted such cognizance to each other (or even to themselves). They have to take ownership of their manifestations, whether they like it or not.

In line with this, such an evaluation also raises issues related to victimhood and the reliance we sometimes place on it when we try to distance ourselves from what we think of as ill-conceived creations or when we feel sorry for ourselves over unrealized, hoped-for aspirations. Because it becomes evident that Deedee and Emma knew what they had been doing, they can't credibly retreat behind such excuses as "I didn't have a choice" or "Things happened outside of my control" for not creating their lives differently. Those explanations simply won't wash here, and Deedee and Emma have to come to terms with that, no matter how difficult, humbling, or uncomfortable that might be for them.

Carrying these ideas further, this type of examination thus forces the protagonists to take a critical look at themselves—who they really are, what beliefs spark their creations, and how they feel about all that. This turns out to be an often painful process for Deedee and Emma, two individuals who were simultaneously good friends and fierce competitors, a volatile mix of qualities indeed. Reconciling their feelings for themselves about this potentially combustible combination of traits—and how they once allowed it, and continue to allow it, to affect their relationship—is a dicey challenge for sure, one that sometimes makes traversing a tightrope seem like a cakewalk by comparison.

As all of the preceding soul-searching transpires, Deedee and Emma also have a glorious opportunity to verify their satisfaction with the choices they've made, to joyfully validate for themselves the lives they've led. So often we go through life with nagging regrets or unresolved speculations that can gnaw at us for decades. Yet the leads in this film have the chance to see that maybe regrets really aren't all they're cracked up to be in the first place, that maybe the grass is greenest on *this* side of the fence after all. As difficult as going through that process might be, it's ultimately very healthy, especially if we come to realize that the manifestations we've created were the ones we were supposed to bring forth from the outset. Such after-the-fact awareness may still represent creation by default (as a form of semi-conscious creation), but if the analysis endorses our personal satisfaction in our creations, that's truly icing on the cake.

Meanwhile, the experiences of Emilia are fascinating to watch as she faces choices similar to those that Deedee and Emma once addressed. Should she create a life devoted exclusively to her art, as her godmother did? Or is romance a more fulfilling option, following the example of her mother? Or maybe Emilia can integrate both into her life, an option different from both of her elders and a possibility that becomes more tempting as she becomes smitten with Yuri (Mikhail Baryshnikov), a handsome young Russian ballet star. Perhaps having the example of those who followed both paths—and who are now engaged in critical evaluations of paths taken and not taken—is an advantage for Emilia as she tries to create a rewarding life for herself.

An asset decidedly in Emilia's favor is her ability to work the magical approach skillfully. She follows her intuition faithfully and yet takes prudent, practical, intellect-inspired steps as needed. Her proficiency in this technique suggests a wisdom and maturity beyond her years. This is not to suggest that everything in her life flows smoothly, but she seems to have a good grasp of this conscious creation strategy, especially as she sorts out her opportunities.

"The Turning Point" is a rich, engaging movie in many respects. In addition to its profound and moving story line, it's a visual feast for dance lovers. Ballet sequences are generously scattered throughout, brilliantly performed and beautifully photographed. The script also reveals much about the behind-the-scenes workings of the dance world, which sometimes has an ugly side equal in caliber to its onstage grandeur. Various other subplots involving an array of colorful characters weave seamlessly into the main story, providing additional insight and perspective about the lives and worlds of the protagonists and their peers.

The film was lavishly showered with praise at the time of its release, earning eleven Academy Award nominations. In addition to bids for best picture, director, and original screenplay, the movie deservedly earned acting nods for MacLaine, Bancroft, and Baryshnikov, as well as for Browne (though it *had* to have been for her dancing). Unfortunately, the film went home empty-handed on Oscar night, though it had previously won two Golden Globes on six nominations.

The drama that is life (or, more precisely, the drama that we often make out of it) often seems stressful and overwhelming as we go through it, but sometimes it's necessary to our growth and to show us things about ourselves and our lives that we might not be able to see otherwise. Once we have such awareness, however, we also come to realize that such drama is no longer necessary, that we can respond to our challenges and opportunities in different ways—ones that don't involve such upheavals of emotion. By simply coming to know ourselves better, we might be able to treat once-difficult situations in entirely new ways, ones that are less painful, more fulfilling, and even more joyful. We may indeed be able to approach these situations by following the advice of the pop band Roxy Music and simply "dance away the heartache, dance away the tears."[13]

## Bonus Features

### *Un-conscious Creation Films*

"The Fountainhead": An innovative, integrity-driven architect creates designs that are brilliant but few people want to build, because they are seen as too revolutionary. Eventually, however, courageous patrons step forward to support him, and his creations gradually materialize. Over time, success and an unwavering devotion to his vision cloud his judgment, leading him to extremes in seeing his plans realized. An excellent study on properly balancing the elements of the magical approach and the consequences that failure—and success—can bring in managing one's conscious creation practices. (1949; Gary Cooper, Patricia Neal, Raymond Massey, Robert Douglas, Kent Smith; King Vidor, director; Ayn Rand, book and screenplay)

"Gallipoli": An aspiring sprinter who creates magic with his feet can't help but give in to his compulsion to go off and fight in World War I, thinking it's the best venue to put his talents to use, serving as a field courier. His best friend tags along to try to steer him out of harm's way. Gripping battlefront drama ensues as the characters—in tandem and individually—seek to find the right mix of intuition and intellect to help them direct their lives. (1981; Mel Gibson, Mark Lee, Robert Grubb, Tim McKenzie, David Argue, Bill Kerr, Bill Hunter; Peter Weir, director and story; David Williamson, screenplay; one Golden Globe nomination)

"Zardoz": A group of elite scientists and scholars in a dying world learn how to overcome death and thus seal themselves in pristine sanctuaries designed to preserve humanity until a better time. But immortality carries a cost; even having all the time in the world can't solve certain problems, particularly creations that stem from faulty beliefs in the first place. The situation becomes that much more complicated when an unexpected bringer of death arrives to change things. Whacked-out, satirical sci-fi at its best. (1974; Sean Connery, Charlotte Rampling, Sara Kestelman, John Alderton, Niall Buggy; John Boorman, director and screenplay)

### Semi-conscious Creation Films

"The Last Temptation of Christ": If the Lord works/co-creates in mysterious ways, His star pupil, Jesus Christ, finds out just how true that is. In struggling to bring forth his messages of love, compassion, brotherhood, and salvation into the world, the sometimes reluctant prophet learns valuable lessons in conscious creation—ones that help him realize his goals, even if in unexpected ways. (1988; Willem Dafoe, Harvey Keitel, Verna Bloom, Barbara Hershey, David Bowie, Harry Dean Stanton, Victor Argo, Andre Gregory, Juliette Caton; Martin Scorsese, director; Nikos Kazantzakis, book; Paul Schrader, screenplay; one Oscar nomination, two Golden Globe nominations)

"Howards End": The dying wishes of a kindly matron seek expression through conscious creation. Her focused intentions wend their way into and through the intricate, interlocking relationships of three early twentieth-century London families. Hoped-for materializations struggle for fulfillment, particularly against the consternation of those who would try to steer events in other directions. Elegant, masterful filmmaking in all respects. (1992; Vanessa Redgrave, Emma Thompson [Oscar and Golden Globe winner], Helena Bonham Carter, Anthony Hopkins, Samuel West, James Wilby, Adrian Ross Magenty, Nicola Duffett; James Ivory, director; E.M. Forster, book; Ruth Prawer Jhabvala, screenplay [Oscar winner]; three Oscar wins on nine nominations, one Golden Globe win on four nominations; Anniversary Prize winner and Palme D'Or nominee, Cannes Film Festival)

"Apollo 13": An ill-fated moon mission doesn't go as planned, but it provides a valuable learning opportunity for all involved, both technically and personally. An excellent account of how what could have been one of America's worst space program tragedies turned into one of its finest hours. (1995; Tom Hanks, Bill Paxton, Kevin Bacon, Gary Sinise, Ed Harris, Kathleen Quinlan; Ron Howard, director; Jim Lovell and Jeffrey Kluger, book; William Broyles Jr. and Al Reinert, screenplay; two Oscar wins on nine nominations, four Golden Globe nominations)

# 2

# Perception Is Everything, Isn't It?

## *When What We Think We Know Doesn't Match What We Perceive*

Soon your inner transformation becomes reflected in everything that surrounds you.

*Kathleen Vande Kieft*

Picture three people sitting in a 68-degree room. One gently tamps away tiny beads of sweat from his brow and complains about how warm it is, while another shivers slightly and harrumphs about getting the fur out of storage. The third, meanwhile, insists the temperature is perfect and silently muses about whether his cohorts are exaggerating, getting sick, or becoming delusional.

So, at the risk of the inevitable three bears analogy, is this room too hot, too cold, or just right? If perception is everything in assessing reality, then whose reaction is the "correct" one?

It's certainly puzzling how three people could have such different responses to the temperature, a quality of the room's environment assumed to be uniform and easily verifiable with an ordinary thermometer. Yet instances of variation like this occur all the time, in all kinds of contexts. I'm reminded of one that happened to me some time ago. One of my hobbies is nature photography, and I often give framed enlargements as presents. One year, I gifted a friend for her birthday with a close-up of a dew-soaked rose that I took at British Columbia's Butchart Gardens. "My, what a lovely shade of pink!" she exclaimed. "Pink?" I replied. "That's not pink, it's light orange, like a Creamsicle," I said, somewhat miffed. "Nonsense," she snorted, insisting that I was dreadfully mistaken and claiming that the flower was indeed coral pink. I, of course, thought she needed her eyes examined.

Again, who's right?

These anecdotes aptly illustrate varying differences in sensory perception. Granted, the variations in these cases are minor and, to most of us, would likely be insignificant. But the perceptions are definitely not identical, either, and one can't help wonder why that's so, especially if both examples supposedly involve the assessment of objectively measurable criteria. In short, there just shouldn't be any disparity, should there?

Arriving at this conclusion requires reliance on a very big assumption—a belief that we all perceive reality in exactly the same way. But do we? And if we do, how do we reconcile that notion with conscious creation, a philosophy that asserts we each create (and, by extension, perceive) reality in our own way?

If the items in the preceding instances truly were identical, there would be no noticeable differences in their intrinsic qualities; subjective perceptions of them simply wouldn't exist, because there would be no variations to perceive! Of course, such inherent uniformity would also nullify the argument in favor of conscious creation, for the kinds of observable distinctions that it makes possible would be patently impossible.

In my view, differences in perception, even if miniscule, actually make an eloquent case *for* conscious creation. If we each manifest our own existence, then naturally there would be variations in what we perceive; they would come with the territory. Even though there may be general agreement among us that we are observing roughly the same things, the specific discrepancies we each sense reflect the particular beliefs that we employ in creating our individual realities. The minor differences in these examples are likely based on beliefs that simply mirror personal preferences, but they're beliefs nonetheless.

To paraphrase this chapter's opening quote, our inner selves really do become reflected in everything that surrounds us, and our perceptions verify that for us with startling accuracy, down to the subtlest of nuances. The question is, however, do we truly understand (and trust) everything our perceptions are trying to tell us (such as how our outer realities reflect our inner states of mind), or do we treat them as mere observational measures of surface qualities? How we answer that will shed light on the value we place on them and how we make use of them as conscious creators. Superficial perception might be everything to some, but to others, it may be just a starting point, the proverbial tip of a gargantuan iceberg.

★     ★     ★

Most of us tend to take the perceptions of our five outer senses as gospel truth, objective evidence of what's around us. But if what we actually perceive doesn't jibe with what we think we perceive (or are supposed to perceive), the almighty sensory gospel suddenly seems suspect. For instance, why does the 68-degree room, which normally feels fine, suddenly seem chilly? Disconnects like this can be disorienting; they might even cause us to wonder, if we can't trust our senses to depict our world accurately, what *can* we count on? At the same time, if we look closely enough, we might see that a variance in something like temperature sensitivity could be trying to alert us to important information, such as the onset of illness and the need to attend to our health. Whether we pick up on the message of that perception, however, depends on how thoroughly we examine and understand it. If we dismiss it too easily, the ramifications could be unpleasant.

What may be even more distressing to those of us locked into sensory tunnel vision is what happens when our perceptions vary from those of others. Small discrepancies in how we feel temperature or view color could be dismissed as annoying nuisances, but suppose our perceptual variances are greater in magnitude; we might feel seriously out of synch with those around us. For instance, it would be strange, if not downright scary, if I were the only one having a significantly different sensory experience from everyone else around me, such as seeing a grotesque green apparition hovering near the ceiling. Incidents like that, freaky though they are, nevertheless raise many relevant questions about what we perceive and why we perceive it in the ways that we do. But even under circumstances as bizarre as this, someone adept at analyzing observations (and keeping a cool head) might be able to cut through the surface qualities to see what intended meaning lies underneath. In this case, since I'm the only one perceiving the image, perhaps it's trying to tell me that it has information pertinent to me alone. If I've been up for seventy-two hours, for example, the appearance of something as whacked out as this may be trying to tell me I desperately need sleep, that continued deprivation would be unwise. Others around me would not sense this image, for the message is not intended for them (especially if they're properly rested). Whether I see this for what it is, however, again depends on how well I'm able to assess the perception's true nature.

To analyze the meanings of our observations properly (especially those that baffle us), we need to dig deeper than just the raw data provided by sensory input. We must look at what's behind them—namely, the beliefs and intents that shape them. If we do so, we should be able to see that our perceptions faithfully provide tangible feedback of what we're genuinely thinking, feeling, and creating, as the previous examples illustrate. Once we realize that, we should also be able to embrace them more fully for what they are—true measures of our own individual realities.

Unfortunately, some of us never take that plunge. Instead, we stay stuck at the appearances level, believing that sensory perceptions only provide surface information and that they necessarily must match those of others. And we can get ourselves into trouble if those expectations aren't met.

★    ★    ★

The first and perhaps most vital step in analyzing our perceptions is to become comfortable with the idea that variations in them indeed exist among us, that it's OK to see something in a different light from someone else. Since they are our own creations, we should trust them, too, no matter how much they vary from typical expectations, how outlandish they seem, or how widely they differ from those of others. But as simple as that sounds, it's often easier said than done.

I suspect we're sometimes hesitant to flex our perceptual independence muscles because we're afraid that doing so might shock our peers or, worse yet, offend the powers that be in heavily entrenched institutions, such as traditional science or mainstream religion. Mind you, there's nothing inherently wrong with these institutions, but the ways we've handled our relationships with them have caused problems for some of us, mainly by giving them too much power to define what constitutes an acceptable interpretation of reality, including impressions of it. And since both demand strict conformity from their constituents, it's no wonder that we might be reluctant to express truthfully what our observations tell us, particularly if they don't comply with the established standard.

Moreover, these institutions are seriously invested in rigid rational structures, such as the intellect and dogma, and dismissive of more intangible influences, such as the intuition and personal spirituality, which they see as too irrational to be properly trusted. In adopting this position, however, they have willingly endorsed a superficial approach to assessing perceptions that purposely marginalizes influences capable of providing some of the most significant insights into understanding such meanings and underlying beliefs. Restricting the analysis process to the surface level is like trying to practice the magical approach by using the intellect alone and intentionally cutting out the input of the intuition. The results in either case are sure to be half-baked at best.

Still, for many of us, it's simply easier to follow the dictates of those institutions that seemingly set the parameters in these regards. Besides, plying one's own course can be a scary prospect. Author Caroline Myss addresses this point repeatedly in her excellent audio course, "Energy Anatomy,"[1] when she speaks of the severe disapproval such institutions ("tribes," as she calls them) can inflict on individuals who have the audacity to suggest the emperor wears no clothes. I believe the members of these collectives fear bold moves like this, for they set an example that one day the collective will have to follow. Such forays into uncharted territory are terrifying, making it imperative to keep renegades in line. When would-be mavericks face a threat like that, saving their own necks would seem the most prudent course.

The second step, as hinted at in the previous examples, is to examine and embrace our perceptions as thoroughly and as honestly as possible, no matter how out of step they might make us feel. As challenging as that can be, however, there are many rewards that come with it. For example, heightened awareness of the true nature of our perceptions could help us make fuller use of our intuition. If we realize that they are being shaped by more than just sensory and intellectual input, we can tap into our intuition more effectively. This allows us to understand better exactly what we're sensing and the beliefs behind that, because our perceptions will appear more fully "in-formed," showing us all of the influences contributing to their coalescence. As a bonus of this, enhanced use of the intuition would also enable us to employ the magical approach more skillfully, allowing us to become more proficient conscious creators.

Such enhanced astuteness can also help us better grasp the gravity of many of the situations we face in ways not possible before. For instance, it may help us avoid unsuitable behavioral responses to what we perceive; we might be less inclined to resort to judgment and prejudice, for example, if they're seen as inappropriate. On the flip side, it would also raise awareness about more appropriate responses that we previously underused or hadn't considered; such qualities as compassion and forgiveness could potentially be major beneficiaries of this. Our ability to sniff out deception (and self-deception) might be greatly enhanced, too, keeping us from making or repeating costly errors.

The films in this chapter show us that perception isn't the superficial practice we often treat it as. They challenge their characters—and audiences—to look at themselves and their situations more critically, to see why they've created what they have. The insights gleaned from such introspection can significantly influence their (and our) responses to the opportunities their circumstances afford.

For the characters in these films, their inner realities truly are reflected outwardly in the worlds around them, just as it is for each and every one of us. By bearing witness to (and, one would hope, learning from) their experiences, we come to see how their stories are in fact reflections of our own, too.

So is perception everything it's cracked up to be? I guess it ultimately depends on your point of view . . .

# Leading Lives of Quiet Desperation

**"Ordinary People"**
*Year of Release:* 1980
*Principal Cast: Donald Sutherland, Mary Tyler Moore, Judd Hirsch,*
*Timothy Hutton, Elizabeth McGovern, Dinah Manoff, Scott Doebler*
*Director: Robert Redford*
*Book: Judith Guest*
*Screenplay: Alvin Sargent*

Sometimes the most arduous task we face in life is simply hanging on. Whether it's literally—to save our lives—or figuratively—to save our souls—we're nearly all faced with this stressful and frightening prospect at some point. It's a time generally characterized by desperation, that panicked feeling that scares us right down to our bones that we'll be consumed by whatever fears threaten us unless we take any and all measures—no matter how drastic—to survive. For those who endure such angst for extended periods, the practice becomes manageable, almost evolving into an art form, one in which it might not even be possible for onlookers to discern whether anything is wrong. But those suffering through the pain surely know its presence, despite the fact that they have honed their practice of quiet desperation to such a degree that their anguish may be barely perceptible—that is, until something happens to shake it loose, exposing it raw for all to see. Then the real challenge of hanging on begins. Such is the scenario that becomes all too familiar to the protagonists in the heartrending drama, "Ordinary People."

The peaceful lives of a well-heeled family living on Chicago's affluent North Shore are shattered by the death of their eldest son, Buck (Scott Doebler), in a tragic Lake Michigan boating accident. The Jarretts are left to pick up the pieces and carry on as best they can, each practicing his or her own form of quiet desperation. But their coping abilities are soon tested again when the sole surviving teenage son, Conrad (Timothy Hutton), attempts suicide to escape his unrelenting despair. He doesn't succeed, but the family is left to wrestle with the fallout of a second tragedy, one whose impact is felt painfully inside the home and uncomfortably in the community at large.

Conrad's parents, Beth (Mary Tyler Moore) and Calvin (Donald Sutherland), follow their own paths in dealing with the twin tragedies. Beth, an ice queen and control freak, tries to pretend that everything is peachy (at least in public), putting on a faux happy face for everyone (except those who need her most) and keeping a lid on whatever she perceives as too humiliating to be seen by the outside world. She flashes her plastic smile in a most convincing way, leading all around her to think that things are just fine. Calvin, a gentle loving soul, tries to smooth things over with everyone both inside and outside the family, but he grows ever more frustrated, disillusioned, and sad that he's ineffective at playing the prototypical strong father figure, unable to fix the pervasive dysfunction at hand. To his credit, he refuses to escape into denial over what's going on, but the overwhelming emotions bombarding him—including feelings he can neither identify nor understand—only make meaningful solutions that much more elusive for him.

Conrad's unwillingness to conduct himself as Beth would like gnawingly irritates her, putting a strain on their relationship and compounding the other pressures already present. So, at his father's behest and in the interest of helping restore harmony in the family, Conrad agrees to undergo psychiatric treatment, albeit somewhat reluctantly. He engages in sessions with Dr. Berger (Judd Hirsch), a wise-cracking straight shooter who refuses to let Conrad hide behind the psychological walls he tries to erect around himself. He cuts through the camouflage Conrad creates to conceal his feelings to see what truths lie beyond and to help his young patient put his life back together.

The various plotlines gradually converge, taking the story in some unlikely directions. Characters and viewers alike come to see that things are not everything they appear to be, often in ways that are totally unexpected, and that things may not be over and done with, even when they appear resolved. This is accomplished through a masterful interweaving of the main narrative with strategically placed flashbacks. From this, we gradually become aware that our superficial perceptions of the characters, as well as those that they have of each other and even of themselves, don't tell the whole story.

The primary challenge for each of the family members is to confront why they have created their circumstances in the ways that they have. Since the mundane aspects of day-to-day life don't provide any insights of a particularly revealing nature, they're forced to dig deeper. This requires them to move past surface perceptions and preconceived notions, to look at what's beyond their superficial actions and emotions, no matter how painful or uncomfortable that is, to get at the underlying beliefs and the deeply buried truth.

Although the heartbreak that comes in the wake of Buck's death and Conrad's attempted suicide is certainly nothing to be minimized, overcoming the hurt of these events is not insurmountable, either. As the story unfolds, viewers catch glimpses of a tremendous reserve of love that has amassed within the family over the years. The task for the characters is to sense its presence and raise it to the surface where it can be put to use to heal themselves and their relationships with one another. How well they succeed or fail at this depends, of course, on what they choose to materialize for themselves, an outcome tied directly to how they perceive their circumstances and form responsive beliefs based on those perceptions.

Some might wonder why the family members have manifested these particular realities to address their challenges. Why, some would argue, did they go to such extremes to discover these things about themselves? There could be any number of reasons, but the one that resonates most strongly with me, as simple as it might sound, is that there just may not have been any other way to do so. If such intense feelings of both pain and love were so submerged under the layers of pretense and forced geniality they have allowed to accumulate, then it may very well have taken consciously created events as powerful—and disruptive—as these to unearth them. I find we often experience or create upheavals in our own lives for purposes like this, and they usually seem so unnecessarily dramatic at the time, causing us to wonder why we drew them to us. But if there's no other way to address such challenges effectively, then we must create what we create to bring about resolution (and, one would hope, a desired outcome). The characters here are no different.

Our ability to identify with the protagonists and their ordeals in virtually any film often reveals much to us about ourselves, but I find that particularly pertinent with this picture. As we watch, we may find ourselves responding to them in ways we typically would under such tribulations, or our reactions might totally surprise us, putting us in touch with emotions with which we've had little or no experience. One would hope that it's the beneficial feelings, such as empathy, that we tap into and not those that would be of little value under these conditions, such as undue judgmentalism. In any event, whatever responses they evoke from us will ultimately depend on our perceptions of them and the resulting beliefs we form about them.

The reaction I had upon my most recent screening of this movie (shortly before this writing) surprised me. I was moved by the level of compassion I felt for the characters, far more profoundly than on any of my previous viewings. Knowing now what the conscious creation process is like, and realizing that it takes effort to become practiced at it, I applied these beliefs to my view of the characters this time around. I came away seeing that they were genuinely doing the best they could, even if I didn't share their sentiments or wouldn't have responded to their circumstances in the same ways that they did. I even found myself feeling that about characters for whom I hadn't felt it before. (I guess perceptions do change when one looks at things closely enough.) In the end, I came to realize that these truly are ordinary people dealing with extraordinary circumstances.

Dr. Berger's contributions in this story are especially noteworthy and particularly critical to how it is resolved. In many ways, this character helped bring psychiatry out of the closet; at the time this picture was released, it showed this profession in a quite different light from the mysterious or lampooned ways in which it had often been previously portrayed, stripping away many long-established misconceptions and taboos and giving it a greater degree of respectability than it had perhaps ever enjoyed on the big screen. But of even greater significance, this film and this character also quietly helped nudge forward the validity of conscious creation as a viable concept (even if that specific term was not used in the movie). Throughout his sessions with Conrad,

Dr. Berger pushes his patient to discover why he's creating the life that he does. Working as a guide, he helps Conrad uncover the underlying beliefs that are fueling his behavior and feelings, helping him perceive that what's going on in his life is springing forth from him and not occurring as some happenstance string of events. In that sense, we could easily draw many parallels between psychiatry and the kind of self-discovery that we often experience in conscious creation. Of course, the level of success we achieve in an endeavor like this depends to a great degree on the skill of the practitioner doing the guiding. A keen sense of perception—being able to see incisively what's happening—is critical, and Dr. Berger, of all the characters, is far and away the most astute in this regard. He has the kind of perception we all should hope for.

"Ordinary People" is a remarkable film in many ways. It's engrossing from start to finish, virtually guaranteed to involve the viewer in a profoundly emotional way. It has the makings of a real tearjerker, so keep those handkerchiefs at the ready, but it never becomes sentimental or schmaltzy in the process.

The performances deserve particularly high praise. Hutton, in one of his first major screen roles, captured the Oscar for best supporting actor for his portrayal of the troubled teen, effectively conveying the trauma of a lost and confused soul without ever becoming belligerent, maudlin, or self-pitying. Moore, who deservedly earned an Oscar nomination for best actress, more than capably demonstrates her range in this role, obliterating any reputation she might have had as being strictly a lightweight. Hirsch, a fellow nominee with Hutton for best supporting actor, plays the hard-edged smart-ass he typically portrays so well, but by doing so in the role of a psychiatrist, he breathes fresh air into a character type that might have ordinarily been treated as cold, distant, and stodgy; he also provides much-needed comic relief at particularly opportune times, but without ever becoming cartoonish. And Sutherland, admittedly the weakest of the lead performances, comes through as well, thoughtfully playing the endearing paternal figure who tries desperately to hold his family together.

In addition to Hutton's Oscar, the film earned top honors as best picture, as well as Academy Awards for screenwriter Alvin

Sargent and first-time director Robert Redford. The picture also took home five Golden Globes on eight nominations.

When tragedy strikes, most of us would no doubt like to put it behind us as quickly as possible to get on with our lives. But sometimes that just isn't possible; sometimes we need to see the lesson in the tragedy we've drawn to us so that we ultimately *can* move forward. Failing to do that may actually keep us mired much longer than we might hope, launching us to into our own protracted lives of quiet desperation. May we all be perceptive enough to see our way clear of that.

## Seeking Asylum

**"King of Hearts"**
*Year of Release: 1966*
*Principal Cast: Alan Bates, Geneviève Bujold, Pierre Brasseur,*
*Jean-Claude Brialy, Adolfo Celi, Françoise Christophe,*
*Julien Guiomar, Micheline Presle*
*Director: Philippe de Broca*
*Story: Maurice Bessy*
*Screenplay: Daniel Boulanger*

Ever know someone who you thought was . . . er . . . not all there, but then later found out that this person was capable of making tremendous sense? As incongruent as those qualities might sound, they do occur together at times, which makes you wonder what kind of special secret wisdom this individual possesses. Of course, in the next moment, this seemingly apparent sage may revert back to a prior state of erratic behavior, leaving you more confused than ever. Now, if you can imagine an entire population of such unique souls, you can grasp the conundrum set upon the often befuddled hero in the charming French comedy, "King of Hearts."

In the waning days of World War I, retreating German troops devise a plan to slow the advance of English forces and keep the enemy from capturing their munitions supplies by plotting to blow up one of their soon-to-be-abandoned strongholds, a small French town. Word of the plan quickly leaks to the local French resistance, who in turn manage to inform Allied forces of the Germans' scheme, albeit in a message that's highly cryptic. Puzzled by the strange communiqué and concerned that an all-out offensive might not be the wisest course under the circumstances, the British commander (Adolfo Celi) decides to send one of his specialists, Pvt. Charles Plumpick (Alan Bates), a bookish, easily confused explosives expert, on a solo reconnaissance mission to investigate.

Meanwhile, as word of the German plot spreads through the town, the locals flee in panic, leaving the village totally uninhabited—that is, except for the residents of the community asylum. In their rush to escape, the townsfolk forget the patients, leaving them behind to fend for themselves—at least initially.

The disparate worlds of the warriors and the asylum residents soon collide. Not long after Plumpick's arrival, as he stealthily skulks about town trying to conduct his investigation, he accidentally encounters the remnants of the German forces as they put the remaining elements of their plan into place. When Plumpick is spotted, he runs to the asylum to get away, paying no attention to where he's escaped. He evades capture from the pursuing Germans with the aid of the patients, but because he's unaware of his surroundings, he doesn't realize where he's ended up. Plumpick admittedly finds his rescuers rather eccentric, especially when they jubilantly proclaim him the returned king of hearts. But because he has no clue about the true nature of his sanctuary, he's also in the dark about who his unlikely saviors are.

Of course, when Plumpick breaks in to the asylum, he also makes it possible for the residents to break out. So when he rushes off to complete his mission, the asylum residents decide to avail themselves of their unexpected newfound freedom. They circulate through the abandoned town, adopting new personas for themselves, often far different from those of their captivity. They become so convincing at it that Plumpick doesn't even realize who they are—at least at first. But once he's aware of whom he's dealing with, he realizes he must depend on their assistance to help him complete his mission—not the easiest of feats, especially since they are more concerned with carrying out his coronation and promoting his courtship to the bashful ingénue Coquelicot (Geneviève Bujold) than with the worries of the outside world. Matters become further complicated when both the Germans and the English send small bands of troops to check on Plumpick's whereabouts, only to have their search efforts foiled by the whims of the peculiar townsfolk. Thus with all this in place, the stage is set to see who will ultimately control the fate of the village.

Viewers are fortunate to be let in on all the minutiae of the story as it unfolds, for if we weren't, we'd be just as confused as the players taking part in it. Plumpick (at least initially) and the search teams, for example, are sufficiently flabbergasted by the strange behavior of the town's residents, not realizing, of course, who they're really dealing with. Their odd comments and unpredictable behavior are certainly not what those from the outside world would consider normal, even if superficially the escapees resemble everyday folks. So from that perspective, then, it's abundantly clear that surface perception alone can't be used as the sole measure for assessing this reality. (If it were, it would be a pretty strange world indeed!)

The reality the asylum residents materialize for themselves raises some intriguing questions about what we manifest through conscious creation and why. For example, many of us would probably look upon the existence the patients have created with pity. Yet most of them appear genuinely happy most of the time. Whether they're behind the walls of the asylum or out transforming their the town, they appear blissfully content in the playfulness of their creations. Considering what those in the real world in this story have manifested for themselves, perhaps the asylum residents have a better idea of how to create true enjoyment out of life. Indeed, in the midst of a world gone mad with war, their example can't help but beg the question, "So who's the crazy one here?"

This is a question Plumpick wrestles with as well. While he never specifically verbalizes his thoughts on this, his actions illustrate his willingness to address it. He's clearly created these circumstances for a reason, even if he's not entirely sure what that is until well on into the story. To say what that is would reveal too much, but suffice it to say that, once he figures out his intent, he doesn't hesitate to act upon it. His story in particular illustrates what a great teacher conscious creation can be when it comes to sharpening our understanding of our perceptions and what's behind them.

As we watch the patients' escapades unfold, we're also treated to their special wit and wisdom, particularly in terms of how it

relates to their practice of conscious creation. I'm especially fond of
one resident's observation that "to love the world, you have to get
away from it." In light of the insanity we often see manifested in
daily life, I can think of few statements that make a more appealing case in favor of creating a reality separate and apart from the
madness, one wherein we take the time to truly appreciate the
beauty of existence, something many of us habitually overlook
as part of our everyday routines.

Similarly, the priorities the asylum residents set in character-
izing the nature of their reality are far from conventional, but,
again, one can't also help but wonder if their way isn't a better
one. In addition to the emphasis they place on following their
own bliss, they are sincerely concerned with the happiness and
well-being of others, especially their beloved king, even if he
doesn't always understand their ways or their benevolence and
devotion toward him. They know he will do right by them, so
they gladly do for him what they believe would make him feel
as happy and fulfilled as they are. In fact, about the only thing
they won't do is unquestioningly follow him when he tries to
impose the ways of the outside world upon them, even if he
believes it's in their best interests. They draw the line at that; they
refuse to let their existence become tainted by such distasteful
ways. Their perceptions are sharp enough to see what that could
lead to. So I again ask, who's the crazy one here? Who indeed
has the preferable reality? Ironic as it may be, sometimes it takes
those who are blind to the ways of our world to help show us
the way out of it.

"King of Hearts" is a warm, funny, joyful picture, full of
amazing depth for a comedy, but it achieves this goal without
becoming preachy or heavy-handed. The movie's circus-like
atmosphere is reminiscent of a Fellini film, only more down to
earth. It's filled with many laugh-out-loud moments, as well as an
array of touching, tender, and thoughtful scenes. Its blend of both
sublime understatement and farcical overstatement make for a
highly distinctive style of filmmaking. Credit director Philippe de
Broca for a skillful combination of cinematic textures all wrapped
up in one sumptuous package.

Bates turns in one of his best performances as the unlikely
hero. Backing him is a colorful cast of eccentrics, ranging from the

elegant Duchess (Françoise Christophe) and Duke (Jean-Claude Brialy) to the streetwise Madame Eglantine (Micheline Presle) to the pompous General Geranium (Pierre Brasseur). Supporting their performances are superb technical contributions in the areas of costuming, set design, and cinematography, as well as an excellent original musical score by Georges Delerue.

The craziness of everyday life is sometimes enough to drive us to escape. We truly seek asylum from the madness, looking for a simpler way of being. The characters in this film have come to discover the benefits of such thinking quite literally (their unexpected jaunt into "reality" notwithstanding). They see from their experience that there are different—and better—ways of approaching life and of achieving happiness in it. We should all be so fortunate to have that kind of wisdom.

# When Life Doesn't Add Up

"A Beautiful Mind"
*Year of Release: 2001*
*Principal Cast: Russell Crowe, Ed Harris, Jennifer Connelly,*
*Paul Bettany, Christopher Plummer, Judd Hirsch, Austin Pendleton,*
*Adam Goldberg, Anthony Rapp, Josh Lucas, Vivien Cardone*
*Director: Ron Howard*
*Book: Sylvia Nasar*
*Screenplay: Akiva Goldsman*

As we all know, it's well-established mathematical fact that two plus two equals five. One can easily prove this truth by taking two objects and adding them to two more to achieve the requisite total. But in case this simple exercise is insufficient evidence, one need only look at the myriad theorems supporting this calculation. As for those naysayers who insist that two plus two equals four, pay them no heed; their thinking is inherently flawed. (They probably also think the world is round.)

Have you ever met individuals so solidly confirmed in their beliefs that their viewpoints are completely unwavering, regardless of what others might say? Perhaps you've even seen this in yourself at times. Either way, the convictions these individuals hold are so strong that they regard their views as obvious, if not unquestionable, not only conceptually but also in terms of how they're reflected in the surrounding reality. But what if they were to discover they were alone in their convictions? How would they then see themselves and their world? It would have to be disorienting to find out their reality is not as they thought it was. But then, what if their perceptions told them they're right and everyone else was wrong? What would happen then? And how would they cope, by capitulating to others or converting them to their way of thinking? These are just a few of the challenges put to both the protagonists and the viewers of the enigmatic character study, "A Beautiful Mind."

The film is based on the unusual life story of award-winning mathematician John Nash (Russell Crowe). Beginning with his graduate school studies at Princeton University in 1948, the movie follows his career as a student, researcher, instructor, and scholar, culminating in his receipt of the 1994 Nobel Prize in economics. But as brilliant as his professional accomplishments were, his personal life was an embattled one due to an ongoing struggle with schizophrenia, a condition that profoundly affected his family life, particularly his relationship with his wife Alicia (Jennifer Connelly). And yet, as difficult as that was, he persisted in his efforts to tame his personal dragons and succeed, ultimately achieving success in his endeavors both inside and outside academia.

Nash's character, as portrayed in the film, is a loner, one who's more comfortable with numbers than with people. He often comes across as a social misfit of sorts, retreating into his own world and having as little as possible to do with "outsiders." In fact, the scale of his retreat is so extensive (and so skillfully and convincingly presented by director Ron Howard) that the scope of it is likely to surprise even the most attentive of viewers. Of all the movies in this chapter, "A Beautiful Mind" best illustrates the notion that perception definitely isn't everything in scrutinizing reality, for both characters and audiences alike. But even more important than that, this film raises a plethora of questions about the nature of one's reality and how one views it.

Throughout the works of Jane Roberts and Seth, there are numerous references to the concept of "probabilities." The books frequently speak of "probable selves" and "probable realities," noting that each of them has its own intrinsic validity and its own likelihood of being made manifest through conscious creation. Indeed, the full range of possible existence seeks expression in one form or another, even if we're not always aware of that fact or able to perceive evidence of it. Our conscious focus may be directed into one particular line of probable existence, but that doesn't mean other lines don't exist; we're simply unaware of them because we choose, because of our individual beliefs, not to send our consciousness in those alternate directions. So with that in mind, the content of this film can be viewed in a whole new light.

For instance, Nash's wife and psychiatrist (Christopher Plummer) work with him intensively to bring him back to reality. But who's to say that his reality is any less real or valid than anyone else's? Moreover, since Nash is a mathematician who is highly adept at probability theories, who better than he to sense the other probabilities out there? Who is to say that he can't experience other probable existences far different from those of his peers? After all, they can't gain direct access to his mind, so how can they claim Nash's perceptions are wrong?

Given all this, instead of branding Nash psychologically out of touch with reality, it could just as easily be argued that those around him are psychologically deficient in their abilities to perceive the wider scope of probable existences. So who would win a debate like that? I guess it would depend on one's point of view. Those who are content with a simpler concept of what constitutes reality would probably call Nash crazy, while his character (or anyone else with comparable capacities), in turn, could easily say that his detractors are ill-equipped to access the broader spectrum of realities available to be experienced. (Considering Nash's temperament as portrayed in the film, his character likely wouldn't say something like that, but, in view of this argument, he'd be perfectly justified in doing so if he so chose.) Criticizing someone, such as Nash, in this regard is patently unfair and, in my opinion, the height of reality-centric hubris.

If we each create our own reality, our perceptive capabilities are all going to differ, too. In fact, depending on the reality in question, the capabilities for perception that exist in some contexts may be far greater than most of us suppose. Jane Roberts writes about this in her book *Adventures in Consciousness*, citing an exchange between Seth and one of the participants in her ESP class sessions who asked her channeled entity about how he perceived a flower pot sitting on a table: "When I use perceptions in your reality, then I automatically translate inner data into physical terms. Otherwise, I am not limited to that kind of perception," Seth replied. "I need not perceive that object as a pot, but I can perceive it as a pot. You must perceive it as a pot."[2] In light of this, then, why should we be surprised if Nash also has capabilities in this regard that differ from the rest of us?

This also raises the question of why Nash's capabilities for perceiving reality differently should matter so much to his peers (or to us). Is it because we're afraid of losing someone cherished from our existence as he slips over the edge as a result of what we see as mental illness? Is it a simple question of trying to exert "control" over someone else so that we can feel more psychologically comfortable in our own skin? Or is it a fear that, if he's bold enough to step into a new frontier of existence, we may one day have to take the same scary steps ourselves, giving up the comfort of something we know so well for something so unfamiliar and potentially unsettling? The answers will vary from individual to individual, but questions like these, in my view, are all legitimate ones worthy of being addressed.

Why Nash chose to create the particular reality he did is unclear, not only to us but also to himself. Perhaps it has something to do with his inclination toward being uncomfortable around people, giving him an escape into something more personally palatable. Or perhaps it's something else entirely that, again, even he doesn't understand. In any case, Jane Roberts and Seth address the issue of one's perception of reality in relation to what we call "mental illness" in their book, *The Nature of Personal Reality*. They offer the following, which may provide a clue to Nash's situation: "Mental 'diseases' often point out the nature of your beliefs as they agree or conflict with those held by others. Here the belief systems are different than those of society to such a degree that obvious effects show in terms of behavior. There are crisis points here as with many physical illnesses, and left alone an individual may well work through [them] to his own solution."[3] To be sure, Nash does search for his own solution, too, employing a skill he's especially practiced at—his ability to see alternate probabilities. He draws upon this both to ground himself and to look for a workable way out of his circumstances.

However, some might also wonder why it takes him so long to use his capabilities to reach resolution. There are a number of possible explanations here. It could be that his perception and probability-seeing abilities occurred to him so naturally that he didn't think they were unusual; why should one want to tamper with one's sense of normal if it seems perfectly comfortable? Second, there could have been some internal resistance to change on his part; he may have asked himself why he should have to conform to the world of others (a distinct possibility, given the disdain he sometimes exhibits toward the more conventional aspects of life and society). Third, there might not have been sufficient incentive to do so; without a suitable carrot, why bother? And last, and perhaps most likely, he simply may not have known how; just because the ability to see other realities came naturally to him doesn't mean that his ability to change them to something else came as readily (developing proficiency in different conscious creation skills doesn't necessarily occur at a uniform pace). He could only work through his situation until he fully understood what his perceptions meant.

Nash's experience illustrates that the ability to envision probabilities is a key skill in conscious creation. The better we can see the outcomes we desire—and perceive what it takes to get there—the more effective we'll be at manifesting what we want. In large part, this is accomplished by being able to spot connections or patterns within frameworks in which they don't make themselves readily apparent. Seeing such configurations goes a long way toward materializing them, and Nash is an expert in this area. We repeatedly witness examples of his ability to spot patterns where seemingly none exist, in such places as piles of numbers, reams of text, and even clusters of stars in the nighttime sky. In the context of bringing forth form out of formlessness, this could be a case in which perception *is* everything. In this regard, Nash truly does possess a beautiful mind.

The high praise this movie garnered was well deserved. It's a flat-out winner across the board. Howard's skill as a director took a quantum leap with this picture, far outstripping any of his earlier very capable works and putting him in select company as one of Hollywood's top contemporary filmmakers. His efforts also earned him and the film Oscars for best director and best picture. The film took home two other Academy Awards for supporting actress Connelly and screenwriter Akiva Goldsman on eight total nominations. It also earned four Golden Globes on six nominations.

The other stellar asset of this film is Crowe's magnificent lead performance, far and away his best to date. He earned a very deserved Oscar nomination for best actor and probably should have won. But having taken home the top prize just a year earlier for his role in "Gladiator," and being in a talent-packed field of nominees for 2001, he was passed over. Under different timing and less competitive circumstances, however, this performance likely would have been a shoo-in.

It's been said that beauty is in the eye of the beholder, but, in my view, that's not quite accurate. As a conscious creator, I believe it's in the mind of the beholder. The more one is able to make use of that mind, particularly in the practice of seeing probabilities, the more beauty there is to behold. Difficult though his journey may have been, we can thank John Nash for helping us see how that all adds up.

## Cynicism on Wry

*"Wag the Dog"*
*Year of Release: 1997*
*Principal Cast: Dustin Hoffman, Robert DeNiro, Anne Heche,*
*Denis Leary, Andrea Martin, Kirsten Dunst, Willie Nelson,*
*William H. Macy, Woody Harrelson, Craig T. Nelson*
*Director: Barry Levinson*
*Book: Larry Beinhart*
*Screenplay: Hilary Henkin, David Mamet*

Think you can trust everything you see on television and read in the newspapers? The press wouldn't lie, would it? After all, the media are made up of trained truth seekers who doggedly pursue "the facts" of what's really going on in our world and faithfully report the results to an inquisitive public, right? And what of politicians, those noble souls tirelessly dedicated to public service in whom we place our solemn trust to serve the public good—we can take everything they say at face value, too, can't we? If you hold any of these beliefs dear, then you just might want to give a look at the bitingly cynical satire "Wag the Dog" and see if you still feel the same way afterward.

For those unfamiliar with the expression that inspired the film's title, it's explained in an opening electronic text sequence:

"Why does a dog wag its tail?

"Because a dog is smarter than its tail.

"If the tail were smarter, the tail would wag the dog."

From there the story line proceeds to illustrate just what all that means.

In the closing days of a national election campaign, an incumbent president is accused of being involved in a tawdry sex scandal with a minor. To deflect attention from the issue, the administration hires Conrad Brean (a.k.a. Mr. Fix-It) (Robert DeNiro), a spin doctor par excellence, to resuscitate the president's tarnished image. His solution is to concoct a phony war that will galvanize public support for his client and win him reelection. To pull off this feat convincingly, Brean turns to Hollywood producer Stanley Motss (Dustin Hoffman) to stage the imaginary conflict. Motss gets the job because, as Brean succinctly puts it, "War is show business."

Brean and Motss, with the assistance of White House aide Winifred Ames (Anne Heche), drum up a scenario in which the United States faces an imminent threat from that rising superpower, Albania. They claim that Albanian insurgents have smuggled a suitcase nuke into Canada and that they threaten to bring it clandestinely across the border into the United States for detonation, an act of aggression that prompts swift retaliation by American forces on Albanian soil. The enemy's motivations are never made clear, but since the war only has to last eleven days until the election, such trivialities go unaddressed. And just to make sure everything seems legitimate, the dastardly duo brings in a team of collaborators to pull things off, including an aspiring actress to portray an Albanian refugee (Kirsten Dunst), a songwriter to compose an upbeat patriotic battle anthem (Willie Nelson), a prisoner of war turned war hero (Woody Harrelson), and an assortment of quirky consultants (most notably, Denis Leary and Andrea Martin).

Not everything goes according to plan, but with the right touch of spin and Motss's repeated reassurances that "this is nothing," even the most harrowing of foul-ups somehow get set right. After all, all that really matters is whether the press reports the "facts" as intended and that the public buys it. As long as that happens, Brean and Motss have done their jobs. They're so good at what they do, in fact, that they should have been hired to do the sell job on the run-up to the Iraq war.

The very premise of this story should make its nexus to perception indisputably obvious. The public's failure to question any of the events that allegedly transpire shows the danger of what can happen when perceptions are limited to surface measures only. "Un-informed" beliefs result, which only serve to stymie any creations aimed at clarification or correction and to perpetuate a cycle of recurring limited perceptions. (And people wonder why they get the reality they create!) Sadly, I believe this exemplifies all too well the kind of sleepwalking that leads to creation by default (as discussed in chapter 1).

If nothing else, this movie cries out for viewers to shake off those slumbers and to look behind the superficiality of our observations to see what's going on behind the scenes. This may lead to the shattering of some long-held illusions, particularly when it comes to respected institutions (like government and the press) that are often regarded with sacred cow status, but that's one of the consequences that comes from waking up. And in this case, I'd apply that assessment to both the characters in the film and those of us in the real world.[4]

The spin doctors' greed and desire for control are plainly apparent, so there's no question what they're out to create. But the unseen masses' motivations are less evident. (Even though they're largely invisible throughout the film, they're just as much a part of the story, for it is their reaction that is ultimately essential to the president winning reelection.) The masses' lack of a stated objective makes determining their creative intent speculative at best, but I believe they subconsciously materialized this scenario to learn a lesson about the corrupting effects of unchecked power and what happens when it gets so far out of hand. Learning by way of negative example may not be the best or easiest way to see what one wants, but it's often a very effective way to learn what one doesn't want, making it possible to determine which probabilities can be ruled out for future consideration (not unlike the way one can learn from creation by default, as explained in chapter 1). How well the masses get the lesson—and, for that matter, how well any of us would learn under similar circumstances—depends, to a great degree, on how thoroughly they scrutinize their perceptions to see what's really happening.

The spin doctors participate in the creation of the masses' lesson just as much as the masses themselves do. Their efforts make it possible for the conditions of the test to exist in the first place. Likewise, the masses allow this scenario to play out not only for their own benefit but also for the puppeteers to have access to a lesson of their own, one in which they have an opportunity to see that their actions carry consequences, too. This becomes apparent to them when, somewhat unexpectedly, an intrepid CIA watchdog (William H. Macy) shows up to question some of the spinners' specious claims and questionable actions. As with the public, the degree to which they understand their lesson depends largely on what they perceive of their circumstances and how they respond to them.

This illustrates how large-scale creations arise with the input of multiple consciousnesses. Put simply, these are prime examples of "co-creations." It also shows how a creation can have more than one intent associated with it, for in this case, both parties are equally student and teacher for one another. Being able to perceive scenarios like this accurately for what they truly are goes a long way toward a greater understanding of one's consciousness, the intents and beliefs that funnel through it, and the role that both play in the creation of individual realities and mass events.

"Wag the Dog" is wickedly funny from start to finish, unabashed in its cynical frankness. Director Barry Levinson and Oscar-nominated screenwriters Hilary Henkin and David

Mamet make no apologies for the smugness with which their picture tells its story, serving up a coterie of arrogant, self-important sleazeballs who relish their guile and audacity and dish it out to a complacent public that lets them get away with it with impunity.

The cast is excellent, particularly the lead pair of rogues. Hoffman, who earned a best actor Oscar nomination, and DeNiro have a great chemistry with one another, plotting their scheme with the impish, impudent playfulness of a couple of frat boys planning pledge pranks, only with much higher stakes involved. Credit Heche and Harrelson with solid supporting performances as well.

In addition to its two Oscar nominations, the film earned three Golden Globe nominations. Unfortunately, it came up empty-handed on all fronts.

Some might wonder what a picture as dark as this is doing in a book of this kind. In my view, it effectively addresses the perception issue that is the subject of this chapter. What's more, and ironically so, it shows us that sometimes it takes a little darkness to shed light on the true nature of things.

**Extra Credits:** A film that tells roughly the same story as "Wag the Dog" is the slapstick comedy, "Canadian Bacon." A U.S. president (Alan Alda) beset by falling approval ratings seeks to bolster his image as a strong leader by ordering his staff to launch a propaganda campaign addressing the dire threat of attack posed by our new would-be foes, the Canadians. Practically overnight, our polite neighbors to the north are demonized as a menace seeking to subvert our way of life and culture, capable of inflicting such unbearable indignities upon us as putting mayonnaise on everything we eat and flooding our radio signals with nothing but Anne Murray music. Although the film does have its share of razor-sharp laughs, particularly in the ways it pokes fun at Canuck culture, its overall tone is frothier and sillier, less poignant than that of "Wag the Dog." However, for those who enjoy this sort of fare, it's worth a look. (1995; John Candy, Alan Alda, Rhea Perlman, Kevin Pollak, Rip Torn, Kevin J. O'Connor, Bill Nunn, G.D. Spradlin, James Belushi, Steven Wright, Wallace Shawn; Michael Moore, director and screenplay)

# The Big One That Got Away with It

"Big Fish"
*Year of Release: 2003*
*Principal Cast: Ewan McGregor, Albert Finney, Billy Crudup,*
*Jessica Lange, Helena Bonham Carter, Alison Lohman,*
*Robert Guillaume, Matthew McGrory, Ada Tai, Arlene Tai,*
*Steve Buscemi, Danny DeVito, Marion Cotillard, Hailey Anne Nelson*
*Director: Tim Burton*
*Book: Daniel Wallace*
*Screenplay: John August*

Anglers the world over are known for their fish stories, those tall tales of adventure that stretch credibility even more than a taut fishing line. Such stories usually speak of the elusive big one that inevitably manages to slip away, their outcomes elevated to epic proportions. Most who listen to these escapades see them for the entertainment that they are; others are dour killjoys, rationally trying to disprove the stories and spoil everyone's fun (their questionable credibility for commenting on the experiences of someone else's reality notwithstanding). These polished story-tellers are slicker than wet floor wax in their delivery, and their capacity for exaggeration is exceeded only by the good-natured humor of their recitation. Most of the time, they get away with it, too. But on rare occasions, they just might throw in a little truth for good measure. In the touching fable "Big Fish," we get some of both.

Silver-tongued salesman Edward Bloom (Albert Finney) has led quite a memorable life. He's always been the prover-bial big fish in the small pond that is Ashton, Alabama, and he's frequently been the center of attention no matter where his far-reaching travels have taken him. From the time he was a lad, Edward always seemed to be a witness to, or a participant in, any number of fantastic exploits—occurrences that, thanks to his natural gift of gab and unrivaled capacity for embellishment, he has successfully spun into elaborate tales of endeavor. And he's never hesitated to share them with anyone who'll listen.

Unfortunately, the one person who's unwilling to hear him out is Edward's son Will (Billy Crudup). Will has lots of issues with his old man's stories. He sees them as ridiculous nonsense and, consequently, a source of personal embarrassment. He views their patent implausibility as being directly opposed to the fact-driven work he does as a journalist. He's especially annoyed by Edward's occasionally ill-timed recountings, a practice that Will sees as little more than his father's relentlessly shameless penchant for self-aggrandizement, even at the expense of others. After a bitter falling out over this, Will distances himself, both emotionally and physically, for a long time. That all changes, however, when the embittered son learns that his aging dad is dying of cancer. Will reluctantly returns home from Paris to square up matters with his father while he still has the time.

Running interference between the two combatants are Edward's adoring wife Sandra (Jessica Lange), his sage physician Dr. Bennett (Robert Guillaume), and Will's loving, expectant wife Josephine (Marion Cotillard). They provide a gentle buffer between father and son, creating a civil environment for Edward to tell his stories one last time and for Will to come to know the father he's spent his whole life searching for. The experience also allows the soon-to-be papa an opportunity to learn what it's like to be a dad himself from the man from whom he most needs to get this lesson.

And so Edward shares his stories, shown through flashbacks featuring a younger version of himself (Ewan McGregor). Through these sequences, we see how and why Edward turned out as he did. Along the way, we're treated to his rich and varied life experiences, including a stint as a carnival worker, a journey to a surreal small town named, appropriately enough, Spectre, and a brief unplanned flirtation with a life of crime. We also get to meet the colorful cohorts who joined Edward in these exploits, including a misunderstood giant (Matthew McGrory), a witch with a gift of prophecy (Helena Bonham Carter), an aspiring poet turned bank robber (Steve Buscemi), a creepy circus ringmaster (Danny DeVito), and a Korean Siamese twin singing duo (Ada Tai, Arlene Tai). (Honestly, what's so far-fetched about any of that?) We're also fortunate to witness Edward's fairy tale courtship of Sandra during her college years (Alison Lohman), a real heart-melting romance.

Needless to say, differences in perception—and perspective—run wild throughout this movie, with the credibility of Edward's stories serving as the fulcrum. The contrast in viewpoints is easily most stark between Edward and Will, polar opposites if there ever were any. Will's beliefs make the stories just as impossible for him to believe as Edward's beliefs make them impossible for him to deny as anything but the truth. Such is the impasse that characterizes the nature of their relationship.

Will says he wants to see what's below the surface where his father is concerned. He aches to know the truth about his "real father," the man behind all those stories. Will sums up his quest like this: "My father talked about a lot of things that he never did, and I'm sure he did a lot of things that he never talked about. I'm just trying to reconcile the two."

From this, it might appear that Will is aggressively seeking to fine-tune his powers of perception, using his understanding of his father as a litmus test. But there's more to it than that. Lofty though his stated intent is, what Will really seems hell-bent on is getting his dad to confess the falsehood of his tall tales. Edward's razor-sharp perceptions cut through his son's smokescreen to see what he's concealing. He holds steadfast, nailing Will's onslaught for what it really is and refusing to concede that his version of reality should be regarded as any less valid than anyone else's. "Who do you want me to be?" Edward asks Will, to which his son replies, "Just yourself." Edward, uncharacteristically angry, responds, "I've been nothing but myself since the day I was born, and if you can't see that, it's your failing, not mine." ('Nuff said.)

One of the greatest ironies in this debate is the fact that Edward and Will are both storytellers in their respective professions. Edward, as a salesman, tells stories to clients to win their confidence and to persuade them to buy his wares. Will, as a journalist, tells stories for his readership as a correspondent for UPI. Their styles and story contents may differ, but they're essentially doing the same thing. Maybe father and son aren't so different after all. Perhaps all they need is common ground. The question is, will they find it in time?

Will's pressing desire to know his real father is also somewhat curious from a conscious creation perspective. Indeed, if we each create our own reality, then isn't the version of Edward that Will already knows his real father? What else is he looking for? If Will wanted a different kind of dad from the one he has, then that's who he would have drawn to himself in the first place. Instead, he drew the father he needed to have come to him. Maybe Will needed somebody to embody the lightheartedness and whimsy that he so desperately requires to counterbalance his overly serious self, someone to serve as an example, who could help instill that quality in him. Edward clearly fits that bill, reflecting the part of Will that most needs attention. But Will doesn't see Edward that way, and by failing to do so, he also fails to recognize that part of himself in need of amelioration. That's sad, for what better purpose can a father serve than to help a son learn about himself, especially those portions that so desperately require love, nurturing, and support?

Fortunately, when we need our reality to present us with outwardly manifested evidence of the inner guidance required to turn around situations like this, it invariably appears, even at the eleventh hour. All we need do is be willing to ask for it and be open to perceiving it. When we do, miracles happen. And when we can see that reflected in the world around us, as this chapter's opening quote suggests, transformation truly is possible.

"Big Fish" is a good time on many levels. Its widely diverse moods range from funny to warm to sad, even touching and uplifting, all without becoming overly sentimental, pretentious, or self-indulgent. The major credit for this goes to director Tim Burton, whose maturity as a filmmaker grew by volumes with this production. The movie definitely bears his mark, yet it's more refined and less manic than many of his other works. The excellent ensemble cast and John August's solid screenplay figure significantly in this, but Burton maximizes their contributions by punctuating them with the quirky exclamation points typical of his signature directorial style.

The performances by Finney and McGregor as the older and younger Edward complement each other perfectly, creating a seamless fit between the two versions of the same character. The judicious use of big-name talents (such as Lange, DeVito, Bonham Carter, and Buscemi) and character actors (such as McGrory and Ada and Arlene Tai, among others) in comparatively small roles is quite effective, too, allowing their star power to shine through without overwhelming the audience or letting their contributions become hopelessly diluted by the larger story surrounding their characters.

The film is a savory technical buffet as well, featuring top-notch work by highly talented teams in costume design, makeup, art direction, set design, cinematography, and film editing. Backing their work is a warm, sometimes ethereal Oscar-nominated original score by Danny Elfman. In addition to the soundtrack's Academy Award nomination, the movie earned four Golden Globe nods.

So much of the time, we take life so seriously. "Big Fish" shows us how to avoid getting hooked on that line by reminding us of the playfulness we need to incorporate routinely in our lives. Lightening up lightens the load we carry and makes the journey that much more enjoyable. We'd be wise to heed that wisdom, for otherwise we just might miss out on one of life's biggest catches, and that's one we truly don't want to get away.

**Author's Notebook:** I have a strong personal connection to this film, and conscious creation played a significant role in that. I saw "Big Fish" for the first time, not knowing anything about it, a few days before the anniversary of my own father's passing. Even though I had a fairly good relationship with Dave, we had some unresolved issues at the time of his transition, which occurred somewhat suddenly in 1987. Like Edward and Will, there was a distance between us when I was growing up, not brought about by issues like those of the characters in the movie but by a lack of time spent together due to his dedication to his work. Consequently, I didn't feel as though I knew him well during childhood and adolescence.

That changed, however, as I grew into adulthood. He and I really began to know and appreciate one another for the first time when I entered my twenties (ironically, at a time when I was now no longer around as much). We were just getting to know each other when a heart attack took him (at work, no less, ever true to form). At the time, there were things left unsaid, feelings unexpressed, stories unshared. There was also some resentment on my part for him leaving just as we were starting to become buddies.

"Big Fish" played a big part in helping me heal those old hurts. Even though seventeen years had passed between the time my dad left and when I saw this picture, the emotions came rushing forth like the big event had just happened yesterday. But watching the movie let me put those feelings behind me at last. And given that I wasn't familiar with the story when I rented it and the synchronicity of the timing, the effects were that much heightened. (Some creation, eh?)

This is very much a picture for fathers and sons, especially for those who would like to feel closer to one another and who still have the time to make that possible. I know Dave would have gotten a kick out of it. I only wish he and I had had the chance to see it together.

## Bonus Features

"Meet John Doe": A minor league baseball player past his prime signs on for a newspaper publicity stunt to portray John Doe, a decent but down-and-out everyman who threatens to kill himself on Christmas Eve to protest the sad state of the human condition. After publication of the alleged suicide note, readers flood the paper with offers of help to persuade John to reconsider his decision. A local circulation-boosting ploy quickly mushrooms into a national compassion-driven social movement with wide-ranging implications that no one involved could have foreseen—except those who hope to exploit it for their own gains. Darkly satirical, yet simultaneously heart-warming and hopeful, and an intriguing study on the seeds that perceptions can sow. (1941; Gary Cooper, Barbara Stanwyck, Edward Arnold, Walter Brennan, James Gleason, Spring Byington; Frank Capra, director; Richard Connell and Robert Presnell, story; Robert Riskin, screenplay; one Oscar nomination)

"Birdy": Two high school pals—one a hotheaded jock, the other a sensitive introvert obsessed with birds—return from the Vietnam War severely injured, one physically, the other psychologically. One draws upon his powers of perception to devise an unusual means for escaping from everyday life; the other uses them to help bring his friend back to his former reality. A thoughtful drama that pushes our views on how and where we might find happiness and contentment for ourselves. (1984; Matthew Modine, Nicolas Cage, John Harkins, Karen Young; Alan Parker, director; William Wharton, book; Sandy Kroopf and Jack Behr, screenplay; Grand Prize of the Jury winner and Palme D'Or nominee, Cannes Film Festival)

"Three Days of the Condor": An intelligent but somewhat naïve CIA operative discovers a terrible tragedy in his New York office upon returning from his lunch break. Realizing that his life is in danger, he flees, believing he can trust no one, even those he thought he once could. He draws upon his keen powers of perception, particularly his expertise in spotting complex patterns, to figure out what happened and why, who's responsible, and how he can keep himself alive. A tense thriller with a sharp psychological vibe that's still relevant more than thirty years after its release. (1975; Robert Redford, Faye Dunaway, Cliff Robertson, Max von Sydow, John Houseman; Sydney Pollack, director; James Grady, book; Lorenzo Semple Jr. and David Rayfiel, screenplay; one Oscar nomination, one Golden Globe nomination)

"The Crying Game": The kidnapping of a British soldier in Northern Ireland leads to the unexpected entanglement of two very different subcultures—Irish Republican Army terrorists and London's gay underground. Appearances are nothing what they seem for all involved, leaving the characters to sort their way through a maze of mistaken perceptions, misdirections, and surprising intentions. An edgy, quirky thriller from start to finish. (1992; Forest Whitaker, Miranda Richardson, Stephen Rea, Jaye Davidson, Jim Broadbent, Adrian Dunbar, Ralph Brown; Neil Jordan, director and screenplay [Oscar winner]; one Oscar win on six nominations, one Golden Globe nomination)

# 3

# Self-Actualized Cinema

## Celluloid Lessons
## from Metaphysical Masters

Each one of us must awaken and know that we are our
own teachers, that we are our own healers, that we are
our own priests.

*Chris Griscom*

Old habits die hard. Clichéd though that may be, as a former
two-pack-a-day smoker who quit nearly a dozen times before
finally succeeding, I can attest to the validity of that belief. I was
elated when I at last reached my goal (one that I have maintained
for eighteen years now), but I also couldn't help but wonder
why it took me so many attempts over eleven years to fulfill my
objective.

No matter how much we try to avoid them, we sometimes
get stuck in conscious creation ruts, unable to free ourselves
from the shackles of repetitive patterns of behavior—or, more
precisely, repetitive patterns of creation. This includes everything from taking on romances destined to fail to pursuing bad
investments to engaging in nasty little habits like nail biting or
overeating. Some form of creation by default is nearly always
the culprit, with sleepwalkers and neophyte creators generally
suffering the most. But even proficient practitioners can fall prey
to this dilemma by simply being unaware of, or unclear about,
the specific beliefs behind their materialization efforts, especially
those that drive them into their ruts to begin with.

If it seems like I've been beating a proverbial dead horse for several chapters now where the belief issue is concerned, then my point must be sinking in, for no matter how you look at it, beliefs really are what it's all about in conscious creation. You'll even note in the opening paragraph how I used the word *belief* instead of *fact* in relation to my experience with quitting smoking. This was intentional. A fact is something absolute, applicable to everyone (if there even is such a thing); a belief, by contrast, is something personal, an element integral to the formation of our individual realities. So when I say "old habits die hard" and "quitting smoking is difficult," I'm expressing personal beliefs, and because those were the thoughts present in my consciousness when I sought to stop, I naturally created circumstances that bore them out. I might not have liked believing those things, and I might not have been readily aware that other belief options were available to me, but, for what it's worth, that's what was in force at the time, and I simply got what I concentrated on.

As intractable as those positions may have seemed, however, they were still just beliefs, personal and changeable, far from immutable. If they had been absolutes, then they'd be facts, and everyone dealing with circumstances like mine—both then and now—would experience comparable difficulties. But that isn't necessarily the case. Those who hold beliefs contrary to mine, for example, might be able to change their habits with comparative ease (lucky bastards). And now that I've had the experience of seeing how my old beliefs played out, if faced with the same challenge today, I'd like to hope I'd choose new ones—beliefs with drastically different outcomes—to gain the experience of seeing how those alternatives would manifest. (After all, those original ones weren't very much fun.)

The foregoing discussion is essentially my way of illustrating why I have chosen to open this book in the way that I have. In the first two chapters, I intentionally approached the subject of conscious creation from the standpoint at which most of us begin—that of knowing virtually nothing about the process. At the outset, we're still locked into a more traditional worldview, one in which we believe things happen to us (rather than as a result of anything we do) and in which we rely on our sensory perceptions and intellect to tell us all we think we need to know about our world. Like it or not, those *beliefs*, limiting and inadequate though they may be, are the ones we employ when we shape existence under those conditions, and we rarely if ever question their merits. They steadfastly persist, too, entrenched like a nasty chest cold in the dead of winter. If anything out of the ordinary arises under their auspices, we generally attribute the anomaly to some sort of inexplicable glitch, a passing curiosity that's easily dispensed with (usually by ignoring it) except under the direst of circumstances. Indeed, when we create reality through a paradigm like this, it's no surprise that one would believe old habits die hard.

But those who become skeptical of this prevailing view are likely to begin questioning their situations, and many eventually find their way to practices like conscious creation to help them redefine and reshape their metaphysical outlooks. Those who are open to such change are ready, eager and willing to take the big plunge to learn more about how to proceed in a new direction. That's the point we have come to now.

★      ★      ★

To know where one wants to go, one needs to start by knowing where one is. Chapters 1 and 2 were intended to provide a sort of metaphysical status report for where we are when we approach conscious creation for the first time. The basics were covered, but in a sort of backhanded way—how not to practice it. That's all about to change.

This chapter is the launching pad for taking the next step—examining conscious creation head-on to see how it functions as a process. This, in turn, will provide a platform from which to later view the qualities that further define it and the tools we can use to make it work more effectively. It is, in essence, the linchpin between the two opening chapters and the remainder of this book.

The films in this chapter provide various overviews of conscious creation, functioning in many ways like metaphysical tutorials. Their approaches are straightforward, and, on the face of them, they're aware of that quality about themselves.

Consequently, the write-ups of these pictures are a little different, more descriptive and less analytical than those of perhaps any other chapter in the book. These movies generally don't lend themselves to analyses of the sort found elsewhere, and attempting to comment on them in that manner would be like trying to evaluate the philosophical insights of a set of stereo instructions. These are excellent films, but they just don't call for critiquing in quite the same way.

These pictures are primarily meant to inform, though they do entertain as well, just in a different way. Viewers should expect more experiences of light bulbs going off than of heart tugs or belly laughs, though the feelings of inspiration and enlightenment one takes away from them are certainly nothing to be minimized (and everything to be celebrated). I'd like to emphasize their overview nature, too. They provide the broad brush strokes of conscious creation, whereas those in subsequent chapters explore the details and nuances. Such particulars are assuredly important, but without the context of the larger picture into which they fit, their significance at this juncture would be about as relevant as a punch line without a joke.

★   ★   ★

Even though these films principally take a general approach to conscious creation, there are several significant themes that run through them. Perhaps the most important of these is the role of consciousness. It should go without saying that this is important; after all, we are talking about *conscious* creation. Through these movies' examples, we see how this nebulous, ethereal force that we each possess is employed to form the beliefs that drive the manifestation process. In many ways, consciousness is depicted as functioning something like an arbitrator, a magistrate in charge of overseeing the magical approach and the intellectual and intuitional elements that feed into it. It collects input from these sources, which it then analyzes and assimilates into beliefs used for materialization, taking concepts out of the realm of the potential and thrusting them into the world of the corporeal. It is the mechanism through which thoughts ultimately become things.

Another theme these films illustrate is the role our consciousness plays in shaping *all* aspects of life, including everything from health to wealth to relationships and even the general state of the world. The breadth of the scope involved here makes abundantly clear the pervasive impact of this component in framing reality. By extension, these movies also depict, both overtly and implicitly, the sheer personal power and incumbent responsibility we each possess in managing our consciousness to bring all these things to bear. Indeed, whether we're aware of it, we truly are powerful beings; there really are no ninety-eight-pound weakling conscious creators.

Awareness of such personal power also helps to open doors to show all of the probabilities available to us, including those previously off our radar screens, a third theme that runs through these pictures. To a great degree, the development of such enhanced cognizance relies on studiously learning the ropes of the process and making a commitment to practicing it, both of which should allow old patterns of beliefs and behavior (like those outlined in chapters 1 and 2) to fade away, almost as if being unlearned. This does require some practice, patience, and diligence, but the effort is well worth it, for when we begin to sense our empowerment as conscious creators, we awaken to a wider range of possibilities—and potential responses—than we may have previously considered. Author and visionary Jean Houston expressed this concept best when she said that such a broader awareness increases our "response-ability" to the challenges we face in life.[1]

The producers of many of this chapter's films borrowed from that idea in terms of how they distributed their movies, which is why some of these titles may be a little unfamiliar to you. When faced with lukewarm responses from typical channels, they employed unconventional means for getting their works into circulation, such as direct Internet downloads, aggressive DVD sales promotions, and special screenings at alternative venues, such as churches and healing centers. They also relied on innovative means for marketing their titles, such as targeted email promotions, Web site advertising, and good old-fashioned word of mouth.[2] Mall multiplexes and neighborhood video stores aren't on their way to becoming dinosaurs yet, but they're not the only games in town anymore, either. This shows how new doors open when traditional ones close—that is, if you know how to use conscious creation to spot them.

Finally, these films repeatedly address the inherent conscious creation nexus between science and spirit (or, in some instances, between science and art). This is a view that was first popularized in Fritjof Capra's *The Tao of Physics*, a landmark treatise on the subject originally published in 1975.[3] Many of the ideas in that work were subsequently addressed in books by authors who further demonstrated how science helps explain spirit and how spirit infuses science, including Michael Talbot, Norman Friedman, Fred Alan Wolf, Lynne McTaggart, Gregg Braden, William Henry, David Ash, and Peter Hewitt, among others. Through these pictures, these ideas have now found a voice on the big screen as well.

In many ways, the functions of science and spirit parallel those of the magical approach elements. Science operates much like the intellect, while spirit mirrors the intuition. But neither the intellect nor the intuition can make the process work by itself; they depend on one another for support. Science and spirit behave much the same way, only we're just now beginning to understand the dynamics of that symbiosis. Even the experts in each of these areas have long overlooked (sometimes unwittingly, sometimes intentionally) the synergistic effects that come from harmonizing these two forces. For those who have seen and accepted the connection, however, a whole host of new possibilities for consciously creative expression has become apparent both in the worlds of science and spirit, not to mention in everyday life. This is particularly true in the area of quantum physics, which in many ways is basically a scientific methodology for explaining the metaphysics of probability. In this particular context, science and spirit have come to appear like two sides of the same coin.

Just as consciousness affects all areas of life through conscious creation, so, too, does the interaction of science and spirit, as these films make obvious. Whether it's in the area of physics, biology, art, romance, spirituality, or any other discipline or endeavor, both influences are present in all of them. They might not always carry equal weight, and their influence may be subtle, but they're both there to some degree or another. We can be grateful that enlightened thinkers in both areas have begun to recognize this connection, even to make its understanding mainstream, to further the education of journeyman creators like us.

Truly, these films illustrate, as New Age therapist Chris Griscom wrote, the need for us to become our own teachers, healers, and priests. And, thankfully, they show us how, too.

## Shopping the Catalog of the Universe

"The Secret"
*Year of Release: 2006*
*Director: Drew Heriot*
*Writers: Rhonda Byrne, Skye Byrne, Paul Harrington, Drew Heriot*

Imagine Amazon.com on steroids. That would be quite an impressive collection of merchandise! Now picture adding the range of potential experiences to that mix and putting it on hormones, too. Sounds like quite a place to shop, doesn't it? Well, if you can fathom that, you have a rough idea of what it's like to peruse the boundless catalog of the Universe. To learn how to access that infinite storehouse of stuff, would-be shoppers should be sure to check out "The Secret."

This little gem of a film was initially available only through alternative channels, namely, over the Internet and on DVD. A slick trailer and an impressive email marketing campaign seductively enticed potential viewers into discovering for themselves the true nature of "the secret," a supposedly long-hidden, little-known source of knowledge that many of history's most celebrated minds were said to have employed to achieve greatness. Using images referencing alchemy, conscious creation's ancient cousin, and citing the examples of such geniuses as Newton, Shakespeare, Beethoven, Emerson, Edison, and Einstein, the movie's creators teasingly pledged to show how these visionaries' experiences could be drawn upon and applied successfully to everyday endeavors. Cryptic though this marketing message may have been, however, something about it apparently resonated with viewers, and interest in the film took off worldwide, eventually capturing widespread attention, even in mainstream media outlets, such as CNN and *The Oprah Winfrey Show*.

Of course, none of this probably would have happened if the producers hadn't backed up their promises with an equally viable product, which they most assuredly did. "The Secret" is, quite simply, an excellent cinematic introduction to the manifestation process, particularly for apprentices, a sort of Conscious Creation 101. It explains how materialization works in clear, concise, easily comprehensible terms, with hypothetical vignettes for handy illustration. In this way, we get to see examples of theory and application, presented back to back, with insightful running commentary offered by a wide range of teachers and practitioners.

The core thinking of the secret lies in its explanation of the law of attraction, a principle that maintains we draw to us what we focus on. Our focus, in turn, depends on what we do with our thoughts and feelings, how we integrate the two, and how we project them forth into the world. Sound familiar? To me, these are merely different ways of restating the function of conscious creation and the magical approach. The semantics may be different, but the concepts are otherwise virtually identical. No matter how you word it, the bottom line is the same.

"The Secret" explains the law of attraction through areas of life that most of us can readily relate to and in which we often face our greatest personal challenges, such as wealth, relationships, health, and all of the bread-and-butter issues we confront on a daily basis. But it also shows how our focus contributes to the shaping of our larger world, putting forth the noble suggestion of imagining what's possible if we apply this basic lesson to the wider scope of our reality.

Some viewers have criticized the film for emphasizing these personal issues at the expense of "greater good" considerations in teaching the law of attraction, and their argument admittedly does have some merit. However, I would also contend that conscious creators need to start somewhere, and getting one's own house in order first really is the best place to start. Think of it this way: When we fly, the portion of the safety demonstration on oxygen masks always instructs passengers to secure their own masks before assisting others. This is because we cannot be of service to them unless we operate from our own position of strength first, and I believe this is advice well heeded, whether we're talking flight safety or helping the world sort out its problems. As virtuous an endeavor as saving the world is, trying to do so from a position of personal subservience (that is, weakness), despite what many traditional religions would have us believe, is, in my opinion, the height of foolhardiness. There's plenty of opportunity to pitch in, but only when our own ducks are in a row first.

In getting our houses in order, it's imperative we first identify where our focus is (that is, acknowledging what beliefs we are harboring). "The Secret" refers to this in terms of assessing our attitudes, but it becomes apparent from the film's examples that these attitudes arise directly from our beliefs. The movie reveals how beliefs translate into what we want, for better or worse, depending on what they are in the first place. It's particularly adept at illustrating how giving attention (and thus power) to what we don't want still often translates into its materialization. As strange as that may sound, consider this: Suppose someone says to you, "Think about anything you like except a pink elephant," and then imagine what you're most likely to ponder. (Chances are, it involves a pastel pachyderm.) Even though the intent has been expressed in terms of a negative, it has still been thought of (that is, given power to manifest), and so it arises as part of your reality. Conscious creation and the law of attraction work exactly the same way.

Thus, to avoid the unintended materialization of what we don't want, it's important to put forth our wishes using terms that reflect the desired results as precisely as possible. This involves phrasing our intents using positive language, stating what we *do* want rather than what we don't. One commentator, author Jack Canfield, offers a great example of this in quoting Mother Teresa, who vowed she would never attend an anti-war rally but who was quick to add that, "If you ever hold a peace rally, invite me."

The film thus makes clear how crucial it is to understand this concept when shopping the catalog of the Universe. It makes this point by comparing God/Goddess/All That Is (pick your term)—the supplier force of the Universe—to a genie, one who is compelled to say, "Your wish is my command." The genie, of course, is bound to comply, no matter how brilliant or harebrained the request. By analogizing the notion in this way, "The Secret" shows us exactly why we end up getting what we concentrate on, be it intended positively or negatively, intentionally or unintentionally, rightly or wrongly, and so on and so on. The Universe is simply fulfilling the dictate it's been charged with by the conscious creator making the request. There's no divine retribution, special dispensation, favored treatment, or capricious agenda at work here; it's a simple case of celestial order fulfillment, delivered with absolute precision.

The benefit of understanding conscious creation in this way is that it ultimately makes us more aware of the range of available probabilities. It helps us weed out materializations that arise from creation by default practices, and the resulting new, broader vision allows us to see options for responses we may have once missed. What's more, specifically in terms of the "greater good" issues, this enhanced view helps clarify our overall awareness, not only in terms of spotlighting the contributions we make as individuals but also in aiding our understanding of the pursuit as a collective effort. If indeed our co-creations (as discussed in chapter 2) all funnel into the larger existence we jointly experience, then we can see more clearly just how much our mutual efforts matter and how our collective input can lead to change. When that awareness is coupled with our enhanced cognizance of personal empowerment, truly great things become possible.

But before we approach that point, we need to start at home first, and, again, "The Secret" is an excellent instructional tool for showing us how, especially for beginners. Seasoned creators may find the film somewhat simplistic for their purposes, but they would be wise to recommend it to aspiring practitioners. To adhere to its rudimentary message, the movie emphasizes the overall conscious creation process and focuses only briefly on its specific mechanical aspects. In offering an analogy to explain this, one of the commentators, philosopher Bob Proctor, notes that we don't need to know how electricity works to make use of it; we don't worry about things like ohms and amps when we switch on a light—we simply want the lamp to become lit. So it goes with the law of attraction, too; preoccupying oneself with what's going on at the quantum level probably isn't necessary for beginners, because they're primarily interested in seeing the principle at work and not so caught up in the means by which it does. Besides, those who want to explore these aspects of conscious creation more fully have other more detailed offerings available to them, some of which are profiled later in this chapter.

A number of the film's commentators will appear familiar to those well acquainted with metaphysical and self-help circles. Among those featured are entrepreneur John Assaraf, spiritualist Michael Beckwith, metaphysician Joe Vitale, psychologist John Gray, quantum physicists Fred Alan Wolf and John Hagelin, and authors Lisa Nichols, Marci Shimoff, Hale Dwoskin, Bob Doyle, and Neale Donald Walsch. Their insights are razor sharp and succinct, never rambling or off point, a key ingredient in captivating and holding audience attention.

Like the marketing campaign that got the film noticed, the slick production values of "The Secret" permeate it from start to finish. Individual segments are well written, nicely paced, and superbly edited in their presentation of theory, application, and commentary. The illustrative vignettes are well produced, too, featuring fine performances and good examples.

Some viewers may want to make the inevitable comparisons between this title and a film that preceded it, "What the #$*! Do We (K)now!?" (also profiled in this chapter). Superficially, there are similarities, including some of the subject matter, the use of fictional examples to accompany theoretical teachings, the inclusion of commentators throughout the narrative, and even the use of some of the same commentators. However, I believe the comparisons end there, because each title is ultimately designed to fulfill different purposes. The strength of "The Secret" lies in its ability to convey its teachings concisely for a primarily neophyte audience. Its predecessor, as will be seen in its write-up, is arguably more appropriate for those whose metaphysical education is a little more advanced, even though it does present its own recap of the basics. In each case, however, both are meaningful, worthwhile pictures, particularly when viewed in the context of their intended audiences.

So grab those charge cards, shoppers, and start browsing the Universe for what your hearts desire. But tune in to this film first so that you, too, can learn the secret—of success.

# An Evolving Body of Work

"What the #$*! Do We (K)now!?"
*Year of Release:* 2004
*Principal Cast (Fictional Sequences):* Marlee Matlin, Elaine Hendrix,
John Ross Bowie, Robert Bailey Jr., Barry Newman, Armin Shimerman,
Robert Blanche, Michelle Mariana
*Directors:* William Arntz, Betsy Chasse, Mark Vicente
*Writers:* William Arntz, Betsy Chasse,
Matthew Hoffman, Mark Vicente

Like the ever-changing colors in a kaleidoscope, reality is in a constant state of flux. Indeed, philosophers from Heraclitus to Jane Roberts and Seth have characterized this state of affairs by saying that existence is in a constant state of becoming. And what better way to reflect that than to create a film—or an emerging series thereof—that itself embodies this very notion. Such is the case with the sleeper hit, "What the #$*! Do We (K)now!?" (more commonly known as "What the Bleep").

So what the #$*! is this picture with the funny-sounding name? And why should an average moviegoer want to see it? Sounds pretty %@^& weird.

I'll admit that I was initially of that mindset. Despite the film's metaphysical content, ordinarily a guaranteed draw for me, I was slow in embracing this movie. The initial descriptions I read didn't do the picture justice, and I thought the title was just a little too precious for its own good. But after numerous favorable recommendations from like-minded friends, and thanks to an astonishingly long initial theatrical run (who would have thought a film like this could have enough staying power to keep it in theaters, at least in Chicago, for several months?), I eventually relented and went to see it. I'm glad I did. I was blown away by it and quickly became an ardent convert to this cinematic missive on the quantum gospel.

Perhaps the reason the initial descriptions didn't sound terribly flattering was the fact that this is a difficult film to pigeonhole, and I believe many mainstream critics didn't quite know what to make of it. Is it a documentary? A theatrical piece? An animated feature? Well, yes. And no. I guess you could say it's best described as a quasi-documentary on the nature of existence, with running commentary by experts in various scientific and spiritual fields, interspersed within a fictional, illustrative narrative that's further punctuated by innovative and often humorous animation and gorgeous special effects. But as unusual as this movie is (at least compared to most of the fare released to the viewing public), it works so well on so many levels.

At the risk of gross oversimplification, the film's underlying intent is to provide a rationale for understanding reality. (Simple enough task, right?) This is initially addressed through a detailed explanation of what happens at the so-called building blocks level—in the subatomic world, the realm of quantum physics, a discipline whose principles form the basis of what one commentator, physicist Amit Goswami, calls "the physics of possibility." Through this analysis, we see how quantum mechanics provides a sensible model for explaining probability theory and how it serves as a means for understanding the emergence of prototype forms of existence. It's a model that works reasonably well, too—up to a point, that is.

As the discussion unfolds, however, we come to see, as research physicists did previously, that, at a certain point, this discipline starts to get goofy. Its mechanics become seemingly paradoxical, if not downright wacky, with explanations that stretch the credibility of those espousing them, no matter what their educational pedigrees are. But such is the world of quantum physics, a study that sheds an entirely new light on the way we look at things.

For instance, in one particularly significant sequence, the commentators discuss the quantum nature of electrons, those little subatomic particles that have traditionally been portrayed as being like tiny planets whizzing in orbits around stellar-like nuclear cores made up of protons and neutrons. These supposedly stable atomic building blocks were long thought to be solid particles. However, quantum physicists who studied electrons found that they were far different. They discovered that electrons essentially exist as particles when being observed and as waves when not being observed. (Two forms of existence, and the shape it takes depends on . . . observation? Somebody tell me they're making this up!) This is like saying that a streetlight is on when your eyes are open and that it's off when they're closed. How can that be? And where's the verifiable proof for something like that (which, quite conveniently, can't realistically be verified)? Yet in the quantum world, not only is such a scenario plausible, it's likely. Even Alice's looking glass world seems normal by comparison.

The importance of that discussion is that it serves as a significant springboard to what follows (both here and in the film itself). Reluctant though researchers once were to admit that a viable model could be based on something other than purely traditional scientific values, some of them (the more open-minded ones, that is) came to realize that they had to adjust their thinking. Slowly but surely they became aware through their quantum observations that they had to make allowances—theoretically at least—for the impact of other influences, such as spirit and consciousness. (The example involving electrons alone would lend credence to the need for this.) Although the impact of these intangibles could not be conclusively proven scientifically, in many ways they also appeared to be the only viable explanations. Once these elements were plugged into the model, things again began to assume a semblance of sense, at least in terms of providing a degree of predictability or tendency—or probability—that wasn't present when they weren't factored in.

This, of course, raises the very valid question of why we should care about all these pie-in-the-sky considerations. ("Interesting, but so what?" you might say.) Well, if we understand that our consciousness, the mechanism that observes and assesses reality, can directly affect the state of something as fundamental as subatomic particles, then we obviously have input into how these elemental building blocks take shape. (OK, so this might generate some moderate amusement.) Now, if we consider that these subatomic particles that are so readily capable of being influenced are in everything around and inside of us, then our observation of them carries considerable weight, for it means our consciousness has the potential to mold our very existence and every aspect that goes into it. (OK, so now your interest is piqued.) And what if we then contemplate what it would be like to start using our consciousness to alter those building blocks of reality in ways that result in a state of being more to our liking? With that, my friends, you have conscious creation, at least in terms of how it operates on a mechanical level. (And if that doesn't grab your attention, I don't know what will.)

But even with this new understanding, some of you still might say that, when all of these concepts are expressed in theoretical scientific and metaphysical terms, they seem so dry and dull. That's where the creators of "What the Bleep" had such a brilliant realization: Why not present these concepts through meaningful examples that viewers can easily relate to? That's where the film's fictional narrative comes in.

The fictional sequences follow the life of Amanda (Marlee Matlin), an uptight, pill-popping photographer who has issues with seemingly everything—men, marriage, body image, and New Age thought, to name a few. Yet something inside her is nudging her to reexamine her beliefs in these areas; otherwise, she wouldn't continually attract a cavalcade of mentors who gently prompt her into questioning her current outlooks. Among those who cross her path are her quirky roommate (Elaine Hendrix), her flirty boss (Barry Newman), an art exhibit docent (Michelle Mariana), a passing stranger (Armin Shimerman), a gallant wedding guest (John Ross Bowie), and a young basketball whiz (Robert Bailey Jr.).

Through her encounters with these unlikely teachers, Amanda takes the first steps toward using conscious creation to reshape her beliefs and her life. This, of course, provides the movie with the means to show how the process affects all aspects of daily living. Complementing Amanda's explorations in these areas are the comments of the experts, who routinely chime in with their insights and special wisdom. The eclectic panel of speakers includes physicists Fred Alan Wolf, Amit Goswami, John Hagelin, and David Albert; medical professionals Stuart Hameroff, Jeffrey Satinover, Andrew Newberg, Daniel Monti, and Joseph Dispenza; molecular biologist Candace Pert; spiritualist J.Z. Knight and her channeled entity Ramtha; subtle energy researcher William Tiller; and religion professor Miceal Ledwith.

Through these discussions and the accompanying examples, numerous themes emerge, but I found two particularly striking, especially when they're examined in tandem. First, if our consciousness influences the functioning of the Universe in the subatomic realm, then the building block components present at that level will conform to how our thoughts, feelings, beliefs, and intentions shape them, as if they were hunks of clay being molded in one's hands. With that said, it means everyone's existence will thus be a tailor-made, individualized creation, fundamentally distinct from everyone else's. It also means that the science of reality is not the objective study we thought it to be. Indeed, it is much more subjective than most of us have probably ever considered, and this picture shows us precisely how that is so. That's worth bearing in mind when we think about how each of us specifically goes about creating our own realities.

Second, the film illustrates reality's inherent interconnectedness. When we consider that the building blocks we use to shape existence permeate everything, then it's obvious there's an innate linkage binding everything to everything else. The qualifier that distinguishes each of our individual realities is, again, consciousness, because it provides the focusing mechanism for the specific range of personal connections within the infinite range of all potential connections that we choose to explore. The specific connections we select help to define the tendencies, or probabilities, that comprise the principal elements or themes of our particular existences. However, as we go about our individual explorations of reality, we would be wise to remember that this boundless repertoire of all possible connections is always present; we can tap into any of them at any time, enabling us to choose new avenues of exploration at any given moment, based on whatever beliefs we then hold. (More on connectedness in chapter 8.)

When these two themes are combined, they raise a fundamental question that many of us have probably asked ourselves and that the commentators pose outright: If we have the full range of potential existence available to us, and we're the ones responsible for which realities we manifest, then why do we continually create the same thing over and over again? This is a particularly relevant question if we're not happy with the results we produce.

In large part, I believe this happens because many of us have never allowed ourselves to address these issues in these ways. There's a wide range of possible reasons for that (for instance, religious upbringing, scientific bias, or general lack of interest), and such explanations signal how the scenarios outlined in chapters 1 and 2 have been able to persist for as long as they have. Consequently, since we've never paid much attention to these issues before, we've also never generated an awareness of the metaphysical mechanics we need for addressing them.

Furthermore, as the film shows in its discussion of how consciousness affects human physiology at the quantum level, the current materialization methodology that many of us use for most aspects of everyday life amounts to little more than a form of belief addiction—one that carries a potent biochemical component with it. As addicts of this kind, we've conditioned ourselves metaphysically and biochemically to re-create behaviors and circumstances repeatedly that give us our daily fix. It's difficult to change this behavior, mainly because many of us aren't even cognizant of this dependency in the first place. What we truly need is inspiration capable of enlightening us about this, steering us in a new direction and making it possible for us to get off the addiction treadmill.

"What the Bleep" does an excellent job in addressing these issues and providing clear explanations of what we need to do to move forward in new ways. By shedding light on these conditions and making us aware of the alternatives that are available to us to change them, we have the resources to strike out in new and more satisfying directions.

Such is the stuff of which evolution—that constant state of becoming—is made. And even the creators of "What the Bleep" have gotten into the evolutionary act in their own way. In 2006, a second version of the picture was released, titled "What the Bleep: Down the Rabbit Hole." This new edition is neither a sequel nor a director's cut but is instead a new take on the original. The same basic approach is followed, and all of the original questions are again addressed, but the discussion flows differently. In this iteration, the fictional narrative has been scaled back in favor of more interview footage with the experts, including new commentary by all of the original speakers and the addition of three more gurus, researcher Masaru Emoto, physicist Dean Radin, and author Lynne McTaggart. There is also the inclusion of several animated sequences for explaining various scientific principles featuring the venerable Dr. Quantum (voiced by actor John Astin).

Both the original and remixed versions are technically excellent in all regards. The editing is especially masterful in its intercutting of theory and application. Virtually every comment by every expert interviewed is a gem of metaphysical or scientific wisdom; there's no fluff or filler here. Accompanying all this are fine production values in everything from special effects to musical score to art direction. In every respect, both editions of the film are knockouts.

As much as I thoroughly enjoyed this picture, it still amazes me that this unlikely title has had such a tremendous impact. Moviegoers who I never thought would be into material like this have told me they've seen it and loved it. (I guess that reveals a limiting belief of mine, now doesn't it?) Perhaps its popularity stems from a hunger to find answers and direction that have not been forthcoming through more conventional channels, like mainstream religion or traditional science. Perhaps it truly is time for a new paradigm in the world, and the "What the Bleep" school of thought is providing the means to help birth it. In that sense, its contribution to cinema in particular and the wider world in general is arguably more than just evolutionary; it's revolutionary as well.

## Double Feature: Out of the Minds of Babes

### "The Indigo Evolution"
*Year of Release: 2006*
*Directors: James Twyman, Kent Romney*

### "Indigo"
*Year of Release: 2003*
*Principal Cast: Meghan McCandless, Neale Donald Walsch,*
*Sarah Rutan, Gregory Linington, Dane Bowman, Lynette Louise*
*Director: Stephen Simon*
*Screenplay: James Twyman, Neale Donald Walsch*

Wouldn't it be something if we all came into this world knowing why we're here and what we were meant to accomplish? On top of that, wouldn't it be great if we arrived with capabilities that enabled us to work miracles with remarkable ease, making conscious creation look like the play it's really meant to be? That appears to be happening now with the emergence of a whole new group of children who have been variously called the "crystal children" or the "children of Oz" but who are perhaps best known as the "Indigos." These exceptional kids are the subject of two revealing films, "The Indigo Evolution" and "Indigo."

So who are these Indigo children? Well, that's difficult to define with certainty, but be assured they're not the offspring of bluebloods, the groupies of a folk rock duo, nor smurfs who stayed out in the sun too long. Rather, they're kids who have been born over the past twenty to thirty years, in steadily increasing numbers, who have arrived with a strong sense of self and a ready awareness of who they are, why they're here, and what destinies they're meant to fulfill, truly visionary conscious creators in many respects. They frequently possess strong artistic and spiritual sensibilities, as well as such paranormal skills as telepathy, clairvoyance, a capacity for healing, and astute past life recall. Many refer to these capabilities as "special gifts." But as special as we might find many of these skills, Indigos tend to think of them as perfectly natural components of being. They would likely say that these skills are our birthright and that they're just more ready, willing, and able than most of us to put them to use in shaping their everyday lives. To this end, then, one of their main purposes in being here, apparently, is to make us more aware of what we already possess but that most of us have allowed to remain dormant or become atrophied. (They've got their work cut out for them, but I'm glad they're here.)

According to Lee Carroll and Jan Tober, authors of *The Indigo Children*, the first reference to these youngsters is believed to have appeared in the 1982 book *Understanding Your Life Through Color*[4] by educator and parapsychologist Nancy Ann Tappe.[5] Carroll and Tober write that Tappe was the first to note the dominant placement of this color in the children's auric fields, the energy bodies that form bubble-like capsules around our corporeal selves. The predominant appearance of this dark blue hue in their auras hence gave rise to the term that identifies them. The presence of indigo auric energy distinguishes these youngsters from those born in prior generations, whose prevailing colors are generally different. This is not to suggest that all children being born now are Indigos; individual variations occur in every generation, even today. However, these new kids appear to be arriving in ever-growing numbers, and their presence has been hard to ignore. They have been steadily garnering wider public attention, too, even in such bastions of traditionalism as the mainstream media.

So why all the fuss about dark blue energy? Pamela Oslie, author of the book, *Life Colors*, writes that the prevalence of specific colors in the auric field is indicative of particular qualities that help to define one's character, abilities, and outlook,[6] and the traits associated with the color indigo mark the appearance of a new set of characteristics compared to those born with other auric color makeups. Individual variations in personal qualities occur within particular color schemes, even among Indigos, but certain traits tend to dominate, such as the pronounced artistic, spiritual, and paranormal qualities mentioned earlier. Some other common characteristics of Indigos, according to Carroll and Tober, are a sense of "deserving to be here," difficulty with absolute authority (especially if unexplained), frustration with meaningless ritual, an ability to see how to streamline procedures, and an unabashed ability to seek fulfillment of their needs.[7] They are also often brutally honest, voracious learners, and startlingly compassionate. That combination of qualities, when added to their other sensibilities, generally makes them a bright, articulate bunch, but the sometimes contradictory nature of their character can also make them a lot to handle, especially to those unaccustomed to dealing with children so forthright and demonstrative in expressing themselves.

"The Indigo Evolution," an excellent documentary by spiritual activist James Twyman, takes an in-depth look at these children and the phenomenon they represent. It includes segments about the colorful lives of these enigmatic youths, their creative and spiritual messages for the world, and the challenges (and opportunities) that they and their families face in a world slow to embrace sociocultural innovation and spiritual evolution.

Intercut with these sequences are interviews with some of these kids and their parents, members of various professions (education, medicine, and psychiatry mostly) who must cope with the special needs of these youngsters, and a number of metaphysical teachers who offer their perspectives on the children and what they bring to the world, including Doreen Virtue, Ram Dass, Gary Zukav, Don Miguel Ruiz, Masaru Emoto, and Neale Donald Walsch. There is also an especially engaging sequence about the appearance of Indigos in Native American culture, a development prophesied in folklore long ago.

In addition, the documentary addresses, at least by inference, some of the contentions of skeptics, who often feel that all the talk about these new kids is just so much New Age hype. Unfortunately, many of these skeptics are in positions of authority, and their actions in handling (or mishandling) these children can have profound consequences.

For example, because Indigos have such a strong sense of self-awareness and different sensibilities, they often question officialdom in various aspects of life, such as education. They need to know the value and purpose of learning what they're being taught, including the whys and hows of instruction. Once they understand, if they believe in the authenticity and validity of what they're being told, they generally go along quite willingly. But if they sense deception or rote, inflexible protocol, they'll rebel, often vehemently, and simply saying "Because I said so" to them has little impact on their behavior. Because of this, Indigos present a unique set of schooling challenges to educators.

However, the skeptics charge, is this a genuinely different sensibility or merely a result of excessive coddling? Progressive thinkers have looked for innovative ways to cope with these challenges, such as alternative study programs. But those who are less open-minded have often resorted to resolving the issue by simply branding Indigos as suffering from such conditions as ADHD or even some forms of autism and prescribing drugs to treat them.

This, of course, raises all sorts of questions of whether such diagnoses arise out of real legitimacy or mere convenience. These circumstances present tremendous challenges for these kids, to be sure, and they're courageous conscious creators for willingly going along with these co-created scenarios to help educate the unenlightened on the folly and intolerance of their limited beliefs. The commentators would appear to concur. As author Doreen Virtue put it during one of her interview sequences, she believes that, where Indigos are concerned, ADHD is not an acronym for Attention Deficit with Hyperactivity Disorder but an abbreviation for Attention Dialed into a Higher Dimension.

As dour as some of these prospects are, however, there is also much to be celebrated about Indigos, particularly in the arts. Their accomplishments in music and painting, for instance, are often quite something for those of such tender ages—prodigies in every sense of the word. They also have a beautiful way of expressing themselves verbally, with an elegant simplicity, clarity, and candor that we could all learn from. In addition, they have a special form of communication they use with one another known as "the grid," a sort of psychic Internet that many of them appear able to tap into. (And you thought wi-fi was cutting edge.) Truly, they have much to offer—and much to teach—a world desperately in need of inspiration, direction, and guidance.

In contrast to the documentary approach of the preceding film, "Indigo" presents a fictional story about these special children. This movie, created by many of the same principals involved in "The Indigo Evolution," straddles the fence between a traditional theatrical picture and an introductory piece about these youngsters (it actually preceded the documentary and in many ways prompted its successor's creation, due to viewer desire for more substantive information).

A series of misfortunes, coupled with a pattern of inherently dysfunctional behavior, leads to the collapse of the comfortable home life of Ray Calloway (Neale Donald Walsch), a successful but arrogant Oregon businessman. His family eventually scatters, and Ray is left to pick up the pieces. Assisting him is an unlikely accomplice—his granddaughter Grace (Meghan McCandless), a perky, assiduous young Indigo who teaches her cynical and skeptical grandfather about her enlightened take on the world and the special ways of her peers. Together, they embark on a journey, literally and figuratively, to rebuild the family and heal a host of old wounds.

Interestingly, this rather unusual story line basically follows a fairly conventional formula, that of a road trip–buddy movie. As they make their trek, both halves of this seemingly mismatched pair come to know one another better, developing a bond and an understanding that wasn't present at the start of their odyssey. Flashback sequences are also included to show how Ray's life came to be so troubled, providing the basis for Grace's interventions for helping to restore balance and well-being in the family.

In undertaking all this, the script regrettably becomes a bit convoluted at times, taking a few too many twists and turns for its own good, arguably placing more emphasis on the sometimes melodramatic narrative than on insights into the nature of Indigos. Also, Grace's character is occasionally portrayed as something of a wunderkind, perhaps a bit too evolved even for an Indigo. The film's production values leave something to be desired at times, too, but that's not terribly surprising, considering that this movie was created on a shoestring budget. Getting the word out about these kids was obviously a greater concern here and, on that point, "Indigo" succeeds. It does a very capable job of showing how Indigos put their talents to use in working wonders and performing a wide range of much-needed fence mending. Had it played to this strength more, it likely would have been a much better picture. But, when it's viewed in conjunction with the documentary that succeeded it, the pair makes for a good double bill.

Perhaps the most important point we can take away from both of these films is an awakening to the possibility of the human potential. How ironic that our children should be our teachers in this regard. But, in many respects, they may truly represent our future as physical beings, possibly even marking the emergence of a new species of human, Homo noeticus, or "the knowing human," as speculated by author Caroline Myss.[8] That could well be the main message of these children and these movies, helping us see the Indigo evolution that's today taking place in us all.

# One Quantum Leap for Mankind

"Contact"
*Year of Release: 1997*
*Principal Cast: Jodie Foster, Matthew McConaughey, James Woods,*
*Tom Skerritt, Jena Malone, David Morse, William Fichtner,*
*Angela Bassett, Rob Lowe, Jake Busey, John Hurt*
*Director: Robert Zemeckis*
*Book: Carl Sagan*
*Story: Carl Sagan, Ann Druyan*
*Screenplay: James V. Hart, Michael Goldenberg*

Nineteenth-century French physiologist Claude Bernard, author of *An Introduction to the Study of Experimental Medicine*, maintained that "men who have excessive faith in their theories or ideas are not only ill-prepared for making discoveries; they also make poor observations." Yet it's ironic that this very statement could just as readily be applied to the discipline in which Bernard so fervently placed his own faith—science—as it could to any other system of hypothesis, such as spirituality. After all, science, like any other doctrine requiring any degree of faith, is inherently based on—you guessed it—beliefs. Still, all irony aside, Bernard's advice is sound, for putting blinders on can keep one from truly great revelations, ones that could potentially benefit all of mankind. Searching for the harmonious balance of inspired hypothesis and hard-nosed observation, and the degree of faith to be put into each, is a challenge faced by the disciples of both the scientific and spiritual camps, and perhaps nowhere is this exploration better portrayed than in the absorbing metaphysical drama, "Contact."

I call this movie a metaphysical drama rather than a sci-fi film, as it's perhaps better known, because I believe science provides a mere pretext for the underlying story, the search for that aforementioned harmony, a metaphysical quest if ever I saw one. We can thank the genius of astronomer Carl Sagan for that. As one who was schooled in traditional science, Sagan remained true to his roots, but he also made cautious allowances for the potential existence of "something more" in explaining the workings of the Universe, always couching them in caveats of the need for proof to substantiate claims. Yet in openly linking the realms of science and spirit—a courageous move for someone who risked significant backlash from the turf-protecting powers that be in both arenas—Sagan shepherded this question out of the shadows and into the light of public debate. In doing so, he also fueled interest in cosmology, the field of study focused on exploring the interrelatedness of everything and the connections that make it possible. Beginning with *Cosmos*, his ambitious, highly acclaimed 1980 PBS television series in which these issues were first raised in a substantive way, Sagan and cowriter Ann Druyan expanded on the ideas they examined in that initial effort in creating the story for "Contact," a fictional exploration into this most sublime of inquiries.

The film presents the amazing odyssey of Dr. Ellie Arroway (Jodie Foster), an enthusiastic young astronomer involved in SETI, the Search for Extra-Terrestrial Intelligence, a program designed to seek contact with alien life through monitoring radio telescope signals. As inspired and idealistic as she is about her work, however, Ellie is met with considerable skepticism from the close-minded administrator who controls her program's purse strings, National Science Foundation director Dr. David Drumlin (Tom Skerritt). When Drumlin pulls the plug on SETI's funding, Ellie and her cohorts are forced to seek private financing to continue, which they eventually secure through the magnanimous contributions of an eccentric industrialist, S.R. Hadden (John Hurt). The program resumes but again faces shutdown when it fails to produce any noteworthy results—that is, until something shocking happens to change everything.

As all this unfolds, Ellie meets an aspiring author, Palmer Joss (Matthew McConaughey), a former divinity student and self-described "man of the cloth without a cloth." Palmer is writing a book about the pervasive impact of science and technology on society and the attendant loss of faith accompanying its proliferation. The ardent scientist and the devout spiritual activist seem like a most unlikely couple, yet they nevertheless launch themselves into an on again–off again romance that wends its way throughout the story line. Their involvement is more than just the obligatory love interest that most films feel so blindly compelled to include. Rather, their relationship plays a highly symbolic role, moving the narrative along in significant ways and taking it in some unexpected directions, for reasons other than simple superfluous passion.

In addition, through flashback sequences, we see how Ellie's interests arose in science, astronomy, and the search for contact. These segments, featuring a young version of the protagonist (Jena Malone), do more than just provide interesting supplemental background on her formative years; they show us why those years were indeed formative in the truest sense of the word—namely, how she got onto her particular life path and why.

All of these intertwining plots eventually combine and culminate in an adventure that richly examines the nature of reality, the roles that science and spirit play in that cosmic dance, the contributions we consciously and unconsciously make as individuals to that unfolding drama, and mankind's capacity and desire for exploration in these and other cosmically significant areas. And what a ride it is! Further adding to this heady mix are the contributions of a cast of colorful supporting characters, including the pompous spoutings of a fundamentalist preacher (Rob Lowe), the paranoid ravings of an opportunist national security advisor (James Woods), the incoherent ramblings of a bizarre cult leader (Jake Busey), and the conciliatory efforts of a presidential aide trying to keep everyone grounded (Angela Bassett). Fasten your seatbelts for this one, folks!

This movie is so strong on so many levels that it's difficult to know which aspects to single out. Arguably its greatest asset is its exploration of the science and spirit question in all its myriad ways and how each of these elements (representative of the components of the magical approach) factors into the conscious creation equation. Ellie faces the greatest challenges in this respect. As a pious practitioner of traditional science, she contends that all knowledge is best understood through the language of science (a product of the intellect) and that all other forms of alleged wisdom, such as those that come from spirituality or religion (the progeny of the intuition), are little more than unprovable superstitious delusions. (Never mind, as one character points out to her, that 95 percent of the planet has bought into what she so lightly dismisses as a collective imagined fantasy.) Yet as zealously committed as she is to her scientific beliefs, Ellie is also continually confronted—and confounded—by the appearance of things spiritual in her life. Since these phenomena embody the antithesis of her convictions, she tries diligently to dismiss them, ridding herself of these pesky intrusions upon her rational worldview. But those nagging issues stubbornly persist, rising up squarely in her face, begging to be addressed.

From a conscious creation perspective, the continued appearance of these issues in Ellie's existence indicates a desire on her part to reconcile them for herself; after all, if she didn't feel that way, then she wouldn't continue to attract them into her reality. As the story unfolds, she periodically kicks, screams, and lashes out as she moves through the reconciliation process, but move through it she ultimately does, eventually attaining a broadened perspective for having done so. By implication, this should make her a better practitioner of conscious creation and the magical approach, for her awareness becomes naturally more attuned to the influences of both elements that make it work. She even seems to have a vague sense of this as she's going through the process, for at one point she speculates, somewhat out of character and off the cuff but with utter sincerity, "I always thought life was what you make of it." That's quite a revelation—and an even bigger admission.

The flashbacks take on special significance in light of this, for they reveal to us how Ellie reached this point in the first place. We see how her childhood experiences galvanized the beliefs that she carried forth with her into adulthood. Those experiences set the tone for the particular line of probability she would eventually choose to explore, including the challenges she encountered. I can't say I've ever seen a film that illustrates this aspect of conscious creation any better; it shows clearly how the character's beliefs arose, gelled, blossomed, and played out over the course of her lifetime, and it does so without ever beating viewers over the head to make its point.

As noted earlier, the intermittent romance of Ellie and Palmer is highly significant, too, not only for how it carries the story forward but also for its inherent symbolism. Each partner in this relationship represents the participants in the grand dance of the Universe, with Ellie playing the role of science and Palmer as spirit. Their constant coming together, splitting apart, and impassioned reunions mimic the intricate steps of that elaborate cosmic tango. What's more, the noticeably anxious discomfort they often exhibit toward one another (despite an underlying wellspring of genuine love and affection and an acute awareness of the need to be together) reflects the conflicted feelings that many of us have about the nature of the relationship between science and spirit. They mirror back to us how we feel about this arrangement, one in which we're not entirely sure how the pieces fit together, even though we know they somehow belong with one another. All of this is accomplished without ever becoming obvious or overblown. This is truly poetic filmmaking.

I'm also particularly taken with the fact that this story deals with the issues of science and spirit through the lens of astronomy. Think of the words and expressions we typically use to describe what astronomy studies: *Space*, the term most often applied to what lies beyond our world, is generally looked upon as a scientific expression, cold and objective. This is in contrast to *the heavens*, a more euphemistic term that generally carries spiritual and mystical connotations. In "Contact," we're presented with a realm above us that embodies qualities of both terms, creating an elegant ambiguity of what it's really like and reflective of the indefinable relationship between the forces that went into making it, all as painted on the canvas that is astronomy. Again, the deft way in which this is handled, without ever resorting to blatancy, makes for great cinema.

I genuinely believe that this is the best film from director Robert Zemeckis, far outstripping the achievements of his more popular offerings ("Who Framed Roger Rabbit" and "Romancing the Stone," see chapters 6 and 10, respectively) and even his award-winning work ("Forrest Gump," see chapter 11). Its production values are top-notch from beginning to end and apparent in every aspect of the picture. The writing, editing, special effects, soundtrack, and cinematography are all first-rate, and the performances are excellent throughout, particularly those turned in by Foster, Woods, and Hurt. Sadly, this movie was seriously overlooked for awards consideration, receiving only one Oscar nomination and one Golden Globe nod and taking home neither honor. That's too bad, because

I believe those who hand out the statuettes really missed out on a grand opportunity to reward a deserving film.

Fortunately, a similar fate didn't befall Ellie. She made the most of her opportunity, successfully managing to avoid the irony of Claude Bernard's admonition. She didn't allow blind faith in her belief in science to keep her from making grand discoveries or meritorious observations for her benefit and that of the rest of us. And, in so doing, she truly took one quantum leap for all of mankind.

## Putting Theory into Practice

"Mindwalk"
*Year of Release: 1991*
*Principal Cast: Liv Ullmann, Sam Waterston, John Heard, Ione Skye*
*Director: Bernt Capra*
*Story: Bernt Capra*
*Screenplay: Floyd Byars, Fritjof Capra*

Learning about theories of conscious creation, metaphysics, and quantum mechanics is a wonderful and enriching pursuit, but what do you do with it when you're done? In the end, how do such abstractions really relate to everyday living, especially in the context of the world beyond our doorsteps, one beset by an array of seemingly unsolvable problems? Those are valid questions, and we're just now on the verge of beginning to understand how to use these philosophical tools to address them. One valuable approach is to play with probabilities and speculate how they might evolve out of taking particular actions. This involves following lines of thought from working hypotheses through all of the possible ramifications to potential end points, all the while keeping an eye on related influences that could take envisioned outcomes in markedly different directions. Sounds too complicated? It needn't be, especially since a valuable tutorial about this can be found in the movie "Mindwalk."

Like other films in this chapter, this one is also hard to categorize. It primarily presents a series of conversations among three individuals sharing a day together after a "chance" encounter.

Scientist Sonia Hoffman (Liv Ullmann), politician Jack Edwards (Sam Waterston), and poet Thomas Harriman (John Heard) are all distinguished but disillusioned souls, each feeling as though they've been let down by their chosen professions. They find their way to the French abbey of Mont St. Michel, unaware of what's drawing them there but quietly hoping that it will provide the solace and answers they seek. In the process, they find one another and engage in a plethora of dialogues running the gamut of topics (think "My Dinner with Andre," only with much more interesting, and eminently more relevant, conversations).

Much of the initial discussion delves into science (particularly quantum mechanics), philosophy, metaphysics, and the relationship of them all to one another. Once the theoretical groundwork is in place, the discourse veers off into a host of different directions, exploring how these ideas can be practically applied. The result is a mesmerizing series of exchanges on everything from medicine to the environment to the allocation of global resources, including how decisions in each of these areas are to be made.

The movie is loosely based on Fritjof Capra's *The Tao of Physics*, the ground-breaking book on the uncanny similarities of science and spirit, specifically showing how quantum physics and Eastern mysticism closely mirror one another. Although the film is fictional in the minimalist sense of the word, its content primarily is not. It essentially provides a forum to present many of Capra's innovative ideas through the experiences and perspectives of the three leads.

Sonia, a former laser scientist, has sought retreat at the abbey and lives there more or less full time. She has become a recluse, cutting herself off from those who let her down both professionally and personally. Unfortunately, she has also cut herself off from those she cares about, such as her daughter (Ione Skye) and a world in need of the vast storehouse of knowledge she possesses. In many ways, she comes to personify the concept of an ivory tower, a citizen of the world but one who is definitely not in it. It's also ironic that a scientist would choose a spiritual site as a locale into which to retreat. (Maybe these disciplines really aren't so different after all.)

Jack, a U.S. senator coming off a recently unsuccessful bid for the presidency, feels detached from the vocation he once so loved. He laments the culture of the Beltway, having to spend so much time, energy, and effort engaged in playing politics that he feels unable to accomplish most of what he sets out to do. He is a lost soul seeking reconnection, a healthy infusion of inspiration, and a means that will enable him to reach his objectives and aid the greater good.

Thomas, a poet and playwright once involved in the New York arts scene, has fled to France to seek a saner and more meaningful life. Although he may not have an answer for what he wants, he at least knows what he doesn't, so he purposely leaves behind what no longer serves him to search more fertile ground for personal and artistic fulfillment.

Employing characters from these three vocations to move the dialogues forward is both interesting and symbolically significant from a conscious creation perspective, for each is highly representative of the concepts involved. For instance, Sonia, the scientist, serves as a metaphor for the intellect and pure rational wisdom. By contrast, Thomas, the artist, signifies spirit and the intuition. Jack, the politician and the man in the middle, embodies consciousness, the arbitrator of these two elements in belief formation and the ultimate policy maker, both politically and metaphysically.

The relationships among these three characters draw upon these symbolic qualities as well. For example, Jack (consciousness) implicitly needs the input of both Sonia (intellect) and Thomas (intuition) if he/it is going to form appropriate beliefs and make the magical approach work. He/it can't function properly without both. At the same time, Jack is also well aware of the mediating role that he must play, both overtly as a politician and symbolically as a representation of consciousness. He doesn't hesitate to question—even play devil's advocate—when necessary if something strikes him as being incomplete, slanted, or not entirely kosher. On one occasion, after Sonia expounds at length about one of her proposed ideas, Jack is quick to scrutinize her contentions, asking (albeit somewhat rhetorically) who has the right to set the template for everyone in a particular venture if the proposal doesn't suit everyone's needs. He thus lives up to his innate obligation to employ fairness in the input assessment process. (Thank goodness consciousness does that; now if we can just get those of Jack's profession to follow suit . . . )

Disillusioned though these characters might be, they fortunately have access to the protocol of conscious creation to help turn their realities around. However, as the film illustrates, they are each just beginning to see how they can use it to reshape their worlds. Each seems to have a piece of the puzzle, but none of them has the entire picture. Their encounter with one another helps shed light on the larger process of which each of them, as individual components, is part. And now that they've been brought together, they have an opportunity for coalescence, to pool their respective talents and combine their collective resources to address common problems and effect mutually satisfying solutions.

Education is a key starting point in this, and that's where Sonia's contributions are most valuable. With her voluminous intellect, she has information to share on seemingly everything from the functioning of quantum particles to health statistics about children in third world countries. Thomas, by contrast, as an artist, spins the information she imparts, extracting the salient elements, polishing them with his own particular take, and providing observations nuanced with his intuitionally driven sensibilities. Jack's job is to collect the input from both of them to make educated decisions about which in-forming beliefs to generate to make manifestation possible.

Before those beliefs are finalized, however, we get to see how they can be deployed in trial runs for assessment. In these tests, proposed beliefs are put through a what-if mechanism to see how they ultimately play out. In one instance, for example, the trio discusses the reallocation of funds for medical purposes. With a shifting in priorities (that is, change in beliefs), Sonia explains how something as simple as promoting changes in dietary habits, such as the consumption of less red meat, can potentially lead to considerably fewer heart-related illnesses and, consequently, reduced rates of cardiac care treatment procedures. This, in turn, she contends, can free up financial resources earmarked for these potentially preventable illnesses and be used to treat other conditions that are overlooked due to a lack of funds.

Of course, because conscious creation is a belief-based materialization practice, the contention that red meat necessarily leads to cardiac trouble is just as much a belief as a notion that asserts just the opposite. So would the proposed scenario that Sonia raises have validity? As with any other projected probability, it all depends on the beliefs involved. If enough people buy into it, the proposal could very well take hold; if not, it won't; and if some do and some don't, it would languish somewhere in between. The degree to which a particular projection takes root ultimately depends on the degree to which we concur with the beliefs that underlie it. The purpose of a test drive is to see whether the proposal finds favor at the elemental belief level and merits further consideration for manifestation.

This is an important point to bear in mind while watching this picture. It was made in 1990, and it represents something of a time capsule of the period's beliefs. Some of the ideas are still relevant, some have fallen from grace, and others are still flopping about like fish on a dock, waiting to be acted upon or discarded. In that regard, as discussed in this chapter's introduction, this movie thus reflects the beliefs that were prevalent in the societal consciousness when it was filmed. They don't all necessarily carry the same relevance now as they did then, but they certainly mirror what was being concentrated upon at the time.

"Mindwalk" is an engrossing piece of cinema from start to finish. But, given its distinctive format, viewers should bear in mind that it's not the kind of film that can be treated as background noise or watched casually while ironing or rehanging the drapes. It requires attention for its information to percolate into one's consciousness. Given that, think of it as an ideal movie companion to curl up with on a rainy Saturday afternoon; that way, viewers are more likely to get the greatest impact out of watching this inspired, thought-provoking picture.

The performances of Ullmann, Waterston, and Heard are all capable, and their dialogue, talky though it is at times, is generally well written. The cinematography is also stellar, showing off the abbey in all its glory, with superb locale shots featured throughout. Regrettably, it is currently available only in VHS format.

The promise of science to solve the world's problems has fallen under considerable scrutiny in recent years, especially when it has been seen as undertaken with ulterior motives or purely selfish ends as part of the mix. This in itself has contributed to the desire to draw spirit back into the equation. According to Fritjof Capra, however, science and spirit should not be thought of as mutually exclusive, and "Mindwalk" clearly demonstrates that. As he wrote in his pioneering book, "modern physics goes way beyond technology, that the way—or *Tao*—of physics can be a path with a heart, a way to spiritual knowledge and self-realization."[9] And, as conscious creators would likely contend, that's good news for all of us.

**Author's Notebook:** My experience in discovering this film recalls yet another beguiling anecdote from the annals of conscious creation. I had just returned from a Seth conference (how ironic is that?) and was waiting to meet an acquaintance for dinner. He had a history of tardiness and unreliability, but I was still anxious to meet so we could discuss all of the weekend's interesting developments, especially since we shared an affinity for metaphysical subjects. As time passed, however, he neither called nor showed, and I began doing a slow burn. To put myself at ease, I flipped on the TV and began cable surfing, looking for a suitable distraction. After a few minutes, I landed on "Mindwalk" on one of the premium channels. I was moderately intrigued at first, but the more I watched, the more enthralled I became. I was intimately drawn into the discussions, my attention rapt on the screen before me. I found the film particularly engaging since many of its conversations echoed many of the same topics that I had just addressed at the workshop (talk about less-than-subtle reinforcement). By the time it ended, I was relaxed, refreshed, reinvigorated, and exceedingly satisfied with what I had learned that weekend, both during and after the conference.

As for that dinner companion, well, he never showed. But that's fine, for after having taken the time to watch this movie, I felt more nourished by it than any meal ever could have provided.

## Bonus Features

"Star Wars: Episode V—The Empire Strikes Back": When the student is ready, the teacher will appear. Although this second installment in the original "Star Wars" series was primarily meant to bridge the story from the first film to the third, detailing the evil empire's backlash against the upstart Jedi rebel forces, it also offers an indoctrination into that mysterious all-encompassing power known as the Force. This is accomplished through the tutelage of the young Jedi fighter, Luke Skywalker, by the sage Jedi master, Yoda. This is by far the most mesmerizing aspect of the movie, essentially offering a conscious creation primer in a fictional format. Great sci-fi fun with a thoughtful metaphysical twist. (1980; Mark Hamill, Harrison Ford, Carrie Fisher, Billy Dee Williams, Anthony Daniels, David Prowse, Peter Mayhew, Kenny Baker, Alec Guinness, Frank Oz [voice of Yoda], James Earl Jones [voice of Darth Vader]; Irvin Kershner, director; George Lucas, story; Leigh Brackett and Lawrence Kasdan, screenplay; one Oscar win on three nominations, special achievement Oscar for visual effects; one Golden Globe nomination)

"Forces of Nature": An uptight but eminently trustworthy groom-to-be gets a serious case of cold feet when seeds of doubt unexpectedly get planted in his head. To test his beliefs in matrimony, he unwittingly draws upon the law of attraction to summon forth highly synchronistic circumstances—the forces of nature at work—to show him the pros and cons of marriage. This all plays out over the course of a road trip from his home in New York to his fiancée's family estate in Savannah, site of the wedding, with an intriguing and attractive stranger who's part vamp, part mentor, and part walking disaster area. A thoroughly entertaining romantic comedy with clever art direction and touches of surreal cinematography. (1999; Ben Affleck, Sandra Bullock, Maura Tierney, David Strickland, Steve Zahn, Meredith Scott Lynn, Blythe Danner, Ronny Cox, Michael Fairman, Janet Carroll, Richard Schiff, Jack Kehler; Bronwen Hughes, director; Marc Lawrence, screenplay)

"Enlightenment Guaranteed": Two brothers leave their home in Germany and travel to Japan to visit a monastery, hoping the experience will teach them about the ways of Zen and provide them with much-sought-after enlightenment. Their trip quickly becomes an outwardly manifested learning laboratory, showing them the teachings they seek in ways more potently than they bargained for, a recipe sure to guarantee enlightenment. A gentle comedy for an unlikely subject. (2000; Uwe Ochsenknecht, Gustav-Peter Wöhler, Petra Zieser, Ulrike Kriener, Anica Dobra; Doris Dörrie, director; Doris Dörrie and Ruth Stadler, screenplay)

# 4

## Igniting the Flame of Manifestation

### *Exercising Free Will and the Power of Choice*

> Imagination is the beginning of creation. You imagine what you desire, you will what you imagine and at last you create what you will.
>
> *George Bernard Shaw*

Oh, how I love a smorgasbord! Ever since I was a kid, I've always craved visits to these do-it-yourself feasts (which, food beliefs aside, probably accounts for my pleasantly rotund physique). I've typically looked upon these bountiful buffets' endless offerings with great glee and anxious anticipation, their mouthwatering savories and irresistible confections all waiting to be plucked from their brimming platters and plopped onto my welcoming plate. (I can practically hear the growing chorus of "yums" reverberating out there in the reading audience right now.)

But, as much as I enjoy the delectable fare of these rapturous repasts, that is only part of their appeal. What I like just as much, if not more, is what smorgasbords represent—choice. This was especially true in my younger years; it was one time when I could be the boss—*I* could make the decision about what *I* wanted. It was all so very liberating. And, as a budding conscious creator, I naturally manifested dishes that I thoroughly enjoyed, too. To have what I desired available to me *and* the freedom to choose it—now that was the best of all worlds!

Irish playwright George Bernard Shaw apparently understood this principle as well, as the opening quote illustrates. He also knew how to make it happen; the three steps he outlines essentially amount to an encapsulated summary of what constitutes conscious creation. But he mentions a component of the process that we haven't yet discussed—free will.

Free will is one of those theoretical constructs whose being and validity have been debated for eons by everyone from theologians to philosophers to scientists. Many have tried to marginalize, if not squelch, its existence, but others have valiantly championed its defense, singing its praises and celebrating its capabilities. As I see it, free will has to exist, for if it didn't, conscious creation would otherwise be impossible.

I think of free will as the match that lights the fire of manifestation. After our consciousness assesses the intellectual and intuitional input furnished through the magical approach, it then formulates a proposal of sorts for what it would like to materialize, expressed as a belief. It's then up to free will, a kind of adjunct to its arbitrator cousin, to say yea or nay on proceeding.

Beliefs that get the green light move forward to materialization, while those that see red are scrapped, and those flashing amber are sent back for further deliberation. It's all rather straightforward really, provided one knows how to read the signals. The problem is that we don't always know how to interpret them, and that's how we end up stopping short, running lights, or finding ourselves in pile-ups, literally or metaphorically. Therefore, to understand and make effective use of free will, it's worth examining some of its important qualities. Otherwise, we're liable to get gridlocked at the intersection.

★ ★ ★

When a belief gets the nod to proceed, our free will facilitates its materialization by sanctioning the necessary intentions and emotions of manifestation and by placing an energetic work order with our conscious creation collaborator, All That Is, to marshall the elements, at the quantum level and otherwise, required for physical expression. With that, the process is thus set in motion.

I like to think of this chain of events as the counterpoint to "letting the spirit move you"; instead, it's a case of you moving the spirit and the spirit responding accordingly.

It takes a powerful force to bring all that about, one with a great *will*. In fact, this prerequisite is so intrinsic to the process that it has even made its way into our everyday language, but most of us probably aren't aware of it. Every time we speak about something in the future tense, we talk about what we *will* do. Future manifestations are thus synonymous with the very force responsible for them, embodied in verb form. Indeed, free will truly must be quite a power if it can shape something as fundamental as the way we speak.

This sheer power stems from the primary quality that defines free will—its fierce, almost autocratic, independence. That characterization might sound a bit extreme, but this kind of autonomy is absolutely essential to free will's proper functioning. Quite simply, if it didn't possess such independence, it wouldn't be free, now would it? To be sure, free will does depend on its collaboration with All That Is to carry out its objectives, as we'll see, but in getting any production under way, it has to have its own decisive say to make things happen.

Independence is important for several reasons. To begin with, it's necessary to facilitate the process of learning, particularly the life lessons we have all come here to experience, one of the chief aims of conscious creation. If our free will were hindered from pursuing any avenues for learning open to it, it might be kept from assessing probabilities that constitute effective responses to dicey challenges. It could also be prevented from allowing us to make mistakes, which can provide some of the most valuable learning opportunities we experience (the lessons of chapters 1 and 2 notwithstanding).

A free will hog-tied with burdensome or foolish restrictions keeps it from operating properly. In fact, the failure to preserve its independence could have potentially profound and far-reaching implications. Drawing again from the wisdom of George Bernard Shaw, the necessity for such staunch autonomy can be seen, albeit metaphorically, in one of his most famous quotes: "The reasonable man adapts himself to the world; the unreasonable one persists in trying to adapt the world to himself. Therefore, all progress depends on the unreasonable man."[1] Indeed, imagine if all the great minds throughout history had been willing conformists instead of independent thinkers; Shaw might say (and I'd heartily concur) that they never would have made the cut as revered scholars but instead would have merely been reasonable men.

Such independence, of course, sheds light on another inherent quality of free will—that its very being is based on the principle of choice. Our free will would be fundamentally unable to select from the range of options available to it if it didn't possess this trait as an integral characteristic. Again, this quality necessarily includes the capability to make both "good" and "bad" decisions, for the wherewithal to choose from the range of all possible responses is key to the learning and conscious creation processes. Or, as author Ayn Rand put it, "Man is a being with free will; therefore, each man is potentially good or evil, and it's up to him and only him . . . to decide which he wants to be."[2]

Of course, even with its innate independence and power of choice, our free will still has its own set of challenges to contend with, especially when it has to play the role of metaphysical traffic cop. Sometimes free will has numerous beliefs proposed to it by the consciousness all at once, all equally viable, even if some of them, when considered individually, are seemingly at odds with one another. At that point, free will has to sort them out, deciding which ones go forward and which ones don't, often in rapid succession. However, some of those that proceed may end up unfavorably affecting others, resulting in quagmires, contradictions, or various other unpleasantries. This can be perplexing, because the choices may have seemed perfectly acceptable at the time they were launched into manifestation. But when they begin arising in conjunction with one another, the outcomes could be incompatible. Admittedly, this does present an opportunity for learning, which means free will is carrying out a fundamental mandate by providing the means to make such lessons possible. But it also again illustrates why it's so important to be clear about the precise nature of our beliefs, for sometimes even our free will might not be enough to prevent such conflicting situations from arising.

The role of All That Is as collaborator sometimes becomes apparent under circumstances like these. As noted in chapter 3,

All That Is acts like a genie in carrying out its celestial supplier role (see the summary for "The Secret"). If presented with unclear requests (especially in instances of contradiction), All That Is generally hesitates in executing its fulfillment orders, simply because it doesn't know how to move forward. A proposed request like this generally turns into a delayed materialization. All That Is seeks clarification from the requestor by asking "How do you want me to proceed?" or "Are you sure you want to do this?" as if it were generating pop-up error messages on a conscious creation computer screen. This gives free will a chance to respond.

This is one important way in which our free will depends on its co-creator source. In addition to the materialization energy it supplies, All That Is provides guidance on manifestation, especially when requests don't make sense. Our free will relies on that feedback when it realizes that what was set in motion isn't happening as anticipated. Free will should at least send the queried request back to the consciousness for reassessment of the beliefs behind it, if not reject it outright. Of course, given how powerful beliefs can be (especially those with strong emotions behind them), that's sometimes easier said than done. As Jane Roberts and Seth noted, "Any strong emotion carries within it far more energy than, say, that required to send a rocket to the moon."[3] With that kind of power at work, free will may become so conditioned to the validity of certain beliefs (especially those that have passed through its portals previously) that it might not even take the time to stop and review them, assuming them as givens. This is how dogma arises; its beliefs settle in and make themselves comfortable, knowing that they'll always get waved through by a gatekeeper that unquestioningly rubber-stamps their passage.

Suddenly, free will doesn't seem so free; you might say that it's a potential prisoner of the beliefs that come to it. But properly functioning free will should be able to sense when the consciousness is trying to slip one past it, a belief that it should know better than to propose, because diligent free will can smell the bullshit at fifty paces. In that regard, free will is like an internal bloodhound, aggressively tracking down the scent of self-deception (but without drooling all over your psyche).

When a bogus belief does slip by, I'd argue that it's because free will gets lazy, usually from being overtaxed by a barrage of belief proposals. In taking such shortcuts, however, free will may approve of beliefs that cause it to lose sight of its own mission. Think of how many times you've said of a situation (especially one that you've faced repeatedly), "I didn't have any choice in the matter." Although that's often a successful means of garnering sympathy for one's cause, I beg to differ about the belief's validity. We *always* have choice, even if we don't always recognize that notion nor are able to see the alternatives. That, in itself, shows just how potent beliefs can be and how strongly they can hang on, that they're even capable of putting one over on an aspect of ourselves designed to filter out such self-deception.

When free will is functioning fully, it's genuinely attuned to the freedom that's part of its designation. This means it's capable of clearly seeing the scope of probabilities open to it for solutions and responses. Consider, for example, in a choice between A and B how many options there are. If you say two, you've come up a little short; unless A and B somehow cancel one another out, we actually have four choices in a scenario like this: A, B, both, and neither. And even where A and B are mutually exclusive, there are still three choices: A, B, and neither. (How's that for broadening the range of options?) Truly discerning free will can readily spot the breadth of possibilities available to us.

Finally, when all of these qualities are considered collectively, optimally firing free will can be seen as possessing a great sense of adventure. Because its operation is largely tied up with our learning experiences, it often seeks out the new and different. This daring streak pushes us to test new waters and pursue uncharted opportunities for exploration, imploring us to use the imagination of which Mr. Shaw so ardently spoke. And that is where the liberating effects of conscious creation really begin to make their presence felt. We grow wings for our flights of fancy, taking our imagination to places never before dreamed of. Now that's real creative power at work.

The films in this chapter examine these and other aspects of choice and free will. Some of them are admittedly rather extreme in how they delve into the subject, but I believe they state their cases better by going over the top than by playing it safe. Too much of the time, we allow ourselves to think we're operating without, or denied access to, this vital aspect of our

being, so I'd rather a film hit me over the head in reinforcing its message on this topic than play it conservatively and
keep me from getting the point. Besides, I believe it's better
to jump into the pool with both feet than to test the waters
with a tentative toe. After all, how else are we going to learn
how to swim?

Understanding the qualities of free will is an important way
to make more effective use of the manifestation process. There
are others, but this is perhaps the most fundamentally significant,
for without the freedom to choose, where would any of us truly
be as conscious creators?

## Choice, Personified

"Sophie's Choice"
*Year of Release: 1982*
*Principal Cast: Meryl Streep, Kevin Kline, Peter MacNicol,*
*Josef Sommer (narrator)*
*Director: Alan J. Pakula*
*Book: William Styron*
*Screenplay: Alan J. Pakula*

Have you ever seen a movie that left such an indelible mark
on your memory that you could recall it in explicit detail, even
years after having viewed it? I've seen a few like that in my time,
but none perhaps more so than the haunting drama, "Sophie's
Choice."

The film tells the saga of Sophie Zawistowski (Meryl Streep),
a Polish concentration camp survivor who immigrates to New
York after the end of World War II. Sophie lives in a Brooklyn
boarding house with her lover Nathan (Kevin Kline), a pharmaceutical company employee who nurses her back to health after
her arrival in the United States. Joining them at the boarding
house is its newest resident (and the film's narrator), Stingo (Peter
MacNicol), an aspiring writer transplanted from the American
South who comes in search of his creative destiny. Sophie and
Nathan quickly befriend their new neighbor, showing him the
ropes of life in the Big Apple. Before long, the trio is nearly insepa-

rable, going everywhere together and enjoying all the attractions of the city that has become their playground.

All seems well, but all is also not what it appears to be, as Stingo soon discovers. He comes to see sides of his friends he didn't know existed. Sophie, an angelic beauty whose boundless kindness and compassion couldn't be in sharper contrast to the horrific indignities she suffered at the hands of her Auschwitz captors, carries secrets around inside her that she aches to confess, including some with the potential to portray her in a shockingly different light. Nathan, a passionate and articulate if somewhat eccentric soul, has a great appreciation for the beauty in life, but he also has a menacing dark side that arises with a vile ugliness, usually without warning. Stingo, as their loving friend, desperately wrestles with his conflicted feelings, trying to be loyal and supportive yet maintaining a prudent distance, a challenge made increasingly difficult throughout the film as his longing affection for Sophie steadily grows.

But as intriguing as all of these interwoven relationships are, without a doubt, the most compelling aspect of this film is its exploration into the issue of choice. That's so central to the story, in fact, that it's how the very word made its way into the title of both the picture and the book on which it is based.

On its face, choice seems like a simple enough concept, yet it carries many implications that aren't always easily seen, and this movie shines the spotlight squarely on them. For instance, the film draws sharply into focus the difficulty often associated with the act of choosing. We frequently allow ourselves to believe that choice is something inherently easy, but that may not always be the case. Perhaps we confuse the freedom that choice can afford—and the benefits that can be derived therefrom—with the actual ease involved in the choosing itself. This point is driven home a number of times, with Sophie being put on the spot to make decisions of kinds that we should all hope we're never asked to make.

The difficulty factor raises further implications as well. For example, it clearly makes us aware of the notion that our choices carry consequences. And because of that, by extension, it also shows the degree of responsibility that's inescapably associated with the choices we make. Both of these issues are weighty enough in and of themselves, but when you put them into the context of conscious creation, they arguably take on greater magnitude and relevance. Since the manifestation process is based on the beliefs and intents we put forth, the notion of deliberateness is also factored into the equation where the foregoing considerations are involved. Suddenly their significance takes on added importance, their pertinence elevated to a level of much greater urgency and substance. And if the decisions to be made involve outcomes that are difficult to project or envision, the ante is upped further. Before long, the stakes are unimaginably high.

Contending with such substantive questions about choice is a natural outgrowth of circumstances like these, undoubtedly the chief lesson to be gleaned from their presence in one's life. Being put in the position of learning how to face—and make—tough decisions is the teaching that difficult choices afford. This is the position into which Sophie is repeatedly put during the film, shown through both flashbacks and contemporary sequences. The pain she endures in making these choices is often considerable, wearing on her profoundly.

But there are benefits, too. Her responses show Sophie that she has the fortitude and mental toughness to be able to deal with the hard choices, especially when the difficulty factor is perpetually raised and her very survival is on the line. It also shows that she is capable of drawing on this inner strength to make the hard choices she wishes to make freely for herself and not just those that are seemingly thrust upon her. Further, being forced into such circumstances helps expand Sophie's awareness, exposing her to a wider range of available probabilities, enlightening her about choices she didn't know she had and might not otherwise have considered, no matter how desirable or undesirable those options are.

Sophie's exploration of free will through processing tough choices is an interesting (and, in its own way, inspiring) creation, taking her and us into the depths of our personal power. It shows us what it means to have genuine command of free will to the degree that it can be employed with absolute authority in the face of whatever choices come our way, no matter how impossible to address they seem to be. Metaphorically speaking, her psyche may be contorted all out of recognition by what she's put through, but she never breaks, even in the face of choices that expose her to unspeakable horrors and personal degradation.

This is why I left the theater awestruck when I saw the film for the first time. I was so moved by the sheer will that Sophie exhibits that I could barely express the feelings I was experiencing from having viewed this picture. That was made all the more ironic by the fact that some of the choices involved were ones that most of us would never dare consider, let alone make, and that many of us would strongly disagree with, especially those of a "negative" nature. But then who are we to judge someone else's choices, especially if we rightfully each create our own reality? Can we truthfully say we wouldn't make the same choices if we had been in her shoes? As Jane Roberts and Seth put it, "Many disavow the experience of the feelings they consider negative. They try to 'affirm' what they think of as positive emotions. They do not permit themselves the dimensions of their creaturehood and by pretending not to feel what they feel they deny the integrity of their own experience."[4] And that, I believe, is why I was so affected by the story; the strength of character that Sophie demonstrates when it comes to the question of pure choice is almost unfathomable. Again, as Jane Roberts and Seth wrote, "Because you have free will you have the responsibility and the gift, the joy and the necessity, of working with your beliefs and of choosing your personal reality as you desire."[5] Through her experience, Sophie truly comes to personify the concept of choice.

Sophie's personification of this principle is further exemplified by her willingness to recount the measure of her choices. In opening up to Stingo as a confessor of sorts, Sophie not only unburdens herself of the secrets she carries around with her but also takes ownership of the choices she has made, regardless of their nature, for better or worse. This, to me, is perhaps one of the most stirring examples I've ever seen of someone taking responsibility for their creations, painful as it might have been for her to admit having produced them. In an age when people are quick to blame others for their difficulties and unhesitatingly immerse themselves in unadulterated victimhood, it's refreshing to see someone—even if only a fictional character—being willing to own up to what she's done, no matter how it's viewed by others. This takes courage equal to that required for making the tough choices in the first place, a tremendous inspiration to be sure.

"Sophie's Choice" is a difficult picture to watch at times, disturbing and woefully sad. But it's also a difficult picture to take your eyes off once you start viewing it, particularly for its thoughtful treatment of the question of choice and the touching portrayal of the life of a character who so willingly and courageously explores it.

Streep's portrayal of Sophie is phenomenal, one of the greatest performances by an actress ever caught on film, and it is rendered all the more captivating by Nestor Almendros's luminescent cinematography. Kline and MacNicol offer fine support, capably playing their roles but never outshining the real star of this show. Superb writing and directing, as well as a gorgeous original score by Marvin Hamlisch, complete the package of this outstanding picture. The film won one Oscar on five nominations and one Golden Globe on three nominations, both for Streep's stellar acting.

It's been said that each of us is the sum of our individual choices, that who we are depends on how all of the decisions we make in life ultimately add up. The ability to choose is a fundamental birthright and a great creation of our species, one of the defining qualities that makes us human. We can only hope that the choices we make amount to something of value. But to reach that goal, we must first have the courage to use that gift to ourselves with the wisdom, confidence, and judiciousness necessary to manifest greatness. Sophie's shining example, despite the many tribulations that beset her, helps light the way for all of us, illuminating what is arguably the most cherished aspect of our authentic selves.

## Be Careful What You Wish For

*"After Hours"*
*Year of Release: 1985*
*Principal Cast: Griffin Dunne, Rosanna Arquette, Verna Bloom,*
*Thomas Chong, Cheech Marin, Linda Fiorentino, Teri Garr, John Heard,*
*Catherine O'Hara, Will Patton, Robert Plunket*
*Director: Martin Scorsese*
*Screenplay: Joseph Minion*

Be careful what you wish for—how many times did you hear that one from your elders when you were growing up? It probably ranks right up there with "It's all fun and games until someone loses an eye." Although the wisdom of that ocular injury admonition is open to debate, that other piece of advice has some worth. What's more, those who made such astute cautionary pronouncements probably didn't even realize they were drawing on conscious creation principles when they said them. Since the manifestation process fundamentally involves conscious choice aimed at wish fulfillment, this safety recommendation is actually quite germane. After all, the lessons of creation by default have already shown us what can happen when we don't consider the consequences of what we're trying to materialize, so it truly is sage guidance to be careful what you wish for, as the beleaguered protagonist finds out the hard way in the dark comedy, "After Hours."

Paul Hackett (Griffin Dunne) is looking for a little excitement in his life, and as a resident of the most exhilarating city in the world, New York, he really should be able to find it. But, alas, he spends his days stuck in a dead-end job as a word processing trainer. His nights are even more thrilling, sacked out on the couch while cable surfing in his uptown apartment. Such joy, such rapture. But then one evening, everything changes.

While sitting in a coffee shop, Paul meets an interesting and attractive young woman, Marcy (Rosanna Arquette). They chat, flirt a bit, and exchange phone numbers, and, before long, Paul is on his way to visit Marcy in her Soho loft. It's the beginning of an evening he'll long remember, though it's one he'd probably rather forget.

Paul's visit to lower Manhattan starts off with one of New York's notoriously wild cab rides during which virtually all the money he has—a $20 bill—flies out an open window. He's now about to go on a first date, far from home, with almost no funds in his pocket. In the spirit of adventure, however, he carries on, only to find out that Marcy isn't exactly his flavor. The bright conversationalist he met earlier in the evening turns out to be something of a kook, routinely spouting disjointed thoughts, bizarre contradictions, and creepy anecdotes, punctuated by seemingly inexplicable outbursts of emotion. When he sees that things aren't going to work out, he decides to head home, but he soon discovers he doesn't have enough money to get there—not even by subway. And from there, things only get worse.

Paul's night on the town gives him more excitement than he ever bargained for. In fact, it turns out to be like a nightmare on acid. He crosses paths with an unending stream of offbeat and macabre characters, most of whom make Marcy look vanilla by comparison. Here's a sampling:

★ Kiki (Linda Fiorentino) is a gruffly sensuous, punked-out, leather-clad sculptress working on an ominous three-dimensional version of Edvard Munch's painting, "The Scream." She shares Marcy's loft and takes a liking to Paul, but she grudgingly keeps her distance to spare her neurotic roommate's feelings. Besides, Kiki's already got a boyfriend— Horst (Will Patton), an intense but soft-spoken disciplinarian with the looks and charm of a fascist youth group member. The two of them hang out at a punk rock bar called Club Berlin that specializes in giving its patrons Mohawk haircuts, whether they want one or not.

★ One of Berlin's regulars is June (Verna Bloom), a quiet and seemingly lost soul who lives in the bar's basement. Like Kiki, she is also a sculptress but has some very strange ideas about what constitutes art—and even stranger ideas about what constitutes proper skin care.

★ Julie (Teri Garr) is a ditzy cocktail waitress from another neighborhood bar whose clothes, home décor, and musical tastes are all straight out of the '60s. A row of hairspray cans lines a shelf in her apartment, a necessity for preserving the beehive that she's so proud of and that she coyly pleads for Paul to touch. Julie works for Tom (John Heard), a likable, strapping bartender. He comes across as a nice enough guy until it becomes apparent he's got an anger management problem, among other issues.

★ Gail (Catherine O'Hara) leads the local neighborhood watch, commanding her band of vigilantes from behind the wheel of her Mr. Softee truck. They're in hot pursuit of whoever is brazenly burglarizing their neighborhood. But while dog-gedly hunting down the wrong suspect, they let the real culprits, Neil (Cheech Marin) and Pepe (Thomas Chong), operate virtually unencumbered. In fact, the only problem this duo encounters occurs when they try to buy something, a situation that prompts Neil to wax philosophically, "See what happens when you pay for stuff?"

These colorful characters thwart Paul's efforts to go home, unwittingly and otherwise, at every turn. He grows ever more frustrated as he makes his way through the night. He even pleads for help from a stranger on the street (Robert Plunket), who misconstrues Paul's request as a sexual advance. Indeed, nothing seems to go right for the hapless hero. But then he gets what he asked for—thrills beyond measure.

Paul's experience illustrates what can happen when free will is presented with having to sort out the viability of multiple beliefs, each of which has its own validity but collectively aren't necessarily harmonious. Although it's true that he does put out the intent to seek some excitement in his life, when we look at our protagonist's persona, he's not exactly the exciting type, and the experience he gets isn't commensurate with where he's coming from. Paul genuinely seems bored with his life at the film's outset, but then that stems from him creating such pervasive tediousness in the first place. Moreover, the predictability of his routine carries a certain comfort to which he's become quite accustomed. To counteract its oppressive sameness, he seeks an adventure, but in creating it, he goes a little overboard.

The artistic, grungy reality of Soho is light years away from Paul's comfy mainstream existence. It's exotic, trendy, fashionable, and even a little dangerous, the polar opposite of a lifestyle characterized by a shirt-and-tie working world, reasoned responses, and furniture showroom décor. And when the Soho experience gets going in full gear, Paul is in way over his head, despite his desire to be dropped into the midst of it. He quickly finds himself overwhelmed, desperately scrambling to reconcile the manifestation of totally incompatible elements. In one harrowing incident after another, Paul looks skyward and asks "Why me?" as if seeking a response from some omniscient deity who'll explain it all to him, all the while not realizing that he simply got what he asked for. Poor guy.

Conceivably, one might think that this is an instance in which our conscious creation collaborator, All That Is, would step in and delay manifestation in the face of apparently mismatched belief requests, sending some type of sign—an intuitive message or physically manifested symbol—to Paul's free will to reconsider the submitted proposal. In turn, his free will would be prompted to throw the proposal back to his consciousness for further consideration. However, on some level, Paul must have been hell-bent on gaining the experience he gets, so the beliefs fueling that desire were pushed through his free will, despite any possible divine objections. In the absence of resistance, manifestation happens, so All That Is complies with what it is implored to provide, regardless of the consequences involved.

Ramifications aside, however, this experience shows how free will, with the cooperation of All That Is, does its job in providing the requisite circumstances for enabling learning experiences. It's an example of free will living up to a fundamental mandate. For Paul's sake, we can only hope he got the lesson he sought.

"After Hours" is not a movie for those who like their comedies light and frothy. It has an edge that runs throughout, fraught with situations that induce nervous, guilty giggles, the kind in which we find ourselves laughing at things we probably shouldn't be snickering at. Of course, I wouldn't expect anything less from a director like Martin Scorsese, who's built a career out of making edgy films. This picture shows he has a good touch for humor, and I'd certainly enjoy seeing more from him in this vein. (It's the only feature-length comedy he's made.) Others apparently thought so, too, for his efforts with this movie earned him the best director award at the Cannes Film Festival. The picture also received a nomination for the Festival's top honor, the Palme D'Or.

The film features an excellent ensemble cast. The performers have a cohesiveness that leads us to believe that they indeed do all belong together, as if they really are all neighbors in the same neighborhood. The peculiarities of their characters no doubt help that, for they all come across like the cast of an urban version of a carnival freak show, but they sell it so well as to be totally convincing. Dunne, as the rational antithesis to all these eccentrics, turns in a fine effort as the uptight hero driven to the brink, a performance that earned him a Golden Globe nomination for best actor in a comedy.

The cinematography of Michael Ballhaus is also especially noteworthy. The picture's atmospheric nighttime shots effectively capture the somewhat seedy side of lower Manhattan, providing a kind of updated spin on the film noir style of the 1940s and '50s. A number of clever photographic techniques are employed, too, such as with Paul's wild cab ride, which was shot at a slightly accelerated speed to accentuate the frenzied driving, offering just the right touch of exaggeration without going over the top. The film editing of Thelma Schoonmaker further complements the camera work, particularly in its use of quick, dramatic cuts (mostly involving Paul's reaction shots), which deftly accent his stunned state of mind amidst the chaos.

So the next time your life seems a little dull, stop and think about how you want to alleviate the monotony. Watching this movie first just may help you save that eye of yours, not to mention your peace of mind. And what's more, your elders would be proud.

# The Perils of Domestic Bliss

"Housekeeping"
*Year of Release:* 1987
*Principal Cast: Christine Lahti, Sara Walker, Andrea Burchill, Margot Pinvidic, Anne Pitoniak, Barbara Reese, Georgie Collins, Bill Smillie*
*Director: Bill Forsyth*
*Book: Marilynne Robinson*
*Screenplay: Bill Forsyth*

Society places a lot of expectations on us (or, more precisely, we allow said expectations to be placed upon us by a culture rigorously preoccupied with conformity). We're supposed to live certain ways, dress certain ways, eat certain ways, behave certain ways, all in an effort to conform to some arbitrary standard of civility that someone decided at some point (probably a long time ago) was the proper way to do things. The more we buy into that kind of orthodoxy, the greater the pile of expectations heaped on us, especially in such areas as marriage, child-rearing, and domestic life in general. What's more, we can get ourselves into serious trouble if we don't adhere to established norms, with consequences ranging from simple peer pressure to oppressive ostracism, sometimes with significant legal and financial ramifications. But maybe some of us just don't want to play by those rules; we want to lash out, be our own authentic selves, and let society be damned. The choices involved in making those decisions are often difficult ones, regardless of whether we seek to strike some kind of equitable balance or to live out our lives genuinely in spite of others' wishes. Those are among the issues faced by three searching souls in the quirky drama, "Housekeeping."

When two young girls, Ruthie (Sara Walker) and Lucille (Andrea Burchill), are suddenly and unexpectedly abandoned by their quietly troubled single mother Helen (Margot Pinvidic), they're shunted off to live with family. They trade in their life in Seattle for that of the small Northwestern mountain town of Fingerbone. Once there, the girls are handed off to a succession of elderly relatives, starting with their grandmother (Georgie Collins) and then a pair of neurotic, self-serving great aunts (Anne Pitoniak, Barbara Reese). The constant changes in guardianship give Ruthie and Lucille little chance to become close to anyone except each other. But that all changes when they finally land in the care of their mother's sister, Aunt Sylvie (Christine Lahti), a free spirit who's spent much of her adult life as a vagabond of sorts but who returns home, reluctantly, at the family's request, to set up housekeeping with her two nieces.

Ruthie and Lucille are thrilled at Sylvie's arrival, if for no other reason than the fact that she's one of the few people they have ever known who is even remotely close to their own age. But, perhaps more important, they hope their aunt will be able to fill in some of the information gaps for them about the mother they barely knew and the father they don't remember. Sadly, Sylvie's of little help since she, too, spent little time around the family into which she was born, having ridden the rails for many years, living like a hobo in a skirt. But, ironically, that lack of connection to family also gives Sylvie and her nieces a connection to one another that allows the three of them to grow close, at least for a while.

However, as Ruthie and Lucille enter adolescence, the long-standing bond they share between them begins to dissipate, in large part because of their aunt's behavior. While Sylvie truly does seem to adore her girls, she's not much on domesticity. The lure of the open road keeps calling to her, and the responsibility entailed in things like household chores and raising teenagers just doesn't hold her interest. The girls see this, and they're divided on what to do about it. Should they allow Sylvie to roam free, or should they rein her in and demand that she live up to her responsibility as a surrogate parent? Regardless of what they decide, however, they know that Sylvie will do as she pleases and that they might easily end up on their own. And that, they further realize, could push each of them into the very scary position of having to make their own choices about what kinds of lives they want to lead. Do they want lives tied to the trappings of conformity and conventional community life? Or do they want one like their aunt lived for so many years (and is quite obviously longingly drawn to again)?

What's essentially at stake for each of these characters is the pursuit of personal happiness, a challenge made all the more difficult by the pressure of townsfolk staring down their noses at them and sizing up the unconventional way they live, something not tolerated well in the constrictive 1950s. The local sheriff (Bill Smillie) is particularly meddlesome in his inquiries, resorting to polite but intrusive harassment to check up on the oddball who's allegedly trying to raise the two kids. Such are the circumstances that prompt some tough choices.

Personally, I congratulate Sylvie for the example she sets. She spent years living the life she wanted—and all by choice. Her existence was as free as free will, which made it possible. We could learn a lot from a refreshing role model like her, even if we don't embrace the same choices she does. So much of the time we squander precious time—even years at a stretch—leading lives that hold little appeal to us, often with fulfilling others' expectations as the primary and stiflingly pointless purpose. Yet by readily giving herself over to her free will and power of choice, Sylvie unhinges herself from the trap of compromises that keep so many of us locked into probabilities that slowly smolder from glowing embers of agitation into raging fires of discontent. We need only look at the experience of Helen to see how that can play out.

I also applaud Sylvie specifically for the example she sets for Ruthie and Lucille. It's important that adolescents learn how to function on their own, and because she's loath to raise them in typically overprotective fashion, Sylvie provides them with an opportunity to learn real independence. She encourages and empowers them in this by telling them that there's nothing to be afraid of, advice that she sells them on by way of her own example. This is significant for both practical and metaphysical reasons. To begin with, independence is vital as a basic survival skill, one that we need to cultivate just to get through daily life. But it's important on a metaphysical level as well. Vigorously indulging one's sense of independence is good exercise for our free will and power of choice to keep fit so that it continues to function properly in the manifestation efforts we engage in every day. Indeed, "use it or lose it" applies even when it comes to conscious creation practice.

I salute the efforts of these three characters as conscious creators, too, for they each do an excellent job of materializing the circumstances they need to learn the life lessons they've chosen to experience. A loosely knit family, ready access to escape routes, a healthy resistance to arbitrarily inane social conventions, and a certain degree of selfishness all help to foster the autonomy that each of them seeks to develop. They even made it strenuous on themselves—to flex their independence and nonconformity muscles—through their choice of the time and place in which they sought to learn these lessons. If they can pass these tests while living in a small town in the 1950s, they will have done well for themselves and could probably get by just about anywhere.

But what is perhaps most satisfying is seeing the sheer joy that Sylvie experiences when she talks about her life on the rails. Her face lights up, relishing the freedom that a life without restrictions affords. She can do as she pleases, go where she wishes, and live as she desires, her only limitation being train schedules. And if she misses one, another one will come along soon enough to take her to her destination—or to someplace different if she changes her mind. Either way, it's all on her.

The prevalence of trains in this story is interesting as a conscious creation symbol. I've always thought that trains are like lines of probability: They each go down a particular track toward a particular destination, directionally focused upon reaching the designated end point, just as the driving intents of individual probabilities do as they move down their respective "tracks." Destinations are reachable by multiple tracks or probabilities, and the particular lines that each follows can veer off on tangents, revealing new routes to be traveled and different destinations to be explored.

That, I believe, is part of the appeal of life on the rails for Sylvie; it affords her the opportunity to explore multiple probabilities and destinations, both literally and figuratively, with her choice being the determining factor as to which path is explored. This explains why she's so taken with big cities like Seattle and Portland, train line hubs that metaphorically double as metaphysical roundhouses. It also sheds light on why she finds life in Fingerbone so claustrophobic—it's a single-line town, just like its residents. Her only use for that lone track is its capability to lead her to other tracks and, ultimately, other probabilities for exploration. It's no wonder she wants out.

"Housekeeping" is an unusual picture, to say the least. Its eccentric story line is perfect for a filmmaker like Bill Forsyth, who's best known for directing other quirky slice-of-life movies, such as "Local Hero" (see chapter 10), "Comfort and Joy," and "Gregory's Girl." He's dealing with material much meatier here than in his other works, but he rises to the occasion, telling a tale that's both heartbreaking and heartwarming, mixed in with touches of mystery, whimsy, and wonder.

Lahti, Walker, and Burchill all turn in fine performances, showing us multiple sides of their characters as they work through their choices. We see the various stages of deliberation they go through—including bouts of doubt and indecisiveness—on their way to making the decisions they know they must ultimately reach. In this way, we see the characters almost as if they were processes and not just as individuals, quite an acting accomplishment indeed.

The Northwestern landscape also has a prominent role in the film, made all the more lush by the cinematography of Michael Coulter. The ethereal musical score of Michael Gibbs provides a perfect soundtrack for the breathtaking scenery.

The film is currently available only in VHS format, so its availability, regrettably, may be a bit limited. However, it does show up on cable from time to time, too.

For many of us, all of the things that we're supposed to aspire to in life are not at all what we hope to achieve out of it. As well as we may know that for ourselves, however, it's often difficult to make the decision to embrace it openly, especially when those around us adhere to a different set of expectations. Having the courage to make the necessary choices to live out what we know is right for us is something to be commended, for making the right decisions to follow one's heart carries the promise of great rewards and tremendous satisfaction. If only the others knew what they were missing . . .

## Double Feature: The Canvas of Life

### "Frida"
*Year of Release: 2002*
*Principal Cast: Salma Hayek, Alfred Molina, Mia Maestro, Patricia Reyes Spindola, Roger Rees, Valerie Golino, Geoffrey Rush, Antonio Banderas, Edward Norton, Ashley Judd, Karine Plantadit-Bageot*
*Director: Julie Taymor*
*Book: Hayden Herrera*
*Screenplay: Clancy Sigal, Diane Lake, Gregory Nava, Anna Thomas*

### "Pollock"
*Year of Release: 2000*
*Principal Cast: Ed Harris, Marcia Gay Harden, Jennifer Connelly, Bud Cort, Amy Madigan, Jeffrey Tambor, Sally Murphy, Val Kilmer, John Heard, Sada Thompson, Norbert Weisser*
*Director: Ed Harris*
*Book: Steven Naifeh, Gregory White Smith*
*Screenplay: Barbara Turner, Susan J. Emshwiller*

In conscious creation circles, life is often compared to a painter's canvas. It is a medium that exquisitely facilitates the expression of physical existence as an art form in all its intricacies, meaning, and mysteries. And sometimes it even incorporates the very medium to which it is so frequently compared. A painter's canvas is truly an ideal physical medium for reflecting one's reality, presenting artistic, allegorical impressions of life and all its attendant beliefs, perspectives, and aspirations. Those interpretations manifest in all forms of articulation, too, from authentic to expressionist to surreal and even abstract, each with its own intrinsic validity. That breadth of scope in itself illustrates the tremendous range of probabilities we all have access to for expressing ourselves, all made possible by our innate sense of choice. This is an incredibly liberating prospect. What's more, one doesn't even have to be a painter to draw inspiration from that idea, for we're all inherently creative beings capable of expressing ourselves in our own particular idioms. Two movies that splendidly explore these concepts are the biographies of a pair of provocative painters, "Frida" and "Pollock."

"Frida" tells the story of Mexican painter Frida Kahlo (1907–1954) (Salma Hayek), an enigmatic artist known for her highly distinctive style that combined elements of surrealism, realism, and symbolism with rich, vibrant colors. She was especially known for works with female themes, most notably her unusual collection of self-portraits, some of which depict her elegantly, some ghastly.

The film examines how various events and forces in Kahlo's life shaped her art, particularly her lifelong chronic pain (the result of injuries suffered in a near-fatal bus accident at age 18), her zealous endorsement of Communist politics, and her two turbulent marriages to muralist Diego Rivera (Alfred Molina). The movie portrays her as a fiercely independent spirit, a hard-drinking, salty-tongued individualist who readily speaks her mind and never hesitates to scoff at the behavior expected of her, eschewing both proper ladylike manners and devout Catholic piety. She freely engages in extramarital affairs, such as a tryst with exiled Russian revolutionary Leon Trotsky (Geoffrey Rush), and experiments with bisexuality, most notably with a black Parisian chanteuse (Karine Plantadit-Bageot) who bears more than a passing resemblance to Josephine Baker, the American-born singer, dancer, and actress with whom the real-life Kahlo allegedly had an affair.

But it is primarily her relationship with Rivera that the film explores. He is portrayed as an artistic mentor, a political comrade, and an openly philandering spouse, all qualities that figured significantly in Kahlo's life lessons and that she, in turn, would draw upon in making choices for how to live her life. Theirs was a real love-hate relationship, but, ironically enough, that ultimately enabled her to see both the good and the bad in romance. In fact, that realization actually freed her so that she could more easily make her own romantic choices, allowing her to be an empowered partner rather than a feeble victim bemoaning the decisions imposed upon her.

Over time, as a consequence of her stormy involvement with Rivera, as well as her successive health setbacks and recoveries, she would develop an ability to see clearly both sides of the coin in most anything in life, even in life and death itself. This insight, perhaps more than anything else, characterized the development and flourishing of her art, freeing Kahlo to create works unlike those painted by any other artist. Her paintings often reflected her life personally—and the choices she made in creating it—employing multiple styles and techniques to yield a unique look, from refined to outlandish. But, regardless of their appearance, they always drew from her keen vision of life and her acute awareness of choice as a means of responding to it, a combination that significantly empowered her free will to make the decisions *she* wanted. This is a principle that is at the very core of conscious creation, and Kahlo applied it both artistically and otherwise. Despite the emotional drain she regularly allowed it to take on her (yet another choice), she lived out this concept to the fullest in every facet of her life.

"Pollock" presents the biography of another innovator on the canvas, abstract expressionist Jackson Pollock (1912–1956) (Ed Harris). The film focuses on the last 15 years of his life, from the time right before his emergence as a rising star in the art world to his tragic self-inflicted downfall.

When we first meet Pollock, he's a struggling artist in New York. As with an aspirant in almost any field, part of that struggle is related simply to getting recognized. But, in Pollock's case, other factors are present, such as occasional bouts with mental illness (a condition apparently considered severe enough to earn him a selective service designation of 4F just as World War II escalated). It doesn't help that he also does battle with the bottle, is prone to fits of antisocial behavior, and is something of a raging womanizer. His prolonged searches for inspiration in getting projects started could just as easily be interpreted as procrastination as they could thoughtful deliberation.

All of those concerns aside, however, he attracts a major ally to his cause before long, his doggedly loyal lover and fellow painter Lee Krasner (Marcia Gay Harden), who fervidly believes in his talent and tenaciously promotes his work to the New York arts community. Largely through her singular efforts, Pollock begins drawing a coterie of benefactors to himself, most notably art dealer Howard Putzel (Bud Cort), gallery owner Peggy Guggenheim (Amy Madigan), and art critic Clem Greenberg (Jeffrey Tambor). Pollock at last seems on his way.

To bring some much-needed stability into Pollock's life, Krasner proposes that they get married and move to rural Long Island. The tranquility of the country and the space of a free-standing studio give Pollock some much-needed breathing room, and the steady presence of a dedicated life partner provides the hoped-for stabilization. But Pollock's rise moves slower than anticipated, resulting in money issues and strain in his marriage. That all changes, however, with an "accidental" discovery that would launch Pollock's career into the artistic stratosphere.

While working in his studio one day, Pollock dribbled some paint on a canvas. He was intrigued by the pattern it created and so went on to dribble some more, and then more, and then more, all in an ongoing process of discovery, an awakening to the technique that would come to characterize his signature style. The art of "Jack the Dripper" was thus born.[6]

With the emergence of this new technique, coupled with a feature article in *Life* magazine, Pollock leaped to fame and fortune. With this fame came an increased number of requests to speak about his art, something he previously did rarely and usually in only limited detail. He started doing radio interviews and was then the subject of a documentary by filmmaker Hans Namuth (Norbert Weisser). But while demonstrating his technique during the filming of the documentary, Pollock began to feel as if he was performing for the camera and not creating genuine art. Self-doubts over the integrity of his work crept in, eventually leading him back into drinking and beginning a downward spiral from which he would never recover.

Pollock's conscious creation choices are indeed interesting ones, for they have a dual-edged sword aspect to them. For instance, his mental illness episodes earned him a 4F draft designation from the U.S. military. As difficult as his treatments must have been to endure, as depicted in one scene in which he's bound in a straightjacket while frantic, they may have also given him the very deferral that kept him from being injured or killed in combat, circumstances that might have kept the world from seeing the art he was capable of creating.

Similarly, his boozing, bawdy antics, and womanizing may have been frowned upon by some, but they also got him noticed, particularly by people who had clout to boost his career. It's even possible that the images he brought into being on canvas were inspired in part by visions generated during the alcohol-induced stupors he put himself through, images that might not have otherwise arisen in his consciousness, let alone seen the light of day. How ironic it is, then, that those same binges would eventually usher in his downfall as well.

The life experiences of both Kahlo and Pollock raise an interesting question where choice and free will are concerned: Why did these artists feel a need to create suffering in their lives? In fact, why do so many artists in general, from painters to musicians to entertainers, seem to feel a need to embrace it? Would they be unable to create, otherwise? Those aren't easy questions to answer rhetorically, but from a conscious creation standpoint, it appears that those who choose to harbor such beliefs, for whatever reason, feel that there's a necessary connection between suffering and the creation of art.

Some of Pollock's choices in that vein have already been discussed, and many of the same parallels could apply to Kahlo. For instance, it was while she was recovering from her accident injuries that she took up painting in earnest. Had she not been so injured, would she have ever even picked up a paint brush? Also, many of her paintings (especially her self-portraits) symbolically reflected the pain she experienced through her ordeals physically and in marriage. Would they have ever come into being without her having had the experiences that inspired them?

Similar questions could be raised about artists and radicalism, and the answers, from a conscious creation perspective, would be virtually the same as those regarding suffering. Kahlo, for example, was heavily influenced by radical political thought, so it should come as no surprise, then, that she also introduced a radical form of art. Pollock was by his nature a renegade spirit, so it's only natural a maverick quality should emerge in his art. In both cases, the nexus between art and revolutionary ideas exists as a belief in the minds of the creators, and the concept ultimately materializes in physical form when given the green light by the free will.

In addition to being solid vehicles for exploring choice issues, both pictures are excellent biopics. "Frida" is a vibrant, colorful film full of exotic locales and exuberant characters. Hayek is thoroughly convincing as Kahlo, looking almost as if she's channeling the flamboyant painter. Molina does a fine turn as Rivera, the frumpy, oversexed sod who never seems to have enough common sense to know when to stop sticking his hand in the cookie jar. Roger Rees, as Kahlo's doting father, and Rush both turn in capable supporting performances as well.

The film has a few shortcomings, however. It really should have featured Kahlo's artwork (especially the self-portraits) more than it does; after all, it is a movie about a painter![7] Also, the picture has several surreal transition sequences at major turning points in the story that, frankly, just don't work. Artistic license aside, these elements are patently annoying and would have been much better left on the cutting room floor.

"Frida" won two Oscars, for its lively original score and its detailed makeup artistry, on six total nominations, including a best actress nod for Hayek. The film also received a Golden Globe for its score, as well as a nomination for Hayek's performance.

"Pollock" offers a probing look into the life of a tortured creative genius. It could have used some judicious editing, especially near the sometimes painfully slow beginning, but the pacing improves markedly as the film progresses. Harris's Oscar-nominated take on the inscrutable painter is generally strong, though he does go a bit over the top at times, especially early on. The film's best performances are undeniably turned in by Harden, who received the best supporting actress Oscar as Pollock's ever-faithful wife, and Madigan, as the often overbearing Guggenheim.

One of the picture's greatest strengths is in its presentation of Pollock's paintings. They're showcased beautifully, their colors coming alive on the screen. A number of sequences depict Pollock in his studio, offering viewers an opportunity to see what it might have been like to watch the artist at work, with his spontaneous flinging of pigment onto canvases tacked to the floor.

The canvas of life is certainly an intriguing one, made all the more resplendent by the choices we make about what to put on it. As we choose the colors and patterns we wish to create, we should always bear in mind that a full palette is ever at our disposal; all we need do is choose to avail ourselves of it. If we do that, the results can be positively sensational.

## The Beauty of Hard Choices

"Brave New World"
*Year of Initial Broadcast: 1998*
*Principal Cast: Peter Gallagher, Leonard Nimoy, Tim Guinee, Sally Kirkland, Miguel Ferrer, Rya Kihlstedt, Steven Flynn*
*Directors: Leslie Libman, Larry Williams*
*Book: Aldous Huxley*
*Teleplay: Dan Mazur, David Tausik*

Consider what it would be like to live in a reality where children are genetically engineered and fetuses are incubated instead of being born, where families no longer exist and words like *mother* and *father* are seen as profanities, where people are stratified into classes based on vocation and programmed from birth to know their place, all with the goal of preserving a social order primarily aimed at catering to a superficial, drugged-out, promiscuous elite. Such is life in "Brave New World."

This made-for-TV adaptation of the famed Aldous Huxley novel (first published in 1932) explores life in a tightly controlled utopian society of the future. War, poverty, and many of the infirmities of existence have been eliminated. Some would contend that even unhappiness has been obliterated. But at what cost? In the interest of maintaining order, the world has been manipulated into a routine of unending tedium where new ideas are discouraged, old ideals have been discarded, and the meaning of things has been sucked right out of them. People collectively go through life on autopilot, their main concerns (especially in the upper echelon) being where they can get their next fix of the mind-numbing drug known as soma, when they can next go shopping to fulfill their need for ever greater levels of conspicuous consumption, and who their next sex partner is going to be. There's nothing innately wrong about any of that, but when that's all you've got, it does seem a bit empty, sort of like living a perpetual L.A. lifestyle. And what's more, no one challenges the established order or even thinks about doing so, mainly because no one has ever been taught the value of independent thought. Some brave new world indeed.

This version of the story, which has been updated and modified somewhat from the original, focuses on Bernard Marx (Peter Gallagher), a rising star in the agency charged with social conditioning and educational programming. He is a member of the ruling alpha class, the managers of society. They work closely with the efficiency-minded middle-management beta class, society's paper-pushing operatives, and oversee the functioning of the gamma and delta classes, the worker bees. Recent behavioral incidents involving the delta class are a cause of concern for the alphas, who fear losing their grip over their subordinates. Bernard believes it could be due to flaws in the programming, which he thinks is focused more on the message given to those it programs than on the individuals who are the recipients of it. His assessment should probably come as no surprise, either, for in a world where individuality has been bred out of society, why would those responsible for monitoring impersonal conditioning be concerned with something as alien as an individual's needs? Bernard's calls for further study and possible reform are ridiculed, even seen as somewhat heretical. But he quietly decides to pursue his own research, much to the circumspect consternation of his agency's deputy controller (Miguel Ferrer) but with the blessing of its head honcho (Leonard Nimoy), a guru-like official whose enigmatic persona seems like a cross between Mr. Spock and Hugh Hefner.

Bernard's views are controversial not only in his work but also in his love life. He spends much of his time with only one woman, his co-worker Lenina Crowne (Rya Kihlstedt), a practice that's seen as antisocial (such exclusivity being perceived as "overly possessory" and degrading to the other person, inhibiting the pursuit of other involvements, a justification for socially sanctioned promiscuity). He even tries to enlist her support in some of his research efforts, which she's skeptical about because of the potential danger they pose to the social order she's so willingly bought into and helps perpetuate in her role as a teacher. And from her perspective, she has every right to be concerned, for one day an incident occurs that could change everything.

While on a visit to the land beyond civilization, the hinterlands past the tightly sealed borders of society, where the residents ("savages," as they're called) live off the land, the helicopter carrying Bernard and Lenina unexpectedly crash-lands. They survive, but their safety is almost immediately threatened by the advances of a band of leering locals. However, almost as unexpectedly, a savage named John Cooper (Tim Guinee) comes to their rescue. John takes them to his home to help them find their way back to civilization. While there, Bernard and Lenina discover that John is remarkably intelligent, a revelation that runs counter to everything they've ever been taught about savages. John then tells his guests the story about how he was born of the union of his mother Linda (Sally Kirkland) and an official from civilization who made a cross-border visit. Bernard reasons that such an official would have to have been a member of the alpha class to gain that kind of access to the outlands. He feels it only fair that John have the right to find out the true nature of his heritage, a lineage that can easily be established through genetic tracing. And so he offers to take John and Linda back to civilization with him, an invitation that they accept and that sets in motion a chain of events with widespread repercussions for all involved and for society at large, prompting a series of hard choices for all concerned.

As with other films in this chapter, "Brave New World" explores the challenges and ramifications of making difficult decisions. It takes the ideas in a few different directions, too. For instance, while other movies in this chapter have examined how hard choices yield "good" or "bad" outcomes, this picture squarely shows how both are possible, sometimes even from the same decision and with impact on a single individual. That is intriguing, for it suggests beliefs are not always as clear-cut as we might think they are; their character is not strictly black or white but indeed can have those oft-misunderstood in-between shades of gray. A mostly positive result may carry with it difficult consequences, while a storm cloud might conceal the proverbial silver lining. In either case, it all depends on what beliefs underlie the outcome to which free will has given license for manifestation.

The picture also illustrates the impact of choice when it's made for a large collective on a society-wide basis. The other films in this chapter have principally examined the question from an individual perspective, but in this movie, we see the notion applied to a broad-based constituency. We witness how an idea can originate as a choice and then morph into policy and eventually dogma, with increasingly strong means of institution- alized enforcement evolving with it to preserve its continuation. One can't help but wonder if those who initially made these choices—even if done so out of benign, beneficial intent—could have foreseen the way their decisions would transform over time. Also, might they have made the same choices if they could have seen how they would unfold? This question again raises some of the creation by default issues discussed in chapter 1, as well as the need to have a clear understanding of the nature of one's beliefs when deliberating them, for when proposed to an industrious free will, they just might get the green light when perhaps they should have received an amber or red one.

In contrast, it's also fascinating to watch how one individ- ual's choices can have impact on the masses. Bernard's choice to bring John back to civilization is just one such example. On top of that, John's choice to be merely his savage self in a world built on artificial façades, simple though that notion seems, has tremendous impact in a world where the fog of deception and superficiality keeps residents from seeing the true character of the world in which they live. They're drawn to him to discover the secret wisdom they believe he possesses, and they do so willingly, exercising a degree of choice that they heretofore had probably not even recognized that they had, due to the rigid social conditioning that they had so pervasively (and perversely) allowed to color their thinking.

Even the powers that be don't recognize the potential power of the beliefs that John espouses. One of them, the notion that we're each in charge of our own destiny (does that sound famil- iar?), is summarily dismissed as a quaint old idea that most resi- dents won't understand and that the few who do are unlikely to embrace because of the debilitating level of responsibility associated with it. Little do they know, however, that notions as exotic as this also hold tremendous appeal, especially to a citizenry starved for something new and different as a means to alleviate the suffocating tedium.

"Brave New World" is thoroughly entertaining from start to finish, with performances and technical aspects that are solid in every respect. But its greatest asset is its thought-provoking character, providing fodder for many issues worthy of contemplation and robust post-viewing discussion. In addition to the choice-related topics it explores, the story poses a host of other hypothetical questions: Can unhappiness truly be eliminated? Can long-established aspects of human nature be defused simply because society sanctions it? Is social conditioning, as powerful as it is, effective enough to overcome an innate force like free will? There's a lot to talk about here.

This version of the story is only available in VHS format, and copies may be hard to come by. However, it does show up often on cable, particularly on networks with a sci-fi bent.

Hard choices are seldom easy, but they potentially carry the seed of great rewards, too. In a society in which those rewards are not only prohibited but also unknown, they hold the promise of offering fulfillment that's unimaginable. And if *that's* not a brave new world, I don't know what is.

**Extra Credits:** A film in the same vein that paints an even bleaker picture of reality—and presents a series of even harder choices—is the sci-fi thriller, "THX 1138." This first feature from director George Lucas grew out of a live-action short that he made several years earlier. In this expanded version, Lucas shows us a sterile world of the future in which all the inhabitants are treated like cogs in a giant machine, with designations like license plate numbers instead of names. A confused and stressed-out resident belonging to the THX series (Robert Duvall) struggles to figure out the meaning of his existence, but seemingly few choices are available to him because the conditions of his society are meticulously ordered and sternly controlled. Everyone is permanently medicated to remain docile (with drug avoidance prosecutable as a crime), and a brutal robot police force coldly dispenses justice without reservation. THX 1138 undergoes corrective measures (voluntary and otherwise) to straighten out his life, which he quietly endures, until one day, when he's finally had enough. Minimalist dialogue, sets, and costumes, coupled with cinematography presenting a decidedly "removed" perspective, combine to create a palpable sense of isolation and detachment, a perfect setting in which harsh choices are raised, framed, and forced into being made. (1971; Robert Duvall, Donald Pleasence, Don Pedro Colley, Maggie McOmie; George Lucas, director and story; George Lucas and Walter Murch, screenplay)

## Bonus Features

"Stardust Memories": A filmmaker once known for making comedies finds himself in a middle-aged funk, personal disappointments and a hefty dose of weltschmerz having piled up to create a jaded outlook. But while at a weekend retrospective of his movies, he goes on a journey of self-discovery to realize his attitude is all of his own making. Will he choose to seek out happiness, or will he decide to stay stuck in his melancholy? (1980; Woody Allen, Charlotte Rampling, Jessica Harper, Marie-Christine Barrault, Tony Roberts, Daniel Stern, Laraine Newman; Woody Allen, director and screenplay)

"Cousin, Cousine": Distant cousins by marriage meet at a family gathering only to discover that their spouses have cheated on them. They find solace in one another's company, forging a strong friendship that other family members misinterpret as an affair. When the cousins find out what everyone is thinking, they choose to play along with the prevailing assumptions, mischievously flaunting their connection until they discover there actually may be something to it. A delightful French farce that inspired the 1989 American remake "Cousins." (1975; Marie-Christine Barrault, Victor Lanoux, Marie-France Pisier, Guy Marchand; Jean Charles Tacchella, director and story; Jean Charles Tacchella and Danièle Thompson, screenplay; three Oscar nominations, one Golden Globe nomination; VHS format only)

"Far From Heaven": Frank and Cathy Whitaker, a middle-class couple in uptight 1950s Connecticut, is forced into dealing with some difficult lifestyle choices. Frank must come to terms with his repressed homosexuality, while Cathy must deal with both her husband's quiet struggle and her growing discomfort with the racist attitudes of locals toward her close friend Raymond, an African American single father. Free will is put to the test as all involved seek to find acceptable paths for themselves. (2002; Julianne Moore, Dennis Quaid, Dennis Haysbert; Todd Haynes, director and screenplay; four Oscar nominations, four Golden Globe nominations)

"Jésus de Montréal": A group of Montreal actors is hired by a local parish to stage a version of the Passion Play. In an attempt to portray the drama with historical accuracy, the group incorporates elements considered too radical by the church, which wants the play presented traditionally or not at all. The actors choose to defy church dictates and put on the production as they deem fit, a decision that causes their odyssey to parallel that of the prophet whose life their play depicts. (1989; Lothaire Bluteau, Catherine Wilkening, Johanne-Marie Tremblay, Rémy Girard, Robert Lepage, Gilles Pelletier; Denys Arcand, director and screenplay; one Oscar nomination, one Golden Globe nomination; Jury Prize winner, Ecumenical Jury Prize winner, and Palme D'Or nominee, Cannes Film Festival)

"Thelma & Louise": Two girlfriends seek to escape their humdrum lives for a weekend adventure, but a series of debatable choices sends them fleeing for their lives as fugitives across four states. What choices should they make then? Good drama and great fun. (1991; Susan Sarandon, Geena Davis, Harvey Keitel, Michael Madsen, Christopher McDonald, Stephen Tobolowsky, Brad Pitt, Timothy Carhart; Ridley Scott, director; Callie Khouri, screenplay [Oscar and Golden Globe winner]; one Oscar win on six nominations, one Golden Globe win on four nominations)

"Rachel River": Residents of a small Minnesota town hardened by life's disappointments look for solutions to alleviate their sadness and loneliness, including making some drastic and desperate choices, decisions that could be viewed as last stabs at finding or recapturing happiness. Unexpected results abound. Touching and thoughtful, but keep the hankies handy. (1987; Pamela Reed, Viveca Lindfors, Craig T. Nelson, James Olson, Zeljko Ivanek; Sandy Smolan, director; Judith Guest, screenplay; VHS format only)

# 5

## Let's See What Happens When We Do *This* . . .

### *Changing Ourselves, Changing Our Circumstances*

When you change the way you look at things, the things you look at change.

*Wayne Dyer*

Try this: Look at something with one eye closed, then switch and look at it again with the other eye closed. Notice any difference? In all likelihood, what you've viewed is essentially the same in both cases, but the positioning of the item in question has shifted. That's because you're seeing it from an altered perspective. Now, a difference like this may not be earth-shatteringly significant when it comes to simply viewing an object, but when this principle is applied in the area of beliefs, the variance can be substantial.

To that end, as apparent as the opening quote might seem, it nevertheless rings resoundingly true from a conscious creation standpoint. It even calls to mind the classic example of the glass being half full or half empty. From a purely visual standpoint, the glass looks virtually identical under either characterization, but the connotations associated with each ascription differ markedly. A half-empty glass implies a negative outlook, calling to mind such qualities as absence, scarcity, pessimism, and deprivation. A half-full glass, on the other hand, suggests a positive view, including such traits as presence, availability, optimism, and even abundance.

One's take on the status of the glass depends entirely on the beliefs of the individual perceiving it. As discussed in chapter 4, thanks to free will and the power of choice, we can formulate beliefs that make it entirely possible to view the glass in either way, with both perspectives having equal validity. Because beliefs are changeable, so, too, are the perspectives that we're capable of holding. It's totally plausible to see the glass as half empty one moment and half full the next and for both views to retain their legitimacy. Regardless of what causes such a shift, be it a reinterpretation of sensory data, the appearance of new intellectual or intuitional input, or something else, the altered perspective is just as bona fide as its predecessor. However, the changed vision is also likely to carry a host of implications that weren't present previously. That can open up a new range of vistas that were once unknown and imperceptible, often providing benefits formerly unimagined.

Of course, the onus for shaping (and reshaping) the beliefs that define such perceptions truly is on each of us. According to Jane Roberts and Seth, when we come upon an aspect of our reality that we dislike, "[t]he only way out . . . is to become aware of your beliefs, aware of your own conscious thought, and to change your beliefs so that you bring them more in line with the kind of reality you want to experience."[1]

Indeed, change can be good.

★   ★   ★

The ability to change ourselves and our circumstances is one of the most beneficial aspects of conscious creation. Very simply, if we're unhappy with where we are, we can always change our situation to something else as long as we allow it. The degree to which this transpires, of course, again relates back to our beliefs. How flexible are they? Will we allow the proposed change to manifest? If so, how readily? These are all questions worth pondering, not only for the beliefs related to a particular creation but also to those that we employ as underlying operating principles, what are sometimes called "core beliefs" (more on this later). The more we embrace or resist change, based on our beliefs, the more or less likely we are able to effect it in our lives. In short, change occurs only as easily as beliefs change.

Tapping into our capability for this generally requires deftness in a few specific areas, namely (1) our comfort with free will and the power of choice, (2) our openness to, and our ability to spot, alternative probabilities, and (3) our capacity to envision the change we seek. The first two points have been discussed in previous chapters, but the third merits some further attention.

The ability to envision the change we seek basically has to do with feeling it in our being. Gregg Braden, author of such works as *The Lost Mode of Prayer*,[2] says that this is like experiencing the change as if it's already happened, the request already fulfilled. This essentially involves picturing and then immersing ourselves in the physical sensations, emotional reactions, and mental impressions that we believe we're likely to experience when the change is implemented. Abstract though this sounds, the energy of intention released through such a practice is incredibly powerful, giving the manifestation process a hefty jolt toward realization.

For example, suppose you're working in a job you dislike, yet you've been unable to draw a new one to you. In that case, try envisioning the position you desire, in all its details, right down to the image of your new nameplate on your new desktop and the comfort of the new cushy chair in which you sit. The sensations such an image evokes are no doubt quite satisfying. Hold it as long as possible, and by all means don't undercut it with the negativity of doubt. (Beliefs like that will only serve to send the creation away.) By maintaining in your mind the image of the change you're seeking, such change will be more likely to happen.

Some of you might be saying that this sounds suspiciously like wishful thinking, but there's a difference between that and genuine envisioning. Wishful thinking generally takes place entirely on an intellectual level; there's no emotional or intuitive energy infused into the creation being sought. Simply saying, "Oh, I'll believe in that new idea from now on" just isn't enough, because you're only investing a part of your being in the outcome; there's no feeling behind the thought. This is akin to a cheerleader merely mouthing the words of a routine and not putting any of the motivating energy into it to transform it into a genuine cheer. The more of yourself you put into the hoped-for manifestation, the more probable its materialization is.

To foster expertise in invoking change, it helps significantly to cultivate a few other attributes (generated, as usual, through our beliefs). Flexibility, open-mindedness, and playfulness contribute much to the process, oiling the wheels of change when threats of stagnation or limitation loom. At the same time, discernment plays an important role by helping show us when change truly is and is not needed, providing a crucial heads-up for those times when things are better left alone.

Perhaps above all, patience is a real virtue in this context, for sometimes, even with the most sincere and resolute envisioning, change takes time to appear. Energetic resources need to be marshalled, conflicting beliefs need to be reconciled, and so on. Without it, doubt can creep in to undermine the process and send the change away. Patience is also a helpful hedge against undue delays caused by constantly checking the progress of an intent's manifestation, a situation not unlike regularly digging up a seed to see if it has germinated, a surefire way to keep creations—and changes—from sprouting.

★   ★   ★

A key question in implementing change is often "How much is enough?" The answer to that can be tricky, because much ultimately depends on one's personal comfort level with change. However, there are a few guidelines to keep in mind.

We've often heard that changing too much all at once is difficult, like taking on too many New Year's resolutions simultaneously. I've found in my experience that there's a great deal of validity to that, mainly because changing even one variable in an equation can drastically change the equation's very nature. What if Einstein, for example, had postulated that $E = MC^3$ instead of $MC^2$? That single variable, that little number, would have made a huge difference, even though it represents only one component of the overall equation.

Another way of looking at this is to think of a tapestry and what happens when you pull on a single thread. Its removal may not seem like much initially, but the impact on the fabric's overall integrity could be quite considerable in the end, for one thread links to another, and then another, and so forth. Before you know it, pulling on it might leave you with a very different looking—or even nonexistent—tapestry.

In light of this, then, changing a single variable is probably the most prudent course, at least at the outset. Of course, there are those who are exceedingly comfortable with change, and they're able to adapt to shifts in multiple variables simultaneously. Those are people we could learn much from, for this is an indication they're practiced conscious creators, at home with the manipulation of their beliefs and the results that spring forth from them.

The next question for most of us would probably focus on which variable to change. This depends entirely on the individual, but the sky really is the limit here. Two basic options are changing ourselves or changing our prevailing circumstances in some particular way. In both instances, there's likely to be a synergistic effect from either choice, for changing the individual will almost invariably lead to a change in the circumstances and vice versa. When it comes to altering an individual's attributes, examples of variables for change would include physical qualities, personality traits, or personal talents. In the case of alterable circumstances, examples could encompass everything from vocation to geographic location to peer group. The more emboldened among us might even choose to change something like our time frame or even our fundamental reality, say from physical to noncorporeal (which could actually be what something like death is really all about). Obviously, the more drastic the change in variable, the greater the impact will be.

It's also possible to change one variable multiple times over. This is like flipping through the pages of a catalog for a particular product line. With each iteration, the same variable is being changed but in constant succession until a desired choice is arrived at. This is metaphysical window shopping of the highest order.

Underlying all these considerations, of course, are the beliefs generating these variables in the first place, and they have degrees of changeability associated with them, too. For instance, the beliefs related to a specific creation would most readily affect only the manifestation in question. The beliefs someone has about his or her car, for example, aren't likely to extend much beyond the qualities associated with the vehicle itself.

However, there are beliefs that have wider impact, the so-called core beliefs noted earlier. The effects of core belief changes can be substantial, since they provide color and shading to *all* of the creations that arise out of them. Think of core beliefs as being like the operating software on your computer. Any changes made to them are going to affect all of the applications that run on them. The implications of that can be quite wide-ranging. To illustrate, think again of the glass example from earlier. A change in one's view from half empty to half full would usher in a plethora of changes in outlook, extending far beyond how one simply sees the contents of the glass. A change in a core belief, then, would have the potential to be just as effective as changing multiple variables all at once.

No matter what variables or beliefs are altered, the resulting changes can be either evolutionary or revolutionary in the way they unfold, depending on the speed and degree of modification. The outcome hoped for in virtually all instances, regardless of which path is chosen, is transformation. And when transformation is taken to its utmost degree, it becomes something even greater—transcendence, something truly worth aspiring to.

The movies in this chapter examine change from a multitude of perspectives, including those noted here. They show how change unfolds in the lives of their characters, sometimes for the better, sometimes for the worse, and sometimes with no alteration at all. In each case, however, the results always come down to what the characters believe they want to manifest for themselves, just as is the case for all conscious creators.

Change truly is the one constant in life. Of course, how that plays out in each of our lives ultimately depends on how each of us looks at things. But in the end, seeing life from a fresh perspective may be just what we need to make it what we want.

## Staying Tuned

### "The Truman Show"
*Year of Release: 1998*
*Principal Cast: Jim Carrey, Laura Linney, Noah Emmerich,*
*Natascha McElhone, Holland Taylor, Ed Harris, Harry Shearer*
*Director: Peter Weir*
*Screenplay: Andrew Niccol*

Broadcasters are notorious for their ubiquitous use of the expression "stay tuned" to keep viewers watching. The act of staying tuned (or, more precisely, staying *attuned*), whether applied to watching television or any other life endeavor, involves more than just being a passive observer. It requires active engagement, a resolute decision to take part in what's transpiring in the reality around us. Too often, however, many of us are content to sit back and watch, letting things happen on their own (or at least seemingly so), giving free rein to a way of living governed by creation by default. Learning how to commit as a full-fledged participant in the manifestation process, all the while staying attuned to the fulfillment of our needs (particularly those requiring change), is one of the many lessons to come out of the quirky comedy-drama, "The Truman Show."

Truman Burbank (Jim Carrey) is a world-famous TV star but doesn't even realize it. He's the focus of the long-running program *The Truman Show*, the moment-by-moment chronicle of his life story, broadcast 24/7, without commercial interruption. This ultimate reality show began at the time of his birth and has run for thirty years, with viewers across the globe captivated by his every move, no matter how mundane. And everyone's in on what's going on—that is, except for Truman himself.

The show is the brainchild of an enigmatic producer simply known as Christof (Ed Harris). His prodigy came into being thanks to his network's legal adoption of Truman, the product of an unwanted pregnancy who became the first child ever to come under the sanctioned guardianship of a corporation. A manufactured reality was then created for the network's newest star, constructed inside the world's largest TV studio, a building so big that it's one of only two man-made structures visible from space.

Inside the studio resides Truman's hometown, the blissful island community of Seahaven. Surrounding him are the show's cast members who make up his family and friends, including his wife Meryl (Laura Linney), his mother (Holland Taylor), and his best buddy since childhood, Marlon (Noah Emmerich). Together, they live out a life that, conscious creation aside, is seen as both real and created. Rough plotlines are drafted for Truman to experience, but all his reactions to them are his own.

Life in Seahaven seems pleasant enough, but Truman grows restless with its relative sameness. He has an adventurous spirit and natural curiosity about the world that supposedly exists beyond his island's shores, and he yearns to see more. But that's a problem for the show's producers: How do they build a studio capable of simulating all of the places Truman wants to visit? The space requirements and costs required for such an undertaking would be astronomical, so the producers need to drum up ways to discourage Truman's wanderlust. Their solutions take a number of forms. Published newspaper headlines, for example, boldly pose rhetorical questions like "Who needs Europe?" And when stronger measures are called for, this objective is accomplished by playing to Truman's fears. The walls of the local travel agency, for instance, are covered with posters frighteningly depicting the myriad dangers of flying. (Makes you wonder why they would even need a travel agency in the first place.)

By employing these tactics, the producers significantly influence the beliefs that Truman holds about his world, and, for the most part, he reacts to the supplied stimuli as hoped for. However, that all changes when things begin happening to make Truman question the nature of his existence. He's puzzled by production glitches, cast members stepping out of character, and awkwardly timed product placement plugs (the show's only source of revenue, since commercials aren't possible with the show's 24/7 broadcast schedule). Such snafus make him wonder about exactly where he's living. The encouragement of desired behavioral responses by the powers that be becomes increasingly difficult (and more coercive) as Truman begins to assert his true self, letting his indomitable spirit surface and threatening the very existence of the production in which he has heretofore unknowingly played the lead part. He begins to create a totally unexpected scenario all his own that forces his producers to struggle to keep up with him. And for viewers, that's high drama really worth staying tuned for.

Truman provides us with an excellent example of someone genuinely coming awake as a conscious creator. As the process begins, we first watch him use his powers of perception more effectively, not only to observe his world but also to analyze it, to see what's behind the surface qualities. This, in turn, helps fuel his use of his intuition and, subsequently, a more balanced application of the magical approach, in framing his beliefs. At this point, he's not so much focused on forming primary beliefs as questioning existing ones to see if they merit retention, reconfiguration, or replacement. The more confident he grows in this, the more willing he is to exert his free will and power of choice. And the more he does this, the more aware he grows of the wider range of probabilities open to him, making it eminently easier to evaluate and embrace change in his life. He takes charge of his existence to seek out a reality that fulfills his dreams, desires, and aspirations, one that allows him to live authentically, with conditions that work to *his* benefit. This is indeed conscious creation in full flower.

What's especially intriguing about this is that we see Truman experiencing the process through everyday, ordinary events. These are things most of us probably take for granted, but for Truman, they're new endeavors. We see him experience the wonder of becoming metaphysically sentient, which provides him with a true sense of joy and empowerment and which provides us with a helpful reminder of just what a miracle the act of conscious creation truly is, no matter how trivial the manifestation involved.

By contrast, Christof provides an excellent example of someone desperately resisting change, staying mired in his inflexible existing beliefs, even if the results they yield are no longer what are desired. He holds on to his creation with a vengeance, doing everything in his power to fashion it in the image he holds for Truman. What he doesn't realize, however, is that he's trying to impose his vision upon a co-creator who has free will equal to his own, one who is just as capable of rewriting the rules as Christof is at trying to set them. As a consequence, Christof receives a lesson in conscious creation equal to that of the one Truman learns but in a much different—and much more painful—vein.

In creating the world he builds for Truman, Christof would appear to be engaging in some heavy-duty materialization—the manifestation of an entirely manufactured reality—which might lead one to believe he's a whiz at this sort of thing. But we should not confuse the physical scale of his creation with the nature and breadth of the beliefs that generate it. The focus of Christof's intent is actually quite limited, at least metaphysically speaking; he's essentially looking to make the world's largest set, the stage required for what is really just an elaborate television show. The focus of Truman's intent, on the other hand, is the creation of something much larger and more meaningful—the very manifestation of his existence. The goals of these two co-creators aren't in synch, for each is employing his abilities in different ways to achieve different objectives of totally different scales. Disconnects between them would thus seem to be inevitable.

Of the world he's created, Christof says conceitedly, "We accept the reality of the world with which we are presented." Oh, do we now? I'm sure Truman would beg to differ. No matter what Christof may try to manifest in Truman's external world, he can never alter anything about Truman on the inside; only Truman can do that. In this regard, Christof tries to play God, manipulating conscious creation to fulfill manufactured and self-serving ends, while Truman *is* God, allowing the divine spirit to flow through him to manifest his authentic intent in physical form. In this sense, Christof is a religious symbol, offering an interpretation of God that he seeks to impose on others, while Truman is a spiritual one, allowing his own interpretation to hold sway. And, in view of this, it's no wonder why the degree of their conscious creation success ultimately differs so markedly.

Caught in the middle between these two metaphysical titans are the show's supporting cast members. They dutifully play the roles scripted for them; after all, as actors, that's their job. But when Truman's rogue agenda surfaces, they're often lost on how to proceed, for his actions don't fit the projected story arcs that they and he are expected to play out. As the lines begin to blur between the realities that they know of as actors and that they help to create as characters in Truman's saga, they start to get a taste of their own medicine; the cruel joke they've all been in on for so long comes back to bite them in the butt. They scramble to improvise, but they have trouble maintaining their façades, increasingly dropping out of character and letting their own reactions take over. For example, in one scene in which "Meryl" feels threatened by Truman, the persona of her character quickly evaporates under the strain of the circumstances and is replaced, quite understandably, by that of Hannah Gill, the actress who plays Meryl. Amidst shrieks of anguish, instead of the fright of Truman's terrified spouse, we hear a tearful, impassioned plea from an actress fearing for her safety, frantically exclaiming "How can you expect me to carry on under these conditions? It's unprofessional!"

The beliefs that the cast members have employed in helping create this charade begin to come full circle, creating a level of confusion for them about the nature of their reality comparable to what Truman has experienced all these many years. What's more, they're getting their payback from both sides. As Truman changes the rules on them, they're left unsure how to respond and do their jobs. Those who once helped ensnare the show's unwitting protagonist have now themselves become ensnared. At the same time, they've also allowed themselves to be manipulated by Christof, almost as much as Truman has, despite an awareness of the truth. They've followed his dictates faithfully, but it has left them unable to create for themselves at the time when the skill would serve them most. In a sense, they've been played just as Truman has. Ironically, it's Truman's unpredictable behavior that helps shake them out of their self-imposed complacency, inadvertently forcing them to get real, even if Truman himself is totally unaware of what he's doing for them as he's doing it.

Of course, all of these considerations raise the question of why Truman would create (or co-create) the world of Seahaven in the first place. If he's so insightful about reality, why did he initially produce such a confining existence for himself? I'd contend that sometimes we need the fog of illusion to help us see the light of clarity. Stripping away the illusory often makes the appearance of the fully illuminated that much more brilliant, and it's this process that we see Truman go through as his story unfolds. With the veil of deception gone, it makes his (and our) awe and appreciation for what is real that much greater. In this regard, I believe the experience of *Tru*-man thus speaks for itself.

This point is especially critical when it comes to changing our reality. As neophyte conscious creators, sometimes we need to see what we don't want first to be able to rule it out as an option for the future. This could even require becoming immersed in the less desired option for a time, to let its impact soak in, so much so that we tire of it and consciously look for an alternative. Indeed, only by having endured our tenure in a marinade of un-conscious and semi-conscious creation may it then be possible to materialize something more desirable, something that we truly want. In this sense, then, such an experience helps broaden our horizons to see the options open to us for change.

As those new horizons open, it's also interesting to note the differences in approach that Truman and Christof take to them. Christof is fearful, afraid of losing what he's so painstakingly worked to create, while Truman is fearless, courageously moving forward to find answers to the questions that have long eluded him. This is important in embracing change, for one who stays locked in fear also stays locked in place. Truman has no idea what lies ahead for him, but he also doesn't let such uncertainty stop him, a heroic gesture if there ever was one (more on fear and heroism in chapter 6).

"The Truman Show" raises a number of other considerations, too, all equally fascinating, such as the role of media in society, the responsibility we have as producers and consumers of information, the regard we place on celebrity, and the degree to which we allow ourselves to be influenced by all of these. It also effectively blends drama, humor, and romance in a seamless way, showing how all three are intrinsically part of life (even when that life's only a fabrication). When these elements are added to all of its metaphysical aspects, the combination makes for a rich cinematic tapestry of ideas, simultaneously entertaining and thought provoking.

The movie was showered with honors at the time of its release, but, somewhat surprisingly, it fared much better at the Golden Globes than it did at the Oscars. It took home three Globes on six total nominations, including a nod for best dramatic picture. In the Oscar race, however, it earned only three nominations and received no statues.

This film was most noteworthy as a breakthrough performance for Carrey, showing that he's just as capable of tackling headier material as he is of handling outrageously silly comedy. For his efforts, he was recognized with the Golden Globe for lead actor in a drama, but, strangely enough, he was shut out of a comparable nomination in that year's Oscars. Harris also took home a supporting actor Globe for his fine portrayal of Christof, a performance that also earned him an Oscar nod.

Technically, the picture is solid as well. Andrew Niccol wrote a brilliant script, and Peter Weir masterfully directed the picture, with both of them earning Oscar and Golden Globe nominations for their work. Burkhard Dallwitz produced an excellent Globe-winning original score that is effectively supplemented with musical elements written by Philip Glass. Peter Biziou's clever cinematography is also noteworthy, fusing images from Truman's first-person perspective with those from an objective perspective, an inventive approach employing a multitude of camera angles and photographic techniques.

Switching programs, metaphysically speaking, can indeed be healthy, especially when the current show grows tiresome or outlives its usefulness, as Truman's example so aptly illustrates. So keep that remote handy and stay tuned to the need for changes in viewing. And, as always, be sure to check your own local listings for time and channel.

## Double Feature: Views From the Other Side

### "All of Me"
*Year of Release: 1984*
*Principal Cast: Steve Martin, Lily Tomlin, Victoria Tennant, Madolyn Smith, Richard Libertini, Dana Elcar, Jason Bernard, Eric Christmas, Selma Diamond*
*Director: Carl Reiner*
*Book: Edwin Davis*
*Screen Story: Henry Olek*
*Screenplay: Phil Alden Robinson*

### "Switch"
*Year of Release: 1991*
*Principal Cast: Ellen Barkin, Jimmy Smits, JoBeth Williams, Lorraine Bracco, Tony Roberts, Perry King, Bruce Martyn Payne, Kevin Kilner, Lysette Anthony, Victoria Mahoney*
*Director: Blake Edwards*
*Screenplay: Blake Edwards*

To appreciate the beauty of some things fully, like an antique coin or a Kandinsky painting, you have to see them from both sides. Many aspects of existence are like that, too; life and death, rich and poor, male and female, and gay and straight are but just a few examples. And sometimes the only way to gain such an appreciation is to change your reality radically by thrusting yourself into a scenario in which you can attain that opposite perspective. Two films that enable their characters to do just that are the comedies "All of Me" and "Switch."

"All of Me" tells the story of Roger Cobb (Steve Martin), a middle-aged lawyer saddled with paper-pushing duties that unfortunately make him little more than a glorified clerk. His interest in law is marginal at best (he'd really rather be a musician), but if he is going to continue practicing as an attorney, he wants his work to be meaningful, taking on idealistic causes rather than catering to the petty whims of fat-cat clients. His love life could use some help, too, because he's little more than the henpecked errand boy of Peggy (Madolyn Smith), the daughter of his less-than-scrupulous boss, Burton Schuyler (Dana Elcar).

To make matters worse, Schuyler assigns Roger to a new client, Edwina Cutwater (Lily Tomlin), a prickly, demanding heiress who, because of a frail heart, is not long for this world. She requires legal assistance in rewriting her will to stipulate that her $20 million fortune be left to Terry Hoskins (Victoria Tennant), the daughter of her longtime stable hand, Fred (Eric Christmas). Her reason? It's simple, really: Terry is a beautiful, healthy young woman, and Edwina plans to have her soul transferred into Terry's body upon her death, a procedure to be facilitated by a somewhat dubious swami (Richard Libertini). Terry, an apparently selfless, enlightened spirit, has graciously agreed to Edwina's offer so that her spirit may slip the confines of physical existence to merge as one with the cosmos. This way, Edwina gets a second chance at life with the resources (and the body) to enjoy it, while Terry has the opportunity to move nobly on to a higher state of being.

In their initial meeting, Roger and Edwina discover they're about as compatible as oil and water. Roger, cynic that he is, sees Edwina's reincarnational plan as a bunch of New Age crap and wants nothing to do with any of this lunacy. But that wish flies out the window—literally—when Roger ends up more involved in his client's plans than he ever dreamed. At the time of Edwina's death, the bowl the swami uses to hold her departed spirit during the transference goes on an unanticipated jaunt, and instead of her soul peacefully transitioning into Terry's body, it's inadvertently flung into Roger's—while he's still in it. Roger is now host to his own soul as well as that of a woman he already despises and grows to dislike more and more by the minute. He is left to cope with two consciousnesses vying for control of his body while they both try to figure out what to do next.

In a somewhat similar vein, "Switch" presents us with the life, death, and reincarnation of Steve Brooks (Perry King), a successful, middle-aged advertising executive who also happens to be a self-serving, self-absorbed male chauvinist pig. When he's murdered at the hands of three wronged ex-girlfriends (JoBeth Williams, Lysette Anthony, Victoria Mahoney), he dies and goes to purgatory, where he meets God, who appears as a shaft of white light and speaks to him with both male and female voices. God determines that Steve hasn't quite earned enough credits to get him straight into heaven, his main failing having been the way he treated women during his lifetime. So God decides to send Steve back to see if he can rectify this fault by finding one female who will like him, thereby earning him the credits he needs to enter paradise. With that, Steve is reincarnated.

Not long after the divine pronouncement is handed down, however, the Devil (Bruce Martyn Payne) makes an appearance in purgatory and claims that he has just as much right to Steve's soul as God does. God tells the Devil he's too late, that Steve has already been sent back and given his marching orders. The Devil presses his claim, however, forcing God into cutting a deal, one in which they agree to make Steve's reincarnational experience "interesting"—he must still find one female who likes him, but he must do so while in the body of a woman, and, in an instant, Steve is transformed into Amanda (Ellen Barkin).

Amanda is naturally quite disoriented at first, the initial discovery of her new gender coming as she's standing over a toilet preparing to urinate and is unable to locate the necessary means. Gradually, however, she overcomes her panic and starts about her new life. But while she may be Amanda on the outside, she's still Steve on the inside—and still charged with fulfilling the task set upon him/her by God. Maybe the best way for this one-time chauvinist to learn about what women are like and what they expect from the opposite sex is to experience life firsthand from the female perspective.

Viewing life from the other side of the fence is the obvious theme of both of these pictures, most notably from a gender standpoint.

Although each film takes a slightly different approach—"All of Me" with both a male and female consciousness in the same male body and "Switch" with a male consciousness in a female body—they both essentially show what it's like to experience life from the perspective of the opposite sex. While this fence-hopping notion is most plainly apparent where gender is concerned, it's reflected in other ways, too.

Learning how to see life from a contrasting viewpoint, even in a purely generic sense, is something that we could all benefit from, and the experiences of these characters provide templates for this fundamental (and eminently transferable) skill. This ability can be applied to a wide range of areas of our lives, too. In Roger's case, for example, through his joining with Edwina the aristocrat, he has an opportunity to see what it's like to be someone who calls shots rather than someone who's shot at. Similarly, he's exposed to the mindset of wealth and privilege, a far cry from his more familiar existence of kowtowing and scraping to get by. The lessons he carries from these experiences have the potential to transform his life in ways he never would have dreamed of had it not been for the newfound perspectives his unexpected fusion afforded him.

In both films, characters also get to experience both sides of the coin of life. By having gone through death, Edwina and Steve both have an opportunity to see life in a new way after having been to the other side, even if only briefly. What they do with it is obviously in their hands, but it seems plausible to assume that having both lived and died must have had some kind of impact on them as they get a second go-round back on Earth.

The principle of integration is examined in both movies, too. In "All of Me," Roger experiences the male and female aspects simultaneously, with each flipping back and forth in rapid succession before homogenizing into an uneasy coherence. In "Switch," the synthesis is much more gradual, soaking in over time as Steve learns what it's like to be a woman through his life as Amanda. In each case, the characters benefit from seeing how the two aspects ultimately can complement, and not necessarily be in conflict with, one another.

Both films make intriguing use of mirrors, a technique that simultaneously provides clever cinematic touches and poignantly illustrates a significant conscious creation concept. In "Switch," Amanda often stands before mirrors, looking at them through the eyes of Steve, to see himself as the woman he has now become, trying to take stock of the mind-boggling transformation he has undergone. And when Roger looks in the mirror in "All of Me," he sees Edwina reflected back to him, symbolically showing the merger that has taken place between their two consciousnesses, the integration of male and female energies in one body. The literal use of mirrors fittingly depicts the notion that our surroundings are metaphorical mirrors of our beliefs, creations that outwardly reflect what's going on inwardly in our consciousness, an imaginative cinematic double entendre to be sure.

Although the scenarios these characters manifest may be somewhat drastic, they were also ultimately necessary. Their old lives were no longer serving them as they should, so change was definitely overdue. Their methods could be seen as a bit extreme to reach this realization, but in the end it was for their own good to materialize such changes for themselves. I particularly like the fact that this idea is explored through comedy. Humor often requires going overboard to make its point, and these films certainly do that, if on no other basis than just their central plotlines. But, to add icing to the proverbial cake, the execution of these stories is so well done that the characters (and viewers) can't help but get the messages they're trying to impart.

"All of Me," in my opinion, is the stronger of the two films. The credit for that largely goes to Martin's stellar performance, without a doubt his best on-screen comedy work. The role of Roger Cobb provides him with the perfect vehicle to go over the top without making it look like he's doing so. Providing valuable support to Martin's portrayal are Tomlin's equally strong performance, Carl Reiner's judicious direction, and Phil Alden Robinson's tightly written script, which is based on the novel *Me Two* and is chock full of raucously big laughs from start to finish. Martin and Tomlin both deservedly earned lead performance Golden Globe nominations for their efforts.

The main strength of "Switch" is the showcase it provides for Barkin, who shines as a man learning what it's like to be a woman. However, even though the basic premise of the story is sound, the script meanders a bit at times, as if it's not entirely sure where it wants to go but knows what points it wants to cover before the film's end. The inclusion of the Devil, for instance, adds little and probably could have been left out entirely (Payne's fine but underused performance notwithstanding); Steve's task, including the gender switching angle, probably could have been given to him by God directly just as easily, without any loss in the story's humor value or overall viability. Still, the film is well worth seeing for its teachings about the benefits of changing our circumstances and for Barkin's acting, which won her a Golden Globe nomination.

Looking at life from the other side can provide valuable insights about our current routines that we might not see otherwise, as well as how we might wish to change them. As these films show, gaining such perspectives sometimes requires sweeping modifications in how we see things and act upon them. But, in the end, a fuller, more integrated whole can result, a true fusion of the best of both worlds.

# The Fog of Hindsight

### "Peggy Sue Got Married"
*Year of Release: 1986*
*Principal Cast: Kathleen Turner, Nicolas Cage, Barry Miller,*
*Catherine Hicks, Joan Allen, Kevin J. O'Connor, Jim Carrey,*
*Lisa Jane Persky, Wil Shriner, Helen Hunt, Barbara Harris,*
*Don Murray, Maureen O'Sullivan, Leon Ames, Sofia Coppola*
*Director: Francis Ford Coppola*
*Screenplay: Jerry Leichtling, Arlene Sarner*

In looking back on the past, most of us have probably said from time to time, "If I had to do it all over again, I'd do a lot of things differently." That's easily said when we examine a line of probability we've already gone down and can see everything that came with it. With this kind of hindsight, it's usually obvious to spot what changes we'd like to make. But what about the implications that go along with effecting such changes? Can we envision what all of them would have been? And, in light of that, can we realistically know what impact they might have had on how our lives turned out? Would it be wise to risk making changes capable of drastically altering who we've become, the selves with whom we've grown so familiar and comfortable? Suddenly, hindsight might not be as clear as we think it is. Those questions and more are among those put to the title character in Francis Ford Coppola's romantic fantasy, "Peggy Sue Got Married."

Peggy Sue Bodell (nee Kelcher) (Kathleen Turner) is about to attend the twenty-fifth reunion of the Buchanan High School Class of 1960. She's anxious, not only because of the anticipation of seeing all her old friends again but also because of those she hopes to avoid, most notably her husband Charlie (Nicolas Cage), her high school sweetheart from whom she recently separated after he had an affair. Her daughter Beth (Helen Hunt) accompanies her, encouraging Peggy to have a good time and even to get on with her life, despite recent upsets. However, once at the event, the emotion of it all becomes overwhelming, and Peggy collapses amidst the resounding cheers of the assembled crowd after she's named reunion queen.

What happens next surprises our protagonist—she inexplicably finds herself transported back in time to her senior year of high school. She's initially disoriented, unsure of where she is or how she got there. This is made all the more strange by the fact that Peggy retains full memory of her adult life. Once she's over the initial shock, however, she realizes she has a valuable opportunity to reexamine her past, to look at the choices she's made, and to decide what she would like to change. She focuses primarily on her relationship with Charlie, seeing her adolescent flame from the perspective of a middle-aged woman. And, for the sake of comparison, she decides to explore her unrequited attraction for one of her classmates, Michael Fitzsimmons, a mysterious aspiring writer with a Beat generation attitude (Kevin J. O'Connor). Peggy also takes a look at her relationships with family members, including her parents (Barbara Harris, Don Murray) and younger sister Nancy (Sofia Coppola), and battles wits with a conniving, gossipy rival, Delores (Lisa Jane Persky).

But as Peggy goes through this experience, she also carries the burden of knowledge of the future, which makes her a self-described walking anachronism. As she becomes more ensconced in this baffling temporal conundrum, she unwittingly starts to vacillate between who she is and who she was. In one moment she reacts to her situation with the wisdom of an adult, but in the next, she responds with the immaturity and naïveté of a teenager. And when it dawns on her that she could be stuck, trapped out of time, never getting back to the future life she remembers so well, her odyssey becomes frightening.

To resolve her dilemma, Peggy enlists the aid of several confidantes. She first turns to the brainy high school science nerd, Richard Norvik (Barry Miller), to see if he can help. She then seeks the sage advice of her grandparents (Maureen O'Sullivan, Leon Ames), who just might be able to help Peggy achieve her goal, even if in an unexpected way. She also routinely turns to her best friends, Carol (Catherine Hicks) and Maddy (Joan Allen), and their respective boyfriends, Walter (Jim Carrey) and Arthur (Wil Shriner), for their guidance and support, even though she tells them nothing of her situation; after all, they find some of her recent erratic behavior difficult enough to fathom as it is. But as helpful as everyone is, it remains unclear to Peggy if she'll ever get back what she's lost.

So, in the wake of our heroine's experience, is hindsight all it's cracked up to be? Is it really 20/20? Peggy might disagree with that characterization, despite her earlier belief to the contrary. Although there certainly is value to exploring our past to help illuminate how it got us to where we are and to show us who we've become, just how anxious would we be to tamper with that past if given the chance? If we were to change our past dramatically, would we even be able to recognize our new lives and the new selves we've become in the present? In Peggy's case, for example, what would become of the children she so adores if she hadn't married Charlie as she had? What kind of life would she have had if she had instead taken up with Michael? Would she have been content spending her life as the casual love interest of a moody, sometimes detached writer, despite the prospect's enigmatic allure?

At the same time, having an adult perspective on choices made during adolescence can prove quite valuable, especially if we've outgrown them. This is particularly true if the behavior associated with those choices continues in adulthood, mimicking the adolescent conduct that arose when those choices were first made. Such an awareness, however, may ultimately prove more important to us in terms of how we conduct ourselves going forward in life than anything it might have done to alter our actions in the past.

Still, there's some merit to at least considering retroactive change. In the case of this film, it sheds considerable light on the primary reason Peggy Sue and Charlie are contemplating divorce as adults. Because they married so young, they each missed out on a lot of what life has to offer. Even though this was their choice, it had to have been painful to endure, especially in the early years of their marriage, the free-wheeling 1960s with its sexual revolution and other liberating social changes. The constraints of traditional marriage no doubt kept them from experiencing many of the things that others of their generation so readily reveled in. And, sadly, they blamed one another for what they missed out on, not realizing that they each created those circumstances out of their own choices. While Peggy Sue remained faithful to her wedding vows, Charlie broke his, having a fling to satisfy his curiosity and fulfill desires that he apparently denied himself in his youth. In the aftermath of this, Peggy feels betrayed, not only by Charlie's indiscretion but also, seemingly, by her own lack of courage to seek for herself the same things her husband sought for himself. For her, that lamentation is arguably even more distressing than any cheating her spouse engaged in, a forlorn victim to thoughts of what might have been. But now she has the opportunity to find out if she really would do things differently. The question for her (and viewers), of course, is, "Will she?"

All of this illustrates how a keen sense of discernment comes in handy when evaluating our choices and desires for change (regardless of whether any temporal considerations are involved). There are more than enough situations in which making changes to ourselves or our probabilities is certainly in order. There are also plenty of times when it's not. The trick is to know when to do each. Running our beliefs past this filtering mechanism can help provide the answers we're looking for, and following up on those answers with actions should put us—or keep us—on whichever path is most appropriate, no matter when we started down it.

The choice of time as a variable in assessing the need for change is indeed an interesting selection. We probably do it more than we realize, even if our experiences don't feel quite as literal as those of Peggy Sue. But then perhaps it would be to our benefit to employ time as a variable in the envisioning process as she does. It would assuredly give us a vivid perspective on the choices we've made, allowing us to feel and experience them firsthand from a different viewpoint, enabling us to make appropriate assessments, pertinent choices, and necessary alterations. There are no guarantees that an experiment like this would make hindsight any clearer, but it has the potential of giving us valuable direction for how to proceed into the future.

"Peggy Sue Got Married" is a charming little film, full of wit, humor, and irony. It successfully avoids the trap of becoming schmaltzy or overly sentimental, largely because of its inherent strengths, as well as its anachronistic plotline. It's refreshing that a director like Coppola, known for powerful dramas such as "The Godfather" and "Apocalypse Now," can also adroitly handle a gentle romantic comedy. His efforts brought the film a Golden Globe nomination for best comedy picture.

Turner's lead performance steals the show here. Her ability to play a woman of two different generations effectively, without the aid of significant alterations in makeup or costuming, is quite a feat, often accomplished with no more than simple changes in facial expressions, work that earned her both Oscar and Golden Globe nods for lead actress. The supporting cast is top-notch, too, providing Turner with a menagerie of colorful cohorts to interact with in innumerable ways.

Technically, the picture is a fine period piece, capturing the look and feel of the early 1960s in superb detail. It particularly excels in the areas of costume design and cinematography, both of which earned the film Academy Award nominations. In all, the movie received three Oscar and two Golden Globe nods but took home no awards.

The one area that could use some work is the writing. The story is solid, and the screenplay generally is, too, but the dialogue suffers from periodic lapses in continuity and flow, usually in the ways that jokes or scene-ending exit lines are set up. These payoff lines are mostly fine themselves, but the routes the writers take to get to them are sometimes a little forced, even lame, which is unfortunate, since most of the script is otherwise quite good.

A little more polish in this area would have let the writing really shine, allowing it to live up to the captivating story it tells.

"Peggy Sue Got Married" provides us with an excellent opportunity to "browse through time," as Peggy's grandmother says. It allows us to examine who we are and how we got there and whether we wish to alter the route we took. In the end, however, it also forces us to ask ourselves if we have the conviction to change our destiny, knowing what we know now. It would appear to depend on how we each assess our own individual hindsight—and to determine just how clear or foggy it really is.

## Double Feature: Stepping into Life

### "Zelig"
*Year of Release: 1983*
*Principal Cast: Woody Allen, Mia Farrow, Ellen Garrison,*
*Patrick Horgan (narrator)*
*Director: Woody Allen*
*Screenplay: Woody Allen*

### "The Purple Rose of Cairo"
*Year of Release: 1985*
*Principal Cast: Mia Farrow, Jeff Daniels, Danny Aiello,*
*Edward Herrmann, John Wood, Deborah Rush, Van Johnson,*
*Zoe Caldwell, Karen Akers, Dianne Wiest, Michael Tucker,*
*Alexander Cohen, Irving Metzman*
*Director: Woody Allen*
*Screenplay: Woody Allen*

Seeking happiness and fulfillment in life requires engagement; it doesn't happen by osmosis. For conscious creators, this means getting involved in the manifestation of their desires, first on a belief level and then following up corporeally. Sitting on the sidelines, waiting for things to happen, with minimal participation in the required physical or metaphysical practices, just won't cut it. Those who are stuck need to take active steps to change their situations and become reconnected, a point made abundantly clear in two comedies from director Woody Allen, "Zelig" and "The Purple Rose of Cairo."

"Zelig" presents the cinematic biography of an unusually gifted little man, Leonard Zelig (Woody Allen), "the human chameleon." Shot in a style resembling a Ken Burns film, this picture recounts the life story of a once-celebrated American icon who quickly rose to fame and vanished almost as fast. Through a combination of early twentieth-century archival footage and contemporary interviews, supplemented with pithily eloquent narration by Patrick Horgan, Leonard's remarkable odyssey is examined in studious detail. There's just one catch—it's all made up, a total fiction, dished up in the form of a humorous faux documentary (or mockumentary) told with scathingly dry wit from end to end.

So how did this fabricated celebrity rise to such sensational status? Leonard possessed the remarkable ability to change his demeanor and physical appearance, seemingly at will, to match the looks and mannerisms of his peers. He could, for instance, take on the appearance of a bearded Scotsman in one moment and that of a smooth-faced Chinaman in the next. He was also capable of adjusting his size, growing obese when needed, and his skin color, becoming African American at the drop of a hat. And whenever he went through one of his transformations, he carried himself with an air that was thoroughly convincing to those around him. He could, in one instant, display the erudition necessary to hobnob with the likes of F. Scott Fitzgerald and, in the next, exhibit the earthy folksiness of the kitchen help. But because Leonard had a penchant for ingratiating himself in situations where his presence was unexpected or unwanted, this walking enigma was often seen as an unwelcome nuisance, even a potential menace.

After a series of such incidents, Leonard was eventually confined to a mental institution, coming under the care of a compassionate psychiatrist, Dr. Eudora Fletcher (Mia Farrow in archival shots, Ellen Garrison in contemporary interviews). She determined that his condition was not a mental illness but a natural ability that he developed in response to his upbringing. As the product of abusive and neglectful parents who gave him little love and nurturing, Leonard developed his special skill as a means to seek the attention and approval of others. He simply wanted to be liked, but he took his coping mechanism a little too far.

When Dr. Fletcher's professional peers realized there was nothing clinically wrong with Leonard, they released him from the hospital. His talent quickly earned him fame and recognition, rising to prominence in the fad-crazed jazz era of the 1920s. He was often seen in the presence of other celebrities of the time, including entertainers Josephine Baker, Fanny Brice, and Charlie Chaplin, Presidents Herbert Hoover and Calvin Coolidge, publisher William Randolph Hearst, and golfer Bobby Jones. He had quite a ride going for him.

But Dr. Fletcher remained concerned about his mental state. She believed that his continued changeability showed that he still hadn't licked the cause of what prompted his unusual talent to arise in the first place. With the provisional approval of her peers, she took Leonard into private intensive treatment to help him make adjustments in his self-image to address his unresolved acceptance issues. And with that, she set Leonard on the course of his biggest challenge of all—learning how to be himself without the spontaneous transformations. Dr. Fletcher believed this was essential to his well-being, but getting there wouldn't be easy. The process would take Leonard down some unexpected paths, frequently landing him in hot water and threatening to undo all the progress he'd made thus far. Finding happiness, it seems, is sometimes very hard work.

Seeking fulfillment by changing one's circumstances is a theme that also runs through "The Purple Rose of Cairo," a bittersweet comedy set in a small New Jersey town during the Great Depression. Cecilia (Mia Farrow) is a downtrodden waitress trapped in a bad marriage to Monk (Danny Aiello), an abusive, unemployed, philandering ne'er-do-well. Like many other Americans of that time, Cecilia seeks escape from her troubles by going to the movies, a simple, inexpensive pleasure to help her forget her worries for a few hours. She's particularly enamored with a picture titled *The Purple Rose of Cairo*, a romantic melodrama involving a cast of upper-crust Gothamites (Edward Herrmann, John Wood, Deborah Rush, Van Johnson, Zoe Caldwell, Karen Akers), and with one of its characters, explorer and adventurer Tom Baxter (Jeff Daniels).

When Cecilia's life falls apart, she seeks sanctuary in the theater, sitting in on showing after showing of the movie. But while she sits through her fifth viewing, something totally unexpected happens—Tom breaks character and starts speaking to her from the screen. He says he's noticed how many times she's watched the movie, conjecturing that "You must really love this picture." And at that, he steps out of the film and into physical reality to meet her.

Cecilia and Tom flee, taking refuge from the chaos that now envelops the theater. Tom's untimely departure leaves everyone thoroughly bewildered, including the audience members, the theater manager (Irving Metzman), and the film's characters, who are unsure how to continue the story with a character now missing. The cinematic fugitives, meanwhile, embark on an adventure through which Cecilia gets to experience a fairy tale romance and Tom has an opportunity to taste real life, sometimes in more ways than he bargained for.

When Raoul Hirsch (Alexander Cohen), the film's producer, gets wind of the incident, he fears the worst. He envisions one of his creations running around on the loose, creating havoc and spawning endless lawsuits that his studio would be liable for. Hirsch and his associates make a beeline for New Jersey to see what they can do to resolve the situation. His contingent includes Gil Shepherd (also played by Jeff Daniels), the actor who portrays Tom, whose chief task is to coax his doppelganger back into the picture. But before Gil has a chance to attempt this, he, too, has an encounter with Cecilia, taking a liking to her on par with that of his fictitious counterpart. Cecilia is smitten with Gil as well, especially since he, unlike Tom, is real. Their mutual attraction further complicates an already-complex situation as now Cecilia, Tom, and Gil all want to alter their realities (some in more profound ways than others). Given the circumstances, how can everyone's wishes possibly be accommodated?

In both of these films, it's interesting to see the lengths that the characters are willing to go to in changing their realities. Leonard certainly goes all out in his efforts to receive a little attention, while Tom, fictitious though he may be, is willing to chuck everything from the existence he knows just to meet the woman of his dreams. Some might see these actions as over-compensating or recklessly impulsive, but then how far would you go to fulfill a desire you really wanted to see materialized?

Indeed, desperate times call for desperate measures. Although there are risks of loss associated with such bold moves, there's also potentially much to be lost (that is, not realized) by staying put. In the end, in situations like this, we must all ask ourselves which course carries the greater cost (or, more accurately, pays the bigger dividend).

Resistance to change often stems from beliefs that we cling to relentlessly, and again both films illustrate this, albeit symbolically. During much of "Zelig," Leonard can't control his spontaneous transformations, because he has allowed the belief that such behavior is essential to being liked to become hard-wired into his consciousness. That's an intent that, ironically enough, he doesn't seem to be able to change.

Likewise, in "The Purple Rose of Cairo," once Tom is in the real world, he repeatedly and rigidly asserts that he must behave in the same ways he did in the reel world, because those qualities were written into his character (symbolic of the way we adopt beliefs for ourselves). His stance is not unlike the one we sometimes take when we allow stubbornly steadfast beliefs to dig in their heels and convince us that there are some situations we're simply unable to change, an outcome that often stems from persistently inflexible core beliefs. To their credit, Cecilia and Gil hold beliefs that leave them more amenable to change, but the question they must address is whether they have the courage to follow through on their convictions. Facing fears plays a major role in changing ourselves and our circumstances, and as difficult as this can be, it's often unavoidable if hoped-for changes are ever to appear in our lives (more on this in chapter 6).

In both of these films, cinematography plays a significant role in making these alternative probabilities believable. Effective visual imagery is essential for these stories to be convincing. But this is a principle that's applicable to more than just telling these stories for the screen. It's a concept that each of us must also employ when we engage in the envisioning process, an integral step in being able to implement contemplated changes in our realities. Cinematographer Gordon Willis does a superb job of selling viewers on the plausibility of these fantastic stories in both of these pictures, particularly in "Zelig," for which he earned an Oscar nomination. The insertion of the images of contemporary performers into the archival footage alone is quite an amazing sight.

"Zelig" is also noteworthy for its incredibly tongue-in-cheek script. It's hard to imagine how narrator Horgan was able to deliver the lines of his voice-overs without cracking up. The same can be said of the performers in the contemporary interviews, most of which employed actors but some of which were conducted with literary luminaries like Susan Sontag, Saul Bellow, and Irving Howe playing themselves, all with the intent of providing the film with a semblance of legitimate, yet nevertheless totally fake, credibility. (How they kept straight faces during filming truly escapes me.) These elements, when coupled with the ingenious cinematography, make the picture a stylistic knockout.

"The Purple Rose of Cairo" is also long on style, creating two very authentic-looking worlds—that of Depression era New Jersey (shot in color) and that of New York high society, as depicted in the film's fictional namesake (shot in black and white and including such cinematic details of the era as over-applied makeup). The performances of both the on- and offscreen characters are all terrific, especially when they interact with one another. But perhaps the movie's strongest attribute is its crisp writing, ever funny and nicely punctuated by period slang and razor-sharp zingers. The film won a Golden Globe award and earned an Oscar nomination for its original screenplay.

In all, "Zelig" earned two Oscar nominations and two Globe nominations, including nods for best comedy picture and for Allen as best comedy actor. "The Purple Rose of Cairo" received a single Oscar nod, but it captured one Golden Globe on four total nominations. In addition, "Purple Rose" won the FIPRESCI Prize from the International Federation of Film Critics at the Cannes Film Festival.

Stepping into life frequently involves taking well-calculated risks—sometimes big ones—to reach the contentment we seek. Little is accomplished by staying put and engaging in endless analyses of "what if?" This is just as true in changing our situations as it is in creating them anew. If fortune truly favors the bold, then those of us who have the courage to take chances like those of the characters in these films have the least to lose—and everything to gain.

# It All Began with a Prognosticating Rodent . . .

### "Groundhog Day"
*Year of Release: 1993*
*Principal Cast: Bill Murray, Andie MacDowell, Chris Elliott,*
*Stephen Tobolowsky, Brian Doyle-Murray, Marita Geraghty,*
*Angela Paton, Robin Duke*
*Director: Harold Ramis*
*Story: Danny Rubin*
*Screenplay: Danny Rubin, Harold Ramis*

Catalysts for change come in all forms. The inclusion, deletion, or alteration of even the slightest variable in one's reality can lead to life-changing events: A "chance" conversation leads to the love of one's life. A momentary delay in getting somewhere saves someone from a potentially fatal accident. A fortuitously timed email forward results in a contract to write a book about metaphysical cinema (one I can vouch for personally). At the time these seemingly random events occur, it's very possible we won't recognize their significance, for they may be just the first link in a long chain of events that leads to the eventual outcome. But when the payoff at last occurs, we often look back fondly, even laughingly, at the trivial sparks that started it all. And so it goes in the comedy that gets its start with the predictions of an unconventional weather forecaster, "Groundhog Day."

Phil Connors (Bill Murray) is full of himself. As a popular weatherman for a local television station in Pittsburgh, he's on track to advance his career to a possible network job (or at least that's what he'd like to think). But as talented as he is, Phil is also surly, sarcastic, and self-important, believing that the world revolves around him and that everyone he works with is present to serve his whims. Considering his attitude, his comeuppance is about due, and it takes place, fittingly enough, on that annual meteorological rite of passage, Groundhog Day.

Phil and his remote crew, producer Rita (Andie MacDowell) and cameraman Larry (Chris Elliott), are assigned to do a location report from the small western Pennsylvania town of Punxsutawney, the home of famed weather prognosticating groundhog, Punxsutawney Phil. The world-renowned rodent emerges from his winter hideaway every February 2 to check for his shadow to determine whether there will be six more weeks of life in the deep freeze. This forecast is the centerpiece event of an annual town festival, complete with parties, ice sculpting competitions, and an official proclamation of Phil's prediction made by event organizers. It's a fun time for the folks of this tiny hamlet, but for Mr. Connors, it's all a little too homespun for his tastes. He never hesitates to verbalize his contempt for this assignment and chomps at the bit to get it over with so he can return to his version of civilization.

With their work done, Phil and company begin their return trip to Pittsburgh. But no sooner do they start back than they're stopped by a blizzard, one that Phil, ironically enough, predicted would hit elsewhere, unexpectedly stranding the crew in Punxsutawney overnight. Little does Phil know, however, that his stay is about to be much longer than expected.

When Phil wakes up the following morning, it seems just like the day before. He initially chalks it up to coincidence or déjà vu, but he soon discovers that it really *is* the day before, all over again. Phil is spooked, but he tries to remain composed, a task quickly made difficult by the realization that he's somehow become stuck in a pattern that repeats itself incessantly. Every time he goes to sleep at night, he wakes up to yet another edition of Groundhog Day. What's more, he's the only one who's aware of what's happening; he retains the memories of each previous iteration, but for everyone else, the day starts over each time. He longs for February 3 to come, but it never does. Suddenly, six more weeks of winter seems palatable by comparison.

Phil is now faced with the dilemma of how to spend his time on a day that keeps recurring. Since there's no apparent way to break the cycle, he reconciles himself to his fate. Considering that he feels small-town life is insufferably limited, he believes his options are similarly restricted. But soon he realizes that he has an opportunity to try out things he's never done before. Since he knows that he'll wake up to the same day again tomorrow with no one aware of what he'd done previously, he has the freedom to live out life as he wants with no threat of consequences or repercussions. For conscious creators, it really is the ultimate experiment for probability exploration. But for Phil, it's the ultimate opportunity for probability exploitation.

At first, Phil engages in activities that are as totally self-serving as he is. But once he's done all of those, he eventually has to ask himself, "What next?" One can be a glutton, womanizer, or thief only so many times before it becomes boring. Phil knows he needs to fill his days somehow, but ideas elude him. Gradually, however, he starts using his days to take on a challenge even bigger than ending the cycle of recurrent Groundhog Days: figuring out who the real Phil Connors is. He's fortunate to have seemingly all the time in the world to try out the countless probabilities, but he's also taken on some of the hardest work he'll ever tackle, learning how to be his true self.

Conscious creators could learn much from Phil's experience, not only in terms of the need to find ourselves but also in terms of how to do so—by playing with beliefs and probabilities. His experimentation in these areas embodies sentiments eloquently expressed by Jane Roberts and Seth: "[B]eliefs obviously have another reality beside the one with which you are familiar. They attract and bring into being certain events instead of others. Therefore, they determine the <u>entry</u> of experienced events from an endless variety of probable ones. You seem to be at the center of your world, because for you your world begins with that point of intersection where soul and physical consciousness meet."[3] Phil may not consciously look upon his experience quite so philosophically, but the net result is the same.

Once he gets the hang of probability shifting, Phil comes to see that the only restrictions he faces are those he genuinely creates for himself. Still, with such an understanding, one might also wonder why he's created the basic limitation of having to experience the same day repeatedly, as if he were living the life of a temporal Sisyphus. My answer would be that he's created for himself the gift of time, the chance to test drive all his options to determine which one he wants before settling on it. It might appear like a restriction to have to live through the same day over and over again, yet it truly isn't; it's a prime learning opportunity through which Phil discovers that he has the power to choose his circumstances, make changes to them, and find those that are most suitable for him. (We should all be as proficient at this as he is!)

Phil's probability-shopping odyssey is poignantly symbolic in many ways, too, especially in matters related to his self-exploration. Consider, for example, how his adventure begins: He goes on assignment to cover Punxsutawney Phil—a fellow meteorologist (of sorts) who coincidently shares the same first name as his big-city counterpart. And since the groundhog is a creature that some would say is little more than an overgrown rat, a case could be made that Phil and his small-town cousin also share the same demeanor. The parallels in this are more than a little uncanny. In essence, Punxsutawney Phil is a fitting symbolic reflection of our protagonist, the image he projects to the world, and, ultimately, the beliefs he holds about himself (even if he's not aware of them or wouldn't readily acknowledge them). However, after having the opportunity to sample multiple alternative probabilities, Phil and his beliefs about himself begin to change, prompting a comparable shift in his counterpart's image. The once-vile creature is seen as more warm and cuddly, even lovable (and the groundhog seems cuter, too). As Phil evolves, so does his woodland cohort.

Phil's impressions of the town similarly reflect beliefs he holds about himself, and they evolve along with him. He initially sees Punxsutawney as limited, but then that's because Phil is also limited, despite the inflated and allegedly worldly opinion he holds of himself. However, after spending countless days exploring different aspects of the town, just as he spends countless days exploring different aspects of himself, he sees there's more to it than he originally surmised, just as there's more to himself than he previously thought there was. The town he once saw as a provincial outpost is now seen as a living, diverse community, just as the formerly one-dimensional egotist is now seen as a multifaceted individual whom people actually like. Now *that's* change.

Phil employs a healthy approach to the way he handles his conscious creation and self-exploration efforts, too. He does so with a strong sense of playfulness, which transforms the experience into something that's meant to be enjoyed and not just endured. Again, Jane Roberts and Seth speak to this issue on point: "All of this is done somewhat in the way that a child plays, through the formation of creative dream dramas in which the individual is free to play a million different roles and to examine the nature of probable events from the standpoint of 'a game.'"[4]

"Groundhog Day" abides by such playful thinking itself. It's a fun movie that imparts meaningful metaphysical messages in a deceptively light way. There's much more going on here than might be perceived on first glance, which in many ways makes it a genuine fable and a surprisingly articulate piece of filmmaking, simultaneously ridiculous and sublime.

Murray is perfect as Phil, playing the role with just the right amount of insincerity to be believable. His cynical demeanor commensurately contrasts with the folksy attitudes of the locals (Stephen Tobolowsky, Brian Doyle-Murray, Marita Geraghty, Angela Paton, Robin Duke), who revel in the charming simplicity of their lifestyles but without ever coming across as bumpkins. Their performances are greatly enhanced by Ramis' skillful directing and by the clever film editing of Pembroke J. Herring.

The next time something comes along in your life that seems only superficially significant, don't be so quick to dismiss it, for it may be just the catalyst you've been waiting for. Contained within it could be the seeds of change, the means to help foster a long-awaited bright and vibrant future. They might take some time to sprout, but the harvest will be well worth it.

## Bonus Features

"Frequency": Separated by thirty years' time, a New York City fireman and his adult son, a detective, work to change the tragic probabilities that have unfolded in their lives. However, unaware that changing one variable also changes others, they must resolve unanticipated issues across time with one another's help, employing the resources of a ham radio set, the high-energy impulses of the aurora borealis, and the baseball miracle of 1969's "Amazing Mets." (2000; Dennis Quaid, Jim Caviezel, Shawn Doyle, Elizabeth Mitchell, Andre Braugher, Noah Emmerich, Daniel Henson;

Gregory Hoblit, director; Toby Emmerich, screenplay; one Golden Globe nomination)

"Sliding Doors": Who would believe that something as simple as catching or missing the subway could have profound effects in changing the course of one's life? But that's the scenario that plays out in this romantic comedy-drama about a young career woman in London. Two versions of her life unfold on the screen, running parallel to one another, all based on whether she catches that fateful tube. (1998; Gwyneth Paltrow, John Hannah, John Lynch, Jeanne Tripplehorn, Zara Turner, Douglas McFerran, Paul Brightwell, Nina Young; Peter Howitt, director and screenplay)

"Malcolm X": This epic biopic explores the transformative life of Malcolm X (1925–1965), one of the nation's most influential African American civil rights and spiritual leaders. What begins as a life of crime and drug abuse changes dramatically when Malcolm learns the ways of Islam while in prison. He pursues a new course, one filled with tremendous accomplishments, terrible tragedies, and a global legacy that has lasted decades after his death. Denzel Washington's portrayal of this historic heroic figure is awesome. (1992; Denzel Washington, Angela Bassett, Albert Hall, Al Freeman Jr., Delroy Lindo, Spike Lee, Kate Vernon, Lonette McKee, Tommy Hollis, James McDaniel; Spike Lee, director; Alex Haley and Malcolm X, book; Arnold Perl and Spike Lee, screenplay; two Oscar nominations, one Golden Globe nomination)

"The Snake Pit": A young woman inexplicably finds herself in a mental institution under unbearable circumstances. Lost and confused, she struggles to find her way out, only to be met with perpetual obstacles and puzzles as she wends her way through the mazes of the mental health care profession and her own mind—that is, until she decides to take matters into her own hands and change her reality. A bit overdramatic by contemporary standards, but its look into a world seldom seen at the time it was made had to have been shocking. (1948; Olivia de Havilland, Mark Stevens, Leo Genn, Celeste Holm, Leif Erickson, Natalie Schafer, Damian O'Flynn, Betsy Blair; Anatole Litvak, director; Mary Jane Ward, book; Frank Portos and Millen Brand, screenplay; one Oscar win on six nominations)

"On Golden Pond": Changing how we look at others—and ourselves—changes the people they and we are. But it's an often difficult process to go through, as members of three generations find out during the annual ritual of summer vacation at the family's waterfront cottage on New England's Golden Pond. A tearful and moving drama featuring Henry Fonda's Oscar-winning final performance, playing opposite his daughter Jane and screen legend Katharine Hepburn, who earned her record fourth acting Oscar for her portrayal of a woman who provides the much-needed glue to keep the family together. (1981; Katharine Hepburn [Oscar winner], Henry Fonda [Oscar and Golden Globe winner], Jane Fonda, Dabney Coleman, Doug McKeon; Mark Rydell, director; Ernest Thompson, play and screenplay [Oscar and Golden Globe winner]; three Oscar wins on ten nominations; three Golden Globe wins, including best dramatic picture, on six nominations)

"What's Up, Doc?": A bookish, often befuddled Midwestern musicology professor henpecked by his overbearing fiancée drastically changes his life—and his fortunes—while on a trip to San Francisco to contend for a lucrative study grant, thanks to the influence of a spontaneous free spirit and the madcap mix-up of four identical travel bags. A screwball comedy that's the funniest G-rated movie I've ever seen. (1972; Barbra Streisand, Ryan O'Neal, Madeline Kahn, Kenneth Mars, Austin Pendleton, Michael Murphy, Phil Roth, Sorrell Booke, Stefan Gierasch, Mabel Albertson, Liam Dunn; Peter Bogdanovich, director and story; Buck Henry, David Newman, and Robert Benton, screenplay; one Golden Globe nomination)

"Working Girl": A Wall Street secretary seeking to advance her career is stymied at every turn, so she decides to take matters into her own hands to change her destiny, ruffling feathers and breaking rules all along the way. The plotline is a bit implausible but entertaining nevertheless. (1988; Melanie Griffith [Golden Globe winner], Sigourney Weaver [Golden Globe winner], Harrison Ford, Alec Baldwin, Joan Cusack, Philip Bosco, Nora Dunn; Mike Nichols, director; Kevin Wade, screenplay; one Oscar win on six nominations; four Golden Globe wins, including best comedy picture, on six nominations)

# 6

## Storming the Castle

### *Enhanced Outcomes Through Facing Fears and Living Heroically*

Only when we are no longer afraid do we begin to live.
*Dorothy Thompson*

Life sometimes takes an abrupt, unexpected left turn. For me, that happened one balmy August night in 2002. I had the pleasure of attending a social gathering put on by one of Chicago's gay community organizations at a popular night spot. It was a gorgeous night, a slight breeze wafting through the patio where the partygoers were assembled, their upbeat energy nicely filling the air. The libations flowed freely, and various forms of entertainment were on hand, making for a very festive occasion.

One of the evening's more popular attractions was a psychic, who was performing life readings and palmistry. As one who often reads for others (using tarot cards), I decided to turn the tables for once, treating myself to a session to get a fresh perspective. I took my seat at his table, opting for a life reading.

Much of what the psychic told me was spot-on, providing valuable confirmation of what I had been thinking at the time, a true mirror of my prevailing beliefs. But then he told me something that came as a complete surprise: "You know," he said, "you've lived a heroic life, and yet you don't give yourself credit for it."

Me? Heroic? He had to have been joking.

But then the more I thought about what he said, the more it began to make sense. He was on target, even if I hadn't realized it at first, for if heroism involves approaching different aspects of life without fear, then I had already lived up to the term's meaning on many prior occasions. As I pored over memories of my life, many examples came to mind, but a few particularly significant ones stood out—moving to a big city by myself, where I knew virtually no one, to start my working life; successfully launching the editorial side of a new magazine in the face of what some saw with quiet skepticism as insufficient experience; coming out about my sexuality after many long years of agonizing (albeit self-imposed) repression; and openly embracing (and adhering to) conscious creation as a life practice at a time when such "outlandish" ideas were (and to an extent still are) fair game for ridicule. All of these acts, I realized, were intrinsically heroic, for even if they didn't resemble the behavior one typically associates with a swashbuckler, they all nevertheless entailed challenges that I approached willingly, without fear.

Thanks to that session with the psychic, I became aware that I had unconsciously adopted the sage advice of the courageous journalist Dorothy Thompson, the inspiration for Katharine Hepburn's character Tess Harding in the movie "Woman of the Year," who noted that, when we have the bravery to face what intimidates us, we then truly have the means to begin living. And with that, I made that fateful left turn, consciously choosing to set fear aside and live my life as heroically as possible from that point forward.

Now there's a Saturday night I won't soon forget.

★    ★    ★

The concepts of facing fear and living heroically are extremely important in conscious creation, even if they don't always receive the level of attention that they probably deserve. In my opinion, these issues are so integral that practitioners of this technique must often address them simply to be able to create what they've envisioned for themselves. In fact, by not doing so, the beliefs they try to forge into manifestation will likely become stymied, and materialization won't occur. As Jane Roberts and Seth put it, "The processes initiated [in conscious creation] are beyond your normal awareness. They occur automatically with your intent if you do not block them through *fear*, doubt or opposing beliefs."[1]

In my view, the prospect of such unfulfilled desires should be incentive enough to take up the lance and storm the castle of our fears. But just in case you need some added inspiration, here are a few more thoughts to consider.

In previous chapters, I discussed the significance of choice (chapter 4) and change (chapter 5) as important elements in shaping the beliefs we employ to create realities that fulfill our desires. But picture what might happen if fear were figured into the equation, too. A fear of change, or, even more basically, a fear of choice, would almost assuredly undercut any manifestations we seek to materialize; they just wouldn't happen. And, when we consider how inherent choice and change are to our conscious creation efforts, many of our materialization aspirations would atrophy if we were to allow fear to hold sway in the process. In the extreme, we could even run the risk of becoming metaphysically paralyzed, unable to move forward with virtually anything we'd hope to create.

Such debilitating stagnation is almost impossible to fathom (and quite scary in itself). But by surrendering to our apprehensions, we become prisoners of ourselves, subservient subjects of fear-mongering masters of our own creation. The feelings this engenders echo sentiments expressed by the sentient renegade android Roy Batty (Rutger Hauer) in the science fiction classic "Blade Runner," who says, as he's pinned down and is threatening to do in his would-be executioner (Harrison Ford), "Quite an experience to live in fear, isn't it? That's what it is to be a slave."[2]

Of course, fear, like anything else we create, stems from—you guessed it—our beliefs. So sometimes half the battle in making choices and changes in our realities begins with making choices and changes in the beliefs we hold about fear and how we apply them in shaping our existence. The failure to do so, as Jane Roberts and Seth noted, is the aforementioned lack of fulfillment, so it truly behooves us to make the necessary adjustments. For some, fear may only pertain to certain situations, such as those related to specific phobias, so the required alterations in those cases are comparatively minor.

For others, fear may be a core belief that pervades a whole range of areas, necessitating major changes in one's overall outlook. But no matter what level of adjustment is called for, I believe the most sound advice we can follow in this regard comes from that famous quote of President Franklin D. Roosevelt, who boldly asserted to a country in the throes of the Great Depression at his initial inauguration, "The only thing we have to fear is fear itself."[3]

★ ★ ★

Another motivation for facing our fears is the promise of the rewards we stand to reap from doing so. This is a potent incentive, regardless of whether tangible or intangible items of value are involved. Frequently, they're not freely offered up to just anyone who wants them; they must be sought out by purposely eliminating the fear blocking their access. This notion essentially provides the basis of the oft-used expression, "nothing ventured, nothing gained," for it is usually some kind of fear that prevents seekers from venturing forth in the first place.

If that seems a bit abstract, then think of it this way, again using the castle metaphor: Where does the kingdom keep the royal treasure? It's seldom on display out in the open; it's generally protected behind the walls of security. An adventurous seeker of said riches, then, is going to have to overcome the challenges posed by such fortifications to reach the coveted prize inside. But the effort is well worth it, for the rewards available to those who successfully surmount the walls of fear frequently far exceed expectations, providing a king's ransom of satisfaction and fulfillment.

Some may look upon all this chest-thumping bravado as totally unnecessary. "Why should we have to storm the castle to reach the rewards in the first place?" they might rightfully ask. Well, it's chiefly because, metaphorically speaking, we built it that way to start with, again a product of our beliefs. (Indeed, as the comic strip character Pogo so aptly noted, "We have met the enemy and he is us."[4]) If we wanted to construct a different, more easily accessible castle—or even plan a totally different means for reaching the treasure in question—we should have employed different beliefs at the outset. But, the situation being what it is, until we learn to create without fear as part of the mix, we must use measures appropriate for tackling the prevailing conditions and challenges.

Nevertheless, facing fears in this way offers two distinct benefits. First, it often requires us to get more creative in our approaches to solving problems, pushing us to stretch our capabilities for coming up with new ways of tackling the issues at hand (more on stretching our capabilities in chapter 9). Second, as suggested earlier (and as noted on many other prior occasions), it encourages us to become better conscious creators by looking for ways to avoid these pitfalls altogether, searching out alternative probabilities that exclude such unnecessary qualities from the outset. Of course, sometimes we're unable to appreciate the easier route until we've traveled the more difficult path first, unfortunate though that is. (The nagging persistence of creation by default can be quite palpable at times.)

A common (though often unconscious) fear many of us must contend with in connection with all of the foregoing has to do with managing our conscious creation power. As author Marianne Williamson wrote, "Our deepest fear is not that we are inadequate. Our deepest fear is that we are powerful beyond measure."[5] The films in this book have repeatedly demonstrated the power present in the manifestation process, including the potential for misapplication, even abuse, and that might seriously scare some of us. But although I would agree that a healthy respect for the power of conscious creation is certainly prudent, I'd also never suggest cowering at the prospect of using what I see as one of our essential birthrights. Learning how to temper our desires and capabilities with wisdom is key to employing the process judiciously, to be able to seek fulfillment without fear.

As an aside, I'd also like to make a subtle but significant distinction between the concepts of facing fear and living heroically, because they could be interpreted as identical. In my view, the difference has to do with intent. When we face fears, we often feel like we're forced into doing so, reluctantly, even involuntarily, compelled seemingly against our will into addressing what scares us. By contrast, in living heroically, we feel like we're facing the fear of our own volition, taking it on without hesitation, sometimes even when hopeless causes are at stake. As conscious creators, however, we need to remember that we actually manifest both types of scenarios for ourselves, with intent serving as the determining factor for which approach we eventually employ. The level of urgency involved with the issue at hand may have some bearing on which tactic emerges, with a greater sense of desperation perhaps more likely to favor the former approach over the latter. In either case, they still both spring forth from our consciousness, and we are ultimately the ones who choose which one we materialize, even if we're not always fully aware of it.

In my view, living heroically is the more empowering of the two tactics, but it also requires a greater sense of willingness, confidence, self-reliance, and resourcefulness—commodities that could be in short supply unless one is already practiced at facing fears. Therefore, in consciously taking on these kinds of challenges, we should probably start small, gaining experience in facing simple fears first so that we can grow comfortable with the concept, making it possible over time to boost our confidence and tackle fears head on—even when stakes of greater magnitude are involved—in true heroic fashion.

The films in this chapter look at both facing fears and living heroically in a variety of contexts, including in ways that spill off the screen and into real life. Four of the movies address the issue of facing fears, whereas three others—grouped into this book's only triple feature entry—examine living heroically. And because these themes are so prevalent in storytelling lore in general and the cinematic world in particular, this chapter concludes with an expanded Bonus Features section, the largest in the book, with listings that address both topics.

The desire to push our personal limits is, for many of us, a big part of the challenge of being human, of living life in physical reality, and of becoming active practitioners of conscious creation. But to push those limits, we must often break through the barriers that block the way, those self-generated obstacles we call fears. By overcoming them, however, we also realize for ourselves lives worth living well beyond our wildest dreams. Approaching life with that outlook in mind is a truly heroic act, one that holds the promise of bestowing rewards upon us we never thought possible. And from where I stand, that's one journey I'm willing to take, no matter how many left turns are involved.

# How To Survive the Dark Night of the Soul

**"Signs"**

*Year of Release: 2002*
*Principal Cast: Mel Gibson, Joaquin Phoenix, Rory Culkin,*
*Abigail Breslin, Cherry Jones, Patricia Kalember, M. Night Shyamalan*
*Director: M. Night Shyamalan*
*Screenplay: M. Night Shyamalan*

From time to time, we all face ordeals in our lives that appear unbearable. The challenges they pose are daunting, their circumstances, at least superficially, seeming as though they've been unfairly thrust upon us. As these scenarios unfold, they almost invariably go from bad to worse, too, making it look to us as though we're sinking further and further into an abyss from which there's no escape. However, the one element that these situations nearly always have in common is that they involve facing some kind of fear, testing us to see if we have the fortitude to overcome it and the wisdom to spot the clues for finding our way out. Seeing the way clear to address such challenges is the fate that befalls the protagonist of the sci-fi thriller, "Signs."

Graham Hess (Mel Gibson) is going through a tough time in his life. As a single father raising two children, Morgan (Rory Culkin) and Bo (Abigail Breslin), he struggles to balance his responsibilities as a parent and his workload as a farmer in rural Bucks County, Pennsylvania. He also wrestles with the fallout of a tragedy so heartbreaking that it prompted him to question—and ultimately to turn his back on—the faith that provided the foundation of his life and his one-time vocation as a minister. His younger brother Merrill (Joaquin Phoenix), a former minor league baseball player, has moved into an adjacent guest house to help out in whatever way he can, but even his well-intentioned assistance can't aid Graham in making sense of his personal travails. And, as if all that weren't enough, an enormous crop circle has now mysteriously appeared in one of Graham's fields. It's a lot to handle, but little does our hero know that this is just the beginning.

Before long, crop circles start appearing all over the world, followed shortly thereafter by lights in the sky over major cities.

What began as a mildly curious diversion from the daily routine quickly turns ominous as other strange events ensue across the globe, including in Graham's own backyard. As much as he tries to dismiss these happenings as harmless explicable phenomena, he soon discovers that these characterizations are wholly inadequate. He finds himself caught up in a situation that upends his worldview. It shakes him to the core and sends him desperately in search of meaning and guidance, a quest that forces him to face the lost faith that had once been his rock, a prospect perhaps even scarier than anything else going on around him. He thus embarks on a personal journey into the dark night of the soul, one that will inevitably rattle him to his very foundation—and change him forever.

In all fairness, I must preface my comments about this film by confessing that I have a soft spot for it. I have been a strong advocate of it ever since its release, frequently coming to its defense in the wake of what I have seen as some rather unfounded and unfair criticism. Although a number of critics and viewers thoroughly enjoyed it as much as I did, many others were less than enthusiastic, if not downright hostile, toward it. In large part, I believe most of these misdirected comments stem from a fundamental misinterpretation of the picture. Detractors could often be heard saying and writing things like "it wasn't a very good alien picture." But therein lies the problem—it's not a film about aliens per se. The extraterrestrial narrative is a mere pretext for something deeper—a story about facing fears. On that point, the film scores big. Those who appreciated that about this picture got what it was driving at; they could see its true intent. So it's with that perspective in mind that I offer my thoughts about this movie.

The superficial fear to be faced in this story, obviously, is how to survive the calamity of an alien attack. But, more significantly (and perhaps even more terrifyingly so), the greater fear to be addressed is how an allegedly just and loving God could allow something terrible like this to happen. For those who are devoutly pious in a traditional religious sense, a betrayal like this would seem like more than enough justification to turn away from the faith that supposedly serves them. For Graham in particular, this is something he has already experienced once in a highly personal way, and now he's being tested on it again, both in a very big sense and in many other smaller ways, as this ordeal plays out. His anxiety over this is so strong that one can practically hear his soul crying out, "Enough already!"

To put this idea into terms conscious creators can relate to, the challenge Graham faces is comparable to one we would have to address if we were to discover we'd lost our partnership with All That Is as a collaborator in the manifestation process. Think of the tremendous sense of abandonment we'd likely feel. If we can appreciate that, then we can appreciate Graham's experience as well.

Of course, as conscious creators, we can only hope that, if such a probability arose, we would have the sense to realize we drew it to ourselves through our beliefs. That naturally begs the question of why we would do so, but wouldn't it likely be as a test of our faith in our convictions? Again, in this light, it becomes much easier to appreciate what Graham is going through: If he has put his faith—his beliefs—into the worship of a God whom he believes will ultimately take care of His flock, then is he not testing his own resolve in the viability of that concept through the experiences he undergoes? The distinction between his odyssey and that of a conscious creator conducting a comparable metaphysical self-analysis suddenly doesn't seem so great.

This point is important for conscious creators to bear in mind, for whenever we face situations that have fear associated with them—no matter what the size or scope of the fear involved—we must realize that we have brought them to us in the first place. In all likelihood, we have summoned such circumstances to teach us how to overcome the fear at issue, to learn how to get past it and see what unexplored territory lies beyond its ramparts. That's generally a daunting prospect, for the façade of the fear is no doubt rather imposing (at least superficially), but if we never attempt to scale its heights, we'll also never see what's on the other side of it, either. And that is generally well worth the effort, for great rewards await us, even if we can't see them when we make our initial frontal assault on the fear at hand.

That is the challenge Graham faces with regard to his fears, too. Interestingly, one of the most significant fears he must address is related to the question of forgiveness (arguably a real toughie for many of us). He faces it on two fronts as well, both as one who seeks it and as one who grants it. In the first instance, he must seek the forgiveness of a God whom he feels he's insulted and betrayed through the abandonment of his faith. And in the second, he must learn how to be able to bestow it graciously, in this case to the individual who was the source of his personal sorrow, a gesture that sees its realization played out in a gut-wrenchingly emotional scene.

In seeking the forgiveness of his God, Graham must also face another, and perhaps even more profound, fear—that the image of God he clings to doesn't match the divine reality actually present in his life. To discover that one's God is not what one expects is disillusioning and scary, but it is a challenge our hero must deal with. As Graham sorts things out along these lines, he finds himself having to come to terms with the essence of that old adage, "Everything happens for a reason." This is not easy for him, for accepting the idea that pain and sacrifice are sometimes necessary in the resolution of certain scenarios (at least as how they've been created) is extremely distressing. Although there may well be a very good reason for such suffering, that doesn't make it any easier for him to endure, nor does it jibe with the all-loving, ever-benevolent image of God that he has come to believe in.

As Graham works through his pain and sees how the events of his life truly do occur for a reason, he's impelled to change the image of God that he holds; circumstances push him to adopt an impression of the divine that is more congruent with the conditions of the reality he manifests for himself, one that is more practical and realistic, less naïve and storybook. As compromising as that might sound, however, it ultimately leads him to a deeper awareness of his God, one that is far richer and more meaningful than he ever could have envisioned otherwise, particularly if he had never made the effort to address the fears that kept him from being able to perceive God in that way in the first place.

Again, conscious creators often experience something similar when they examine their realities with a comparably critical eye. Seeming incongruities in the world before our eyes that don't align with the beliefs we think we hold about it serve to reveal the nature of the beliefs that we actually do hold about it. With such clarified awareness, our beliefs and realities harmonize more effectively, bringing about deeper understandings of ourselves and possibly prompting us to make changes that result in greater personal satisfaction. Coming to such understandings and making such changes is sometimes intimidating, but the payoffs are usually so great that failing to pursue them would be itself tragic. Graham comes to see that, and we'd all be wise to follow his example.

Of course, facing fears doesn't necessarily require major drama to overcome them. At its heart , fear is usually based on a lack of familiarity or understanding. If such deficiencies can be replaced by knowledge and awareness, then the apprehensions such shortfalls fuel needn't be manhandled to conquer them; they can be finessed instead. This is the "work smarter, not harder" principle applied to tackling the challenges posed by our fears. Invariably there are clues—"signs"—along the way that help guide us in such pursuits, leading us to the once-absent familiarity and understanding. Becoming practiced at reading the symbols is an invaluable skill, and it's one way in which making full use of all of the elements of the magical approach is worth its salt.

This film's characters (and its viewers) get quite an education in reading signs, their images serving as meaningful physical guideposts pointing to solutions that can be drawn upon for resolving their dilemmas. The more apparent the signs are, the better the characters become at being able to identify them and any subsequent markers, thereby boosting their sense of personal empowerment and increasing their aptitude for this practice.

Such symbolic, meaningfully coincidental images and associations are sometimes referred to as "synchronicities" and are explored in depth in the book *What a Coincidence!* by Susan M. Watkins. "Once you start paying attention to this sort of thing, it quickly becomes apparent that coincidence is never ambiguous," Watkins writes. "Unfailingly, it gives you the sensation of waking up from an important-feeling dream. You're supposed to take note here; something has just *happened*. Risen up, as it were, from *somewhere*. But from where? And why?"[6] That's the puzzle posed to Graham—will he make use of the signs presented to him, not only to figure his way out of the dilemmas he finds himself in, but also to determine where they came from and why?

Will he see them as "messages from the deity [that give] us an elbow in the ribs when we need it most"?[7] For his sake, we can only hope so.

The signs themselves are quite diverse. Some, like the crop circles, are rather obvious, but others are much more subtle: A passing comment that at first seems inconsequential takes on greater meaning at an opportune moment; a chronic health condition proves to be a life-saving blessing in disguise; a nonsensical statement provides salvation in a time of peril. And so it goes in situation after situation and time after time.

A number of the signs, interestingly enough, are delivered by children. Graham's daughter Bo, for instance, an Indigo child of sorts (see chapter 3), is a wealth of wisdom. Her habits and comments are quite telling, even if their meaning isn't obvious. (Who says kids are to be seen and not heard?)

Other signs, ironically enough, come from characters who had once been members of Graham's congregation. When they seek solace from him in their times of need, however, he grows noticeably uncomfortable at their requests, because they remind him of the faith he's abandoned and the spiritual issues he's left unresolved. Since the former parishioners continue to come to him for comfort, they obviously don't feel he has turned his back on them, that he still is—and always has been—with them. This idea makes him squirm because, if they can continue to have faith in him in light of the betrayal he believes he's perpetrated against them, then why can't he continue to have comparable faith in the God whom he once trusted implicitly and knows hasn't gone away? Graham's former parishioners thus point him in the direction in which he must go: back to his faith. Their persistent presence reflects the quandary that he must address—the need to recognize that he might have erred in hastily and unfairly judging his God and that the divine love that he thought vanished indeed is (and always was) unconditionally available to him, even in spite of what he feels he may have done. To be the recipient of love and forgiveness from one whom we believe we have wronged is a scary prospect, an assault on our foolish, arrogant human pride. And now Graham is on the verge of discovering just how terrifying—and transcendent—that can be.

Director M. Night Shyamalan has created a remarkable picture here. In addition to its many sublime metaphysical qualities, it's also a chilling thriller, more effective at genuinely scaring the crap out of viewers than most conventional horror flicks. This is largely accomplished through a technique popularized by director Alfred Hitchcock—that of cinematically hinting at, but never completely showing, the source of the fright. The rationale for this approach is that the viewer's mind is capable of conjuring up images eminently more terrifying than anything the director could possibly put on film, so the filmmaker lets the viewer do the work of creating his or her own personal horror in his or her own head. (Who says beliefs aren't powerful things?) Shyamalan employs the practice masterfully, enhancing it with exceptionally effective use of lighting, editing, and sound.

None of this would matter, however, if it weren't for the strong story making it all possible. The plot is well crafted from beginning to end, weaving in multiple elements skillfully. The screenplay is mostly solid, though some of the dialogue early on is a tad choppy and awkward, with some unfortunately ill-conceived lines that misrepresent these characters as ignorant rural rubes (which they're clearly not). Tidying up the script in the first half hour would have made the narrative shine that much more.

The story is also successfully brought to life by the well-rounded cast. Gibson is surprisingly effective as Graham, showing a range not usually apparent in many of his performances. Phoenix as the protagonist's brother essentially plays a capable sidekick, likable and dependable. But some of the movie's best work is turned in by Breslin and Culkin, proving, as in some of Shyamalan's other pictures, that he's a highly effective director when it comes to working with child actors.

The art direction and set decoration are other major assets, symbolically portraying some of the philosophical ideas explored in the film in intriguingly fitting ways. A window whose flawed glass initially distorts the view of the outside world, for instance, is later replaced by one whose glass provides sparkling clarity. Similarly, the opportunely timed use of light and shadows subtly emphasizes the awareness and unknowing, respectively, that the characters experience as they work through their individual challenges. Even minor elements symbolically carry through on images and ideas present elsewhere in the film, such as curtains with tiny embroidered circles that mimic the patterns present in Graham's field. All these elements aptly illustrate how physical reality really is a reflection of our consciousness, mirroring beliefs back to us metaphorically in corporeal form.

Perhaps the only major disappointment with the film is its special effects. As noted earlier, even though I see the alien story line as a mere pretext for the main plot, the ETs are still integral to the picture, and the visuals used to bring them and their spacecraft to the screen could have been better. Fortunately, the picture's other strengths more than compensate for this shortcoming.

The dark night of the soul is a potentially maddening, chilling time for anyone who takes up the challenge it poses. Its seemingly disillusioning, disorienting, and menacing elements are enough to intimidate even the strongest among us. But there is always a way out, an illuminated path of enlightenment to lead us clear, as long as we know how to look for it and trust in the promise it holds (especially since it's of our own creation). Seeing the signs and interpreting them for what they are provide the keys for surviving such a test of our soul so that we can move forward stalwartly into the dawn of a brand new day.

## Going It Alone

### "An Unmarried Woman"
*Year of Release: 1978*
*Principal Cast: Jill Clayburgh, Alan Bates, Michael Murphy,*
*Cliff Gorman, Pat Quinn, Kelly Bishop, Lisa Lucas,*
*Linda Miller, Penelope Russianoff*
*Director: Paul Mazursky*
*Screenplay: Paul Mazursky*

Stepping out on one's own—especially when venturing onto unfamiliar turf—is an intimidating prospect. Leaving behind the safety and security of the known and the comfortable for the unknown and the uncomfortable is daunting, to say the least. Sometimes, however, we must face the fear of such probabilities, especially if the alternative means staying stuck and stagnating in circumstances that in the long run will only serve to undermine us. Choosing an appropriate way out of just such a dilemma is the task put to the heroine of the heartrending drama, "An Unmarried Woman."

Erica (Jill Clayburgh) has led a fairly pampered life. True, she does hold a part-time job at an art gallery, but, for the most part, she has had a rather cushy existence in her marriage to Martin (Michael Murphy), a successful Manhattan stockbroker. She spends a good deal of her time socializing with friends (Pat Quinn, Kelly Bishop, Linda Miller) and her teenage daughter Patti (Lisa Lucas), enjoying the spoils of a comfy upper-middle-class life. However, it all comes crashing down one day when Martin reveals he's been having an affair and is in love with another woman. Suddenly, Erica sees the world she's known for almost two decades shattering before her very eyes.

Faced with being a middle-aged single mother with limited means of support, Erica quickly realizes she has two choices—fall to pieces or stare down her fears and make a new start. Drawing upon reserves of inner strength that she had been quietly and unconsciously amassing for years, Erica picks herself up and systematically begins creating her new reality as an unmarried woman. Her defiant determination surfaces, revealing the depth of her personal power. This becomes most apparent in one sequence in which she methodically and resolutely goes through her apartment to dispose of all the remaining vestiges of her soon-to-be ex-husband, her last act being the unemotional removal of her wedding ring, which she calmly takes off and tosses across a tabletop while her daughter looks on, a gesture designed to show definitively there's no going back. At this point, Erica is clearly a woman not to be messed with.

Yet, as empowering as all these actions make her feel, Erica is nevertheless plumbing uncharted territory, and her exploration periodically causes its share of panic. Fortunately, she has the good sense to build a support network that includes her friends and daughter, as well as a new therapist, Tanya (Penelope Russianoff). In those moments of doubt, she draws upon the wisdom and guidance of her kindred spirits to help her deal with such issues as loneliness, anger, self-esteem, parenting, and dating. Slowly but surely she gets back on her feet, building a new life for herself.

Now, some may look upon Erica's experience and say, "So what's the big deal? Women go through that all the time." However, considering when this film was made, responses like hers were far less common then than they are today. Although the feminist movement had been in full swing for some time and women were increasingly feeling their sense of autonomy and empowerment, it was nevertheless relatively new ground for many of them, even in the late '70s. Inspiring though Erica's response was, it was still more the exception than the rule at that time to see women courageously striking out on their own as she does in this picture. Despite unspoken desires to the contrary, many women reluctantly opted to stay in bad marriages rather than chance going off on their own and creating new lives for themselves, partly for economic reasons, partly out of the fear of being alone, and partly because of the stigma associated with divorce (which, sadly, lingered even then). And then there was also the matter of how such an "unconventional" lifestyle would be perceived, the "what would people think?" factor. Even the film's title implies that the concept of an "unmarried" woman was somehow anomalous, that Erica's status was something of an aberration by virtue of the fact she had chosen to lead her life without a husband. (It's comforting to see how much things have progressed since that time.)

Yet, in spite of the outward self-assuredness that she projects, Erica also occasionally admits reservations about going it alone, particularly during her therapy sessions and in conversations with her friends. Such hesitancy might seem somewhat out of character for her, but it's present nevertheless, a condition more than likely due to beliefs she embraced while growing up. Although the question of Erica's upbringing is not explored in any great detail in the film, it's probably safe to say that, if her character was at all typical of her generation, she was raised at a time when women were taught to believe that they must fulfill much more traditional roles than they do today. They generally weren't schooled in the ways of independence, despite the rise of feminism that occurred as they entered young adulthood. Even Erica, despite her aura of great personal strength and keen sense of self (apparent even before Martin drops his bombshell), seems to have invested heavily in the beliefs behind these conventional expectations, as evidenced by the life she led before her husband's revelation. So her decision to go it alone, despite the beliefs she was apparently brought up with, represents a brave, marked departure, tenuous though some of her steps may have been.

By the same token, Erica's willingness to admit that she has such reservations indicates a fear overcome. Many often see such admissions as a sign of weakness, that owning up to them would be perceived as cowardly, but, in my view, nothing could be further from the truth. It takes courage to acknowledge one's weaknesses and limitations, and Erica does so freely when up against them. What's more, she acts upon these realizations, too, seeking assistance to help her overcome them once recognized, preventing stubborn pride from interfering with her efforts to get the help she needs, an integral step in identifying and rewriting beliefs in need of change. This is most apparent by her decision to go into counseling, another act that could be considered courageous for the time this film was made, since therapy was still often looked upon then in an unfavorable light, a sure sign that someone was crazy or unstable. Again, how far we've come in thirty years!

But perhaps the biggest fear Erica faces is the challenge of dating new men. This is an area in which she is seriously out of practice, having barely even looked at other guys since marrying Martin. Then there's the question of her anger management: Erica is so resentful toward Martin initially that she projects her fury onto men in general, an understandable reaction, though not exactly a healthy or appropriate one for someone looking to get back into the courting game. But when loneliness and the absence of sex start to get the better of her, Erica breaks down. In response, Tanya suggests that Erica take a chance on men again, despite the risks, for not doing so will only keep her locked in fear, cutting off all hope of ever finding someone whose company she enjoys. Erica takes the advice to heart, and, before long, she begins to enjoy the male of the species once again. Another fear conquered.

In seeking out new men, Erica tries out a probability she's never explored before—she experiments sexually. She consciously and unabashedly chooses to comparison-shop men to see whose companionship she enjoys most, and she successfully draws accommodating partners to her to share the experience. Her first encounter is with an oversexed chauvinist named Charlie (Cliff Gorman), who primarily loosens up Erica for further exploits. Realizing that Charlie is not whom she's looking for, she then turns to a passionate and sensitive artist named Saul (Alan Bates), with whom she has a steamy affair.

Erica's actions not only represent a major breakthrough for her, having previously only slept with Martin, but they also represented an epiphany of sorts for many women at the time of the film's release: She showed female viewers that it was perfectly acceptable to enjoy a healthy, robust sex life, even with multiple partners, without guilt or fear of being perceived negatively. Erica may not have been the first sexually liberated woman on the screen, nor may she have been the most provocative, but she certainly had some of the most positive impact, portraying the active sex life of a middle-aged woman in a favorable light, something her offscreen contemporaries could look to hopefully as a source of inspiration.

By facing her fears and making herself over in all these various ways, Erica creates not only a new life for herself but a new persona as well. She opens herself to possibilities never before envisioned and relishes them so much that she even has difficulty seeing herself tied down in the traditional ways that she once had been. She longs to taste all the fruits that life has to offer and to do so without restriction, focused purely in the moment, grounded in the here and now, and not worrying about what has passed nor what might happen tomorrow. Her newfound attitude in many ways epitomizes what conscious creation is all about for all of us, regardless of gender (or any other supposed defining quality, for that matter)—enjoying what's before us at the present time, for it is truly the only moment over which we have any direct control. Even the very next moment is a different reality from the one we are in now (and one over which we won't be able to exert any control until we find ourselves in it), so we'd be wise to focus our attention and appreciation on the only existence we can access at any particular given time—the present.

This film is an excellent character study of a woman in transition, powerfully portrayed by Clayburgh, who won the award for best actress at the Cannes Film Festival and received comparable Oscar and Golden Globe nominations. Her performance is superbly supported by an excellent cast of co-stars, most notably Murphy and Lucas.

The sensitive writing and direction of Paul Mazursky showed tremendous depth in his understanding of women and their concerns, a major asset in bringing Erica's story to life for the screen. Mazursky's efforts earned him Golden Globe nods for both writing and directing, as well as an Oscar nomination for original screenplay. The movie itself received best picture nominations at the Oscars, Golden Globes, and Cannes, a rarity for a film to be so honored in all three competitions. In all, the film tallied three Oscar and five Globe nods, along with two Cannes nominations, but Clayburgh's award was the movie's only win.

One rarely knows what venturing out on one's own will bring, at least at the outset, but pleasant surprises are certainly one of the possibilities. Erica discovers this for herself, for although she may have lost a lot when her marriage to Martin dissolved, she gained even more once she faced her fears about going it alone. Her experience is one that can benefit us all in finding true happiness in life, no matter how unconventional a form it takes.

## Scaling the Dizzying Heights

"Vertigo"
*Year of Release: 1958*
*Principal Cast: James Stewart, Kim Novak,*
*Barbara Bel Geddes, Tom Helmore*
*Director: Alfred Hitchcock*
*Book: Pierre Boileau, Thomas Narcejac*
*Screenplay: Alec Coppel, Samuel Taylor*

The search for ecstasy can be an elusive one. So often the blissful prospects that it holds out to us are just beyond our grasp. And if enough disappointments in attaining it occur, we may just give up the quest to create it and reconcile ourselves to the idea that we'll never realize it, despite its seductive allure. But when it suddenly appears compellingly accessible once again, it's tempting to cast aside such resignation and take another stab at it, especially for those who see their opportunities running out, even if it means facing down long-standing fears. The Alfred Hitchcock classic, "Vertigo," takes us on just such a journey, one aimed at scaling those dizzying heights.

After incurring a serious injury on his beat, San Francisco Police Detective John "Scottie" Ferguson (James Stewart) is forced into retirement. But as if the middle-aged investigator's physical pain weren't enough, he also suffers from a profound sense of guilt, feeling personally responsible for the death of a fellow officer who was killed in a fall while trying to rescue him. Scottie's acute acrophobia—fear of heights—kicked in and triggered an attack of vertigo—a severe dizzy sensation—causing him to freeze in fright as he clung to the edge of a rooftop just as his colleague tried to pull him to safety. The attempt failed, and the officer plunged to his death while Scottie looked on in horror, filling him with a deep sense of remorse that he has been unable to shake ever since.

Faced with premature retirement, Scottie now contemplates what to do with the rest of his life, but he seems directionless. The confirmed bachelor spends much of his time with an old college chum and one-time romantic interest, Midge (Barbara Bel Geddes), having drinks, making small talk, and reminiscing about the good old days. It passes the time, but it hardly seems enough to fill up his days. The tedium of that limited routine changes when Scottie receives an unexpected phone call from another old college friend, Gavin Elster (Tom Helmore), with a proposition that's about to change his life.

Gavin wants to hire Scottie to shadow his wife, Madeleine (Kim Novak), whom he believes could be mentally ill. Gavin says that she speaks of being possessed by a departed spirit, one who threatens to take over her body and potentially subvert her persona. He wants Scottie to follow Madeleine to see where she goes and what she does in hopes that it will unlock the mystery of her obsession and help him determine if she genuinely needs treatment for her mental state. With no other offers coming his way, Scottie reluctantly agrees and begins to follow his new client's wife. The surveillance starts out innocently enough, but Scottie soon finds himself embroiled in circumstances far more complicated than what he bargained for.

Scottie discovers that Madeleine indeed is obsessed with the idea of possession, in danger of being overcome by the spirit of a dead woman named Carlotta Valdes, who, as it turns out, is one of Madeleine's long-departed relatives. Carlotta was a tragic figure who perished by her own hand, but her suicide was kept quiet, so it was unlikely that Madeleine knew of her obscure ancestor's identity, let alone the way in which she died. Gavin grows worried at this news, since he's familiar with Carlotta's story and fears that his wife may just be mentally vulnerable enough to follow the same path as her forbear. He keeps Scottie on the case to watch her closely and see what more he can uncover.

Scottie, meanwhile, must contend with an obsession of his own—his budding attraction for Madeleine. Falling for the wife of one's client may not be the wisest course, but Scottie can't help himself. As a lonely middle-aged man, he's compulsively drawn to Madeleine's radiant beauty. He also identifies with the lost quality she exudes, as he, too, is personally adrift, longing for those things, like love, that have always seemed to so capriciously and cruelly elude him.

After a time, Scottie's gazing from afar leads to a face-to-face meeting with the object of his affection, at which point they discover the attraction is mutual. As Scottie grows closer to Madeleine, he decides to help her resolve her obsession, particularly her burgeoning fear that she's losing herself, becoming consumed by the spirit of Carlotta. She tells him of a dream she had involving an old Spanish settlement, which Scottie recognizes from her description as the mission of San Juan Bautista. He offers to take her there in hopes that it will help bring closure to her ordeal, but instead of resolution, their fateful visit unleashes a terrible tragedy. In a fit of hysteria, Madeleine flees to the mission's tall bell tower, setting in motion a chain of events that leads to death, disillusionment, mental breakdown, and the resurfacing of unresolved fears.

Many of Hitchcock's films are more than mere thrillers; they can be interpreted on multiple levels, and "Vertigo" is no exception. From the standpoint of facing fears, one of the picture's central themes, Scottie's acrophobia is the most obvious concern in need of attention. But even this condition has a secondary (and arguably more significant) meaning than just a fear of heights. It's also symbolic of Scottie's fear of scaling the heights of ecstasy. Being the lonely bachelor that he is, Scottie is just as afraid to ascend to the apex of love as he is to climb a flight of stairs, even if he isn't as consciously aware of the former as he is of the latter. And romance, metaphorically speaking, is a prospect that makes his head spin almost as much as the vertigo that his acrophobia induces. If Scottie truly wishes to find personal happiness in his life, then he must conquer his fear of heights in all of its permutations, both literal and symbolic. Madeleine's presence in his life provides an opportunity for doing just that, but whether Scottie avails himself of it is a question only he can answer. Should he fail at this task, however, he faces a future in which his love life is likely to consist of little more than idle chitchat with Midge over cocktails.

Scottie, however, is not the only one with a fear to master. Madeleine must contend with the fear of losing herself and her grasp on reality. This is fascinating from a conscious creation perspective, for she is apparently choosing to let go of her persona in favor of that of another, even if she's not sure why. If nothing else, this shows how elusive the nature of reality can be at times, often far more ethereal and less fixed than we generally assume it to be. This becomes even more obvious as the film progresses, with unfolding events revealing that everything is not always what it seems, a fact that becomes apparent to both characters and viewers alike. Under these circumstances, one can't help but wonder why the realities we create would flow in such seemingly unlikely directions, but such conditions also provide a basis for us to examine the precise nature of our beliefs to determine why we manifest what we do, especially when fears arise as part of the materializations.

The need to look into why we create what we do comes up repeatedly in one particularly intriguing context—how it relates to the manifestation of our mental state. Hitchcock frequently dealt with psychological themes in his movies, especially where issues of motivations and intents were concerned, the very basis of what underlies conscious creation, so it's interesting to see how he applied them here specifically with regard to the characters' mental states. In some instances, their motivations become clear and their issues are resolved, while in others they do not. In any event, understanding the particular beliefs that drive our creations, as noted in the previous paragraph, is always important, but that's especially true in a context as vital as this, in which one's very sanity and mental well-being are at stake. Breakdown and recovery are both possible outcomes on this particular continuum, and characters in this film, in fact, experience both, but no matter which arises, it's always essential to remember that it's the beliefs we hold that determine which result occurs.

"Vertigo" is a taut thriller from a legendary cinematic genius. It's filled with a plethora of twists and turns—far more than I've noted—ever captivating with each revelation. Stewart and Novak are great together, each turning in excellent performances as lost souls exploring their fears and obsessions, playing their parts with just the right amount of desperation to come across as credible without going overboard. Edith Head's costuming suits Novak perfectly, providing her with a simple, graceful elegance that allows her radiance to shine through exquisitely. (It's no wonder Scottie's so taken with her.)

One of the picture's greatest strengths, though, is its dazzling and inventive camera work. The film portrays the city by the bay magnificently, its many landmarks showcased at their cinematic best. However, the shots that really make the cinematography pop are those that depict Scottie's sense of acrophobia, showing his exaggerated perception of height in a metaphorical yet thoroughly convincing way. Amazingly, this aspect of the film was overlooked for Oscar contention, even though the picture did receive two other nods for sound and for art direction and set decoration.

Bliss, particularly of a romantic sort, can be a frightening notion to someone who's never experienced it. But, as with any other fear, the attempt to overcome it is worth the effort for the rewards it bestows, no matter how fleeting or unexpected they might be. Of course, allowing for the possibility of such joyful contentment in the first place is half the battle, since hoped-for results will never materialize as long as fears are permitted to stand in the way of its manifestation. Scaling the heights of ecstasy may be a dizzying prospect, but taking a shot at it—no matter what the outcome—is, in the end, far preferable to taking no shot at all.

**Extra Credits:** Hitchcock fans who also possess a funny bone are sure to appreciate the hilarious send-ups of the master's works in the raucous Mel Brooks comedy, "High Anxiety." Dr. Richard Thorndyke (Brooks), a prominent psychiatrist who is named the new administrator of an elite asylum for the very wealthy (and very nervous), gets sucked into a tale of mystery and intrigue involving a rich industrialist, his heiress daughter (Madeline Kahn), and a staff in serious need of oversight. While the film parodies many of Hitchcock's pictures (as well as the thrillers of several other directors), it borrows heavily from "Vertigo," including a protagonist who also suffers from acrophobia and a concluding sequence that absolutely slays the bell tower scene from its predecessor. Big laughs all around. (1977; Mel Brooks, Madeline Kahn, Cloris Leachman, Harvey Korman, Ron Carey, Howard Morris, Dick Van Patten, Charlie Callas, Rudy DeLuca; Mel Brooks, director; Mel Brooks, Ron Clark, Rudy DeLuca, and Barry Levinson, screenplay; two Golden Globe nominations)

# Dying To Prove Oneself

"Defending Your Life"
*Year of Release: 1991*
*Principal Cast: Albert Brooks, Meryl Streep, Rip Torn, Lee Grant,*
*George D. Wallace, Lillian Lehman, Buck Henry, Raffi Di Blasio*
*Director: Albert Brooks*
*Screenplay: Albert Brooks*

Have you ever faced a situation in which you had to prove yourself to someone? Most of us have probably experienced that at some point or another. Now, imagine if you were faced with having to do that about your entire life, justifying its validity to a circumspect band of inquisitors, upon its completion. That's exactly what the recently departed are up against in the Albert Brooks comedy, "Defending Your Life."

While taking his new BMW convertible on its maiden drive, middle-aged advertising executive Daniel Miller (Brooks) is killed in a head-on collision with a Los Angeles bus. Upon his death, he's whisked away to Judgment City, an afterlife world based on modern urban life. The reason for Daniel's visit, like all those who go there, is to defend his life, a proceeding somewhat similar to a trial in which a panel of judges (Lillian Lehman, George D. Wallace) determines if he's ready to move on to the next phase of his evolution or if he must return to Earth to work on life lessons as yet unresolved. Helping Daniel is Bob Diamond (Rip Torn), a wily and gregarious defender, and opposing him is Lena Foster (Lee Grant), a tough-as-nails prosecutor.

The main purpose of the proceeding is to evaluate whether Daniel has sufficiently fulfilled the principal task worthy of forward movement—learning how to overcome fear. As Bob explains to Daniel during their initial meeting, the primary reason for living life on the earthly plane is to work out such issues. Conquering fear, as he puts it, is essential to achieving true happiness and personal fulfillment, making it possible to then move on to the even grander adventures that the Universe has in store. However, if someone is unable to meet that basic qualification for the journey, that individual is sent back for remedial terrestrial training.

In the course of the trial, defendants are shown recorded episodes from their lives, viewing them as if they were watching a movie. These incidents are offered up as evidence to illustrate whether they represent facing or dodging particular fears, followed by questioning and commentary by both the prosecutor and defender. The number of episodes presented varies from individual to individual, depending on the degree of certainty associated with whether forward progress is merited.

As the life episodes reveal, Daniel is a likeable guy with many good qualities, but he is also someone who sometimes let his fears get the better of him, especially in sequences depicting him as a child (Raffi Di Blasio). He's thus one of those borderline cases whose worthiness of onward movement calls for particularly close scrutiny, especially since many of the incidents reviewed can easily be taken in more than one way (showing how our beliefs about particular subjects and situations may not always be as clear-cut as we might like to think they are). It also makes pleading his case that much more difficult.

When defendants are not in their courtroom sessions, they're free to enjoy the many amenities of Judgment City, a place that has been purposely designed to be comfortable and familiar so that defendants can be free of stress and distractions in getting on with the business of their proceedings. It's a place of endless recreational opportunities, such as comedy clubs, golf courses, and the wildly popular past lives pavilion, as well as always-perfect weather and the best food one will ever eat (which everyone can enjoy to their heart's content without gaining any weight—talk about heaven!). Daniel, however, ends up meeting a very big distraction—the woman of his dreams, Julia (Meryl Streep)—an encounter that ultimately brings him face to face with perhaps his greatest fear of all. The question for Daniel is whether he'll rise to the occasion of the new challenge (or is it opportunity?) presented to him.

The issue of facing fears is without question the central theme of this picture, and the film approaches it on a variety of fronts and in a variety of contexts (it's even the subject of a game show on one of Judgment City's television stations). But perhaps the most important way is expressed by Bob in his first session with Daniel—that overcoming fear is essential to finding personal happiness. Conquering our personally created demons is an empowering act that is necessary if we ever hope to make personal progress. "If you understand that," Jane Roberts and Seth wrote, "then in a large manner many of your fears will . . . vanish."[8] It simply doesn't get much plainer than that.

When we consider how pervasive the search for personal happiness is in our everyday lives, the importance of developing expertise in a fundamental skill like facing fears thus takes on added significance, for its impact on personal satisfaction can be felt in everything from vocation to romance to finances and virtually everything else imaginable. Without this skill, however, we're likely to be saddled with the burden of having to address our fears and the issues underlying them over and over again, stuck in a sort of metaphysical purgatory until we finally figure out what's hindering our forward progress. Discovering that can be a rather disheartening revelation as Daniel finds out when Bob tells him he's been to Earth about twenty times trying to work on these issues, far in excess of the mere six incarnations Bob needed.

One of the simplest ways to overcome fear, from a conscious creation perspective, is to not create it in the first place. That's a basic, straightforward solution, yet many of us fail to see it, let alone employ it. And that's because we have allowed ourselves to become so ingrained into believing that fear *must* be a part of our reality that we keep creating it with that as part of the mix. It's just like that old joke about the guy who goes to see his doctor and says, as he raises his arm, "Doc, it hurts when I do this," to which the doc replies, "Well, then don't do that." Simple, right? If so, then why do we keep raising our arms?

If the solution really were that easy, we all should have figured that out by now, shouldn't we? Or is there something more at work here? Daniel, interestingly enough, provides the answer: The reason he and so many of us stay stuck in fear and fail at creating reality without it is that we don't give ourselves permission to do otherwise. We don't allow ourselves to see probabilities in which fear doesn't exist, so we never develop beliefs that allow it to manifest. We never give to ourselves the gift of freedom from this weighty, self-imposed millstone; we just keep on creating according to the dictates of those outmoded beliefs, perpetually short-changing ourselves.

So where do such short-shrifting beliefs come from? Brooks never addresses that directly (probably to avoid offending anyone). However, one could speculate that, if Daniel's experience is at all like that of many of us (especially during his formative years), his beliefs probably arose from influences he took in and allowed himself to embrace from sources like traditional religion, teachers, older relatives, authority figures, and other members of officialdom. Such sources are often heavily invested in conventional notions like never giving ourselves permission to act or believe in ways that differ markedly from the mainstream and allowing fear to keep us locked in place, even in spite of the many inherent pitfalls that accompany such thinking. (Quite an inspiring collection of beliefs, wouldn't you say? Given their prevalence, it's a wonder we've ever made any progress as a species at all.)

Consequently, if we continually create circumstances in which fear is intrinsically part of the equation, we must also continually create ways to manage and cope with fear. The amount of energy and focus we have to funnel into such management and coping mechanisms is so great that these resources tend to get used up, making them unavailable for other more enjoyable, more meaningful pursuits that we would be able to explore if we had only allowed ourselves to create realities in which fear was absent altogether (preferably from the outset). If our energies are routinely channeled into these kinds of mundane activities, it's no wonder we never have them available for seeking out and obtaining the rewards that conquering fears makes possible or for enjoying those ever-grander adventures of the Universe that Bob spoke of so glowingly.

This is essentially what puts Daniel on the fence as a borderline candidate for advancement. He always seems to be on the verge of breaking through the fears that hold him back, but he has trouble going the last mile, mainly because he won't give himself permission to go there. His experience serves as a valuable cautionary tale to those of us who feel held back, for it helps to show where the source of responsibility lies for that—squarely with us.

"Defending Your Life" is a wonderfully funny movie but by no means a lightweight. It addresses these rather substantive issues with a deftly humorous touch, never allowing the subject matter to become too heavy to spoil the fun. The story is a winner, as is most of the screenplay, though a few tangential dialogue sequences in the courtroom scenes would have been better if reworked or left out (something that tends to come with the territory in Brooks's pictures, so it's not entirely unexpected). However, there is also a great deal of understated wit in the writing, especially in the comparative ways that Daniel's and Julia's respective life histories and Judgment City experiences differ from one another.

The film is big on sight gags, and nearly all of them hit home runs. Brooks makes effective use of signs, placards, and even billboards for getting good hearty laughs out of his viewers. He also includes one of the funniest, most inspired visuals I've ever seen in a movie, coming at the beginning of a scene in which Daniel and Julia pay a visit to the past lives pavilion. (That's all I'm going to say, because I don't want to spoil it; you'll have to see for yourself what I mean.)

In addition, this is one of the most romantic movies I've ever seen. The fledgling romance between Daniel and Julia is one of the most touching love stories ever put to the screen. This is principally due to the great chemistry between Brooks and Streep, who look great together and have an affinity for one another that comes across as completely genuine, never forced. They turn in great performances, as do their co-stars Torn and Grant.

In short, I like this movie a lot. And with that, I rest my case.

## Triple Feature: The Three Musketeers

### "The Constant Gardener"
*Year of Release: 2005*
*Principal Cast: Ralph Fiennes, Rachel Weisz, Hubert Koundé, Danny Huston, Gerard McSorley, Archie Panjabi, Richard McCabe, Bill Nighy, Anneke Kim Sarnau, Pete Postlethwaite, Donald Sumpter*
*Director: Fernando Meirelles*
*Book: John le Carré*
*Screenplay: Jeffrey Caine*

### "Syriana"
*Year of Release: 2005*
*Principal Cast: George Clooney, Christopher Plummer, Jeffrey Wright, Chris Cooper, Matt Damon, Amanda Peet, Alexander Siddig, Akbar Kurtha, William Hurt, David Clennon, Robert Foxworth, Nicky Henson, Peter Gerety, Mazhar Munir, Jayne Atkinson, Tom McCarthy, Jamey Sheridan, Nadim Sawalha, Sonell Dadral, Mark Strong*
*Director: Stephen Gaghan*
*Book: Robert Baer*
*Screenplay: Stephen Gaghan*

### "Good Night, and Good Luck"
*Year of Release: 2005*
*Principal Cast: David Strathairn, George Clooney, Jeff Daniels, Patricia Clarkson, Robert Downey Jr., Frank Langella, Ray Wise*
*Director: George Clooney*
*Screenplay: George Clooney, Grant Heslov*

In 1844, French author Alexandre Dumas penned a novel about a trio of chivalrous heroes who pursued noble causes in the face of strident opposition, their escapades undertaken in the collective spirit of "one for all, and all for one!" That novel, of course, was *The Three Musketeers*, a classic that has come to epitomize the very nature of heroism. In late 2005, a trio of films was released embodying that same spirit, featuring heroic figures taking on modern-day goliaths under seemingly hopeless circumstances, characters who recognized the fear of what they were up against and faced it anyway. That cinematic triad went on to much acclaim, not only critically but also for the offscreen social impact they had in helping raise consciousness for their causes. Such were the achievements of "The Constant Gardener," "Syriana," and "Good Night, and Good Luck."

"The Constant Gardener," based on the novel by John le Carré, tells the story of Justin Quayle (Ralph Fiennes), a capable though conformist British diplomat working as a foreign service officer in Kenya. He dutifully endeavors to represent Her Majesty's government, yet he's simultaneously pressured by those in high places to curb the enthusiasm of his wife Tessa (Rachel Weisz), a social activist who has begun looking into the questionable dealings of a large pharmaceutical company that operates unrestrictedly with the blessings of the Crown. Justin, a sensitive, soft-spoken man who's a bit of a milquetoast and is most at home in the seclusion of his garden, is torn in his allegiances but conscientiously tries to assuage the interests of both his spouse and his employer through his mannerly diplomacy.

In many ways, Justin's caught up in a no-win situation. But when his wife is found dead, his hand is forced. With the vendetta having become personal, the one-time ostrich retaliates, his fury channeled into finding out who is responsible and why, a search that leads him to some very high levels of power in both the corporate world and the British government.

In a similar vein, "Syriana" examines the lives of those seeking to rectify comparably shady dealings in the oil business in an unnamed Persian Gulf emirate. The struggle of governments, corporations, and even individuals to control the flow of this valuable resource (and the power that goes with it) is played out through numerous intertwining story lines, each of which features heroic figures defiantly taking on those who would put self-interest before the common good.

Aging CIA foot soldier Bob Barnes (George Clooney) grapples with figuring out the true intents behind his assignments in the Middle East, trying to keep his government honest, even in the face of threats to his reputation and life. Corporate lawyer Bennett

Holiday (Jeffrey Wright) seeks to balance the aims of his big oil clients while making sure they behave legally, a task that has him under the thumb of both his high-powered boss (Christopher Plummer) and a Justice Department investigator (David Clennon). Prince Nasir Al-Subaai (Alexander Siddig), the idealistic heir apparent of the emirate, who wishes to launch various progressive reform initiatives, faces dashed dreams in a succession battle with his younger brother Meshal (Akbar Kurtha), an opportunist more interested in lining his own pockets and those of his minions than seeing to the welfare of his homeland. Coming to Nasir's aid is commodities dealer Bryan Woodman (Matt Damon), who joins the would-be emir's quest by providing much-needed financial advice, ultimately seeking to help himself by helping another. In the midst of all this are a pair of wild cards, Wasim (Mazhar Munin) and Farooq (Sonell Dadral), immigrant refinery workers who lose their jobs in a corporate restructuring and subsequently embark on a radical new path as freedom fighters. The diverse threads of these various plotlines eventually weave together to tell a compelling story of heroism on multiple fronts with wildly divergent outcomes.

Government figures, while ancillary targets in each of the prior two movies, are the principal adversaries in the historical drama, "Good Night, and Good Luck." This fact-based story examines the crusade of CBS television journalist Edward R. Murrow (1908–1965) (David Strathairn), host of the popular news magazine *See It Now*, and his producer Fred Friendly (George Clooney) in taking on fanatical Senator Joseph McCarthy (R-WI) and his supporters during the government-sanctioned anti-Communist witch-hunts of the early 1950s. The picture's title comes from Murrow's signature sign-off line that he used at the end of each of his broadcasts.

This lavishly produced period piece, shot in black and white, incorporates extensive archive footage, including many scenes from actual government hearings. But in addition to detailing these historical events, the film shows the workings that went on inside CBS, including the extensive soul-searching of the *See It Now* staff and of network chairman William Paley (Frank Langella), who wrestled with balancing issues of self-censorship, keeping his sponsor happy, and letting his staff do their jobs. In the end, Murrow convinced Paley of the urgency of this story and succeeded in getting it on the air, exposing the senator for the exploitative opportunist that he was and boldly proclaiming "we must not confuse dissent with disloyalty," sentiments that sound eerily familiar even today.

But as popular as Murrow's coverage was, it also signaled the beginning of the end of his relationship with the network that made his name a household word. In a speech that Murrow made at an awards dinner several years after the McCarthy broadcasts, part of which is re-created in the film, he voiced his concerns about the direction television was taking, assailing the networks for emphasizing entertainment and commercialism at the expense of news and public service. Murrow foresaw what the future of television held in store and offered a prescient warning to change things before it was too late, offering opinions that would be expressed again years later by media reform critics.

The heroism explored in these three films is self-evident. Their fearless devotion to their causes speaks volumes about their commitments to question the established order and to help usher new and improved realities into being. What struck me the most about them, however, had more to do with the circumstances under which they were released than with any of their artistic accomplishments or metaphysical attributes: All three came out at a time when taking on authority figures, be they in government, industry, or the media, with strong social messages was quite a brash—and genuinely heroic—move.

As thrilled as I was to see these pictures released when they were, I must confess that I was also quite surprised—impressively so, but surprised nevertheless. Despite growing public dissatisfaction with the ineffectual responses of established, official bodies to deal with the challenges of contemporary society, many of those who were critical also remained quiet; and those who did try to speak out often had considerable difficulty conveying their messages through media outlets whose primary loyalties were seen as belonging to their corporate and government patrons and not to telling the truth.

The nearly simultaneous release of these three movies was like an icebreaker crashing through a frozen lake, chopping up the intractable surface to make the first opening in waters that had been impassable through a very long winter of discontent. They brought a resounding relevance to the screen that few other films or even mainstream journalistic outlets were supplying at the time. Their appearance was a breath of fresh air for those of reasonable mind who felt as though they were being systemically and relentlessly suffocated by those aligned with a rigid agenda of narrow dogmatic views aimed at benefiting the privileged few and ignoring the greater good.

From a conscious creation standpoint, I was fascinated, both at the time of their release and to this very day, to see how these pictures reflected emerging changes in the beliefs of the mass consciousness. They served as rallying points for those fed up with the status quo, giving voice to concerns that few had been willing or able to express freely or comfortably in times prior. Although the specific measure of their impact is certainly up for debate, they at least got people talking again, particularly about overly intrusive, authoritarian government, corrupt big business, and complicit mainstream media. Such talk led to some rather significant change subsequently, especially in the sweeping political turnaround that occurred a year later, so perhaps the catalytic influence of these films was more substantial than anyone realizes. It would seem, to paraphrase Oscar Wilde, that life often does imitate art.

I was also struck by how all three of these pictures put human faces on the issues they covered, treating their story lines as more than just abstract explorations of ideals but as tales where real people are intimately affected by their prevailing circumstances. As in virtually all heroic epics, the plights of the oppressed and less fortunate are addressed by champions who come to their aid, seeking to provide security where peril and vulnerability have held sway.

In "Good Night, and Good Luck," the reputations of government employees and everyday citizens are at stake, with prospects of unemployment and public ostracism potentially awaiting those who are unfairly branded; without Murrow and company, McCarthy and his cronies might have been able to perpetrate their often unfounded indignities on perfectly innocent civilians for far longer. In "The Constant Gardener," the health of countless Africans is at issue; without the advocacy of activists like Tessa to represent them, those who are already most vulnerable face even greater exploitation by those who would put profits before people. And in "Syriana," the influence of the oil industry touches individuals in myriad ways, prompting the emergence of heroes in different milieus, from political to economic to legal and even spiritual; when multiple crises arise, multiple champions appear.

All three films are strong in numerous ways, and each was recognized handsomely for its accomplishments. They explore their subjects in depth, offering insights into them seldom seen through other sources and other media. They also all feature scripts that are rather involved, requiring careful attention, so casual viewing is definitely not recommended.

"The Constant Gardener" is one of the most complete pictures I've ever seen—part spy thriller, part murder mystery, and part love story, all rolled into one package. It's also one of the saddest films I've ever viewed, effectively tugging at the heart strings without ever becoming sappy. Fiennes and Weisz play their parts superbly, with Weisz winning both an Oscar and a Golden Globe Award for best supporting actress. Gorgeous cinematography and an eclectic soundtrack complement the package well. In total, the movie received one Oscar on four nominations and one Globe on three nods, including a nomination for best dramatic picture, as well as the Cannes Film Festival award for best original score.

"Syriana," my favorite film of 2005, is a masterpiece of storytelling. It's particularly adept at explaining how the oil business and the political landscape of the Middle East are both far more complicated than how they're typically portrayed in more conventional sources. The interlocking plotlines show how multiple influences can all play into one composite story with some characters never even meeting each other yet still affecting one another in many ways, an excellent example of the connectedness inherent in conscious creation (more on connectedness in chapter 8). Fine direction and an excellent script set the tone for this picture, with an excellent cast filling the roles of its many (and I do mean many) characters. Wright, Plummer, Damon, and Siddig are all noteworthy, as is Clooney, who won both an Oscar and a Golden Globe for best supporting actor. In all, the film took home one statue on two nominations at both the Academy Awards and the Globes.

"Good Night, and Good Luck" is a very stylish production with its distinctive black-and-white cinematography, its seamless editing of archival and new footage, and its excellent production values in everything from sets to costumes to hair and makeup. The story is well paced and well presented, with musical numbers by jazz singer Dianne Reeves serving as elegant bridges between sequences, pleasantly separating the story's segments without breaking its continuity. Strathairn plays Murrow as if he's channeling the famed broadcaster, down to the subtlest of inflections and nuances, earning him both Oscar and Golden Globe nods for best actor. Clooney makes a major splash here, too, giving a fine performance as Friendly, as well as turning in noteworthy efforts as director and co-author of the screenplay with Grant Heslov, accomplishments that resulted in both Academy Award and Golden Globe nominations in both categories. The movie received six Oscar and four Globe nods overall, including best picture in both competitions, but it took home no awards.

Simple as it may sound, these films ultimately show that, no matter how complex our political and corporate structures can be, their effectiveness and functioning still come down to the beliefs we hold and the decisions we make about them as individuals. Underlying all the elaborate and intricate schemes and ideas are people—human beings capable of both great accomplishments and terrible blunders, of being both inspired and flawed, forthright and vulnerable, effective and not, all engaged in the process of learning what it is to be conscious creators. But those who approach their endeavors like the musketeers, heroically and without reservation, as the characters in these films do, merit special recognition, for they are among the most ambitious of creators. They dare to try their hand at pursuits others won't touch, courageously attempting to manifest that which others are too fearful to even consider giving recognition, particularly in the face of intimidating opposition. And that, in my view, is the pinnacle of what conscious creation strives to achieve.

## Bonus Features

### Facing Fears Films

"Romancing the Stone": Joan Wilder, a talented but sheltered and easily stirred romance novelist, learns her sister Elaine has been kidnapped and is being held for ransom. To save her life, Joan must leave behind the comparative safety of her New York life and travel to the wilds of Colombia, where she gets caught up in an adventure not unlike the plotline of one of her novels, bringing her face to face with many of her fears, including some she wasn't prepared for. Great romantic fun with plenty of unexpected twists and turns. (1984; Michael Douglas, Kathleen Turner [Golden Globe winner], Danny DeVito, Zack Norman, Manuel Ojeda, Alfonso Arau, Holland Taylor, Mary Ellen Trainor; Robert Zemeckis, director; Diane Thomas, screenplay; one Oscar nomination; two Golden Globe wins, including best comedy picture, on two nominations)

"Fearless": A plane crash survivor who, ironically enough, had once been afraid of flying sees his good fortune as a sign that it's possible for him to conquer all of his fears. His belief in this conviction is so strong, in fact, that he comes to help other survivors deal with their fears and the psychological scars that emerge in the aftermath of the crash, earning him the nickname "the Good Samaritan." However, his sense of invulnerability grows so powerful that it begins to consume him, becoming a sort of addiction that encourages him to take foolish risks. And, in an even greater irony, it's a compulsion he grows afraid to give up. An enigmatic, powerful drama with knockout performances. (1993; Jeff Bridges, Isabella Rossellini, Rosie Perez, Tom Hulce, John Turturro, Benicio Del Toro, John De Lancie, Deirdre O'Connell, Spencer Vrooman, Daniel Cerny; Peter Weir, director; Rafael Yglesias, book and screenplay; one Oscar nomination, one Golden Globe nomination)

"Sex, Lies and Videotape": Fears about intimacy, sexuality, relationships, and even what makes life worth living are meticulously probed in this voyeuristic study of the lives of four individuals coming to grips with what they want for themselves and from one another. Intense drama approached through an unlikely angle. (1989; James Spader [Cannes Film Festival winner], Peter Gallagher, Andie MacDowell, Laura San Giacomo; Steven Soderbergh, director and screenplay; one Oscar nomination, three Golden Globe nominations; Palme D'Or winner, FIPRESCI Prize winner, and best actor award winner, Cannes Film Festival)

"Blade Runner": In a depressing future version of Los Angeles, sentient human-like androids known as replicants threaten to run amok when faced with the expiration of their preprogrammed life expectancies. Special law enforcement officers known as blade runners are deployed to eliminate these renegades before trouble arises. For both hunter and hunted, however, the story ultimately turns into an examination of the fear each must face when time is about to run out. (1982; Harrison Ford, Rutger Hauer, Sean Young, Edward James Olmos, M. Emmet Walsh, Daryl Hannah, William Sanderson, Brion James, Joanna Cassidy, Joe Turkel; Ridley Scott, director; Philip K. Dick, book; Hampton Fancher and David Peoples, screenplay; two Oscar nominations, one Golden Globe nomination)

## Living Heroically Films

"The China Syndrome": A long-tenured, fiercely loyal nuclear power plant worker makes plans to blow the whistle on his corporate employer when he discovers potentially serious safety issues at its new facility, aided by a local television reporter and her cameraman, who captures a near meltdown on film. The intrepid trio moves forward to expose the disaster-in-waiting before it materializes amidst threats from powerful forces seeking to silence them. Ironically, this film was released just a few weeks prior to the accident at Pennsylvania's Three Mile Island nuclear power plant. (1979; Jane Fonda, Jack Lemmon [Cannes Film Festival winner], Michael Douglas, Wilford Brimley, Donald Hotton, Daniel Valdez, James Karen, Richard Herd; James Bridges, director; Mike Gray, T.S. Cook, and James Bridges, screenplay; four Oscar nominations, five Golden Globe nominations; Palme D'Or nominee and best actor award winner, Cannes Film Festival)

"JFK": This painstakingly detailed drama documents the heroic investigation conducted by New Orleans District Attorney Jim Garrison (1921–1992) into the alleged conspiracy behind the assassination of President John F. Kennedy (1917–1963), dubbed "the story that won't go away," according to the film's tagline. Quixotic though his quest may have been, Garrison nevertheless moved forward in the face of staggering opposition to try to expose the elusive truth behind one of the twentieth century's most vexing mysteries. (1991; Kevin Costner, Tommy Lee Jones, Kevin Bacon, Gary Oldman, Jack Lemmon, Laurie Metcalf, Sissy Spacek, Joe Pesci, John Candy, Walter Matthau, Sally Kirkland, Donald Sutherland,

Edward Asner, Brian Doyle-Murray, Michael Rooker; Oliver Stone, director [Golden Globe winner]; Jim Marrs and Jim Garrison, book; Oliver Stone and Zachary Sklar, screenplay; two Oscar wins on eight nominations, one Golden Globe win on four nominations)

"Casablanca": Rick Blaine, a crusty American bar owner in Nazi-controlled Casablanca, faces the dilemma of whether to engage in acts that are wholly self-serving or eminently selfless, potentially benefiting millions threatened by totalitarian aggression during World War II. In the end, only he can decide to play the scoundrel or the hero. A classic for any age based on the play, *Everybody Comes to Rick's.* (1942; Humphrey Bogart, Ingrid Bergman, Paul Henreid, Claude Rains, Conrad Veidt, Sydney Greenstreet, Peter Lorre, Dooley Wilson; Michael Curtiz, director [Oscar winner]; Murray Burnett and Joan Alison, play; Julius J. Epstein, Philip G. Epstein, and Howard Koch, screenplay [Oscar winner]; three Oscar wins, including best picture, on eight nominations)

"The Front": When successful television writer Alfred Miller is labeled a Communist sympathizer and blacklisted from working during the McCarthy era of the early 1950s, he turns to his longtime friend, Howard Prince, to front his scripts for him. Howard, a restaurant cashier and part-time bookmaker, jumps at the opportunity, especially since he'll get a cut of the script fees for his efforts. But as Howard's star rises, so, too, do the eyebrows of government investigators, who begin looking into where this previous unknown came from and how he got to be so popular so quickly. Interestingly, three of the film's performers, along with its writer and director, were themselves at one time blacklisted. (1976; Woody Allen, Zero Mostel, Andrea Marcovicci, Herschel Bernardi, Michael Murphy, Remak Ramsay, Lloyd Gough, David Margulies, Marvin Lichterman, Charles Kimbrough, Josef Sommer; Martin Ritt, director; Walter Bernstein, screenplay; one Oscar nomination, one Golden Globe nomination)

"Hotel Rwanda": This fact-based drama about hotel manager Paul Rusesabagina chronicles his heroic humanitarian efforts to save lives during the insanity of the Rwandan civil war of 1994, a bitter and bloody conflict between rival Hutu and Tutsi tribal factions. By housing refugees in his hotel and doing whatever it took to survive, Rusesabagina miraculously managed to spare the lives of many who would have otherwise perished in this unfathomable genocide. (2004; Don Cheadle, Sophie Okonedo, Nick Nolte, Joaquin Phoenix, Hakeem Kae-Kazim, Tony Kgoroge, Desmond Dube, Fana Mokoena, Antonio David Lyons, Leleti Khumalo, Cara Seymour; Terry George, director; Keir Pearson and Terry George, screenplay; three Oscar nominations, three Golden Globe nominations)

"Schindler's List": This stellar film biography explores the life of German industrialist Oskar Schindler (1908–1974), whose heroic efforts spared the lives of 1,300 Jews during the Holocaust. Over the course of World War II, the flamboyant businessman who began his career as a would-be profiteer from the German war efforts transformed himself into a quiet but dedicated advocate of those who faced certain death in Nazi concentration camps by clandestinely employing them in his manufacturing plants, regardless of whether they were skilled to do the work. A powerful, moving, and inspiring saga. (1993; Liam Neeson, Ben Kingsley, Ralph Fiennes, Caroline Goodall, Embeth Davidtz; Steven Spielberg, director [Oscar and Golden Globe winner]; Thomas Keneally, book; Steven Zaillian, screenplay [Oscar and Golden Globe winner]; seven Oscar wins, including best picture, on twelve nominations; three Golden Globe wins, including best dramatic picture, on six nominations)

"To Kill a Mockingbird": Heroes come in all sizes in this fictional memoir of growing up in a small Alabama town during the 1930s, told from the perspective of a tomboyish young girl nicknamed Scout. In addition to her own childhood adventures, we witness the courageous court battle waged by her thoughtful, soft-spoken father, attorney Atticus Finch, in defending (before an all-white, all-male jury) a black man who is falsely accused of beating and raping a white woman, as well as the heroism of a mysterious stranger who protects Atticus's family against those who would do them harm for his courtroom deeds. In June 2003, the character of Atticus Finch was voted the No. 1 Greatest Hero of American Film by the American Film Institute, beating out such other notable heavyweights as Indiana Jones and James Bond. (1962; Gregory Peck [Oscar and Golden Globe winner], Mary Badham, Phillip Alford, John Megna, Brock Peters, Rosemary Murphy, Frank Overton, James Anderson, Collin Wilcox, Robert Duvall, Paul Fix, Estelle Evans, William Windom; Robert Mulligan, director; Harper Lee, book; Horton Foote, screenplay [Oscar winner]; three Oscar wins on eight nominations, three Golden Globe wins on five nominations; Palme D'Or nominee and Gary Cooper Award winner, Cannes Film Festival)

"The Insider": Based on the *Vanity Fair* magazine article "The Man Who Knew Too Much," this tense drama tells the story of tobacco company insider Jeffrey Wigand, who courageously stepped forward, despite the constraints of a confidentiality agreement, to blow the whistle about industry practices aimed at intentionally making cigarettes more addictive. After protracted courting by producer Lowell Bergman of the popular television news magazine *60 Minutes,* Wigand gave the show a candid interview on the subject, only to have it pulled when threats of litigation from big tobacco were made against the show's network, CBS. With Wigand threatened by his former employer and his personal life in turmoil, Bergman then set out on a crusade to right the perceived wrong perpetrated against his source and get his interview aired, an undertaking that nearly tore apart the long-running news magazine from the inside. A largely overlooked but worthwhile gem. (1999; Al Pacino, Russell Crowe, Christopher Plummer, Philip Baker Hall, Diane Venora, Lindsay Crouse, Debi Mazar, Stephen Tobolowsky, Gina Gershon; Michael Mann, director; Marie Brenner, story source article; Eric Roth and Michael Mann, screenplay; seven Oscar nominations, five Golden Globe nominations)

"The Burning Season": This excellent biography examines the life-and-death struggle of environmental activist Chico Mendes (1944–1988), who valiantly fought powerful forces in both the Brazilian government and the corporate world to protect the Amazon rainforest from reckless clearing that threatened the well-being of his people, his country, and the globe at large. An excellent portrayal of the slain hero by Julia in one of his last performances. (1994; Raul Julia [Emmy and Golden Globe winner], Carmen Argenziano, Sonia Braga, Kamela Dawson, Luis Guzmán, Nigel Havers, Tomas Milian, Esai Morales, Edward James Olmos [Golden Globe winner]; John Frankenheimer, director [Emmy winner]; Andre Revkin, book; William Mastrosimone, story; William Mastrosimone, Michael Tolkin, and Ron Hutchinson, teleplay; two Emmy wins on six nominations; three Golden Globe wins, including best made-for-TV movie, on four nominations; VHS format only)

# 7

# Road Trip!

## Journeys of Self-Discovery Through Conscious Creation

> Our life evokes our character and you find out more about
> yourself as you go on.
>
> *Joseph Campbell*

Hitting the road is one of our favorite ways to escape the stresses and monotony of everyday life. Sometimes our journeys lead us to places we're already acquainted with, like the family cottage on the lake, while others show us the exotic delights of strange and foreign locales, such as the tropical island resort. However, no matter where we go, our travels nearly always take us away from the ordinary and the known to destinations less recognized and routines less familiar. And, in doing so, this separation from the usual also often has the seemingly unintended (but nevertheless significant) side effect of helping us understand ourselves better. How ironic that something that yields greater personal self-awareness should arise on such unfamiliar turf!

In a way, though, escapes from the everyday should actually promote these kinds of revelations, as anyone who has ever gone on a pilgrimage, retreat, or vacation knows. When we go on vacation, for example, we purposely engage in a pursuit whose root word is *vacate*, to empty out or remove. So when we "get away from it all," we literally (and intentionally) remove ourselves from the mundane and recurrent sameness of daily life. Simultaneously, we make it possible to empty out our consciousness (one would hope of the psychological flotsam we least need at the moment) to free up some space for introspection, either to let in new impressions or to take time to explore existing elements that have gone unaddressed.[1] The net effect of this, in either instance, is self-discovery, learning things about ourselves we never knew.

As a conscious creator, I find that travel is an interesting means for achieving this. There are no doubt other ways to accomplish it, but I've discovered that journeys are certainly one of the most color-ful, memorable, and effective ways of attaining this result. The role of conscious creation in this is undeniable, for our travels, like every-thing else in our existence, are products of our own manifestation. Intentionally materializing circumstances that help foster improved self-awareness, then, would appear to be one of the primary aims behind the journeys we make in life. It would also lend further credence to mythologist Joseph Campbell's contention, as stated earlier, that "you find out more about yourself as you go on."

★    ★    ★

Journeys take an array of forms. Physical travels are the most obvious type, but they need not be quite so literal; they can be metaphorical, too, unconstrained by the limitations of physical reality, taking place in the mind, in dreams, in alternate realities, or across time. They can also manifest as living yardsticks, gauges of our experience with relationships or other aspects of our lives as measured by such criteria as time, interactions, or milestones. They thus frame the scope and history of our experiences in vir-tually any area of life, and they can do so from both individual and collective perspectives.

No matter what type of travel we embark on, though, our journeys nearly always have certain traits associated with them. First, they significantly aid the aforementioned process of self-discovery. By liberating consciousness resources, they enable (and even encourage) us to look at ourselves and our beliefs, to conduct a sort of "personal metaphysical inventory" or "belief audit." This allows us to assess the beliefs we hold, which, in turn, helps shed light on why our realities manifest as they do. And since an inventory or audit taken under such conditions is generally done without many of the distractions that show up in everyday living, the results of the process should be clearer and more precise than they likely would be otherwise.

To illustrate, think of how often you've come back from a trip (especially a vacation) with a fresh new perspective on things, a clear head, as it were. In all likelihood, that's due to you being able to spend some time during the trip sorting and purging, ridding yourself of thoughts, ideas, and beliefs that no longer serve you and opening up room for new ones to enter that do serve you, allowing them to take their rightful place in your consciousness. How likely do you think that would have been were it not for having made the journey?

The scope of such inventories can be extensive. On a general level, they can examine which beliefs (including those of a core variety) that you want to keep, which ones you want to dispose of, and which ones you want to change (and in what ways). These principles can then be applied to a host of specific areas, from romance to finances to career to creativity and so on. Thus the assessment potential is quite broad, making possible profound, multifaceted self-evaluations ripe for enlightenment and self-discovery.

The concepts covered in chapters 4, 5, and 6 frequently play a significant role in the way an audit is conducted. The core beliefs we hold about choice, change, and fear, as well as the ways we apply them to the specific areas addressed, can have major impact in terms of how we handle items up for scrutiny. Suppose, for example, you're contemplating a change in a personal relationship. Take a look at your present beliefs and then consider the alternatives. Now run those options past the core belief considerations discussed in the previous chapters: What are your choices, and are you open to them? How would you need to rewrite your current beliefs to implement a change based on one of those choices? Do you have the courage to proceed with those rewrites, especially if they relate to an area of your life in which you were previously afraid to take action?

The inventory process also often prefaces a number of other conscious creation considerations that are examined later in this book. For example, the inherent connectedness among the various elements of our realities (see chapter 8) can be directly affected by decisions made during an inventory. Similarly, the specific means by which we manifest our creations (see chapter

9), the realities in which we hope to do so (see chapter 10), and the ways in which we seek to live our lives with purposefulness and fulfillment (see chapter 11) can all be comparably affected by initiatives implemented at this juncture.

When all these factors are combined in an audit, our prevailing beliefs are truly put to the test. Sometimes their resiliency and malleability may be pushed to their limits, but this provides valuable feedback for addressing a key question: Do they measure up to meet our needs? If they do, great and, if they don't, it's time to move on to new beliefs.

All of the foregoing helps illustrate how the unfolding process of conscious creation is like a journey itself, with many interim stops that metaphorically express the beliefs leading us toward our inevitable destinations, which brings us to the second trait that journeys of nearly every kind have in common—they show us the *evolution* of our beliefs (and, consequently, of ourselves) over a given range of experience, be it time, activity, physical locality, or whatever other criterion is used for appraisal. They thus provide us with the perspective of progression, a valuable tool in helping us determine whether and how we've made progress with particular endeavors and our success in formulating the beliefs necessary for manifesting them. Such a perspective ultimately makes for better inventories and audits, too.

I should note that the journey approach is by no means mandatory for conducting an inventory, assessing existing beliefs, or examining the evolution of our progress in a particular pursuit. However, when faced with a troublesome situation in which answers have stubbornly eluded you, it may help to get away from it for a while, regardless of the mode of escape, especially if you feel you've grown too close to it. If you have doubts about that, ask yourself this: Is it realistic to assume you would be able to glean the insights you seek by staying put (in the same relative proximity to where you've been all along, a place in which solutions have evaded you), or would getting some space help?

⋆ ⋆ ⋆

Road trip tales have been around almost as long as storytelling has, which is probably why they've also been a staple of the movie industry almost from its inception. These types of stories are frequently classics, a quality that characterizes many of the pictures in this chapter as well. Films, like stories, become classics because they tell their tales and make their points so effectively, and that's very much the case here. These movies show how the conscious creation process is like a journey itself, illustrating how the beliefs related to particular areas of individual or collective endeavor progress over the course of their unfolding toward their eventual fulfillment.

An ancient Chinese proverb maintains that a journey of a thousand miles begins with a single step. Another holds that life itself is a journey, not a destination. Both of these adages could be applied analogously to the conscious creation process. They evince the evolutionary self-discovery that we experience as we work our way through the steps of this practice, or through life itself, both of which could be seen as dual expressions of the same phenomenon. And I'm sure Joseph Campbell would contend there's no myth about that.

## Working Magic

"The Wizard of Oz"
*Year of Release: 1939*
*Principal Cast: Judy Garland, Frank Morgan, Ray Bolger,*
*Bert Lahr, Jack Haley, Billie Burke, Margaret Hamilton,*
*Charley Grapewin, Clara Blandick*
*Director: Victor Fleming*
*Book: L. Frank Baum*
*Screenplay: Noel Langley, Florence Ryerson, Edgar Allan Woolf*

When most of us think about magic, we probably call to mind images of stage practitioners skilled in the art of sleight of hand. But, as entertaining as their antics can be, their wizardry (even that of the best of them) usually boils down to elaborate parlor tricks and feats involving convincing special effects. *Real* magic, from a conscious creation standpoint, is a product of the magical approach, that practice of harmoniously blending the influences of our intellect and intuition to manifest our desires successfully, as discussed in chapter 1. While much of that discussion focused on how to use the technique for overcoming the pitfalls of creation by default, the magical approach works perfectly fine all on its own as an effective materialization practice, provided we know how to employ its various elements. A telling primer on this very subject can be found in the cinematic classic, "The Wizard of Oz."

This masterpiece is not only noteworthy as a standard in the annals of filmmaking, but its enduring popularity has made it a cultural icon as well. It's been analyzed from virtually every conceivable angle, but I'd like to add one more interpretation: a symbolic examination of the magical approach as told by way of metaphysical travelogue.

The story of "The Wizard of Oz" is so ingrained in our culture that it's difficult to imagine anyone not knowing its plotline. References to its characters and famous quotes are at times ubiquitous (especially if you've ever been to a gay Halloween party). But, for the sake of this analysis, a summary is in order.

Farm girl Dorothy Gale (Judy Garland) wishes she could change her life. The bleakness of the Kansas landscape, as well as the inflexible attitudes of locals, such as the evil spinster Miss Gulch (Margaret Hamilton), make Dorothy long for a place where things are beautiful and the people are nice, a place "over the rainbow." Her caretakers, Auntie Em (Clara Blandick), Uncle Henry (Charley Grapewin), and their trio of trusty farmhands, Hunk (Ray Bolger), Hickory (Jack Haley), and Zeke (Bert Lahr), try to make her life tolerable, but Dorothy wants more out of her existence. And when she's confronted with the snatching of her beloved dog Toto, her only real friend in the world, Dorothy takes action—by taking flight.

Dorothy runs away from home with Toto in tow. Not long after leaving, she meets a traveling fortune teller, Professor Marvel (Frank Morgan), who claims to see sadness for Dorothy's family if she doesn't return home. Not wishing to hurt those she loves, Dorothy immediately heads back to the farm, but, just as she does so, the area is besieged by one of those infamous Kansas twisters. When she finally arrives home, everyone has already taken refuge in the storm shelter, so Dorothy must fend for herself. She runs to hide in the farmhouse, and, in seeking cover, she's hit by flying debris, knocking her unconscious.

Dorothy's bout with unconsciousness is apparently brief. She awakens in her house which is spinning inside the vortex of the tornado, but, miraculously, she and Toto are somehow safe. Moments later, Dorothy feels the house come crashing down, but it lands in a place that's anything but familiar. When she opens the front door to investigate, she sees herself in the land she once daydreamed of, that beautiful place over the rainbow, the Land of Oz.

However, as beautiful as Oz is, not all the people are. True, there are some nice folks, like Glinda, the Good Witch of the North (Billie Burke). But there are also some nasty ones, most notably the Wicked Witch of the West (Hamilton), who blames Dorothy for killing her sister, the Wicked Witch of the East. She's convinced Dorothy purposely dropped her house on her sister, an act worthy of revenge. Dorothy decides she'd better get back to Kansas before she encounters any more trouble, but no one knows how to return her. Glinda then suggests that Dorothy visit a powerful but mysterious magician, the Wizard of Oz, to see if he knows how. And so Dorothy sets out for the Wizard's home, the Emerald City, merrily following the Yellow Brick Road.

Along the way, Dorothy meets some interesting new friends—a scarecrow in search of a brain (Bolger), a tin man in search of a heart (Haley), and a cowardly lion in search of courage (Lahr). Upon meeting each of them, Dorothy suggests that they join her on her journey, that perhaps the Wizard can help them, too. But fulfilling their objectives is easier said than done. Their travels are frequently beset by the meddling of the Wicked Witch of the West. And once they reach the Emerald City, the Wizard himself (Morgan) assigns a daunting task to the favor-seeking pilgrims to prove their worthiness. Their fates hang in the balance, depending on whether they succeed or fail in their venture, raising such questions as, "Will the scarecrow get his brain?" or, even more important, "Will Dorothy ever find her way home?" The solution lies, fittingly enough, in conscious creation and the magical approach.

Dorothy's adventures provide a symbolic roadmap to understanding this practice. When the story begins, we see a young girl wishing to change her reality but unsure how to go about it. Her journey to fulfill this quest begins by leaving home, an act of letting go of her old existence (and her old beliefs) and signaling the

Universe that she's ready for change. Even though she goes back not long after departing, her return summons forth the conditions that launch her into her conscious creation lesson.

Once in Oz, Dorothy sets herself upon the path of learning the magical approach. To get started, she follows the guidance offered by Glinda, a personification of our divine conscious creation collaborator, All That Is. She tells Dorothy to seek out the Wizard, a practitioner of the magical approach, and one who symbolically embodies the practice itself. She then departs for the Emerald City, following the Yellow Brick Road, a designated pathway that represents a defined line of probability, and she does so joyfully, informing the Universe of her enthusiastic intent.

With her journey under way, Dorothy first encounters a scarecrow in search of a brain, a symbol of the intellect, one of the key components of the magical approach. Later she meets a tin man looking for a heart, a symbol of feelings and emotions, qualities associated with the intuition, the technique's other core element. Next she meets the lion, the purported king of beasts who, ironically enough, seeks the courage that enables the conscious creation process to move forward. Her three companions are thus outward projections of qualities that make conscious creation and the magical approach work, serving as physically expressed, metaphorical symbols she can look to for inspiration in honing her conscious creation skills. Meanwhile, the Wicked Witch of the West pops up with periodic annoyances, a symbolic taskmaster to prod Dorothy into staying on track and carrying through with her lesson.

With all these representational conscious creation components assembled, Dorothy then arrives in Oz to meet the Wizard, who gives her a task to prove herself worthy, a symbolic test of whether she's learned the process and understands how to integrate all its elements successfully. As cold or unfeeling as this might seem, it's positively essential, for, in the end, it is Dorothy who will work the magic for herself, not the Wizard; the power of this process originates from within her, not from some outward projection of it, which is ostensibly all that the Wizard himself really is. Thus it's wise to make sure she knows how to put her new teachings to use. If Dorothy ever doubts the validity of any of this, she need only remember the advice of Glinda, who gently reminds her that she's had the power inside herself all along.

226 | GET THE PICTURE

In this sense, "The Wizard of Oz" is as much about recalling our own birthright as it is about learning the magical approach anew. This is sound advice to bear in mind, for, as we move forward into our own future, it is we who will solve the problems of our world, not some externalized extrapolation of our consciousness. We would serve ourselves well to learn from Dorothy's lesson and experience.

Dorothy's journey not only shows the attainment (or remembering) of this knowledge, but it also reflects the evolution of her beliefs and abilities over time. It presents her with a new means of approaching challenges, as well as a new way of perceiving, understanding, and appreciating the reality she creates for herself. This is significant for her (and us), for Dorothy's ultimate conscious creation goal, that of finding her way home, is merely a symbolic way of coming to understand and value the nature of her true self and her projected manifestation of it, a notion that, in its full fruition, Jane Roberts and Seth frequently refer to as "value fulfillment." It's an objective to which we all should hope to aspire.

The film is sheer genius when it comes to conveying these ideas for the screen. For example, the picture's masterful casting of performers playing dual roles is brilliant. This symbolically shows the intrinsic connection between our inner beliefs (and the elements that cause them to arise) and their outward material expression. In addition, it shows how Dorothy's external life in Kansas and her internal world of Oz mirror one another more than she might think if only she'd allow herself to see it that way, a message for us as much as it is for her. The performances are all top-notch, too, making the characters truly believable and eminently heartfelt.

Similarly, the use of black-and-white photography to portray Kansas and color photography to depict Oz is brilliant. It effectively contrasts the arguably commonplace nature of everyday life with the vivid richness of life's magical possibilities, the range of potential experiences that exist (and await activation) in the Oz-like character of our minds and imaginations. Its stunningly fanciful art direction and special effects (remarkable for the time the film was made) provide further enhancement of this distinction.

The movie won Oscars for its original score and its legendary original song, "Over the Rainbow."[2] It received four additional nominations in the areas of art direction, cinematography, and special effects, as well as for best picture (its failure to take home more awards likely resulting from the competition it faced that year from a little film called "Gone with the Wind"). It was also a Palme D'Or nominee at the Cannes Film Festival.

Working magic is not a talent reserved for "the gifted"; we all possess it. The challenge for us is to discover whether we have the confidence and courage to use it. But if you're not sure, take some time and follow your own Yellow Brick Road. You just might be pleasantly surprised at what you find down that enchanted path.

## Adopting a Fresh Perspective

### "Flirting with Disaster"
*Year of Release: 1996*
*Principal Cast: Ben Stiller, Patricia Arquette, Téa Leoni, Alan Alda,*
*Lily Tomlin, Mary Tyler Moore, George Segal, Josh Brolin, Richard*
*Jenkins, Celia Weston, Glenn Fitzgerald, David Patrick Kelly*
*Director: David O. Russell*
*Screenplay: David O. Russell*

Sometimes it's best to leave well enough alone. Tampering with success can spell trouble, especially when we've done a good job of creating. But no matter how obvious that may be, at times we just can't help ourselves. The temptation to tinker is so strong that we don't realize we're setting ourselves up for potential calamity. Yet walking the rim of tragedy has its benefits, too, for it often shows us just how good we've got it, providing us with a fresh perspective on the realities we've created. That's just what happens on a wild road trip in the edgy comedy, "Flirting with Disaster."

When Mel Coplin (Ben Stiller) gets an opportunity to meet his birth family, he jumps at the chance. Having been adopted as a baby, he believes it's important to connect with his blood relatives, to acquaint himself with his own roots. He's convinced that filling this long-empty blank in his life will provide him with the sense of biological continuity he's always sought, a particularly crucial concern for him now that he, too, has just become a new parent.

Noble though Mel's intention may be, however, his adoptive parents, Pearl (Mary Tyler Moore) and Ed (George Segal), a pair of prototypically neurotic Gothamites, aren't thrilled at the idea, envisioning utter disaster. Mel's wife Nancy (Patricia Arquette) is a bit reluctant, too, but she agrees to go along with his wishes if it's that important to him. So Mel and Nancy, along with his kooky case worker Tina (Téa Leoni), set out from New York for San Diego to meet Mel's birth mother, Valerie (Celia Weston).

Once on the road, it quickly becomes apparent that this trip will be anything but smooth sailing. With Murphy's Law in full force, unfortunate incidents abound. But the worst of it doesn't materialize until it's revealed that Tina hasn't adequately done her homework. Instead of finding his family in California, Mel learns they're in a small town near Battle Creek, Michigan. With that news, the hapless trio heads east in search of Mel's father, Fritz Boudreau (David Patrick Kelly).

Not surprisingly, Michigan doesn't pan out either (and given what Fritz is like, Mel should be grateful). More debacles ensue, one of which brings them into contact with a pair of ATF agents, Tony (Josh Brolin), an old high school friend of Nancy's, and Paul (Richard Jenkins), Tony's partner (in every sense of the word). The unexpected reunion rekindles Nancy and Tony's friendship, which slowly turns into a less-than-subtle flirtation when the avowed bisexual admits he once had something of a crush on Nancy, a confession that adds a hefty dose of sexual tension to the already-jumbled mix (and makes both Mel and Paul more than a little uneasy). At the same time, a torrid but decidedly dysfunctional attraction simmers between Mel and Tina, giving Nancy pause for justified concern as well.

After backtracking through her records again, Tina discovers that Mel's birth parents are actually living in New Mexico. So with that revelation, the trio sets off once more, but they've got company this time—their two new friends have opted to join them for an impromptu vacation. Before long, this eclectic quintet is on its way to meet the Schlichtings, Mary (Lily Tomlin) and Richard (Alan Alda), and their son Lonnie (Glenn Fitzgerald). But as zany as events have been up to this point, they pale by comparison to what transpires in the New Mexico desert. And when Pearl and Ed get drawn into the fray, the lunacy reaches a crescendo that causes the film truly to live up to its title.

So why would anyone in his right mind (and apparently happy with his life) create a fiasco like this? That's a good question, but, as I see it, sometimes we feel compelled to put our creations to the test, even if we're not always aware that we're doing so or why. I see a scenario like this being a sort of "metaphysical stress test," a means to determine whether the manifestation will hold up under pressure. If it doesn't, it's time to change beliefs and materialize anew. But if it does, it's clear that the creation is solid, one worth holding onto.

Mel does this throughout his cross-country journey. It's almost as if he's conducting one of those aforementioned metaphysical inventories, running down a checklist of the various creations in his life to see whether they (and the beliefs behind them) measure up. Taking it on the road to do so frees up his consciousness of everyday distractions so that he can focus on the process exclusively while simultaneously putting added stress on the items under scrutiny to test their resiliency. Pushing matters to the brink of peril may seem like a treacherous path to traverse, but it could also be the most effective way of determining the true vigor of the creations up for review. After all, the rewards of such an analysis—a fresh perspective, a renewed sense of appreciation, and a strengthened foundation—certainly make it well worthwhile in the end.

As a result of this adventure, we witness Mel—and his beliefs—evolve. Even though that journey may seem like it amounts to little more than a 360-degree spin, he doesn't end up in exactly the same place from whence he started, for going around the circle, even if only once, leaves him with a different viewpoint from when he began, no matter how much things might look the same on the surface. Now that's quite a feat—and some metaphysical road trip, too.

"Flirting with Disaster" didn't exactly set the box office ablaze when it was first released, but it seems to have found a welcome home for itself on cable TV, which is where I first stumbled upon it in my channel surfing. I'm glad I found it, too, for the movie is one of the funniest, laugh-out-loud pictures I've seen in years. At a time when many mainstream comedies have increasingly resorted to rampant silliness and tasteless fart jokes to get giggles, this one elicits laughs with wit and intelligence. It's smart even when it gets slapstickish. What's more, it does all this with a sustained rapid-fire pace, very much in the tradition of the screwball comedies of old.

The ensemble cast is excellent, particularly Moore, Tomlin, Leoni, Jenkins, Kelly, and Fitzgerald. It's also refreshing to see Stiller in a less manic role for a change, in many ways playing the straight man to the cast of crazies around him. Making it all work for them is the smart writing of director David O. Russell.

Putting our creations to the test might be an extreme way of appraising their qualities and valuing their merits. But sometimes that's also the best way to gauge their true strength and validity, to gain a new appreciation of them and, ultimately, to adopt a fresh perspective.

# The Ultimate Quest

"Indiana Jones and the Last Crusade"
Year of Release: 1989
Principal Cast: Harrison Ford, Sean Connery, Denholm Elliott,
Alison Doody, John Rhys-Davies, Julian Glover, River Phoenix,
Michael Byrne, Kevork Malikyan, Robert Eddison
Director: Steven Spielberg
Story: George Lucas, Menno Meyjes
Screenplay: Jeffrey Boam

Have you ever pursued a goal with the kind of fervor and devotion that made you feel like you were on a crusade? If so, have you ever asked yourself why you went after it with such dogged determination? Was it because you believed that achieving it would answer all your questions? Was it because you thought the satisfaction you'd derive would be akin to a lottery win? Or was it because you just got so used to it that you couldn't imagine doing anything else or, even worse, letting go of it? What's more, was it truly *your* dream that you were chasing in the first place, or was it someone else's that you inadvertently assumed or allowed to become your own? Those are some pretty heady questions, but they're among many examined in the action adventure, "Indiana Jones and the Last Crusade."

This picture might seem an unlikely vehicle for addressing such deep inquiries, but that's one of the aspects I cherished about it. This movie does much more than just take viewers on a nonstop thrill ride; it gives pause to think.

I've often thought of this picture as the "forgotten" film in the original Indiana Jones trilogy. To be sure, it generated a lot of buzz when it was first released, but I've seldom heard anyone mention it since then. Many a moviegoer definitely recalls the series' thoroughly entertaining first installment, "Raiders of the Lost Ark" (1981) (see chapter 1). They even seem to recollect its snoozy, forgettable second offering, "Indiana Jones and the Temple of Doom" (1984). But, in my opinion, this third episode is the one most worth remembering, for a lot of reasons.

The story line is fairly simple and straightforward. Archaeologist Dr. Indiana Jones (Harrison Ford) is contacted by Walter Donovan (Julian Glover), a wealthy businessman and ardent sponsor of archaeological expeditions. Donovan is particularly interested in the legends surrounding the Holy Grail, the chalice said to have held the blood of Jesus Christ at the Last Supper (revisionist interpretations of *The DaVinci Code* notwithstanding). He tells Indy that his latest expedition has made significant breakthroughs in the search for the Grail but that its leader has mysteriously gone missing. Donovan wants to recruit Indy to look for the disappeared scientist, an offer he initially declines. But Indy reconsiders when he learns that the archaeologist in question is his own father, Dr. Henry Jones (Sean Connery), a longtime Grail scholar. With the mission suddenly having become personal, Indy changes his mind and unhesitatingly signs on.

Indy's first task is to pick up the trail of his father's research, which leads him to Venice and one of Henry's peers, Dr. Elsa Schneider (Alison Doody). With the discoveries they make there, Indy and Elsa then launch into a search for the elder Dr. Jones in Austria, where they find him held captive in a castle by Indy's old foes from the first film, the Nazis. Unaware of what he's stepping into (in more ways than one), Indy improvises a plan to free his dad, a scheme that pits the father-and-son duo in a frenzied race with the Nazis across two continents to see who reaches the Grail first.

Supplementing the principal story line are a number of intriguing subplots, the most engaging of which involves an exploration of the tenuous bond between Indy and his father, raising issues not unlike those seen in one of this book's earlier offerings, "Big Fish" (see chapter 2). The relationship of the Joneses in this film is an uneasy one and had been even during Indy's upbringing, as shown in a flashback featuring him as an adolescent (River Phoenix). It seems that dad was more preoccupied with his Grail studies than he was with being an active and involved parent. This lack of paternal attention thus helped shape Indy's beliefs in three very significant ways. First, it obviously affected his choice of vocation; after all, what better way to get the old man's ear than to follow in his footsteps? But while Henry respected Indy as a peer, he never gave him the kind of attention as a parent that he so desperately craved, and this affected Indy in a second way, by fostering beliefs that set up an emotional chasm between the two of them. Most interestingly, however, the beliefs behind these first two developments combined to give rise to a third, one whose materialization had an even more profound influence on the junior Jones: Finding his long-lost father, metaphorically speaking, became his own personal Grail quest. Indy thus emulated his father by making him the objective of his own crusade. Given what beliefs Indy was working with, that's quite a captivating creation.

By the time this story takes place, Indy has become as embroiled in his father's mission as Henry himself is. But one has to wonder why Indy is doing that. Is it genuinely to help out dad? Is it one peer assisting another? Or is it yet another attempt for a son to win acceptance and approval? And, by becoming so involved, whose quest is Indy really pursuing—his own or his father's? Indeed, what beliefs are at work here?

The journey of Indy and Henry through life together shows not only the evolution of the beliefs driving their relationship but also the progression that takes place in the development of their individual beliefs (particularly Indy's). The flashback shows how the prevailing conditions of the past gave rise to beliefs at that time that carried forward as manifestations into the future. If one wants to see how the roots of one's conscious creation framework take shape, develop, and flower, this film provides as good an example as any I've seen.

As Indy and Henry embark on the latest segment of their odyssey together, we see their long-standing unresolved issues arise once more. The continued presence of these conflicts shows the continued focus of the characters' beliefs in this regard. The question for them now, however, is whether they will finally alter their outlooks and create the conditions necessary to achieve closure on these matters or whether they will defer resolution yet again. This is crucial, for whatever they decide will determine what destination next lies ahead on their path together.

A key concern in addressing the foregoing, for both Henry and Indy, is how tightly they should hold on to the quests they've each undertaken for themselves. At what point, for example, does a pursuit transmute into an obsession? What does that say about the nature of the underlying beliefs driving such a creation? And, if it genuinely has become an obsession, when is it time to finally let go? This concern, which ends up manifesting both literally and figuratively, is as applicable to Henry's search for the Grail as it is to Indy's search to find Henry, the two endeavors aptly and metaphorically mirroring one another.

There are no easy answers to questions like these, but there is something worth bearing in mind that may make them easier to cope with. The quest for a grail of any kind is not about finding some ultimate panacea that will solve all our problems or provide us with the secret to perpetual happiness so that we never have to concern ourselves with such matters again. It's about the path we take to seek it and what lessons we learn along the way. Eventually, one would hope, we might even be able to use what we've learned through these experiences to move past the goal of the quest itself, to transcend it, to seek ever-higher pursuits and purposes. This, however, means letting go (for real) of the belief that the objective being sought is or ever will be the be-all and end-all of the subject undertaking, a genuine leap of faith for many of us.

If we examine quests and obsessions in the context of the foregoing, the distinction should become apparent. If we focus our beliefs on the process, we're likely operating within the parameters of a quest. But if we blindly channel our beliefs only into the objective, without regard for any other costs or consequences involved (much as we do when we practice unconscious creation), we've probably launched ourselves down the path of obsession, and achieving the undertaking's stated goal likely won't live up to its expectations, for new problems may have sprung up in the course of its pursuit. As in any conscious creation scenario, the key, of course, lies in where our beliefs are directed. For the sake of the Drs. Jones, we as viewers can only hope they have the wisdom to recognize this as well.

None of this is meant to suggest that this movie is a plodding philosophical treatise, however; like its first predecessor, it's full of spills and chills from start to finish but with more substance tagging along for the ride. It's gorgeously filmed, too, especially in its location shots, such as those at the ancient city of Petra, Jordan. The character development is most definitely richer than either of the two earlier pictures, with the inclusion of Henry a most welcome addition (superbly played by Connery). The writing is also stronger, with a good deal of wit skillfully blended into the good humor that has characterized this series from the outset. The film captured one Oscar on three nominations and received one Golden Globe nod.

The road we travel in seeking what we believe to be fulfillment of the ultimate quest is an often beguiling, sometimes vexing one, replete with twists, turns, delights, and potholes, not to mention the unexpected. But it's the solutions we come up with for making our way down that road, and the beliefs we espouse in that process, that renders the journey so satisfying and potentially transformative, far more interesting or rewarding than any destination that might lie along or at the end of its path. If ever we lose sight of that, we need only remind ourselves that, in the end, it's the route of the matter that really counts.

# Paradise Found

### "Lost Horizon"
*Year of Release: 1937*
*Principal Cast: Ronald Colman, Jane Wyatt,*
*Edward Everett Horton, Thomas Mitchell, John Howard,*
*Isabel Jewell, H.B. Warner, Sam Jaffe, Margo*
*Director: Frank Capra*
*Book: James Hilton*
*Screenplay: Robert Riskin*

The search for paradise is a quest many have spent their entire lives pursuing. Finding the prize is often elusive, though, like trying to catch a fading dream upon awakening. So, in light of that, a question that naturally arises is, "Would we even recognize paradise when we've found it?" That's the weighty challenge put to the characters in the screen classic, "Lost Horizon."

Robert Conway (Ronald Colman), a high-profile British envoy to China, flees his post with a group of companions when a civil disturbance threatens their safety. Joining Conway are his brother George (John Howard), scholar Alexander "Lovey" Lovett (Edward Everett Horton), secretive businessman Henry Barnard (Thomas Mitchell), and a mysterious, terminally ill American woman, Gloria Stone (Isabel Jewell). The evacuees' itinerary calls for them to fly to Shanghai, where they will board a ship bound for England. However, while in transit, they find themselves hijacked—by their own pilot no less—and taken to the mountains of Tibet, where their plane crashes. With the aircraft a wreck and their pilot dead, all seems hopeless—that is, until the survivors are miraculously rescued by a mysterious stranger named Chang (H.B. Warner) and his band of porters. These unexpected Samaritans lead Conway and company through a narrow mountain pass to a protected valley where the land is lush and the weather beautiful, the utopia known as Shangri-la.

Needless to say, the new arrivals are perplexed by their fate and their surroundings. They have more than a few questions, too: How does an idyllic place like this exist in the midst of such harsh terrain? How do the residents survive being so cut off

236 | Get the Picture

from the outside world? And how did this remote place come
to have all the fineries and comforts of life beyond the mountains? What's more, the outsiders are somewhat suspicious of
the kindness and courtesy of the locals, believing they must have
some kind of ulterior motive behind those perpetually smiling
faces and ever-pleasant demeanors. Their fantastic tales about
Shangri-la and the joy of life there seem preposterous as well,
far too good to be true.

But the longer the survivors stay, the more at peace they begin
to feel. Gloria's health even shows improvement. Some begin to
think there may be something to this place after all. Still, they
have many unresolved questions, such as why they were brought
there against their will. And will they ever get to go home?

After a period of adjustment, these questions are gradually answered through meetings with Chang and with other
locals, particularly two Western women who also appear to
be Shangri-la transplants, Sondra (Jane Wyatt) and Maria
(Margo). Sondra and Maria befriend Robert and George,
respectively, but each has a different take on the land they
call home. Sondra loves her life in Shangri-la, while Maria
feels she's a prisoner of it, views that parallel the emerging
opinions that Robert and George hold of it as well. As Robert
grows increasingly comfortable with the charms of Shangri-la
(and of Sondra), George becomes ever more anxious about
wanting to leave (and to take Maria with him).

Sondra also confides to Robert that she was instrumental in
helping to bring him to Shangri-la. She had heard of his great
diplomatic accomplishments in the outside world and believed
that he could be of tremendous service to her community. Robert
wonders why, but those concerns aren't addressed until Chang
arranges a meeting with the aging spiritual leader of Shangri-la,
the High Lama (Sam Jaffe). It's at that point the truth behind
Robert's delivery unto paradise becomes revealed. The big question for him, of course, is whether he rises to the challenge posed
to him by this most unexpected of opportunities.

That question, I suppose, is one that we all must face as we
attempt to create paradise: Are we up to it once we find it? It
seems like we search for it for so long, but when we finally come
upon it, we can't help but ask ourselves if we're ready to give up

the quest. After all, as Jane Roberts and Seth are so fond of saying, we're all in a continual state of becoming, so wouldn't giving up the pursuit of utopia, a permutation of that larger undertaking, represent a betrayal of our own basic nature? Or does our entry into paradise simply mark the beginning of just another phase of what we've been doing all along but with circumstances and conditions different from what we've grown accustomed to? What's more, if we were to enter paradise willingly, how readily would we give up creating those things that we believe *aren't* inherent to it but that we have always assumed to be givens in our present realities, such as war, violence, strife, deceit, poverty, hunger, lack, conflict, and so on? Are we really ready for a world free of those attributes, or is it simply impossible for us to let go of them and envision an existence without them? Given the experiences of the characters in this film, the answers may not be as automatic as one might think. As becomes apparent, semi-conscious creation can be a stubbornly persistent beast at times.

"Lost Horizon" illustrates how individuals of different mindsets might approach such issues. Thus the journey aspect of this film involves not only the actual trip to Shangri-la but also the personal explorations of consciousness—soul-searching—that each individual embarks upon in evaluating whether he or she is ready for paradise. Through the course of the story, we witness the progression of the characters' beliefs about this from the time they set out on their adventure through their time spent in Shangri-la itself. Based on their individual odysseys, it becomes apparent that the evolution of their beliefs progresses at different speeds and unfolds on the basis of varying criteria of what actually constitutes utopia.

As we watch these individual evolutions play out, we simultaneously witness the progression of the collective beliefs that feed into the co-creation of paradise. Not surprisingly, those whose beliefs concur with the prevailing agreements regarding its nature embrace its manifestation, while those who don't buy into such beliefs quickly find themselves out of alignment with the emerging reality. The views of each individual figure prominently in their concurrence analyses and may even serve as deal breakers as far as whether someone is willing to sign on. Circumstances like this thus draw into focus questions about how steadfastly one might want to hold on to certain beliefs, especially when there's as much at stake as there is here. Finding paradise can be tricky business indeed.

Yet paradise, like the Holy Grail, is something many of us never cease searching for, and stories about its fabled charms will likely persist for as long as we exist as a species. Whether we're talking the Shangri-la of "Lost Horizon," the Shambhala of James Redfield's *The Secret of Shambhala*[3] or the Belovodia of Olga Kharitidi's *Entering the Circle*,[4] paradise is a concept that transcends cultures, occupying an exalted position within the mass consciousness. And even if we never find it, at least it gives us something to strive for; if we didn't have such a lofty goal to aspire to, I'd suspect we might rival amoebas when it comes to the development of consciousness.

"Lost Horizon" is, in my opinion, one of director Frank Capra's more overlooked films, overshadowed (especially in recent years) by more popular offerings, such as the perennial classic, "It's a Wonderful Life" (see chapter 11). It's also sometimes confused with a disastrous 1973 remake that attempted to turn the story into a Burt Bacharach musical. But it truly is a moving and entertaining movie to watch, with fine performances all around. It earned Academy Awards for film editing and for its positively superb art direction, as well as five additional nominations, including best picture and a best supporting actor nod for Warner.

Perhaps its most inspiring quality, however, is its supreme sense of optimism. This becomes most apparent in the scenes in which Robert meets with the Lama, who tells the newcomer, "You've always been a part of Shangri-la." To have such knowledge, that the possibility of paradise is always within each of us, provides us with a tremendous sense of hope, echoing the message of another famous teacher who similarly told his followers, "the kingdom of God is within you."[5] It also gives us pause to stop and ask ourselves why, if we already possess this capability, we're not using it. This is particularly critical to a world on the brink of unleashing powers capable of unspeakable atrocities and tremendous devastation—and those are the Lama's sentiments, quite prophetic for a movie made in 1937. Sadly, however, those sentiments are at times equally applicable even today.

For now, it would appear that paradise still awaits our discovery. But thanks to the inspiration provided by films like this, the search continues in earnest.

## The Next Frontier

"2001: A Space Odyssey"
*Year of Release: 1968*
*Principal Cast: Keir Dullea, Gary Lockwood,*
*William Sylvester, Douglas Rain*
*Director: Stanley Kubrick*
*Story: Arthur C. Clarke*
*Screenplay: Stanley Kubrick, Arthur C. Clarke*

"Who am I?" and "Where did I come from?" Those are questions that theologians, scientists, and even the exasperated parents of inquisitive youngsters have wrestled with for eons. But another question that's just as vital, yet doesn't get asked nearly as much, is, "Where are we going next?" The answer to that is as important to us as a species as it is to us as individuals. One film that attempts to provide some insight is the enigmatic sci-fi adventure, "2001: A Space Odyssey."

Even though we've long since passed the calendar year that's part of this movie's title, the picture itself is by no means outdated. In fact, in these days of shifting consciousness and changing paradigms, its message and mystique are perhaps more relevant than ever.

Although the film's title makes the picture sound like a movie about space, it has more to do with evolution than astronomy. Director Stanley Kubrick's cryptic yet poetic approach to the subject makes for a unique style of filmmaking, one that was decidedly way ahead of its time (and that baffled many viewers at the time of its original release).

In many ways, the plotline and characters are almost incidental to this picture. It's really everybody's story, that of the evolutionary journey of our species from the dawn of man to the time of our exploration of the heavens, first in our establishment of a base on the moon and then on a manned mission to Jupiter.

The common thread linking all these seemingly disparate events is the spontaneous and unexplained appearance of a mysterious black monolith. The exact nature of this rectangular structure is never explained, but each of its appearances is immediately followed by some kind of significant leap in knowledge that helps further the evolution of the species.

Impressive as the monolith's effects apparently are, however, one still can't help but wonder what it is. Is it All That Is coming to us in physical form? A projection of the mass consciousness that somehow prompts us to greater self-understanding? A construct of an alien intelligence guiding our species' progression toward ever-greater awareness? Or do none of these explanations suffice? And does it really matter what it is as long as forward movement results? All these questions are left ambiguously open, suggesting that perhaps the answers are bigger than our present level of comprehension is capable of assimilating but that each leap nevertheless takes us ever closer to discovering the truth.

The significance of this from the standpoint of conscious creation is that the flowering of our evolution is not unlike the constant state of becoming that Jane Roberts and Seth speak of. That's reflected in the narrative of the film, whose sequences are self-contained, with almost no story line elements or characters that overlap or recur, except, of course, for the monolith. The mysterious structure acts like a bridge, linking the sequences, and a catalyst, sparking into existence whatever follows next.

Given that, one might understandably wonder how the monolith itself figures into the conscious creation equation. That's difficult to answer, especially since its precise nature and function are never delineated. I can't speak to this from personal experience, either, for I've never seen a giant black rectangle appear before me when I've been on the verge of a eureka moment. However, given the conditions under which the monolith appears in the film, it always seems to show up when man has been on the brink of needing to make one of those major leaps in cognition. So if we're all conscious creators by nature, then one could speculate that the characters who are on those thresholds of evolutionary advances are the ones who summon forth the monolith (and whatever powers it holds or represents) to help facilitate these changes.

In many instances, the needs for advancement depicted in the movie are driven by survival considerations, so one could argue that the monolith is an abstract embodiment of the belief that "necessity is the mother of invention." Why these characters would feel compelled to manifest a physical symbol of this at all, let alone in the specific form depicted herein, is a bit of a mystery, but perhaps it's simply meant to be an outward reminder of our innate materialization capabilities, serving like the proverbial string tied around one's finger. But why an enigmatic black rectangle? Your guess is as good as mine. While a string around the finger might be eminently more manageable from a practicality standpoint, it would also make for far less engaging filmmaking.

Evolution is apparent in a number of ways in the film. It's most obvious in terms of our physical appearance, first as apes and later as Homo sapiens (and beyond). It's also present in our physical locations, first as earthbound primates and later as humans soaring toward the stars. It's even reflected in the complexity of our physical creations, progressing from crude levels to ever-increasing degrees of sophistication, in everything from our tools to the meals we consume. It might be tempting to assume that it's all possible thanks to a mysterious black rectangle, yet it's we who manifest the creations that result after its appearance. Maybe the monolith is doing nothing more than trying to remind us, like Glinda in "The Wizard of Oz," that we're the ones with the power to create the realities we experience. Armed with that knowledge, it's exciting to envision the possibilities for what comes next.

Kubrick was clearly at the top of his game with this masterpiece, and he earned one of the film's four Oscar nominations for his directorial work. It's more like watching a moving painting than a moving picture. The narrative unfolds before us slowly, like the pace of evolution itself, with its dazzling cinematography and spectacular Oscar-winning special effects shouldering much of the responsibility for telling the story. Backing all this is a classical-based soundtrack that features compositions as whimsical as the Johann Strauss waltz *On the Beautiful Blue Danube* and as inspiring as the introduction to Richard Strauss's *Also Sprach Zarathustra*, a fanfare that has become virtually synonymous with this movie.

"2001: A Space Odyssey" is, in many ways, the ultimate road trip film, showing us where we came from, where we're going, and who we've been all along the way. The one trait that links all the stops along that path is the sense of awakening that arises within each of us with our passage through each stage of the journey. It affirms, for me at least, the idea that, if you've liked what you've seen so far, wait till you see what's next. And that's something to look forward to.

**Author's Notebook:** Several years ago, I had the good fortune to view this picture as I believe it should be seen—on an IMAX® theater screen. The cinematography and special effects of this movie were unquestionably breathtaking when it was made, and they have held up amazingly well in the nearly four decades since then. But imagine seeing them projected onto a screen several stories tall, presenting them on a scale far grander than what was used for theatrical films at the time of its initial release. Add to that the multi-speaker sound system of the IMAX® theater set-up, and you have an amazing venue for viewing this picture. If ever you have the opportunity to see "2001" in a setting like this, clear your calendar—you won't want to miss it.

# Bonus Features

"Star Trek VI: The Undiscovered Country": The final voyage of the cast from the original *Star Trek* TV series details how the United Federation of Planets makes peace with its longtime foes, the Klingon Empire. The crew of the Starship Enterprise is charged with leading the initiative, an assignment assumed with great reluctance. Their mission leads them on a journey to many locales throughout the galaxy and, more important, to the far-flung corners of their souls. In the end, their quest marks the first step in an epic exploration of the vast expanse of the great unknown, the land of the "undiscovered country."[6] (1991; William Shatner, Leonard Nimoy, DeForest Kelley, James Doohan, Walter Koenig, Nichelle Nichols, George Takei, Kim Cattrall, Mark Lenard, Brock Peters, Christopher Plummer, Rosanna DeSoto, David Warner, Michael Dorn, Kurtwood Smith, Iman; Nicholas Meyer, director; Gene Roddenberry, TV series creator; Leonard Nimoy, Lawrence Konner, and Mark Rosenthal, story; Nicholas Meyer and Denny Martin Flinn, screenplay; two Oscar nominations)

"Into Me See": The saga of a couple's journey through life is not only the sum of their collective experiences but also of their individual tales, particularly in terms of how their relationship helped them become the people they are. That's the focus of this film, which features an intimate, though protracted, conversation between two former lovers who meet at a coffee house for the first time after many years apart (think "My Dinner with André" with lattes). Through their discussion, they explore the journey they took together and as individuals, both while in the relationship and after it dissolved, to see who each of them has become. The movie is admittedly a bit talky at times, but it's certainly revelatory for characters and viewers alike, providing a model for new ways of examining the value of relationships, even those that we think "fail." (2005; Nancy Rodriguez, Gregory Linington, James Twyman, Neale Donald Walsch; James Twyman, director and screenplay)

"Missing": Conservative American businessman Ed Horman travels to Chile when his nonconformist son Charles goes missing after the overthrow of Socialist President Salvador Allende in 1973, a coup staged by the Chilean military (and allegedly backed by the U.S. government). Suspecting that Charles must have done something wrong, Ed makes the trip somewhat reluctantly, like an annoyed parent bailing out a teenager in trouble. But once there, he soon discovers much more going on than he was aware of, much of it disillusioning, prompting him to rethink many of his values. Guiding Ed in his search is his free-spirited daughter-in-law Beth, whom, like the son he has been estranged from for so long, he barely knows. Together, this unlikely duo launches into a soul-searching journey that brings them closer to one another and helps Ed understand and appreciate the son whom he had given up on so long ago. A powerfully emotional fact-based saga. (1982; Jack Lemmon [Cannes Film Festival winner], Sissy Spacek, John Shea, Melanie Mayron, Charles Cioffi, Jerry Hardin, David Clennon, Richard Venture, Joe Regalbuto, Keith Szarabajka; Costa-Gavras, director; Thomas Hauser, book; Costa-Gavras and Donald Stewart, screenplay [Oscar winner]; one Oscar win on four nominations, five Golden Globe nominations; Palme D'Or and best actor award winner, Cannes Film Festival)

"Close Encounters of the Third Kind": After having a frightening, though compellingly intriguing, close encounter with a UFO, an Indiana power line worker embarks on an epic odyssey (including a perilous cross-country trip) that frequently defies logic and raises more questions than it answers. His relentless search for the truth, however, takes him on a grand journey to prepare him for an adventure even greater than he can possibly imagine. (1977; Richard Dreyfuss, Teri Garr, Melinda Dillon, Bob Balaban, François Truffaut, Cary Guffey; Steven Spielberg, director and screenplay; one Oscar win on eight nominations, special achievement Oscar winner for sound effects editing; four Golden Globe nominations)

"The Hitchhiker's Guide to the Galaxy": An earthman and his off-world sidekick gallivant across the galaxy as space-hopping hitchhikers when the Earth is inadvertently destroyed as part of a cosmic construction accident. Along the way, they address the big questions of life, making their journey as much a metaphysical odyssey as it is an out-of-this-world adventure. Frequent use of their spacecraft's "improbability drive" takes them to some unlikely places, too. Good fun with some supremely witty writing, even if a bit uneven and annoyingly over the top at times. (2005; Martin Freeman, Zooey Deschanel, Mos Def, Sam Rockwell, Anna Chancellor, Warwick Davis, Alan Rickman, Bill Nighy, John Malkovich, Stephen Fry [narrator]; Garth Jennings, director; Douglas Adams, book; Douglas Adams and Karey Kirkpatrick, screenplay)

"Black Robe": This gorgeously filmed saga set in 1630s Quebec follows a young French priest who is idealistic but dogmatic about his faith in his quest to bring his brand of salvation to the region's "savages." Guided by a band of Native Americans and a fellow countryman, he sets out on a journey to a distant Catholic mission to fulfill his task. Along the way, however, he learns the true meanings of Christ's teachings from those who, ironically enough, aren't themselves Christian, a lesson that ultimately enables him to better fulfill his own destiny. (1991; Lothaire Bluteau, Aden Young, Sandrine Holt, August Schellenberg, Tantoo Cardinal, Billy Two Rivers, Lawrence Bayne, Harrison Liu, Wesley Cote, Frank Wilson; Bruce Beresford, director; Brian Moore, book and screenplay)

# 8

---

# Connecting the Dots

## *How Everything Relates*
## *to Everything Else*

Our separation from each other is an optical illusion of
consciousness.

*Albert Einstein*

Like many other children, I was a huge fan of connect-the-dot
books when growing up. I was utterly fascinated to see what
completed images would result from simply drawing lines
between the little black numbered spots, watching the emerging
pictures slowly materialize into identifiable patterns out of their
abstract origins. It could be, unbeknownst to me at the time,
that my conscious creation training began right then and there.
But my chief lesson from this didn't have to do with watching
something manifesting out of nothing; it had to do with learning
how things connect.

Understanding the connectedness of all things is central to
grasping conscious creation's comprehensive nature. As noted in
the introduction to chapter 3, there's an implication in the statement "you create your own reality" that necessarily maintains
we each create the totality of our reality, not just portions of it.
And because of that, there's an intrinsic linkage thus binding
everything within it.

As reasonable as that may sound, such thinking actually
runs counter to the way many view the world. They tend to

246 | G<small>ET THE</small> P<small>ICTURE</small>

see it as a collection of individual components, distinct and apart from one another, the elements' only commonality being that they somehow just happen to be in physical proximity to one another. Many conscious creators probably saw the world that way, too, before becoming studied in the practice. But once one becomes more proficient in the art and witnesses firsthand how beliefs give birth to the complex interrelatedness of all things, one can't help but agree with Albert Einstein's contention, as noted before, that any semblance of separation is truly just an illusion.

If you're skeptical about this metaphysical explanation of connectedness, consider the idea from a purely scientific standpoint. If atoms are indeed the building blocks of all things, then there isn't anything that's not made of them; and, if they're continually bombarding, combining, and recombining with one another as they construct the physical framework of our world, then they and everything they comprise must be innately connected. What's more, studies in the field of quantum physics suggest that there even appears to be a sort of "cooperation" among elements at the subatomic level that's responsible for the emergence of particular patterns of correlated behavior, a phenomenon known as "entanglement," a condition that operates independently of seemingly immutable considerations, such as physical distance. (It would seem the atoms have a better handle on this than we do!)

So pick your basis of contention: Be it metaphysical or scientific, connectedness is an integral quality of reality. Whether we look at it through what happens at the subatomic level or in the realm of conscious creation principles, there's no getting around the fact that we, and everything surrounding us, are all in this together.

★　　★　　★

The opposite of connectedness, of course, is separation, which, lamentably, has characterized much of the prevailing worldview for the past several centuries. A wide range of beliefs has contributed to this, but those related to traditional science and mainstream religion have arguably played the most significant roles.

When it comes to science, there's little denying we've made fairly intelligent use of this discipline as a means of understanding the mechanics of our physical world and its individual components. But, in doing so, we have also allowed it to color our thinking to such a degree that many of us now view reality only in terms of its parts and not how they integrate with one another. Perhaps the most distressing aspect of this is that many have lost sight of how the most significant component of our world—us—relates to the rest of it. The result has been the steadily growing sense of separation, leaving many of us feeling lonely and isolated, cut off not only from other elements of our existence but also from our peers and, at times, even from our very selves.

Similarly, despite religion's cornerstone assertion that God is in all things, many of us have allowed its teachings to convince us that we've been purposely excluded from that divine essence, that we mere mortals are apart—even unworthy—of being connected to such holiness. Regardless of the intents behind these assertions (or our reasons for embracing them), the result of their proliferation has been to exacerbate the sense of separation we feel.

When you add to this all of the silly feuding that routinely goes on between science and religion, the distance between us and these means of understanding our world becomes even greater. It thus would seem we've been using our beliefs to formulate concepts and construct institutions specifically aimed at cutting ourselves off from everything. I can't help but wonder, "How did we get ourselves into this mess? And why?" Perhaps it was a roundabout way for us to appreciate the value of connectedness; maybe we had been taking it for granted and needed to manifest circumstances to remind ourselves of how important it really is by exposing us to the effects of its absence. Or maybe it was for reasons we have yet to discover. Either way, what do we do now?

As Einstein put it, "Science without religion is lame; religion without science is blind."[1] Attempts *are* being made at showing that science and spirituality, the primary doctrines responsible for explaining the function and fit of reality's various elements, aren't as far apart as they might seem, as illustrated by the films profiled in chapter 3. And those efforts are definitely commendable.

But since the pervasive sense of separation has done its greatest damage at the personal level, I believe it's essential to promote awareness of connectedness and its many benefits in ways that hit closest to home. Stories that address this topic in a highly personal, heartfelt way carry the most weight for getting these ideas across. They strengthen our awareness of connectedness and help melt away the icy sense of isolation that has persisted for so long. And that's what the films in this chapter are all about, stories that show the significance of the ties that bind us.

★     ★     ★

Appreciating the value of connectedness is important for several reasons. The most obvious is that it sheds light on the notion of consequences. The beliefs we hold and the manifestations that spring forth from them impact the realities into which they materialize, especially at their points of interconnection with other elements, the points where consequences arise. Such creations generally have the greatest influence on what's immediately around them. (That helps explain why, for example, residential neighborhoods are more likely to welcome parks and not landfills into their midst.) Sometimes, however, they have effect at a distance, suggesting that entanglement isn't something that occurs only at the subatomic level. (Who would have thought, for instance, that a storm like Hurricane Andrew, which hit south Florida in 1992, could put someone out of a job in Chicago? That was one of my creations, albeit a bizarre materialization at the time, but one that eventually paid off handsomely.) In fact, their impact can fan out in multiple directions, like a spider web, stretching into areas far flung from their origins. (Excellent examples of this can be seen in episodes of the TV series *Connections*,[2] hosted by science historian James Burke, who demonstrates how disparate inventions arose from common, connected roots, depending on the particular line of mechanical reasoning one follows.) Consequences thus unfailingly arise, regardless of source and proximity.

Being aware of the consequences that connectedness spawns is, in turn, significant for appreciating the role of responsibility in conscious creation. If we take a particular consequence and work backward from it, we can trace it first to the manifestation that gave rise to it and then to the creator whose beliefs brought it into being. If there's an issue to be resolved in connection (pun intended) with the consequence in question, we know where to look to find the responsible party. I would like to hope this gives us pause to think a little more carefully about our creations before bringing them into being, a step leading us toward what I'd call *conscientious creation.*

Were we to practice a more conscientious form of conscious creation, think of the benefits we could reap from improvements in such areas as compassion, empathy, the environment, peace, and so on, for once we genuinely realize we're all connected to, and not separate from, one another, would we really want to keep doing things to others and our surroundings that we wouldn't do to ourselves? (Seems like we've heard this before.)

With greater awareness of connectedness and the advent of more conscientious forms of creation come the possibility that we could intentionally choose to redirect more of our thoughts, energy, and beliefs into areas of endeavor other than those into which we've typically channeled them. The benefits to be enjoyed in such areas as beauty, the arts, and spirituality are potentially tremendous. But, most important, we would be our own greatest beneficiaries. It would enable us to become more effective creators, capable of producing significantly better creations. With our separation-induced anguish behind us, we could live happier, more fulfilling lives. We could become whole again, rejoining the human and cosmic families of which we've always been a part but from which we've felt estranged for so long, a truly holistic existence.

And to think all of this could emerge by simply investing a little more of ourselves into figuring out how to connect the dots. As metaphysical investments go, that's quite a bargain, one whose dividends are virtually incalculable.

# Lost, Lonely, and Oblivious

"Six Degrees of Separation"
*Year of Release: 1993*
*Principal Cast: Will Smith, Donald Sutherland, Stockard Channing,*
*Ian McKellan, Mary Beth Hurt, Bruce Davison, Richard Masur,*
*Anthony Michael Hall, Heather Graham, Eric Thal, Osgood Perkins,*
*Catherine Kellner, Anthony Rapp*
*Director: Fred Schepisi*
*Play: John Guare*
*Screenplay: John Guare*

In a world in which separation is taken as a given, it's easy to become accustomed, even oblivious, to the widening distance that grows between its ever-weakening, less-acknowledged connections. Moreover, when a lack of concern over the deterioration and loss of these bonds becomes the norm, the cries of those seeking to preserve them often go unheard. Some may even respond to those pleas with disdain, wrapping themselves up in cloaks of cynicism and seeing such earnest appeals as quaint, simplistic, or juvenile. But every once in a while, one of those cries squeaks through and captures the attention of a willing ear, someone who can make a difference in a world of indifference. Such is life in the reality of "Six Degrees of Separation."

The film, based on the play of the same name, derives its title from the idea that everyone on the planet is connected to each other such that no one is ever more than six relations away from everyone else. It's a notion that takes the somewhat nebulous concept of the global village and attempts to quantify it in a comprehensible way. In a reality in which connectedness is all but invisible, that's an almost heretical idea, but it's a concept that nevertheless tries to make its presence felt in the consciousness of a world largely populated by inattentive inhabitants (or at least in the awareness of anyone who'll listen).

Flan and Ouisa Kittredge (Donald Sutherland, Stockard Channing) are a successful, though somewhat dubious, pair of private art dealers. They relish the comforts of life on New York's Upper East Side. But in their sheltered world of privilege, they've also become detached from virtually everything around them. They can't remember how they came to know some of their friends, and they're largely unaware of the lives of their own children (Catherine Kellner, Osgood Perkins) and sometimes even of each other. They reduce their experiences to anecdotes that they share at smart social gatherings where everybody treats one another like commodities, sizing them up to determine of what value they might be. Oh, how very droll it all is.

However, that all changes one evening. As Flan and Ouisa prepare to dine out with their friend and prospective investor Geoffrey (Ian McKellen), a well-mannered young stranger named Paul (Will Smith), who claims to know the Kittredges' son, unexpectedly shows up at their door. He says he's been mugged and needs medical assistance. They unquestioningly take him in and immediately attend to his wounds. In caring for him, they find their unanticipated guest to be quite erudite and charming. Ouisa, Flan, and Geoffrey are thoroughly impressed with his knowledge of art and literature, as well as with the culinary prowess he displays in the dinner he prepares for them in thanks for their kindness. Ouisa is particularly beguiled, especially by his philosophical outlooks, many of which echo aspects of the magical approach. But most of all, they're starstruck by Paul's revelation that he's the son of actor/director Sidney Poitier, whom he says he's meeting in New York to assist in the making of a film version of the musical *Cats*, a project for which he says he'll be able to secure them roles as extras. The Kittredges in turn invite Paul to stay the night, partly because they like him and he has no place else to go, but mainly because his wit and charm were instrumental in helping them successfully close their business deal with Geoffrey.

By morning, however, it becomes apparent Paul is not who he says he is. In fact, it turns out he's an accomplished con man who has used his routine not only on the Kittredges but also on many other affluent Upper East Siders, including Flan and Ouisa's good friends Kitty and Larkin (Mary Beth Hurt, Bruce Davison). His claim of being Sidney Poitier's son also proves false when the quartet of amateur sleuths discovers, while reading a copy of the actor's biography, that he's the father of only daughters.

But, in virtually every instance in which Paul falsely ingratiates himself with his well-heeled hosts, he never steals anything or commits any other kind of criminal offense. So why the pretense? That's a puzzling question for all involved, but it's particularly troubling for Ouisa, who looks past the superficial aspects of his bizarre behavior and sees a young man in dire need of help, a concern that everyone else ignores, downplays, writes off, or reduces to an anecdote. Although Ouisa would certainly like an explanation for Paul's actions, she also realizes that it's ultimately irrelevant, that getting him the help he needs is what's most important. That consideration takes on added significance as Paul's exploits grow ever more disconcerting, particularly when he winds up in serious trouble with a couple of naïve young transplants from Utah (Eric Thal, Heather Graham). It's also a time when Ouisa starts distancing herself from her supposed kindred spirits, a step that leaves her, like Paul, in search of someone with whom she can meaningfully connect.

At its heart, the search for, and restoration of, connectedness are what this story is all about. Those points aren't always plainly apparent, but, considering that so many of the film's characters are caught up in removed, shallow, distraction-ridden realities, they're often oblivious to such matters anyway, and the movie simply reflects their remote worldview (credit director Fred Schepisi and playwright and script writer John Guare for not beating viewers over the head in depicting this). The story's central themes, however, should be obvious by Paul's behavior during his forays into the bluebloods' lives; if he genuinely has premeditated criminal acts in mind, then why does he never perpetrate any? What does he really want? Only Ouisa is capable of identifying what he craves, for she craves it, too, and that realization, which serves to divorce her from her coterie of supercilious cronies, connects her instead, strange as it may seem, to the mysterious young visitor (and he to her). They thus mutually create conditions to make that possible for each other. A bond, unconventional though it may be, is forged.

The aristocrats' reactions to Paul's visits are quite curious, too. Most are outraged and wish to press charges, but for what offense? Showing them how easily they can be fooled? How shallow they are for being so readily impressed by someone's alleged celebrity ties (connections that they never even bother to investigate)? How willing they are to let their guard down in exchange for something as inane as extras roles in a movie version of *Cats*? At the surface level, they're embarrassed that their supposed levels of sophistication could be so easily compromised. They're also appalled that their private information could be so readily discovered (all of which was revealed to Paul by a mutual friend of the children of those whom he purportedly victimized [Anthony Michael Hall]). But, on a deeper level, they're quietly mortified that they've been exposed for the self-centered, disconnected souls they truly are. Paul's polite but nevertheless in-your-face intrusions into their lives forces them to come to grips with their utter lack of real connectedness, an uncomfortable state of affairs for those who view themselves as supposedly so in touch and worldly. They obviously have much to learn, and their unlikely teacher's unexpected arrival makes that painfully apparent.

This is not to suggest Paul is a saint by any means. He has his share of issues, as the film gradually discloses. It's never revealed exactly how he lost his way, but given that at one time he had to resort to measures as drastic as becoming a street hustler to survive suggests a serious breakdown in all of his meaningful attachments, leaving him lost, lonely, and desperate. Little does he consciously realize, however, that his experience provides the foundation for a much-needed life lesson for many far removed from the kind of emotional circumstances with which he's intimately familiar.

None of this is meant to imply that the film is all heavy-handedness, either. It has a biting wit that runs throughout, particularly in its scathing depiction of New York's social elite. Its humor integrates well with the picture's dramatic elements, with neither aspect overpowering the other, thanks to Guare's faithful adaptation of his own play.

The performances are generally strong, too, especially Channing, who earned both Oscar and Golden Globe nominations for her role. Smith's portrayal of Paul is good, though not great, but since this was his first major dramatic part after doing TV sitcom work, it represented quite a leap for him (and gave him valuable experience that he applied toward the much stronger performances he has turned in ever since). Give kudos also to the work of Sutherland and the fine supporting cast.

"Six Degrees" is a sometimes raucous, sometimes disturbing film that uncompromisingly shows what can happen when something as essential as our basic sense of connectedness goes astray from our lives. It also illustrates how easily this can happen not only to those who've lost their grasp on it but also to those who think they still have it. It's at times like that when a slap in the face or a splash of cold water proves its worth in helping restore perspective. May we all hope such help is available to us when we need it.

# Of Dysfunction and Disentanglement

### "American Beauty"
*Year of Release: 1999*
*Principal Cast: Kevin Spacey, Annette Bening, Thora Birch, Wes Bentley,*
*Mena Suvari, Chris Cooper, Peter Gallagher, Allison Janney, Scott*
*Bakula, Sam Robards*
*Director: Sam Mendes*
*Screenplay: Alan Ball*

As noted in this chapter's introduction, quantum physicists have devoted increased attention to a phenomenon known as entanglement, in which elements at the subatomic level somehow harmonize with one another in ways that lead to various types of correlated behavior, regardless of such considerations as distance. No one's quite sure how or why this happens, but some of the more audacious researchers have quietly speculated there must be some unseen, intangible force—such as consciousness—that activates or assists in this process. If that's true, then our beliefs really are hard at work shaping reality, cajoling these elemental building blocks to combine and materialize the physical existence surrounding us. Thus when we interact with the reality around us, we, too, experience a kind of "entanglement" with our manifested world (arguably of a more metaphorical than scientific nature).

But what if we don't like what we've become entangled in? Sadly, many of us experience that far too frequently (though, one would hope, less often after becoming practiced conscious creators). A lesson in learning how to become disentangled—and re-entangled in more fulfilling ways—is the focus of one of the more unusual film releases of recent years, "American Beauty."

Lester Burnham (Kevin Spacey) hates his life and doesn't know what to do about it. This middle-aged sad sack detests his magazine editing job, feeling like a shameless corporate shill. His home life isn't much better, either. His wife Carolyn (Annette Bening), a materialistic, success-obsessed real estate agent, shows more interest in her living room furniture than she does in her husband. His daughter Jane (Thora Birch), a prematurely cynical, sometimes angst-ridden teenager, is embarrassed by her dad, seeing him as a pathetic loser. But, in spite of their own individual shortcomings, mother and daughter are agreed that the man of the house is irrelevant except for the paycheck he brings home. Poor Lester's beliefs have gotten him caught up in circumstances from which he sees no escape.

But then one night, our hero meets his new hero, a quietly charismatic figure who helps set Lester on the path of fleeing his imprisoning mediocrity. And just who is this Svengali-esque idol who gets Lester to turn his life around? It's Ricky Fitts (Wes Bentley), the eighteen-year-old who just moved in next door. Ricky is no ordinary teen, though; he's a supremely confident young man, the walking embodiment of self-assuredness. He's an enigmatic philosopher-poet who regularly chronicles his singular observations of the world through the lens of his video camera. He's also an enterprising dealer of designer pot who's got his rigid ex-military father Frank (Chris Cooper) completely buffaloed about where he gets all his money.

Inspired by the unrestrained way Ricky lives his life, Lester begins making changes in his own, first at work and then at home. He speaks his mind. He takes his power back. He breaks his old pattern of dissatisfying entanglement in favor of one more to his liking, one of his conscious choosing. Meanwhile, those around him, most notably Carolyn and Jane, are left to fend for themselves; Lester simply won't play their game anymore, so they'll have to search for others who will or try their hand at new sports. And, in their own ways, they gradually adjust, shaping new realities for themselves that they mostly find agreeable. Ricky's actions thus affect the entire Burnham family, directly or by extension, even if his influence is seemingly inadvertent and goes largely unrecognized by all involved (yet it's connectedness in action nonetheless).

Of course, the webs of attachment we weave for ourselves extend out far from us, and that's definitely the case here, as seen in the film's many subplots. No matter how divergent the various story strands might seem, there's no mistaking they're all part of the pattern of Lester's life. Although there are far too many plotlines to detail, some are quite intriguing, if not downright provocative, such as Lester's semi-lecherous obsession with Jane's flirtatious young friend Angela (Mena Suvari), a would-be model who quite clearly enjoys the attention of an older man; Carolyn's obsequious fawning over a rival real estate agent, Buddy Kane (Peter Gallagher), a relationship that, while supposedly just professional, has tawdry written all over it from the outset; and Ricky's quiet fascination with Jane, an involvement that leads to a most unconventional romance.

It's easy to see that relationships—perhaps the most fundamental form of connectedness—are a major theme of this movie. Even though the film focuses largely on dysfunctional associations, it actually explores interpersonal connections from many angles. Some, such as those between Lester and his family, are obviously out of balance. But even the dysfunction of their involvements pales in comparison to that of the relationship (if one can call it that) between Frank and his wife Barbara (Allison Janney), which is so skewed that Mrs. Fitts has withdrawn, becoming a virtual catatonic, rarely speaking and making only irrelevant comments when she does. (We never learn specifically why she has retreated, but given Frank's brutal, unyielding personality, it's easy to guess what may have prompted her response.)

Other relationships, such as those between Jane and Angela and between Jane and Ricky, function some of the time and not others, depending on what issues come up between them. And then there are those that are downright healthy, such as the one between Jim (Scott Bakula) and Jim (Sam Robards), the well-adjusted gay couple down the block, who have the most functional partnership in the film.

With so many degrees of functionality depicted here, it naturally leads one to wonder why some relationships work and others don't. If this film is any indication, however, it largely comes down to the compatibility of the characters' associations (or "entanglements") with one another in terms of goals and outlooks, indications that their underlying beliefs are on the same page. This explains, for example, the success of the relationship between Ricky and Lester, for even though they're just getting to know one another, they have mutual interests. Lesser degrees of compatibility result in less successful connections, as happens, for instance, in the involvement between Jane and Angela. And complete disconnects result in entanglements where the characters are contemptuous of each other, as happens in the rare but tense exchanges between Angela and Ricky.

Ultimately, the degree of compatibility achieved in almost any relationship depends on how well we each live out our value fulfillment (see chapter 7), for the more we succeed at this, the more energy and strength we bring into the connections we forge with others. And if both parties to a relationship thrive at this, the bond truly rocks. Ricky is by far the character most adept at this; he genuinely knows himself and truthfully lives his beliefs, comfortable in his own skin, no matter how much his aspirations and perspectives differ from those of others. This is why Lester is so drawn to him and why their connection is so strong; he shares in Ricky's value fulfillment and wants to find out how he can make it work for him, too.

This also accounts for why other involvements languish and decline. For instance, as Lester grows into his value fulfillment, he becomes ever more distanced from Carolyn, who seems unable to grasp the concept, let alone determine what it entails for her. She desperately turns to external means to feel her sense of personal power, like listening to affirmation-laced motivational tapes, but she merely mouths the words; she doesn't live them or feel them, for they don't genuinely reflect her inner values. So as Lester learns how to follow his bliss, his actions create an ever-widening gap between him and his wife, a sorry sight for a couple that apparently once had it all together.

Ricky's success in living his value fulfillment largely stems from his personal worldview, one that he alone possesses (even though his presence in the story is to help introduce, or reconnect, others to it). He sees the inherent connectedness of everything and the divine beauty that resides within it all, providing him with a sense that everything is as it should be and that, consequently, there is nothing to fear in anything. He knows that whatever he does is what he's supposed to be doing. In many ways, this is taking the heroism concepts explored in chapter 6 and putting them on steroids. By making fearlessness his mantra and living it accordingly, it's no surprise to see where his charisma comes from. Who wouldn't want to feel like that? At the very least, who wouldn't want to know someone like that? If he feels that connected to all that exists (and to All That Is), he must know something that those who lack it need to find out.

Adopting Ricky's philosophy is essentially how Lester becomes a changed man—and how any of us feeling a loss of personal power can do the same. It truly is possible to get it back, to reconnect with it. And even if the ecstasy of renewal is fleeting, the awe it inspires almost defies description. That's one of the main reasons I recommend this film so highly, for it shows how to restore what so many of us feel we've lost. Telling the story from Lester's perspective, I believe, is especially valuable to middle-aged men who have experienced this, particularly those who have undergone the stereotypical mid-life crisis, what I often see as a crisis of responsibility—the sense of feeling responsible to everyone but themselves. Lester and Ricky show how to turn that around.

"American Beauty" succeeds on virtually every level. Its performances are dynamite across the board, as are its writing, cinematography, and distinctive original score. It came up a huge winner in awards competitions, taking home five Oscars on eight nominations, including top honors for picture, director, original screenplay, cinematography, and Spacey's lead actor performance. The film also captured three Golden Globes on six nominations for best dramatic picture, director, and screenplay.

As conscious creators, it should be apparent that our entanglements don't arise by accident. We should also realize we're not stuck with them once they materialize, either; we can reconfigure them to suit our needs as we see fit. All it takes is the desire and courage to proceed, particularly if we picture ourselves, as Lester does in the midst of the quagmire he calls his life, as "an ordinary guy with nothing to lose." If that's not incentive enough to change, I don't know what is.

# A Lot To Swallow

"Hard Pill"
*Year of Release:* 2005
*Principal Cast:* Jonathan Slavin, Scotch Ellis Loring, Susan Slome, Mike
Begovich, Jennifer Elise Cox, Jason Bushman, Lisa Marie Basada,
Timothy Omundson, John Hartmann, Jessalyn Rizzi
*Director:* John Baumgartner
*Story:* John Baumgartner, K. Dayton Mesher
*Screenplay:* John Baumgartner

The web of relationships we weave with others is a fragile
configuration. Removing even one strand weakens the pattern
holding it together. Take away enough of them, and the whole
thing eventually falls apart, causing a collapse with sweeping
consequences for both the weaver and everyone connected to
it. That can be difficult to take, as the characters find out in the
imaginative what-if drama, "Hard Pill."

Anyone who believes that the gay lifestyle is a nonstop party
obviously hasn't met Tim (Jonathan Slavin). He's a nondescript-
looking thirty-something whose social life leaves much to be
desired. True, he has a few good friends, such as Joey (Scotch
Ellis Loring), his longtime buddy and co-worker, and Sally (Susan
Slome), his loyal, lonely, and longing fag hag neighbor and office
mate. But Tim's dating life consists of little more than occasional
trysts with Don (Mike Begovich), an alleged straight guy who
sneaks away from his girlfriend Tif (Lisa Marie Basada) for dis-
creet encounters. He also has a mild fascination with a sexually
ambiguous co-worker, Matt (Jason Bushman), but all hope for
that fades when Matt introduces Tim to Amber (Jessalyn Rizzi),
his girlfriend.

With his life in a rut and his prospects bleak, Tim decides to
pursue a radically different course. He learns that a pharmaceutical company is preparing to conduct clinical trials on an experimental drug designed to transform gays into straights. Feeling
he has nothing to lose, he decides to enroll in the program. Little
does he realize, however, that he'll be changing more than his
sexuality. What's more, he's completely unaware of how far the
ramifications of his decision will reach.

Tim's story in many ways is a case study on the implications of consequences. Although he's certainly not accountable for the realities his peers create for themselves, he does bear responsibility for what he manifests in his, including at least partially at the points where his reality intersects with theirs, a lesson he learns the hard way after undergoing treatment. For instance, when he's finally ready to try out his newfound sexual sea legs, he follows the path of least resistance, turning to the first woman who crosses his path, his gal pal Sally. However, both go into the experience with different expectations. For Tim, it's essentially a test drive at heterosexuality with someone familiar and comfortable, while for Sally it's an unrequited fantasy finally fulfilled. But, as pleasant as Tim finds the experience, he discovers that Sally's not exactly his type; having been socialized in the looks-conscious culture of gay society, he's slow to shed some old beliefs and concludes that Sally's sweet, bubbly personality isn't quite enough to compensate for her rotund physique. She quickly learns she can't compete, either, when Tanya (Jennifer Elise Cox), a perky, curvaceous blonde, enters Tim's life, a realization that sends Sally fleeing in search of the nearest available container of ice cream.

But the effects of Tim's new lifestyle choices don't stop there. They also affect his work life and his relationships, particularly with Joey and Don (and, by extension, Don's involvement with Tif). As these story lines play out, they also come back to haunt Tim in his relationship with Tanya. Indeed, connectedness carries wide-ranging consequences.

At the root of all these dilemmas, of course, is Tim's decision to disregard his value fulfillment and the impact this has on the various connections in his life. He's a gay man, plain and simple, and although he might not have enjoyed the kind of success at it that he'd hoped for, taking a route totally counter to his natural tendency proves equally dissatisfying. In fact, it makes things worse, for it completely disrupts the aspects of his life that he *has* successfully built. It negatively affects those he loves and cares for, the very people who are intimately connected to his network of worthy creations. This reiterates the importance of adhering to our value fulfillment, for failing to do so obviously touches others than just those from whom it springs forth.

Tim also buys into a false assumption that something external, like a pill, can change something about himself that arises from within. Although the pill may serve as an externalized reminder of the experiment in probability shifting that he's conducting on himself, it has no power of its own to fundamentally change who he is; that's a matter reserved for the beliefs he holds about himself, so even after supposedly completing treatment successfully, Tim is still left to come to grips with facing who he really is. Through this, he learns that being gay has to do with more than just sexuality or biochemistry; it's what characterizes him as a person—which leads us back again to the subject of his value fulfillment and all the attendant implications that carries, both for Tim and for those around him.

Naturally, the question arises of why Tim would draw circumstances like these to himself, but, as is the case with many other movies in this book, I believe it's another example of a self-induced test. It provides him an opportunity to examine the validity of his creations, the merits of his value fulfillment, and the strength of his connections (not to mention his commitment to all of them). This is certainly a difficult path for finding that out, without a doubt one of those proverbial hard pills to swallow, but if that's the only way he believes he can effectively assess what's transpiring in his life, then that's the course he must follow. One can only hope, for his sake and for that of those around him, that he sees the light.

"Hard Pill" is a surprisingly delicious nugget of a movie. It hasn't received much fanfare, playing primarily at gay film festivals and on the Logo cable network, but it is well worth viewing. Admittedly, there's nothing particularly fancy about it of a technical nature, but it's a compelling story, well told, well written, and well acted. It successfully avoids simplistic stereotypes and trite dialogue, giving us interesting, believable characters.

It's also refreshing to see a piece of gay cinema whose primary focus involves a topic other than coming out or AIDS. As noteworthy as those subjects are, they have been overworked. "Hard Pill" provides something new and fresh, particularly relevant in the wake of today's headlines about initiatives aimed at mainstreaming same-sex lifestyles and the backlash campaigns undertaken by those seeking to reverse the strides the gay community has made.

The fragility of the connections we build in life reminds me a lot of the party game Jenga, in which a tower of interlocking wooden blocks is assembled and players take turns removing them to see who'll ultimately bring it down. Our networks of relationships are like the pieces of that tower, inextricably linked to one another through delicate, complex connections we often fail to observe, understand, or appreciate fully. "Hard Pill" shows us the need to think about what we do before extracting any of those blocks, for even a seemingly harmless removal may have implications we can't begin to fathom—until it's too late.

## Double Feature: Seeking Engagement

### "Grand Canyon"
*Year of Release: 1991*
*Principal Cast: Danny Glover, Kevin Kline, Steve Martin,*
*Mary McDonnell, Mary-Louise Parker, Alfre Woodard,*
*Jeremy Sisto, Patrick Malone, Tina Lifford*
*Director: Lawrence Kasdan*
*Screenplay: Lawrence Kasdan, Meg Kasdan*

### "Crash"
*Year of Release: 2005*
*Principal Cast: Sandra Bullock, Don Cheadle, Matt Dillon, Michael*
*Peña, Brendan Fraser, Terrence Howard, Chris "Ludacris" Bridges,*
*Larenz Tate, Thandie Newton, Ryan Phillippe, Shaun Toub, Bahar*
*Soomekh, Jennifer Esposito, Tony Danza, Loretta Devine, William*
*Fichtner, Karina Arroyave, Bruce Kirby, Yomi Perry, Marina Sirtis, Greg*
*Joung Paik, Alexis Rhee, Ime N. Etuk, Beverly Todd*
*Director: Paul Haggis*
*Story: Paul Haggis*
*Screenplay: Paul Haggis, Bobby Moresco*

There must be something about L.A. The sprawling metropolis, with its endless freeways that link lots of places fundamentally disconnected from one another in every respect except geography, seems to breed a pervasive sense of isolation among its residents. That disconnection has given license to the rampant separation that keeps so many so apart from one another on so many different levels, be it economically, racially, socially, and, most important, emotionally. In many ways, the city has become a living metaphor for the worldview that has, for both Angelinos and others, unfortunately come to characterize the prevailing perception of reality.

Fortunately, however, Los Angeles is also the world's film capital, and its creative minds have drawn upon this separation theme as inspiration for some of the most emotionally involving pictures of the past two decades. They present stories of the search for engagement, the plea for reconnection, through movies with intertwining plotlines that focus on helping us rediscover our inherent connectedness. They thus present a worldview that is the polar opposite from what many hold of life in both the City of the Angels and the globe at large. Although many films of this genre have been released over the years, such as "Short Cuts" and "Magnolia" (see this chapter's Bonus Features), two of the best examples are "Grand Canyon" and "Crash."

In many regards, these two pictures are very similar. In fact, a friend of mine astutely described "Crash," the more recent release, as an extension of the themes initially explored in "Grand Canyon." Both employ interrelated story lines, and both delve into the frequently charged topic of race relations (more on this to follow), but, most important, they both heavily explore themes of connectedness (or the lack thereof) in human relations. The substance of both pictures could perhaps be best summed up by the opening lines of "Crash," wherein Detective Graham Waters (Don Cheadle), in response to a minor car accident in which he's just been involved, says of his hometown and its often-lonely residents, "It's the sense of touch . . . [In] any real city, you walk, you know? You brush past people, people bump into you. In L.A., nobody touches you, always behind this metal and glass. I think we miss that touch so much that we crash into each other, just so we can feel something."

"Grand Canyon," nevertheless, was the film that introduced viewers to stories of entanglement set in L.A. Mack (Kevin Kline), a successful immigration law attorney, is the pivotal character around whom the movie's various plotlines revolve. For instance, when his car breaks down in a seedy neighborhood and he runs afoul of a local street gang, Mack's shepherded out of harm's way before matters escalate by Simon (Danny Glover), a street-savvy savior in the guise of a tow truck driver. The two become fast friends afterward, prompting Mack to repay the favor, first by offering assistance to Simon's sister Deborah (Tina Lifford) and nephew Otis (Patrick Malone), and later by introducing Simon to a possible love interest, Jane (Alfre Woodard).

Love, however, is an area in which Mack has his own troubles. His marriage to Claire (Mary McDonnell) is teetering now that they're approaching the empty nest stage, their only child, Roberto (Jeremy Sisto), nearing college age. Mack deals with the distance opening up between them by having a fling with his secretary, Dee (Mary-Louise Parker), while Claire attempts to cope by lobbying Mack into adopting an abandoned baby. Meanwhile, they also have to contend with the fallout from the near-fatal shooting of their good friend Davis (Steve Martin), a producer of gratuitously violent action films who casually absolves himself of all responsibility for his work, believing his art merely portrays what's going on in the world at large, an irony that comes home to roost in a far too realistic way.

In all of the plotlines in "Grand Canyon," we see the connectedness theme primarily as it extends outward from one character. But in "Crash," the intertwining story line idea is taken to an entirely different level. The interactions of the characters overlap continuously, going beyond the bounds of mere synchronicity and presenting a mosaic of the connectedness that truly binds us all. The crisscrossing plots are far too numerous to detail, but they involve an eclectic array of characters, including:

* a racist patrol cop (Matt Dillon) and his idealistic young partner (Ryan Phillippe).

* a pair of carjackers, one who's in it for a living (Larenz Tate) and one who's in it to make a sociopolitical statement (Chris "Ludacris" Bridges).

* a well-intentioned yet pragmatic district attorney (Brendan Fraser) and his perpetually angry wife (Sandra Bullock).

* a detective (Cheadle) who struggles to find his place on a police force that's as much concerned with image as it is with justice.

★ a successful television director (Terrence Howard) and his wife (Thandie Newton), both of whom wrestle with issues of racial identity.

★ an embittered shopkeeper (Shaun Toub) seeking someone to blame for his many misfortunes.

★ a young locksmith (Michael Peña) doing all he can to provide a secure life for himself and his family.

★ a smuggler of illegal Asian immigrants (Greg Joung Paik) and his brash, argumentative wife (Alexis Rhee).

As diverse as these stories may sound, however, they all weave together and have one common thread—the characters' burning desire for connection.

The profound sense of separation felt by the characters in each film gives rise to related emotions that push them ever more toward connectedness as a means to ameliorate such distressed feelings. In "Grand Canyon," for instance, the characters frequently experience fear, of perpetually living on the brink of peril. To get by, many of the characters seek the comfort of one another and the sense of security that interpersonal connection often provides. But those who doubt the value of this coping mechanism, by approaching it with attitudes of cynicism or disbelief, experience a very different outcome in their search for solace.

In "Crash," the prevailing feelings are anger and frustration, again brought about by a lack of meaningful contact. Interaction—of any kind—is perceived as the antidote, a reminder to the characters of their own innate humanity, an awareness that they have largely lost or allowed to become obscured and that they desperately seek to regain by any means possible. Some succeed, some don't, again for reasons not unlike those cited earlier.

Of course, why the characters in these pictures would create circumstances like these is a question many of us are no doubt curious about. In my view, the answer hearkens back to this chapter's introduction—that these scenarios are meant to serve as reminders of the importance of connectedness, showing the characters (and us) its value by its absence. Detective Waters' opening statement in

"Crash" would itself appear to support this. Such creations speak to desperate measures by desperately lonely people who feel seriously out of touch with the world around them.

For those willing to put their faith in connectedness, rewards appear that confirm the merits of their beliefs. In "Grand Canyon," this manifests in the form of rescues and rescuers. No matter how implausible they seem or how unusual the forms they take, they always appear when needed, opportunely materializing to usher those in danger into the cradle of safety. In "Crash," where the stakes are often higher, the rewards are even greater, with affirmations of connectedness leading to such transformational gifts as forgiveness, salvation, and redemption. Considering the predicaments the characters in these films face, upholding one's belief in connectedness would seem to be well worthwhile, no matter how daunting that task might be.

Another aspect of connectedness that these pictures explore is our relationship to other sides of our being that we may not be aware of but that exist nevertheless, something that Jane Roberts and Seth often referred to as our "multidimensional selves." This is something that can manifest in myriad ways. In the extreme, for instance, it could be exemplified by the emergence of totally different personas (as was the case with the author and her channeled entity). It could also be looked upon as another way of understanding concepts like the archetype personality principles advanced by Swiss psychiatrist Carl Jung. But in more commonplace instances, such as those explored in these films, this concept most readily applies to sides of our own "localized" personalities that we're mostly unaware of until something happens to trigger their release.

Although this idea is somewhat apparent among the characters in "Grand Canyon," it's quite prevalent in "Crash." A self-avowed prick, for example, reveals his compassionate side in times of crisis, something that surprises both himself and those he assists. Similarly, an idealist must confront the fact that an ethical approach to life isn't license to put oneself above others (or the law). In yet other instances, victims may not be as innocent as they seem, regardless of how much they might protest to the contrary, unveiling aspects of themselves that they'd probably rather disregard. Such revelations are something many of us experience at some point in our lives, but no matter how they manifest, they're all further expressions of connectedness, our linkage to the previously unseen parts of ourselves.

As noted earlier, both films address the issue of race relations, a tense and delicate subject for many communities, but one for which Los Angeles has often been a lightning rod. "Grand Canyon" was released at a time of spiraling street gang violence, and "Crash" came in the wake of such high-profile, racially charged events as the Rodney King incident, the L.A. riots, and the O.J. Simpson trial verdict. Although these movies deal with this subject in a frank and thought-provoking manner, I must admit that I was somewhat disappointed to see film critics tout these pictures primarily as studies in race relations. To be sure, this is an important element in both films (especially "Crash"), but focusing on that aspect to the exclusion of their other attributes sells these movies short. They have much to say about many things; categorizing them along single-issue lines does a great disservice to them and everything they're about.

Both pictures are excellent at what they do, but "Crash" is the stronger of the two films. What I liked so much about it is that the movie took chances—big ones, too, with bold incidents that had my heart in my throat on multiple occasions. I went into the theater not expecting much but was blown away by it, particularly in its writing, its Mark Isham musical score, and its superb ensemble cast, especially Dillon, Bullock, Howard, Newton, Bridges, Peña, and Toub. It won three Oscars, for best picture, original screenplay, and editing, on six nominations, including a supporting actor nod for Dillon. It also received two Golden Globe nominations.

As a pioneering effort in this genre, "Grand Canyon" may be overshadowed by its progeny, but it was definitely innovative for its time and still holds up well today. It, too, features an excellent ensemble cast, with a surprisingly strong serious performance by Martin (it would be interesting to see him do more such work). Solid writing earned the picture both Oscar and Golden Globe nominations. The film's excellent editing, cinematography, and James Newton Howard score complement the package well.

It's regrettable that we often feel the need to go to great extremes to bond with one another. Fortunately, we have films like these to show us what we can reap by taking the chance to reach out and connect. And no matter where we hail from, be it L.A., the Grand Canyon, or someplace far afield from everything, that's a lesson from which we can all benefit.

# Ripples in a Global Pond

"Pay It Forward"
*Year of Release: 2000*
*Principal Cast: Kevin Spacey, Helen Hunt, Haley Joel Osment,*
*Jay Mohr, James Caviezel, Jon Bon Jovi, Angie Dickinson,*
*David Ramsey, Gary Werntz, Kathleen Wilhoite, Colleen Flynn*
*Director: Mimi Leder*
*Book: Catherine Ryan Hyde*
*Screenplay: Leslie Dixon*

Small gestures carry tremendous power. Just as Jane Roberts and Seth noted that there's enough energy in an emotion to send a rocket to the moon (see chapter 4),[3] there's a comparable degree of might in an act of kindness, a helping hand, even a simple compliment or word of encouragement. Now imagine what's possible if we all engaged in intentional acts of mutual support. The ripple effect of such interactions would stretch across the world, strengthening the bonds among us and reminding us that we're one globally connected human family. A model for how we might pursue this is the subject of the uplifting drama, "Pay It Forward."

The first day of seventh grade is an interesting one for Trevor McKinney (Haley Joel Osment), a bright, sensitive, impressionable young man. He's particularly captivated by his social studies instructor, Eugene Simonet (Kevin Spacey), an articulate educator who teaches his subject by establishing the relevance of it in his students' lives, thereby providing context for the material. And to add personal meaning to it, he gives his class a year-long assignment—to come up with innovative suggestions on how they could change the world of which they're a part.

Trevor takes the assignment to heart and creates a plan that's a real original. He proposes that each person help three others with something they can't accomplish on their own. Anyone who successfully receives the necessary assistance must then help three more people in need of aid, who must in turn do the same, and so on in an endless chain of permutations that eventually encompasses virtually everyone on the planet. Trevor calls his plan "pay it forward," an altruistic concept of doing for others that purposely runs counter to socially ingrained expectations based on the more familiar notion of "pay it back." (What pearls of wisdom emanate from the mouths of babes.)

To launch his own efforts, Trevor invites a homeless man, Jerry (James Caviezal), to stay in the family garage, which he does without telling his mother, Arlene (Helen Hunt), who, needless to say, is not thrilled at the idea. Besides the disruption of having a stranger at home, she has a full plate to manage as a single mother who's working two jobs, battling the bottle, and trying to exorcise memories of abuse inflicted by her estranged husband Ricky (Jon Bon Jovi). When she learns Trevor extended the invitation to Jerry as part of his class project, she's livid, marching off to school to confront Eugene. But, as someone who's accustomed to dealing with rowdy students, Mr. Simonet has a relatively easy time quelling an angry parent. In fact, he's even able to garner some sympathy from the initially irate Mrs. McKinney; as a burn victim who's self-conscious about his appearance, Eugene tries nobly to cover the psychological wounds that accompany his facial scars, but he has difficulty concealing them when he comes face to face with someone who's carrying scars of her own. A connection is made, and a bond begins to form, a development that gives Trevor the inspiration he needs to decide who his other two pay it forward projects will be.

Meanwhile, word of the pay it forward movement somehow finds its way into the outside world, eventually wending its way to Chris Chandler (Jay Mohr), an intrepid reporter who decides it would make a good story. He's genuinely puzzled by this phenomenon of supreme selflessness, especially when he becomes a direct beneficiary of it. When his car is totaled while covering a story, a wealthy lawyer (Gary Werntz), who just happens to be on the scene at the time, gives Chris his Jaguar, claiming that he doesn't need it and that, by presenting it to him, he's fulfilling one of his pay it forward obligations. Chris thus begins researching the story to trace it back to its source, a mystery that brings him into contact with a wily inmate (David Ramsey) and an elderly homeless alcoholic (Angie Dickinson), both of whom become pay it forward projects of his own. But the biggest surprise of his investigation is far more astonishing than anything he could have possibly imagined.

The connectedness theme of this film is fairly self-evident. What I find particularly intriguing, though, is how directly the link between it and conscious creation is presented. There's nothing at all ambiguous about it, either in the way it's discussed amongst characters or in the manner in which the concept is imparted to viewers. On the first day of school, for instance, after Eugene explains the nature of the ongoing assignment, he closes by rhetorically asking his students, "The realm of possibility exists where?" to which he unhesitatingly adds, "Inside each of you." The notion is handled so matter of factly that it's treated as a given, with the information passed along to those on the screen and those in the audience as if to say, "There's no need to belabor this stuff; you already know it."

I must say I was pleasantly surprised to see a movie treat a subject like this with such unassuming directness. But if that weren't amazing enough, I was even more astounded to see that it was presented in a junior high school classroom setting. I couldn't help but imagine how great it would be if real junior high school classes taught material like this. Think of how many years of struggle those students could avoid later on in life by learning this material at an age when they're still impressionable, receptive, and (one would hope) free of much of the psychological, scientific, religious, and metaphysical clutter that accumulates through years of indoctrination into dogmatic belief systems peddled by out-of-touch mainstream institutions. (There's a mass creation I'd certainly be willing to buy into.)

But even more important than the conscious creation teachings being passed along are the lessons in values being taught. Teachings about the world's sacred connectedness and the unquestioned merits of assisting all those who are part of that connection go a long way toward putting us on sound footing for developing a new appreciation of—and a new paradigm for—our world and ourselves. That's where this film genuinely excels; I only wish there were more like it.[4]

"Pay It Forward" is an inspiring story, nicely presented and a joy to watch. Spacey and Osment are terrific, both individually and together, as are Mohr, Ramsey, and Dickinson. Hunt is adequate, though I believe she may have been miscast for this role; she comes across as having it all a little too well together for someone whose character is attempting to struggle with as many challenges as she does, stretching believability somewhat. The writing, score, and technical attributes are all generally solid as well, though the pacing is at times a bit uneven, especially in telling the reporter's part of the story, dragging in a few spots where some judicious snipping would have helped tidy up things a bit.

Generosity as currency is a novel concept, one that has great appeal and enormous potential, for it gives back to those who spend it far more than what they initially expend. It makes even the most generous rebate program appear paltry by comparison. But the outlay is worth it, for anything that strengthens the whole strengthens all its parts, and in a world of interconnected components, like the one to which we belong, that means we all wind up gaining in the end.

## Bonus Features

"Wetherby": A small English town full of lonely and disconnected people who have become isolated and disillusioned through various forms of disappointment are shocked into emotional reconnection and re-engagement with the world when a mysterious stranger unexpectedly commits suicide in their midst. This unlikely catalyst forces a community of perpetually stiff upper lips to quiver in ways that they haven't in years, proving that they're still human. A potent, heartrending drama about sad people seeking meaning. (1985; Vanessa Redgrave, Ian Holm, Judi Dench, Stuart Wilson, Tim McInnerny, Suzanna Hamilton, Tom Wilkinson, Marjorie Yates, Penny Downie, Joely Richardson, Katy Behean, Robert Hines; David Hare, director and screenplay)

"21 Grams": A heart transplant patient, an embittered young widow, and a born-again ex-con are among the unlikely participants in a complex entanglement of love, remorse, and revenge. Told out of chronological sequence, the story shows how connections arise and consequences spin out of them in ways we often don't expect until we find ourselves in the middle of them. (2003; Sean Penn, Naomi Watts, Benicio Del Toro, Charlotte Gainsbourg, Melissa Leo, Danny Huston; Alejandro González Iñárritu, director; Guillermo Arriaga, screenplay; two Oscar nominations)

"Magnolia": A network of diverse, interconnected lives, all ultimately linked to a dying television producer, is pushed to its limits by the strain of oppressive stagnation and repressed secrets. With the lives of those in the pattern at the breaking point, old connections falter and new ones emerge amidst a rain of frogs. A quirky mixture of bizarre humor and edgy, surreal drama. (1999; Julianne Moore, William H. Macy, John C. Reilly, Tom Cruise [Golden Globe winner], Philip Baker Hall, Philip Seymour Hoffman, Jason Robards, Alfred Molina, Melora Walters, Melinda Dillon, Michael Bowen, Jeremy Blackman, April Grace, Luis Guzman, Ricky Jay, Henry Gibson, Felicity Huffman, Michael Murphy, Emmanuel L. Johnson; Paul Thomas Anderson, director and screenplay; three Oscar nominations, one Golden Globe win on two nominations)

"Short Cuts": Slices of life, and how they connect to one another in ways both great and small, provide the focus for this amalgamation of overlapping plotlines in modern-day L.A. Based on a collection of short stories, this concoction of eccentric humor, heartrending drama, and rare characterizations brings together more than twenty players in a series of interwoven tales exploring points of connection—and disconnection—in life. A bit uneven at times, but brilliant when on target. (1993; Andie MacDowell, Bruce Davison, Jack Lemmon, Julianne Moore, Matthew Modine, Anne Archer, Fred Ward, Jennifer Jason Leigh, Chris Penn, Lili Taylor, Robert Downey Jr., Madeleine Stowe, Tim Robbins, Lily Tomlin, Tom Waits, Frances McDormand, Peter Gallagher, Lyle Lovett, Buck Henry, Huey Lewis, Zane Cassidy, Lori Singer, Annie Ross; Robert Altman, director; Raymond Carver, source writings; Robert Altman and Frank Barhydt, screenplay; one Oscar nomination; one Golden Globe nomination, special Golden Globe Award for best ensemble cast)

# 9

# Exceeding Our Grasp

## How To Stretch Our Personal Capabilities

Reality leaves a lot to the imagination.
*John Lennon*

At some point in our lives, most of us go beyond what we thought we were capable of. We surpass our perceived limitations, moving into fresh territory for exploration. But how does that happen? Why are we suddenly able to exceed our grasp and extend our reach? As with all other aspects of conscious creation, the answer is simple: It's because we believe we can.

But how do new beliefs like this arise seemingly out of the blue? What brings about such changes? Although the answers to these questions vary from individual to individual, it's mainly because we're able to envision possibilities we once couldn't. By browsing through the range of probabilities—including ones we might not previously have been aware of or able to conceive—we stretch our capabilities, setting foot into new realms of experience. Skydiving suddenly ranks as the favorite pastime of someone once afraid of heights. A culinary flair emerges in a bachelor previously convinced he couldn't boil water. A confirmed disbeliever of divinatory powers becomes an expert in palmistry. In cases like these, we open up our imagination, which, as former Beatle John Lennon suggested, makes much more possible in the realities we manifest.

The ramifications of this are mind-boggling. Innumerable conceptions suddenly come off the drawing board of potentiality and spring into materialization. Far-flung ideas and flights of fancy have the capacity to be made physical. Creations never before imagined take shape as bona fide elements of reality.

However, belief changes like this not only affect what we manifest; they also affect our manifestation capabilities. Enhancements to our personal repertoires of conscious creation skills are very useful, particularly for overcoming supposedly insurmountable obstacles. We thus have the potential to accomplish seemingly daunting feats simply by granting ourselves access to (and by giving ourselves permission to believe in) abilities we'd never imagined or only dreamt about. Some basic examples are improved intellectual and intuitive faculties. Other, more advanced capabilities include telepathy, clairvoyance, precognition, telekinesis, the healing arts, the manipulation of matter or time, access to our multidimensional selves (see chapter 8), contact with other realities (see chapter 10), and whatever else our consciousness can envision. In fact, the possibilities are limitless except for the belief-based hindrances we place before ourselves. Indeed, all it takes is getting out of our own way.

*   *   *

So if the benefits afforded by these sorts of alternate beliefs are so great, why don't we make wider use of them? As German philosopher Arthur Schopenhauer wrote, "Everyone takes the limits of his own vision for the limits of the world."[1] Whether this happens as a result of our own belief formation or as a consequence of how we allow the limiting beliefs of others (that is, skeptics) to imprint on us, this observation, pessimistic though it is, helps explain why many of us fail to explore the other possibilities available to us. When we concentrate our focus on limiting beliefs, we come to see them (and their associated implications) as fixed, unchangeable absolutes—that is, until someone has the courage and conviction to question them by putting his or her faith in alternate notions. New ideas are thus born, taking root and challenging the supposedly intrinsic nature of their predecessors.

Some prevailing beliefs may vanish almost immediately, but others take time to dissolve. As new ideas emerge, they may encounter the kind of opposition that French philosopher and essayist Michel de Montaigne observed when he wrote, "All actions beyond ordinary limits are subject to a sinister interpretation."[2] Many of us simply don't trust new beliefs, because they don't fit our worldview, they haven't been tried out, or they just flat-out make us uncomfortable, hastening a retreat into ignorance and close-mindedness. (I guess this shows we still have a long way to go . . . )

Yet maverick beliefs have their own validity and vitality, even if these qualities aren't appreciated when new ideas are initially proposed. For example, as author, scientist, and psychic researcher Maureen Caudill said in a recent Internet radio interview, just because the technology doesn't exist to measure or assess a particular phenomenon doesn't mean the phenomenon itself doesn't exist, citing electricity as an example.[3] Dismissing beliefs in such phenomena out of hand, due to a mere inability to quantify them, is willfully foolhardy, the epitome of blind denial. In fact, being open to new ideas could prove essential for addressing certain thorny issues, such as the development of suitable measurement or remediation technologies, as physicist Albert Einstein noted when he said, "We can't solve problems by using the same kind of thinking we used when we created them."[4]

★　　★　　★

Opening the mind isn't always easy, but having sources of inspiration to draw from, even if only as starting points, can be immeasurably beneficial, and movies are frequently some of the best sources of this (particularly those in the science fiction genre). The imaginativeness that went into creating their story lines is itself often enough to get us thinking in new directions, prompting us to come up with the means to solve problems and challenges in unthought-of ways.

By the same token, movies have also done their share to preserve the status quo, even to dissuade the pursuit of new courses of thought. Many pictures depicting the aforementioned capabilities, for instance, have shown them in a negative light, portraying these skills as dangerous or evil, as evidenced by films like Brian De Palma's "Carrie" (1976) and "The Fury" (1978) and, to a certain degree, M. Night Shyamalan's wildly popular "The Sixth Sense" (1999). In my view, such movies do us a grave disservice, for they teach us to be scared of inherent parts of ourselves. Although it's arguable that these pictures do serve a purpose as cautionary tales for educating viewers about the healthy respect these abilities deserve, they also overstate the case, almost completely disregarding the prospective benefits they afford.

Thankfully, a number of films have been released in recent years to counter this trend, presenting these qualities in a positive, favorable light, and those movies are the focus of this chapter. They show us the possibility of who we can become and how we can use our innate (if latent) gifts and imagination to tackle the challenges we face, as well as how not to be afraid of such abilities. Now *that's* inspiration!

We'd be wise to learn from the messages of these pictures. After all, we've got a lot riding on it—even reality itself.

## Afterlife Lessons in the Art of Living

"What Dreams May Come"
*Year of Release: 1998*
*Principal Cast: Robin Williams, Cuba Gooding Jr., Annabella Sciorra, Max von Sydow, Jessica Brooks Grant, Josh Paddock, Rosalind Chao*
*Director: Vincent Ward*
*Book: Richard Matheson*
*Screenplay: Ronald Bass*

How ironic it is that "sometimes when you lose, you win." Strange as that may sound, the act of giving something up—even life itself—can pay off in ways beyond imagination. That's the prospect awaiting the protagonists in the afterlife fantasy, "What Dreams May Come."

Chris Nielsen (Robin Williams) believes he leads a charmed existence. He's a successful doctor happily married to Annie

(Annabella Sciorra), a gifted painter, and he's the father of two great kids, Marie (Jessica Brooks Grant) and Ian (Josh Paddock). Life is good. But that all vanishes in an instant one day, when Marie and Ian are killed in a tragic car accident. In the aftermath of this loss, Annie withdraws into her despair, leaving Chris virtually alone, an act that only serves to compound his sadness. He does his best to cope, and eventually he coaxes Annie to re-engage with the world. Life starts to improve once again, but those renewed hopes are mercilessly dashed four years later, when Chris is himself killed in an accident. Annie is left alone, widowed, childless, and devastated. But for Chris, an entirely new chapter is just beginning.

Having departed the earthly realm, Chris finds himself in the afterlife. He's initially confused by the transition, but fortunately he has guides (Cuba Gooding Jr., Rosalind Chao, Max von Sydow) to help him adjust to his new reality. First and foremost, he learns that he's now in a place where thoughts almost immediately become things, where "you create your own reality" is taken to an entirely new level. In the process of learning these metaphysical lessons, he also discovers previously unknown things about himself, qualities that are part of his consciousness that were present in his recently departed incarnation and that are still with him now. He sees how these traits helped shape the life just completed. They also show him how events and themes from his life are now being mirrored back to him in the afterlife (and how his conception of the afterlife was foreshadowed while still in physical existence). He thus discovers that he was employing the same manifestation abilities then as he is now, even if he wasn't conscious of them before; he created his own reality in life just as he does now in death, only now he's aware of it. The big question for him, though, is what he will do with this newfound knowledge.

As Chris adapts to life after death, the thoughts that burn most intensely in his mind center on Annie, his soul mate. He misses her terribly, and it's painful for him to witness the profound sorrow she's experiencing now that she's alone. He's also saddened that she mistakenly blames herself for her loved ones' deaths; she believes those tragedies could have been prevented if she had only made different decisions than the ones she did at the time. Chris believes he needs to use his new abilities to help make things right with her, a plan that subsequently unfolds with many unexpected twists and turns on both sides of the wall between the worlds.

I must admit that my reasons for liking this film have little to do with its story and much to do with its metaphysics (and how they're brought to life for the screen). In many ways, the plot is little more than a somewhat sappy afterlife romance centered on the reunification of separated soul mates, not unlike those that have been done before (and better). However, I don't believe I've ever seen a picture that explains and depicts the rudiments of conscious creation as eloquently as this one does. What's more, it's a tremendous source of inspiration for illustrating how much we can stretch our abilities in that area, achieving results far surpassing anything we might have thought possible.

The picture unreservedly contends that existence in the afterlife is based on the notion of "you create your own reality." The first guide Chris encounters (Gooding) states this unequivocally, presenting it as a given. But to show how a reality that operates on this basis works, the film employs a highly imaginative approach—by portraying Chris's world as an interactive painting. The reality he creates with his thoughts emerges like an image that appears from laying down brushstrokes on a blank canvas. As his thoughts change, so, too, does the world around him, and his creation manifests so quickly that, when he goes to touch any of its elements, they're still wet, rubbing off on him like freshly applied paint.

This approach to explaining the mechanics and outcomes of conscious creation is quite clever. It reminds me very much of concepts espoused by writers like Julia Cameron and Natalie Goldberg, who show how tapping into this metaphysical mindset leads to the creation of art. In such works as Cameron's *The Artist's Way*[5] and Goldberg's *Wild Mind*,[6] readers see how intangible intents transform into tangible results. That connection is similarly demonstrated in this film, only it takes matters a step further—using the thought-driven creation of art as a metaphor for the thought-driven creation of reality. Existence becomes its own canvas, with thoughts and beliefs providing the brushstrokes.

If Chris is using his manifestation abilities in a much more literal way than he ever did before, it's because he does so with a much greater awareness of them than he's ever had. His spectacularly enhanced results speak to that added clarity as well. The ease with which he accomplishes all this is quite inspiring, not only for those flapping their conscious creation wings for the first time but also for seasoned practitioners anxious to augment their abilities and achieve more.

The specific approach Chris uses to create his reality, unconventional though it may seem, is actually not that surprising, because in life he was a lover of painting and even married an artist. He thus draws upon something he already knows, a means familiar to him based on knowledge and beliefs he has carried forth with him from life into the afterlife. By depicting Chris's afterlife experience in such a way, we're shown that death is merely an extension of life, like simply stepping through a door from one reality into the next. Granted, the new reality operates with some very different ground rules, but its existence nevertheless lets us see that it's all just part of the continued journey of our souls, a rather comforting thought to those wary of what happens after making the big leap. Indeed, as Jane Roberts and Seth wrote, "Your existence . . . after death is as much a normal phenomenon as your present life."[7] That sentiment is echoed by Chris's initial guide, who reassures him that his spirit, his consciousness, still exists, even after death, telling him, "You didn't [disappear]; you only died."

With all that said, however, I must add a few significant qualifiers. Although I heartily applaud the film's exploration of conscious creation principles, I must admit being somewhat troubled by the story's implication that one needs to die to develop these kinds of manifestation capabilities. The picture leaves the general impression that they're inherent to the afterlife. However, in my experience, as well as that of many of my kindred spirits, practicing conscious creation isn't dependent on dying, and, in that regard, I believe the narrative is a bit misleading. I wouldn't at all be surprised to discover that these skills are greatly fortified on the other side (though that's not to suggest that can't happen here, either), but I don't believe it's mandatory to pass over to experience them (unless, of course, one's beliefs prohibit that possibility in physical existence).

I'm also somewhat disappointed that, despite the film's breakthrough presentation of conscious creation as a defining quality of the afterlife, the picture still relies on some rather traditional imagery in portraying the next world, most notably in its almost trite conceptions of heaven and, especially, hell. To its credit, the movie includes some highly unconventional (and visually stunning) renditions of the afterlife, too, but its incorporation of these tired images dilutes the impact of its innovations. It may make good theater, but it also makes for an unimaginative depiction of the core principle it seeks to illustrate.

Finally, the script leans toward presenting Chris's story—and the beliefs forming the foundation of it—as absolutes of the afterlife. Fortunately, Chris has the presence of mind to realize that, in a reality in which there are essentially no rules except those we determine for ourselves, any semblance of circumstances being fixed is simply a result of whatever beliefs we're projecting. And, to his credit (and that of the script), he openly challenges assertions to the contrary. However, I don't believe these objections are raised strongly enough; the afterlife's open-ended character, a quality that supposedly defines what that reality is all about, doesn't always receive the support in the writing that it deserves. I believe these notions could have been argued more convincingly by reminding viewers that Chris's story is Chris's experience, that the beliefs underlying this particular afterlife narrative are his; others going into the afterlife would have their own particular beliefs and, therefore, their own particular experiences.

These shortcomings aside, however, I must reiterate how impressed I was with the way in which core conscious creation principles are explained, which, for me, is reason enough for watching this film. In addition to its depiction of the principles previously discussed, I was quite taken with the ways in which life and the afterlife are presented as mirrors of one another. This parallels the conscious creation notion that the physical world is an outward projection of beliefs we hold in the inner worlds of our consciousness. Admittedly, the analogy isn't an exact one, but it comes very close illustrating this principle.

Another aspect I found fascinating is the picture's examination of the physical packaging of consciousness, how the bodies we assume are corporeal metaphors of our beliefs. In the afterlife, we visually become who we think we are. (We do this in physical existence, too, though we're much less aware of it.) Understanding the value of this is significant, for it encourages us to look past the superficial masks we perceive and project, to see and appreciate what truly lies beneath, the beliefs and intents that give rise to such appearances.

So what should we take away from this picture? If nothing else, "What Dreams May Come" reaffirms the basic principles of the manifestation process, providing beautiful examples of how they work. It also shows we have talents far in excess of what we think we're capable of, that we can stretch our limits much further than we thought possible. Grasping these basics is important, not only for the rudimentary information they impart but also for the metaphysical foundations they provide for comprehending the specific conscious creation capabilities explored elsewhere in this chapter. As for the picture's afterlife aspects, I wouldn't totally discount them, but I also wouldn't make them my main reason for viewing the film. We'll all get to that exalted destination soon enough, but, in the meantime, there's plenty to live for in the here and now of physical reality. This film provides important insights into some of the materialization techniques we can use to make the most of life until then.

By far, the film's visuals are its greatest strength, some of the most dazzling special effects eye candy I've ever seen. (Try to watch this picture on a big screen if at all possible.) It received a much-deserved Oscar in this area, as well as a well-earned nomination for its inventive art direction. The performances are all capable, but those of Sciorra and the three guides stand out the most.

We can never guess what gains will come from the experiences we draw to ourselves until after we've gone through them. We may unwittingly end up winners just when we've thought we've lost it all. And sometimes it takes learning that basic lesson to show us how we can push ourselves to wind up victorious all the time. This picture illustrates that for us, providing valuable lessons into how we can shape the experiences of what dreams may come.

# Seeing the Light

"Phenomenon"
Year of Release: 1996
Principal Cast: John Travolta, Kyra Sedgwick, Forest Whitaker,
Robert Duvall, Jeffrey DeMunn, Richard Kiley, Brent Spiner,
Elisabeth Nunziato, David Gallagher, Ashley Buccille
Director: Jon Turteltaub
Screenplay: Gerald Di Pego

Do we really know all that we're capable of? Researchers estimate, for instance, that we're using a mere fraction of our brain power, a consideration that doesn't even take into account the much wider powers of the mind. With so much untapped potential, then, it's no wonder we're constantly making new discoveries about our capabilities, learning things about ourselves we never knew before. Revelations of this type have been disclosed at an ever-quickening pace in recent years, too. But imagine what it would be like if we were to find a whole range of new abilities unleashed within us, all at once, literally overnight. If we could picture that, then we'd be able to appreciate the experience of an everyman-turned-prodigy in the science fiction fantasy, "Phenomenon."

George Malley (John Travolta) is a simple man. He leads a quiet life in a small northern California town, working as a mechanic, helping his friends, and trying to win the affections of Lace (Kyra Sedgwick), a recently arrived single mother of two (David Gallagher, Ashley Buccille). But one night, upon leaving a birthday party thrown in his honor, George looks up in the sky and sees the light—literally: a brilliant burst of illumination that knocks him off his feet. It's not entirely clear what George sees, but its effects become apparent almost immediately: He spontaneously develops a wide range of new abilities, including greatly enhanced cognitive powers, accelerated learning capabilities, clairvoyance, telekinesis, and heightened sensory skills. Suddenly, he's no longer the average Joe everyone has always known; he has become a walking phenomenon.

George's new abilities are somewhat disorienting initially, but after a period of adjustment, he takes to them just fine. He periodically encounters some challenges (mostly in terms of how others react to him), but he eventually learns to use his new talents for the things that matter most in life, particularly helping others. For instance, he teaches his best buddy Nate (Forest Whitaker), a bachelor and perpetual slob, how to speak basic Portuguese (a language George learned in a single textbook reading) so that he can communicate with his new housekeeper (Elisabeth Nunziato), a recently arrived immigrant. It's a lesson that ends up getting Nate more than a clean house.

Of course, there are those who are suspicious of George, unsure of what his true intentions are. Those are attitudes held mostly by people who don't know him, such as government agents. George takes their scrutiny in stride, confident that he can outsmart the best of them at any turn, as a befuddled inquisitor (Brent Spiner) finds out all too quickly. What genuinely upsets George, however, is when he comes under suspicion by those he cares about, the towns-folk who have known him for years. He becomes distraught and frustrated, allowing his emotions to get the better of him and letting capabilities surface that he'd probably rather have left alone.

To allay the public's fears, George decides to appear at a community book fair to speak with those who have concerns. But when the crowd becomes unruly, George is overwhelmed. He sees the light once again and passes out, landing him in the hospital, where his good friend and lifelong physician (Robert Duvall) informs George of what's really going on—and what he might want to do before it's too late.

"Phenomenon" is an excellent exploration of what we as humans are capable of. It lays out the range of abilities in survey fashion, showing how we can employ uncommon skills in com-monplace applications, such as those of everyday life. Indeed, once George embraces his newfound talents, he treats them matter of factly, as if he's had them all his life. He sees these capabilities as perfectly natural, like a birthright. However, recognizing that most of us have not as yet tapped into them, he's also pragmatic enough to state that he sees what's happened to him as representing the *possibility* of what we all could become. None of this, of course, should come as any great surprise to practitioners of conscious creation, for as Jane Roberts and Seth wrote in *The Magical Approach*, "evidence of clairvoyance, telepathy, or whatever, are not eccentric, isolated instances occurring in man's experience, but are representative of natural patterns of everyday behavior that become invisible in your world because of the official picture of behavior and reality."[8] (If only we could let go of those limitations . . . )

It's also refreshing to see a film portraying a character who'd rather use his powers for constructive purposes than for petty endeavors, such as personal vendettas. George takes great pleasure, for example, in using his increased sensory skills to help a geology professor (Jeffrey DeMunn) become more adept at earthquake prediction, an eminently worthwhile pursuit in a seismically active region like northern California. Moreover, when George witnesses what yields the "darker" side of his gifts can reap, he retreats from it immediately. He's aware of the power he's harnessed, and he has the good sense not to misuse it.

One might wonder why someone who suddenly possesses such sweeping new abilities would use them primarily to help others and not for self-serving purposes. (That's a pretty phenomenal notion in itself!) However, being of service to others is something that had always been part of his nature; as a simple man, though, he lacked the capabilities to be as effective as he could be, so to fulfill these aims better, he manifests new ones to enable him to perform better, even if he did so unconsciously. And once these abilities are in his grasp, he takes the ball and runs with it, living out his value fulfillment with the means to maximize his potential. That he would choose to use his powers in this way is, perhaps, the most inspiring and most important lesson we can take away from this film.

This picture provides an excellent overview of what's humanly possible, despite what many would dismiss or disbelieve, and it presents these possibilities through a credible, enjoyable story, well written and skillfully directed. Travolta gives a fine performance as a man of many talents, keeping his character real and successfully avoiding even the slightest hint of superiority or sensationalism. The movie also features a terrific soundtrack with cuts from the likes of Peter Gabriel, Bryan Ferry, Aaron Neville, and Jewel, as well as its fitting signature song, "Change the World," performed by Eric Clapton.

It would truly be something if we as a species could all see the light as George does. The doors that would open for us, and the world that it would make possible, are almost beyond imagination. But considering the rewards at stake, it's certainly something to strive for, something at which I'd be willing to take my best shot.

**Extra Credits:** Those looking for another cinematic exploration into human potential should consider the motion picture "Powder." Cut roughly from the same cloth as "Phenomenon," this film tells the story of a sensitive, psychically powerful young albino (Sean Patrick Flanery) who has spent years in seclusion in his family's basement. When circumstances arise that require him to emerge from isolation, he's thrust into a world that's as mysterious to him as he is to those who occupy it. Gifted with amazing intelligence, tremendous capacities for healing, and an ability to harness vast amounts of energy, he seeks to find his way in this new reality. He looks to create an existence for himself in which he can be of service to others in numerous ways, including everything from helping the infirm pass on to gently but pointedly showing the close-minded the folly of their prejudices. As entertaining and enlightening as "Powder" is, though, it doesn't quite measure up to "Phenomenon," mainly because it's less focused, more a movie of moments than a movie with a solid story. However, the picture does portray extraordinary human abilities with a sense of wonder, rather than with a sense of horror, and any film accomplishing that merits attention in my book. (1995; Sean Patrick Flanery, Mary Steenburgen, Lance Henriksen, Jeff Goldblum, Brandon Smith, Susan Tyrrell, Missy Crider, Bradford Tatum, Danette McMahon; Victor Salva, director and screenplay)

## Double Feature: Filling in the Gaps

### "Gattaca"
*Year of Release: 1997*
*Principal Cast: Ethan Hawke, Uma Thurman, Jude Law,*
*Alan Arkin, Gore Vidal, Xander Berkeley, Ernest Borgnine,*
*Tony Shalhoub, Loren Dean*
*Director: Andrew Niccol*
*Screenplay: Andrew Niccol*

### "Memento"
*Year of Release: 2000*
*.Principal Cast: Guy Pearce, Carrie-Anne Moss, Joe Pantoliano,*
*Mark Boone Junior, Jorja Fox, Stephen Tobolowsky, Harriet Sansom*
*Harris, Callum Keith Rennie, Kimberly Campbell, Larry Holden*
*Director: Christopher Nolan*
*Story: Jonathan Nolan*
*Screenplay: Christopher Nolan*

Life doesn't always seem complete. Gaps sometimes exist that cause hindrance and frustration, keeping us (or so we believe) from fully appreciating and enjoying the experience. But such voids can also be tests of our abilities—and our resolve—to make our lives (and us) whole. Explorations into using conscious creation to fill in the missing pieces in our lives are the focus of two very different but thoroughly engaging films, "Gattaca" and "Memento."

"Gattaca" tells the story of a fictitious society of the near future in which genetics is everything. Advanced prenatal screening techniques, for example, help weed out all that's considered genetically undesirable, from health defects to antisocial behavior. But every so often, for reasons inexplicable, parents shun this sophisticated technology and seek to conceive their children in the old-fashioned way, allowing the apparent randomness of nature to take its course. Such is how Vincent Freeman (Ethan Hawke) is born.

Being born genetically inferior into a world dominated by genetic perfection, however, carries a great stigma. Although the rights of those of lesser stock are supposedly safeguarded by laws against "genoism," as Vincent explains in a voice-over narration, there are ways around such protections in a world in which "we now have discrimination down to a science." For example, the probabilities of predisposition to certain unfavorable health conditions, which are determined immediately after birth, function like permanent markers of one's personal character. An individual's genetic makeup thus carries much weight in determining opportunities in everything from educational options to career paths to social standing. Those with good, "valid," properly modified genes obviously fare better than those without, a circumstance that has given rise to a stigmatized subclass of social inferiors condescendingly called "*in*valids."

Vincent, however, will have nothing of this. Despite his supposedly inferior pedigree, he believes he's just as capable of worthy accomplishments as those who think themselves superior, and he's anxious to prove it. Having been fascinated by space exploration ever since childhood, he longs to travel to the stars, participating in the program operated out of the Gattaca research facility. Considering his genetic record, that prospect is highly unlikely, but Vincent believes anything is possible. His solution is to pass himself off as someone else, using the borrowed genetic record of a paralyzed athlete, Jerome Morrow (Jude Law). Since his accident, Jerome has been treated with about as much civility as that shown to the average invalid. But he also realizes there's still value to be had in the viability of his genetic record, and so he agrees to trade on that commodity through an identity broker (Tony Shalhoub), who arranges a deal between Jerome and Vincent. Vincent buys himself a new genetic identity, a "borrowed ladder" as it's called, becoming part of a much-despised social class known as "de-gene-erates."

Before long, with his new identity in place, Vincent is enrolled in the Gattaca program, training for an upcoming mission to the Saturnian moon, Titan. His impersonation is so convincing that virtually no one suspects he's an imposter. But that all gets thrown into question one day when a grisly murder takes place at the facility, causing everyone to come under heightened scrutiny. Various types of genetic screening are conducted repeatedly on Gattaca's entire staff in hopes of narrowing the pool of suspects. Vincent is innocent, but with a pervasive police presence at the site, led by an aggressive detective (Alan Arkin) and his tireless superior (Loren Dean), he feels mounting pressure that his true identity will be revealed. The ante is upped further when a coolly thorough Gattaca cadet, Irene Cassini (Uma Thurman), is charged with assisting the investigators, all of which forces Vincent to improvise even more to keep his secret concealed (and to keep his dream alive).

In contrast to "Gattaca," which explores a character's attempts at compensating for gaps in his physical makeup, "Memento" presents us with a protagonist striving to achieve something comparable with his mental state. Leonard (Guy Pearce) is a man attempting to live his life in the wake of personal devastation. In addition to coping with the brutal rape and murder of his wife (Jorja Fox), he struggles to get by with the loss of his short-term memory, a consequence of the mental trauma he experienced over his wife's death. He remembers his life up until the time of that incident, but, sadly, the last new memory he recalls is his wife dying.

Having lost so much, Leonard's hell-bent on exacting revenge. In fact, he's so determined that, when the police probe runs cold, he launches his own inquiry. Unfortunately, because he's lost his short-term memory, he never remembers from one day to the next what information he uncovers. To make up for this, he draws upon skills he once used in his career as an insurance claims investigator, taking copious shorthand notes and incessantly snapping Polaroid photos to document his findings. He also frequently references his experiences with a claim investigation involving a short-term memory loss victim (Stephen Tobolowsky) to give himself direction on how to proceed. And when something seemingly very important is revealed, he takes the radical step of having the information tattooed on his body so he won't risk losing it. But even with all these clues at his disposal, he has trouble sorting things out because he fails to put any of the evidence into sequence. With no time context involved, it's all just a big jumble of miscellaneous notes, observations, and pictures, some of which contradict each other.

There are those who appear to want to help Leonard, most notably a bartender (Carrie-Anne Moss), a gregarious stranger (Joe Pantoliano), and the front desk clerk of the hotel where he's staying (Mark Boone Junior). But it also becomes apparent that, because they know of Leonard's condition, they may be manipulating him, without his awareness, to fulfill their own agendas. The red herrings they toss his way make it that much more difficult for him to sort out the truth. But when he finally does, it involves revelations that surprise even him about what happened—and, more important, what has been happening ever since.

As different as these two films are, they have a common thread from a conscious creation standpoint: They show how the characters stretch their manifestation abilities in very practical ways to compensate for perceived deficiencies in their physical or mental states. They employ these skills to overcome what are seen as insurmountable odds, drawing upon the power of their beliefs to take them places they theoretically shouldn't be able to go, at least according to the conventional wisdom. To be sure, their methods and accomplishments may not be as flashy as those portrayed in other movies dealing with capability expansion, but the tactics used and the outcomes sought are just as belief-driven as the techniques employed and results pursued in pictures with more flamboyant characters, story lines, and special effects. In fact, because these elements are purposely not as glitzy, they could conceivably be seen as more credible by the average viewer, more typical of how everyday folks would use their abilities in daily life. This points out how integral conscious creation is to the practice of living, even if it's portrayed in a more understated way here than it is in other films.

In pursuing their respective undertakings, the protagonists draw to themselves forces that could be interpreted as potential enemies or as potential allies, both of which, ironically enough, are ultimately present to help them realize their goals. These elements primarily take the form of other characters, though sometimes they manifest as a presence whose existence is merely alluded to instead of achieving full-fledged materialization (but whose impact is felt nonetheless).

In both pictures, for example, there are frequent references to elements that function in enforcement capacities. These forces appear to be at odds with the characters, but they essentially serve as conscience symbols, taskmaster projections from the protagonists' consciousnesses that less than subtly remind them to stay vigilant in attaining their goals. These elements are primarily hinted at in "Memento," but they're overt and ubiquitous in "Gattaca." The dogged detective and his diligent superior officer are the most obvious embodiments, but Irene plays a similar role, yet another enforcer looking to zero in on the guilty party. Vincent successfully staves off any threat she poses to exposing him while she interacts with him in a purely professional capacity, but when she becomes his romantic interest, entering his world in a much more intimate way, hiding from her becomes much more difficult for him (ironic, too, considering his anxiety has nothing to do with the crime being investigated). With increased pressure now being squarely placed on him, Vincent must work even harder at maintaining his façade as Jerome. But that's also to his benefit, for it reinforces his resolve to keep focused on what he's seeking to accomplish.

Balancing the impact of these so-called enemies is the influence of the allies. In "Memento," Leonard appears to have his share of them, but their support is often lost on him, because he can't remember when or how they last helped him and whether he should trust them. However, this puzzling manifestation, ironically, helps Leonard in significant ways that he's not even aware of. Managing available aid is much less of an issue for Vincent in "Gattaca," for he draws many supporters to his corner. Jerome's assistance is obvious, as is that of the Gattaca flight director (Gore Vidal). But there are less noticeable sources of assistance as well, ones that Vincent is unaware are working on his behalf, such as the facility's physician (Xander Berkeley).

Both pictures are real treats to watch. They each have an edge-of-the-seat quality about them that keeps viewers riveted. Their story lines are compelling, for they present characters at the fringes of society using conscious creation just as a means to keep pace with everyday life, something to which their peers apparently never give a second thought. Their valiant struggles to create to get by are inspiring indeed.

"Gattaca" is a very stylish picture, presenting a look that has sometimes been called "future noir," a hybrid of the film noir and sci-fi genres. It also effectively combines two distinct types of stories, a crime drama and a work of science fiction. As odd as that all might initially sound, the diverse qualities work together well to create a unique moviegoing experience. The film earned an Oscar nomination for its distinctive art direction and a Golden Globe nod for its moving original score.

"Memento" is equally stylish, though in a different way. The story is told through a cleverly edited mix of what appear to be flashbacks and current actions, allowing events to unfold on the screen in much the same way as they do in Leonard's mind. Viewers can never be entirely sure exactly what is occurring when, at least until the story plays itself out, though valuable clues are supplied by alternating color and black-and-white footage and by dramatic sequence-ending cuts in the narrative, providing a semblance of order to the events. These inventive cinematic techniques helped garner the picture a well-deserved Oscar nod for film editing. The acting of Pearce, Pantoliano, and Moss is superb, as is the movie's script, which earned both Oscar and Golden Globe nominations.

No matter how Vincent and Leonard seek to achieve their goals, be it through their own direct manifestations or through the assistance they receive from others, they stretch their conscious creation capabilities to fill in the perceived gaps in their realities. Such materializations may not be the most glamorous applications of these principles, but they're often among the most satisfying. They help level the playing field just when we thought it was beyond being brought into balance, and achieving success at that could be more rewarding than anything else we ever hope to create.

## Double Feature: Touched by the Hands of God

### "Resurrection" (theatrical version)
*Year of Release: 1980*
*Principal Cast: Ellen Burstyn, Sam Shepard, Richard Farnsworth, Roberts Blossom, Eva Le Gallienne, Jeffrey DeMunn, Lois Smith*
*Director: Daniel Petrie*
*Screenplay: Lewis John Carlino*

### "Resurrection" (made-for-TV version)
*Year of Initial Broadcast: 1999*
*Principal Cast: Dana Delany, Brenda Fricker, Rita Moreno, Nick Chinlund, Mitchell Kosterman, Matthew Glave, Margaret Ryan*
*Director: Stephen Gyllenhaal*
*Story Source: Lewis John Carlino*
*Teleplay: Peachy Markowitz*

Healing by touch has been around for a long time. In indigenous cultures, shamans have long made this practice part of their repertoire of techniques. Similarly, the laying on of hands is a long-standing tradition in the healing and blessing ceremonies of many of the world's religions, and those proficient in this skill have often produced stunning results. More recently, this practice has at times come under scrutiny, its reputation tarnished by the scams of charlatans and unscrupulous faith healers. But its merits have enjoyed something of a renaissance of late, thanks to the concerted efforts of such professionals as massage therapists and reiki masters, as well as the practitioners of related disciplines, such as Reconnective Healing®.[9] Whether one is comfortable trusting it ultimately depends on what one believes, as the characters find out in the two film versions of "Resurrection."

The original theatrical picture tells the story of Edna Mae McCauley (Ellen Burstyn), a California transplant who leaves behind her Kansas roots in search of a better life. She's happily married to Joe (Jeffrey DeMunn), a warm, fun-loving guy, and to show him how much she loves him, she gives him a new sports car for his birthday. Thrilled with his new toy, Joe takes Edna for a spin along the coast, but, tragically, he's killed when the car plunges over a cliff. Edna somehow survives the crash, but her legs are paralyzed and her spirit broken. With her husband gone and no one to care for her, Edna reluctantly agrees to return home and live with her father, John (Roberts Blossom), a devoutly Christian but mean old man whose disapproving demeanor sparked his free-spirited daughter's departure in the first place.

Once back in Kansas, Edna becomes reacquainted with the one family member whom she genuinely adores, her deeply spiritual grandmother, Pearl (Eva Le Gallienne). In one of their conversations, Edna recounts a strange dream that she had immediately after the accident. But Pearl realizes from Edna's description that it wasn't a dream; she recognizes it as a near-death experience (NDE), similar to one that an acquaintance of hers had had many years before. Pearl stresses to Edna the significance of this experience, particularly her encounter with the bright loving light of God. As a consequence of these recollections and Pearl's sage guidance, the feelings of contentment that Edna experienced at the time of her NDE come flooding back, filling her with a sense of inner peace for the first time since the accident. But that's only the beginning.

Edna discovers she's developed a remarkable capacity for healing. She accomplishes this by placing her hands on the recipient of the divine healing energy. When her hands grow warm, the energy is thus transmitted. First she heals herself, regaining full mobility in her legs. She then begins curing the ills of others, achieving success about seventy percent of the time and quickly developing a reputation for her skills. She even finds a new love interest through her efforts, Cal (Sam Shepard), a young man whose wounds she heals after he's injured in a bar fight.

But as word of her miracles spreads, others in the community become suspicious of her, most notably the fundamentalists, who cite scripture to support their contention that she's doing the devil's work. On top of that, John is angered by his daughter's wicked ways, not only in her newfound vocation but also in her sordid new romance. Even Cal, the one person whom Edna thought she could trust, grows leery of her abilities (and distant from her emotionally) as her public healing sessions, now held under big tents, grow ever larger. But then, as the son of a preacher, it's difficult for Cal to turn his back on his upbringing, so he convinces himself that something must be done to stop her.

The made-for-television version of this film tells roughly the same story but with a few twists. Edna McCauley has been renamed Clare Miller (Dana Delany), and she moves to Colorado from the Pacific Northwest, a home to which she, too, returns reluctantly after her accident. Clare's reason for leaving home is similar to Edna's, though the falling out that prompted her departure is not with her father but with her close-minded mother (Brenda Fricker). The warm homecoming extended by Grandma Pearl is here replaced by the friendly reception of the wise-cracking but good-intentioned New Age neighbor, Mimi (Rita Moreno). And Clare's new love interest is not the son of a preacher but her rigidly skeptical attending physician, Dr. Jake Sandler (Nick Chinlund), who, unlike Cal, manages to keep a level head, especially after he sees what she can do. Otherwise, most of the events are the same as the original, though a few are presented in a slightly different sequence or tweaked to suit variations in the characters' backgrounds.

Beliefs play integral roles in this story for healers and patients alike. The healers, for instance, must be convinced that they *can* heal, a belief that Clare wrestles with more than Edna does, but one that both of them eventually embrace wholeheartedly. When they come to see themselves as conduits for dispensing divine healing energy, their confidence swells, so much so that even the once-skeptical Clare eventually believes there's no one she can't heal.

For the healing to work, however, patients must also believe they can be cured. They must allow it to happen, which is not necessarily something that all patients want. As Edna observes in one scene with a patient she's unable to help, some people hold on to their illnesses as a means to attract attention that they don't feel they can get any other way. That's a rather difficult course for achieving such a result, but then no one ever said we always take the easy route in fulfilling our expectations.

Patient skepticism is also a hurdle to be overcome. Those who doubt the effectiveness of the process tend to heal more slowly. But their doubt isn't as much in the healer as it is in themselves, that they can't get better. In both versions, we see instances in which Edna and Clare need to encourage their patients to allow the healing, not because the patients disbelieve the abilities of those ministering to them but because they can't envision the healing taking place. Only when Edna and Clare instill these skeptics with confidence in themselves are they able to let their healings proceed.

Both films also show that healing comes in many forms and that the restoration of health isn't always the intended outcome. Aiding others in passing on, for instance, is shown to be just as much a form of healing as one that results in the alleviation of illness or infirmity. Indeed, if the aim of this practice is "to make someone whole," then sometimes it requires measures that defy convention, employing intentions different from what we typically associate with a more traditional interpretation of healing. Just as healers must accept their abilities, patients must accept their cures, no matter what that may entail, if they hope to achieve the desired result of being made whole again.

"Resurrection" is a compelling story in both its incarnations. The theatrical version is better known, but I must admit that I enjoyed the made-for-TV movie more. With the exception of a somewhat implausible subplot involving a hostage taking, the story line and characters of the TV version are more believable than those of the original. Delany, Fricker, and Moreno are wonderful, and they have a great collective chemistry, despite portraying very different characters from one another. The backdrop of the Pacific Northwest provides a gorgeous setting, too, much better scenery than what one typically finds in a made-for-TV film.

While the original version features fine performances by Burstyn, who earned both Academy Award and Golden Globe nominations, and Le Gallienne, who received an Oscar nod, much of the rest of the acting is over the top. The fundamentalist rhetoric is rather shrill, excessive even by today's standards, causing many of the characters (like Cal and John) to appear almost cartoonish. Other elements, such as the often overdramatic soundtrack, are also definitely outdated. But the story's messages about healing, our potential to provide it and receive it, and the role beliefs play in it are thoughtful and well presented, which makes putting up with the other shortcomings worthwhile.

At present, the original version appears to be available in VHS format only. The made-for-TV version does not appear to be available on either DVD or tape, but it is shown on cable occasionally, which may be the only place to catch it.

Many see healing as a gift, a special dispensation reserved for God's chosen ones. But as this story makes clear, it's available to all who wish to embrace it, either as facilitators or recipients. Believing in the possibility and allowing it to happen are what it takes to bring that result to fruition. And fewer harvests are as glorious as this.

# Who Are We, Really?

"K-PAX"
*Year of Release: 2001*
*Principal Cast: Kevin Spacey, Jeff Bridges, Mary McCormack,*
*Alfre Woodard, David Patrick Kelly, Saul Williams, Celia Weston,*
*Ajay Naidu, Melanee Murray, Conchata Ferrell, William Lucking*
*Director: Iain Softley*
*Book: Gene Brewer*
*Screenplay: Charles Leavitt*

Now there's an eternal question—Who are we, really? It's one that virtually everyone has asked as long as we've been around, and, after millennia of existence, we still haven't adequately answered it. Yet, with continuing explorations into the realms of consciousness, I'd like to hope we're beginning to understand it better than before. This is particularly true when it comes to recognizing ourselves as multidimensional beings. Although we certainly have a long way to go in this regard, I believe we're at least making headway into acknowledging, if not comprehending, this phenomenon. But what we really need to understand it better are more examples of how it manifests, case studies, as it were, that we can examine in greater detail. One film that presents such an example is the much-overlooked drama, "K-PAX."

The latest arrival at the Psychiatric Institute of Manhattan is a bit unusual, even by its standards. A smarmy, sunglass-sporting chap who calls himself Prot (pronounced "Proat") (Kevin Spacey) claims he's a visitor from a planet called K-PAX in a distant binary star system. He nonchalantly contends he traveled to Earth in a beam of light and is here to check out some of the sights before returning home, presumably the same way he arrived. He seems totally at ease with his surroundings, despite his confinement in an institution, because he claims with the utmost confidence to possess the ability to come and go at will.

But Prot's powers don't stop there. He also has a special wisdom for relating to his fellow asylum residents, who become like a surrogate family to him. That's particularly true of his relationships with Howie (David Patrick Kelly), the resident people pleaser; Ernie (Saul Williams), a seemingly hopeless paranoiac and hypochondriac; Doris (Celia Weston), the ward diva; and Bess (Melanee Murray), the house recluse. He understands them in ways the institution staff doesn't (or can't). In fact, he's even able to make progress in treating their conditions where the experts have failed.

The psychiatrist who's left to decipher the enigma of Prot is Dr. Mark Powell (Jeff Bridges). He's a capable professional but rather conventional in his outlooks and something of a stuffed shirt, qualities that provide ample fodder for Prot's sarcastic wit. Mark is committed to solving the mystery of the new arrival, but Prot doesn't make it easy, tossing out distractions that deflect attention from him and put the good doctor on the spot. Prot frequently turns the tables on Mark, prodding him into confronting his own personal problems, particularly those in his souring home life. Prot's razor-sharp insights into Mark's family issues make him decidedly uncomfortable, mainly because he knows Prot is right. In this way, just as he helps his kindred spirits, the patient helps heal the doctor.

Mark is also baffled by Prot's considerable knowledge of astronomy, particularly information that few experts possess but with which Prot appears intimately familiar. Mark arranges a meeting with several astronomers, and when they ask Prot how he's aware of such knowledge, he casually responds, "Every K-PAXian knows this. Just as every child on Earth knows that your planet revolves around your sun. It's common knowledge, isn't it?" Heads are scratched in wonderment yet again at the mysterious stranger's special wisdom.

As time passes and the deadline looms for Prot's alleged return to K-PAX, Mark grows increasingly frustrated at being unable to unlock the inscrutable truth about his patient. He asks Prot to undergo regression therapy, to which he freely consents, and it's only then that Mark finally begins to gain some insight into whom he's dealing with. A totally different side of Prot begins to emerge, and Mark believes that the truth is at last starting to come out—at least while he's regressed, for when Prot returns to waking consciousness, he reverts to his old self. So is he delusional in normal consciousness and lucid when in an altered state of mind? Or is each aspect of his self equally valid, depending on his state of mind? Or is his consciousness genuinely home to more than one persona, a bona fide example of a multidimensional self? No matter how one interprets Prot's condition, we're inevitably confronted by the same question we began with—who are we, really?

One of the story's greatest strengths, ironically, is the intentional ambiguity we're left with regarding who Prot really is. The concept of the multidimensional self (first discussed in chapter 8) is an idea we're just beginning to understand, and "K-PAX" recognizes this, capably exploring it while simultaneously resisting the temptation to provide answers wrapped up in tidy little packages. The film gives us a look into what the phenomenon is about, illustrating how our most immediately identifiable personas may be only the tip of the iceberg of our greater consciousness. It squarely shines a spotlight on other aspects of our selves that lurk within but with which we're barely aware. And it shows how these other personas may each possess knowledge, skills, and qualities that could be effectively shared with one another. Such information and awareness could be successfully used, for example, in formulating beliefs for everything from creating new art to solving the stickiest of problems. It could also be employed in highly useful applications, such as healing, as Prot demonstrates in this picture. Indeed, the multidimensional self could be one of the greatest untapped storehouses of personal resources we have yet to discover, a treasure trove of talents, wisdom, and experience that could potentially transform our worldview and how we put conscious creation skills into practice.

Awareness of this concept could also be a key for unlocking many mysteries of the mind, including, possibly, those traditionally associated with mental illness (which makes this story's setting of an asylum all that more fitting). I'm not a mental illness expert by any means, but, from a purely speculative standpoint, it's interesting to consider some of the possibilities that might arise from applying this concept in a diagnostic context. Someone who exhibits signs of mental illness related to multiple personas, for instance, may actually be experiencing trouble integrating all of the various selves, their sheer volume causing the patient to become overwhelmed. Or perhaps the individual is unable to harmonize a particular persona properly with the others because it's inherently incompatible or has been damaged by some kind of psychological trauma (the individual's underlying beliefs in each case providing important clues about the cause). Or there could be some kind of "hosting" problem, in which the alternate self just won't fit into the localized consciousness, not unlike trying to squeeze a proverbial square peg where it doesn't belong. These are all merely theories, but they're interesting to ponder nevertheless.

Shifting our outlook about the multidimensional self thus might yield tremendous benefits to those whose true conditions may have been patently misunderstood. In fact, this concept could possibly provide a basis for explaining a whole range of behavior beyond mental disorders, including phenomena as diverse as speaking in tongues and channeling. Since we're just beginning to scratch the surface of this notion, however, our current knowledge is limited. But thanks to such consciousness pioneers as Frederick S. Oliver,[10] Edgar Cayce,[11] and, of course, Jane Roberts, as well as the ongoing work of such contemporaries as Esther Hicks[12] and Sonaya Roman,[13] information continues to be amassed, providing further insights into the multifaceted aspects of our being. Learning how to integrate these elements successfully remains a challenge, but books like Jane Roberts's *Adventures in Consciousness*[14] provide constructive insights on how to go about this. Prot's saga no doubt provides a helpful perspective, too.

"K-PAX" is an entertaining, enlightening, and unusual film. When asked to describe it, I said it was like a cross between "One Flew Over the Cuckoo's Nest" (1975) and "Starman" (1984) (see this chapter's Bonus Features). It effectively fuses stories from these two very different genres, telling a captivating tale with warmth, humor, compassion, and superb writing. Spacey is great as Prot, portraying him like the extraterrestrial cousin of Lester Burnham, his signature character from "American Beauty" (see chapter 8). Bridges is also terrific, playing the wooden Dr. Powell with the right amount of stiffness but not so rigid as to lack credibility. Their interactions are both dynamic and delightful.

Even though the film had a wide initial release, many have told me they've never heard of it. I suspect that's because it had the misfortune to premiere about a month after the 9/11 attacks, a time when many moviegoers were still staying home. However, given the picture's many strengths, it is well worth seeing, even if on DVD or cable.

Stories that delve into the multidimensional self intrigue, mystify, and enlighten us in many ways. They enchant the spirit, stirring parts of ourselves that have long slumbered, coaxing them to the surface and the light of awareness. And, if we look closely enough, we just might find out who we really are.

## Bonus Features

"Pi": A brilliant number theorist convinced that mathematics is the language of nature believes it can be used to explain patterns in everything from natural phenomena to epidemic cycles to the stock market. In searching for a universal numeric key, he develops a special wisdom that everyone wants, from Wall Street analysts to a group of kabbalistic Jews. But the power he's tapped into is so tremendous that it threatens to overwhelm him. An edgy drama about managing our enhanced capabilities. (1998; Sean Gullette, Mark Margolis, Ben Shenkman, Pamela Hart, Samia Shoaib, Stephen Pearlman, Kristyn Mae-Anne Lao; Darren Aronofsky, director; Darren Aronofsky, Sean Gullette, and Eric Watson, story; Darren Aronofsky, screenplay)

"Ghost": A murder victim who dies with unfinished business looks to set things right before moving on. However, before he can proceed, he must learn, as a nonphysical spirit, how to function in and communicate with those in the physical world to achieve his objectives. (You may never take conscious creation for granted again!) Makes me cry every time I see it. (1990; Patrick Swayze, Demi Moore, Whoopi Goldberg [Oscar and Golden Globe winner], Tony Goldwyn, Rick Aviles, Vincent Schiavelli; Jerry Zucker, director; Bruce Joel Rubin, screenplay [Oscar winner]; two Oscar wins on five nominations, one Golden Globe win on four nominations)

"Starman": An alien accepts the invitation to visit Earth extended by a phonograph recording mounted on the Voyager space probe. Upon arrival, he assumes human form, creating a corporeal body out of DNA found in the strand of hair of a dead man, giving himself (and his genetic decedent) life. During his terrestrial odyssey, he stretches his capabilities by learning the ways of being human, while simultaneously showing us what else is possible when we augment ours. Surprisingly engaging for a sci-fi film. (1984; Jeff Bridges, Karen Allen, Charles Martin Smith, Richard Jaeckel; John Carpenter, director; Bruce A. Evans and Raynold Gideon, screenplay; one Oscar nomination, two Golden Globe nominations)

# 10

# When One Reality Isn't Enough

## Exploring Dreams and
## Alternate Realms of Existence

I dream for a living.

*Steven Spielberg*

How wonderful it is to awake from a restful night's sleep, especially one that's been punctuated by pleasant dreams. These nocturnal journeys into the netherworlds of our souls are often among our most enjoyable explorations of consciousness. By the same token, they can also thrust us deep into the pit of our fears, terrifying us like few other frights imaginable. As contrasting as these experiences are, however, they share one trait in common—both occur in a different state of mind, a totally new reality, one in which the operational ground rules we've agreed to abide by in everyday life are swept aside, our imaginations posing the only boundaries we encounter. And because of the tremendous sense of liberation dreams facilitate, they provide us with infinite opportunities for solving problems, assessing beliefs, satisfying curiosity, gazing introspectively, and engaging in unfettered creativity. With dreams having so much to offer, it's no wonder, then, that there are those, like director Steven Spielberg, who have made them their vocation.

But dreams aren't the only alternate realities we can tap into. All kinds of altered states of awareness are possible, such as those induced during hypnosis, guided visualization, or meditation. Even simple daydreaming, the casual practice of informally envisioning other probabilities, momentarily shifts us into other realms of existence. All of these techniques put our minds someplace else, showing us that there's much more to our consciousness than the waking state with which we're most familiar. How we get to these other realities, and what we do when we get there, depend on how we create them, which, of course, stems back to what beliefs we hold. But the possibilities, like the beliefs that give life to them, are limitless.

Our experiences in these other states of being make it possible for us to create or change anything. If we want to manipulate matter, time, appearances, outcomes, or even the basis of existence, they're all viable options in these different mind frames. It all comes down to what you want, the reality you wish to create. Indeed, as Jane Roberts and Seth wrote, "in many ways the dream universe depends on you to give it expression, in the same manner that you also depend upon it to find expression . . ."[1]

★   ★   ★

Because the range of options for experience and expression is so broad in dreams and other realities, we can employ these alternative consciousness venues for many types of endeavors. For example, as noted earlier, we could use them for problem solving, trying out different solutions to see how they work, as if in a laboratory or test kitchen. Because these other states of awareness allow us to proceed without the baggage of everyday reality bogging us down, there's not much to lose (and potentially everything to gain) by availing ourselves of the experimentation opportunities these alternate realms have to offer. The removal of waking consciousness roadblocks is eminently freeing, allowing our imaginations to stretch without the threat of undue consequences hampering us. We can brainstorm ideas and deliberate options to our heart's content without fear of reprisals. I routinely use dreams for such purposes, drawing upon techniques like those taught by writer and dream researcher Robert Moss in his audio course, *Dream Gates*.[2] These methods have helped me accomplish goals ranging from resolving financial issues to discovering the underlying sources of physical ailments (which generally clear up immediately after their dreamtime revelation, I might add).

Our experiences in dreams and alternate realities can also provide us with fresh perspectives, much the same way road trips do (see chapter 7). Just as travel helps us get away from it all and take our minds off routine matters, journeys of consciousness into altered states can achieve similar results. They can help us understand our beliefs (and thus what we create) better and improve our grasp of such concepts as value fulfillment and multidimensional selves. But perhaps their greatest benefit is the sheer enjoyment they make possible. What grand fun it is to veer off into a different reality, even the unknown, just for the utter pleasure it affords.

All of this shows how fundamental a connection there is between these altered states of consciousness and conscious creation. In fact, the link is so intrinsic that we have even come to use language about them interchangeably. For example, think of how often we've spoken about achieving a particular goal as representing the fulfillment of *a dream*. There's no idle coincidence in that; the practice of envisioning, picturing what we seek to manifest, is so vital to the materialization process that it's no surprise their semantics have become inexorably intertwined.

Although these notions may be fresh ideas to some of us, they're by no means new. In fact, they have long traditions in Native American and other indigenous cultures. These tribal societies know well what power lies in dreams and other realities. They see them as integral, meaningful components of existence. In fact, they often regard the dream state as our true reality and waking life as an illusion.

But just as many of us have been reluctant to embrace the possibilities afforded by stretching our personal capabilities (see chapter 9), so, too, have we often been slow to accept the merits of dreams and alternate realities. This is true not only for what they have to offer, but also of whether they even exist. If you doubt that, think of how many times someone has dismissively said of one of your nightly adventures, "It's just a dream." Such disparagements denigrate the value of these experiences, obscuring the benefits they have to offer.

Limiting beliefs, especially those driven by traditional science, are the chief culprit in this, just as they have been in the snail's pace acceptance of enhanced personal capabilities. To be sure, there are some forward-thinking scientists—sleep researchers and quantum physicists mostly—who are fascinated by these other realms. The same can be said of such organizations as the Institute of Noetic Sciences, which are devoted to their further examination. Unfortunately, these progressive explorers are more the exception than the rule. Those locked into conventional viewpoints have allowed their limiting beliefs to dictate their outlooks on reality to such a degree that they can't even fathom the viability of alternatives. They discount the value of these subjective experiences for many of the same reasons they reject capabilities like psychic powers, such as an inability to quantify them effectively. Trying to measure something as subjective in nature as this using methods grounded in the (supposed) objectivity of traditional science is patently unworkable, foolish, and perhaps ultimately maddening. As Jane Roberts and Seth wrote, scientists who attempt such undertakings "will be, and are, prisoners of their tools."[3]

By contrast, conventional religion, despite its many inherent limitations, is comparatively more tolerant than science when it comes to dreams and alternate realities. Its very belief in the existence of an "unsubstantiated" concept like the afterlife, for instance, would bear this out. What's more, religious texts, such as the Bible, are full of references to dreams as a form of prophecy, a source of meaningful messages that their recipients treat reverently and regard as entirely reliable. Although religion has tended to look upon these nocturnal revelations as falling within the purview of a select few, at least it acknowledges their validity, something that generally can't be said for its scientific cousin.

Those who have been unable to find insightful information on the value of dreams and other realities through mainstream sources can look to the films of this chapter for ideas and inspiration. These pictures explore many aspects of these altered states, including their relation to conscious creation. As with the movies in chapter 9, I have shied away from pictures that tend to portray these phenomena negatively to avoid the impression they're something we should be afraid of.

A fascinating theme that many of these movies share is the role memory plays in shaping, distinguishing, and interpreting the various realities we encounter. They show how a sense of history provides context, continuity, and familiarity to the existence in question (be it alternate or otherwise) and how its loss or reconfiguration can disrupt our ability to relate to it.

"Daring to dream" is something many of us have routinely been encouraged to do by our mentors, peers, and loved ones. It's good advice, whether we apply the idea practically in our daily pursuits or whether we invoke it just for the sheer pleasure of letting our minds roam the cosmos. It's interesting that we frequently use the word *dare* in connection with dreaming, as if it were something difficult, scary, or extraordinary, because, if anything, it should be the opposite of all that. Maybe that expression is meant to inspire or motivate, proposing a challenge to those who have let the skill lapse or who have avoided it out of fear or other reasons. Personally, I can't imagine an existence without dreaming, nor, would it seem, could many of the great minds throughout history. If someone like Steven Spielberg has turned the idea into his reason for being, then that says something about the concept's allure and power. And when those traits are tapped into successfully, the result is a reality well worth exploring and a life truly worth living.

## When Dreams Come True

"The Lathe of Heaven"
*Year of Initial Broadcast: 1980*
*Principal Cast: Bruce Davison, Kevin Conway, Margaret Avery*
*Directors: David Loxton, Fred Barzyk*
*Book: Ursula K. Le Guin*
*Teleplay: Roger E. Swaybill, Diane English*

Whether or not someone is an avid practitioner of conscious creation, at some point we've all speculated about what it would be like to make our dreams literally come true. It's an enticing sentiment, for sure, but one that many of us regard as a feel-good, storybook notion that's nice to ponder but not to take seriously. But what if it could be? That would be quite a feat. What's more, what if our dreams not only came true but also changed the reality that came beforehand? And, just to make matters even more interesting, suppose you were the only one who knew that reality had changed and in what ways. Now that might be a little troubling, if not downright scary. The challenges of coping with such knowledge, as well as the responsibility accompanying that kind of power, are the issues at stake in the science fiction drama, "The Lathe of Heaven."

Life in the near future looks pretty dismal. For the residents of Portland, Oregon, simply getting by is a challenge in a world beset by rampant overcrowding, an uncaring bureaucracy, and incessant rain. One would think that escaping from all that, even if only temporarily in one's dreams, would be a welcome relief. But not for George Orr (Bruce Davison). He's troubled by his dreams; they're so powerful (and thorough) that they not only change the conditions of his life, but they also alter the events and circumstances leading up to their materialization, and he's the only one who knows how things have changed. George is worried about the consequences of this, mainly because of an unsettling dream incident from his adolescence. In fact, he's so afraid of the power he's wielding that he desperately seeks to prevent these so-called "effective dreams" from occurring. He concocts a potent combination of prescription drugs to try to shut them off, but even that doesn't work. And when officials learn of his little unauthorized chemistry experiment, he winds up charged with illicit drug use.

George's penalty for his drug violation is to undergo psychiatric treatment with a dream specialist, Dr. William Haber (Kevin Conway). Haber is fascinated by his new patient's claims, which he quickly discovers live up to every bit of their seemingly implausible billing. The good doctor is thus presented with a golden opportunity to engage in groundbreaking dream study with a unique subject. The question is, however, what kind of work will he do with his patient?

Before long, it becomes obvious Haber has little interest in helping George sort out his dream difficulties. Instead, he unscrupulously attempts to use his subject's abilities as an instrument for fulfilling his own ends, namely, reshaping the world in the image *he* holds for it. During their sessions together, Haber instructs George to have a number of effective dreams, which he does, resulting in some noteworthy changes. Most of the initial dream-inspired developments are generally inoffensive, primarily because they arise from fairly benign suggestions. But when Haber's requests involve plans calling for radical changes, grandiose schemes hatched by his over-inflated ego, the results take some frighteningly unexpected turns.

To his credit, George quickly realizes what's going on and enlists the assistance of a public defender, Heather LeLache (Margaret Avery), to help him seek reassignment to a new therapist. But the wheels of bureaucracy turn slowly, giving Haber sufficient time to proceed with his plans. So it is up to George himself to take on the egomaniac seeking to control him, and he does so in the arena in which he's most adept—the world of his dreams. George may not be able to stop his nemesis, but he's certainly capable of matching wits with him, thwarting Haber's plans by having effective dreams whose outcomes don't exactly abide by his expectations. George isn't clear how he's accomplishing this, especially since some of his dreams are rather scary, even to him. It makes George wonder what kinds of powers he's unleashing upon the world, forcing him to address some thorny questions about what he's creating and why. But despite the potential risks involved, George knows on some level that he must continue along this course to stop Haber from using him as a tool to play God.

Straightforward as all that may sound, there's much more going on here than simply foiling the ploys of a madman. In many ways, that scenario is just a pretext to a more substantive narrative in which George must face, sort out, and resolve some major conscious creation issues, the roots of which extend down to the very core of his being. He's got his work cut out for him, especially when it comes to the most important question of all: Why is he doing all this in the first place?

In addressing these challenges, George passes through multiple levels of personal understanding, as if he's peeling the onion, a metaphor commonly used to describe to the multilayered nature of psychoanalysis. For starters, George appears, on the one hand, to be quite skillful at using dreams as powerful conscious creation tools. On the other hand, he's also clearly undisciplined about this practice, letting his dreams play out as they will, functioning as agents of creation by default. He obviously holds beliefs allowing this, even if he's not aware of them. But the fact that he remembers how his dreams change reality suggests that some part of his consciousness is trying to get his attention, that it wants him to take steps to rein in the internal forces driving this behavior. But how?

By creating the need for therapy, George begins his journey to identify the beliefs he needs to bring under control. But once he's in treatment, another issue becomes apparent—his susceptibility to manipulation. Again, that wouldn't happen unless George held beliefs allowing it. So on some level, then, he recognizes the need to change these beliefs also, in this case to protect his manifestation skills against exploitation. This helps explain why his dream-driven creations often result in materializations thwarting Haber's goals; he won't give the manipulator his way. But this solution is only a stopgap measure; it doesn't adequately address George's beliefs about susceptibility to manipulation or why he holds them.

When all these considerations are looked at collectively, they have a common trait that points to an even bigger issue—George's inability (or unwillingness) to take responsibility for the creations his dreams generate. His beliefs regarding dreamtime discipline and suggestion susceptibility are merely components of this larger concern, conveniently letting him believe that he's not accountable for the results. In fact, he's so in denial about it that he even lashes out at Haber as being the responsible party for what's transpiring. (Granted, one could argue that Haber, as co-creator of these incidents, isn't exactly innocent in this scenario; but then one could also contend that he's merely playing a role that George's beliefs are making possible for him, and he's only too willing to oblige.) By allowing his dreams to create by default (before entering treatment) and by letting Haber's manipulative practices assume de facto control over the direction of his dreams (after entering treatment), George essentially absolves himself of responsibility for his dreams' creations. At the same time, the fact that George has sought help through therapy (at least in principle, Haber's techniques notwithstanding) and that he uses his dreams to derail Haber's plans both point to an emerging awareness on his part to become personally responsible for his dreams and what they produce. However, only when George is willing and able to recognize, acknowledge, and rewrite his existing beliefs can he change his behavior and its outcomes.

These circumstances naturally raise questions about the role of intent and value fulfillment behind George's dreams. Just what are his aims in these areas anyway? What purposes are they meant to serve? And how does his apparent lack of responsibility figure into them? These are issues George must address if he ever hopes to get a grip on his reality, not to mention a good night's sleep.

Ironically, as the story unfolds, it becomes apparent that part of George's problem may actually be due to his ability to recall how his dreams change reality, a significant clue to understanding his underlying intents and value fulfillment. Consider this: If we were to use our dreams to change our existence, truly to let go of aspects about it we dislike, then should we really expect to remember anything about the discarded elements upon awakening? Wouldn't forgetting them totally be more appropriate? In fact, if we were to continue recalling them, wouldn't we be purposely holding on to them? (That, of course, would also raise the question of why.) In light of that, then, maybe the real responsibility George needs to assume is the ability to forget how his dreams change reality. In this way, he can just enjoy the new existence; the alterations he seeks to put into place can finally take hold, without the encumbrance of memories that are no longer relevant impinging upon them. Perhaps that goal is the true value fulfillment he's supposed to seek. So why doesn't he?

As an aside, this illustrates the fundamental role memory plays in our understanding of reality. Many of us no doubt take that for granted, yet it truly serves a significant purpose in shaping awareness of our existence. If our memories were to change suddenly, through dreams or other means, either for us or for those with whom we routinely interact, the reference points we use for maneuvering through reality would vanish, leaving us without the signposts we rely on for getting by on a daily basis. It's no wonder, then, that George is so disoriented.

But, as suggested previously, sometimes the loss of particular memories can be highly beneficial, especially when ridding ourselves of painful or unpleasant recollections that no longer serve us. In fact, holding on to such memories may be what gets us into trouble, for that signifies we've not truly let go of them, a lesson that George (and, in his own way, Haber) learn the hard way.

One way for George to eliminate his recall problem intentionally would be to wish it away in a dream. Indeed, if dreams can be used as tools for manifesting, then why couldn't they be used for something like that? Because George is such a whiz at bringing about change through effective dreams, he should be able to materialize this, too, right? But why stop there? If George is so troubled by the power of his effective dreams, then maybe he should just try dreaming that he loses that ability altogether.

Sometimes the simplest solutions are the hardest to see—and the easiest to miss. Yet their impact can be quite profound, for not only do they clear up the most immediate issues, but they also often solve bigger, more deeply rooted problems that are easily camouflaged by superficial considerations. All we have to do is allow ourselves to view these options. This frequently requires us to send our ego consciousness packing, getting it out of the way to let in other types of information, such as intuitional impressions or insights from dreams and altered states of being, that carry the seeds of these solutions. These impressions and insights nearly always defy logic and conventional wisdom, but they provide the very information we're meant to have and make use of.

George eventually comes to realize this for himself. He's able to make peace with his dreams and the creations that spring forth from them. When he learns to state his intents and then let his collaboration with All That Is take over, rather than processing everything through his own ego (as Haber tries to do), George can let the results be what they are and take in whatever they have to offer. He's comfortable in the knowledge that they embody manifestations he drew to himself, regardless of whether he knows how he did it or what they encompass. He truly learns the lesson of Taoist Chuang Tzu that "to let understanding stop at what cannot be understood is a high attainment. Those who cannot do it will be destroyed on the lathe of heaven."[4]

Thankfully, this picture is once again available after a protracted hiatus. It was originally broadcast on PBS but had long been out of public circulation due to a rights issue over its inclusion of an original Beatles recording and the lapse of the network's broadcast rights.[5] It has held up well, though, despite some of the picture's low-budget special effects. Its story line is riveting, and the writing is rock solid. Conway's performance as the chilling and arrogant Dr. Haber sends shivers up my spine every time I watch this picture. Please note that this original version of the film should not be confused with the dreadful 2002 made-for-cable remake, an incomprehensible mess that abandons much of the original story and that puzzles more than enlightens.

"The Lathe of Heaven" is one of those greatly underrated gems that shouldn't be missed. After viewing it, you may never think about your dreams, or your reality, in quite the same way ever again—that is, if you can recall how you thought about them beforehand . . .

# Through Another's Eyes

"Brainstorm"
*Year of Release: 1983*
*Principal Cast: Christopher Walken, Natalie Wood, Louise Fletcher,*
*Cliff Robertson, Jordan Christopher, Donald Hotton, Alan Fudge,*
*Joe Dorsey, Bill Morey, Jason Lively*
*Director: Douglas Trumbull*
*Story: Bruce Joel Rubin*
*Screenplay: Robert Stitzel, Philip Frank Messina*

It's often been said, usually with a stern finger pointed in our faces, that, if we could see through another's eyes, we would look at things differently. Of course, because virtually all of us lack that capability (or have chosen not to manifest it), we've had a convenient out, enabling us blithely to disregard the wisdom of that admonition. But what if we were to develop the means to acquire that skill? Such a breakthrough would hold the potential to revolutionize the world and how we perceive it, a prospect explored in depth in the sci-fi thriller, "Brainstorm."

Dr. Lillian Reynolds (Louise Fletcher) is a dedicated research scientist for a major corporation. Her workaholic and chain-smoking tendencies aside, she's sincere and passionate about her studies into the development of a new technology for faithfully recording one's sensory perceptions on a special type of tape. Once recorded, these impressions are available for playback by those wishing to experience the subject's sensations firsthand, right down to the minutest details. The possibilities such technology opens up are incredible in such areas as communications, education, counseling, even adult entertainment. Thanks to Lillian's work, it's now possible to know what it's like to walk in someone else's shoes—literally.

Joining Dr. Reynolds in her investigation is her best friend and trusted colleague, Dr. Michael Brace (Christopher Walken), an enthusiastic but naïve idealist. Keeping the resources flowing for the duo's research is Alex Terson (Cliff Robertson), the corporate chief responsible for project oversight. Handling product design to make the technology palatable to consumers is Karen Brace (Natalie Wood), Michael's wife. Despite their many years together at the company, this project marks the first time that Michael and Karen have worked directly with one another, an amazing irony since they are also in the process of getting divorced.

When Lillian and Michael achieve a significant breakthrough in their work, it's a great cause for celebration—or at least it should be. While attending a reception in their honor, they learn from Alex that the government is about to intrude on their turf, splashing more than a little cold water on the festivities. Citing such reasons as preventing the spread of potentially dangerous technology, a contingent of officials led by military brass announces its intentions to step in and jointly manage (prepare to take over) the project. Supporting them are their lackey defense contractors, who clearly want first crack at the new technology for their own questionable applications. In addition, to put a face on their presence in the project, the feds introduce their chief researcher (and spy), Landan Marks (Donald Hotton), whom Lillian unhesitatingly blasts as "a hack."

As Lillian and Michael continue their research, with Landan surreptitiously watching from behind the scenes, they discover that their technology is capable of recording much more than simple sensory impressions. First they find it can tap into emotions and memories. Later they learn that repeated exposure to certain recorded imagery can affect the viewer's state of mind or physiology (presumably, from a conscious creation standpoint, by encouraging the viewer to alter beliefs associated with such manifestations). With those kinds of capabilities in place, it's no wonder the feds want to get their hands on this technology. But as impressive as these capabilities are, they pale in comparison to what the technology can do when it's used, quite unexpectedly, to register the impressions that occur during the ultimate journey of one's consciousness—the sensations that happen at the time of, and after, death. With a recording of information like that at stake, the struggle for control of the technology takes on added dimensions—in every sense of the word.

I find this story's premise fascinating, highly original in its conception of a new technology and inventive in its thinking about how it might be put to use. Some conscious creation purists may object to the use of a physical technology for attaining the stated goal, but that a tool like this is employed to achieve this end doesn't make the means any less valid; one needn't use only subjective approaches to experience subjective phenomena, for the technology making something like this possible wouldn't exist were it not for the beliefs that conceived of it in the first place.

What the technology enables is also remarkable. The ability to sense another's firsthand experiences is an awesome prospect. On the lighter end of the scale, there are tremendous implications in terms of sheer entertainment and adventure value. Travelogues, for instance, would never be the same again. In more substantial ways, the applications of this technology for educational, anthropological, and counseling purposes have huge ramifications. The potential gains in such areas as understanding, tolerance, and compassion alone are enormous, and with the developments that come out of advanced research, showing how the technology can be used to tap into feelings and memories and to affect physiological processes, there are amazing opportunities for employing it in conscious creation. It could almost be used like an amplifier of one's beliefs, making truly significant changes to one's reality possible.

Of course, the inherent neutrality of a device like this also reveals the dual-edged nature of this technological sword. Essentially this technology, like the mind itself, allows all possibilities to be fair game, and when those possibilities are committed to tape, they're all equally capable of being experienced through playback. Easy access to these recorded experiences, as well as the potential for easy amplification of their effects, bring new meaning to the notions of being careful what one wishes for and what one creates. This is particularly true when research shows how the technology is capable of cataloguing what transpires across supposedly impermeable dimensional barriers.

The aura surrounding this picture has an eerie irony about it given the story line and the tragic offscreen developments that occurred during its shooting. Actress Natalie Wood's drowning while on a break from filming cast a cloud over the future of the production, putting its completion in limbo for a time. But director Douglas Trumbull moved forward with the project, improvising and reworking elements as needed to finish it. The result was an engaging, if somewhat chillingly poignant movie that critics praised but that largely flopped at the box office. Its inventive premise is supported by a smartly written script, one that thankfully avoids the temptation to spoon-feed viewers about each of its plot developments. Its cinematography and special effects are dazzling, so try to watch this picture on a large screen if at all possible. Its ethereal and haunting score provides an appropriately moving backdrop to the thought-provoking subject matter.

Viewing the world through another's eyes is tantamount to exploring another reality, for if we each create our own, any others that we experience are sure to be different, even if only in small ways, from those we manifest for ourselves. Experiences like that not only provide us with the fresh perspectives of others, but they may also give us new takes about ourselves and our beliefs and, by extension, the realities we choose to create. Indeed, the insights afforded by an ability like that could change the world in countless ways overnight.

Now, that would be something to see.

# Clearing the Slate

"Eternal Sunshine of the Spotless Mind"
*Year of Release: 2004*
*Principal Cast: Jim Carrey, Kate Winslet, Elijah Wood,*
*Mark Ruffalo, Kirsten Dunst, Tom Wilkinson, Jane Adams,*
*David Cross, Deirdre O'Connell*
*Director: Michel Gondry*
*Story: Charlie Kaufman, Michel Gondry, Pierre Bismuth*
*Screenplay: Charlie Kaufman*

A good purging, no matter what it entails, can usher in healthy changes. Ridding ourselves of the useless and superfluous clears the slate to help us start anew. If nothing else, it enables us to get a better handle on our conscious creation resources, for even the things we no longer want or need take up some of these resources just to sustain their continued existence. Such house-cleanings can be used not only to pitch items like old clothes or eight-track tapes, but they're also useful for divesting ourselves of relationships that have run their course, a prospect explored in "Eternal Sunshine of the Spotless Mind."

Have you ever looked at an unlikely couple and wondered, "How did those two ever end up together?" That's a valid question when examining the relationship of Joel (Jim Carrey) and Clementine (Kate Winslet). Joel is a reserved, somewhat unimaginative soul, an introspective loner who's generally more comfortable in the world of his books and his journaling than in dealing with others. Clementine, by contrast, is an impetuous, eccentric extrovert who dyes her hair crazy colors, furnishes her home in the latest flea market fashions, and plays out every capricious impulse that enters her head. Together they seem like a match made in hell, an accident waiting to happen, yet there they are, an improbable pair. (There must be something to this "chemistry" notion after all.)

All seems to be going surprisingly well between them when, suddenly one day, Clementine treats Joel as if she doesn't know him, or has never met him, in fact. At first, Joel thinks Clementine's playing another of her goofy little games, but when he discovers she's serious, he's devastated. He seeks consolation from his friends Carrie (Jane Adams) and Rob (David Cross), who reluctantly divulge that Clementine had undergone a procedure with Dr. Howard Mierzwiak (Tom Wilkinson) to wipe her memory clean of any recollections she held of Joel. Hurt and angry at this revelation, Joel decides to do the same, purging himself of any memories of Clementine.

The procedure involves the patient collecting all memorabilia related to the subject slated for memory erasure. Dr. Mierzwiak and his staff then show these items to the patient while hooked up to a brain scanner. The portions of the brain that light up during this process allow the doctor to create a map of memory centers to be treated when formal erasure begins, a procedure that takes place overnight while the patient is at home asleep. All memorabilia is discarded, and even recollection of the procedure is wiped from the patient's memory. This way, the patient is unaware that anything ever happened.

With the preliminary work complete, Joel prepares to undergo treatment, which is handled by two of Dr. Mierzwiak's technicians, Stan (Mark Ruffalo) and Patrick (Elijah Wood). Initially, all proceeds as anticipated. Joel's most recent memories of Clementine are erased first, revealing that things between them recently hadn't been as rosy as one might have believed; their many differences were a source of frequent conflict. Given the pain of these memories, it's no wonder that Clementine wanted to undergo the erasure process, and it's no surprise Joel is doing it now. But the further back his memories go, the more Joel rediscovers recollections of their good times together. They're so pleasant, in fact, that he has second thoughts about continuing with the procedure. Since he's asleep, however, he has no way of letting Stan and Patrick know that they should stop. So if Joel is going to preserve any memories of Clementine, he'll have to figure out how to do it on his own, within his own mind.

As Joel's memories are erased, his recollections of the reality associated with them are literally deconstructed piece by piece, a change cleverly depicted with inventive cinematic techniques and special effects. To counteract this process, Joel attempts to preserve his remaining memories of Clementine by relocating them to areas of his mind that aren't scheduled for erasure. This not only staves off the memories' deletion, but it also gives Joel a look at how these other recollections colored some of his long-standing core beliefs, which, in turn, show how he employed them in creating his reality. But to carry out the patient's stated wishes successfully, the techs, now aided by Dr. Mierzwiak himself, hunt down the rogue memories to erase them as well. As the deletion of Joel's history with Clementine moves backward through his catalog of memories, nearing the point where they first met, time is running out for him to maintain any remaining recollection of her. He needs to figure out what to do before it's too late.

In this film, just as in "The Lathe of Heaven" (discussed earlier in this chapter), memory plays a significant role in how we relate to the reality we create. It provides a record that we draw upon, not unlike the tapes in "Brainstorm" (also discussed earlier in this chapter), to comprehend its various elements. It gives us a frame of reference about the reality's history, which in turn supplies a context that we can use for understanding the existence in its present form.

When memory changes, however, so does the associated existence it depicts. In "The Lathe of Heaven," reality changes through dreams and the suggestions inspiring them. In this film, alterations result from intentional memory erasure, the effects of which are portrayed through the systematic disappearance of all the elements in Joel's recollections, including people, places, and things. In both cases, the memory in place initially is supplanted by the new one, which simultaneously changes the reality accompanying it. The old existence thus disappears except for any remnants that are intentionally retained in the recollections of the new one.

Because beliefs create reality, and because memory is a recording of what transpires in reality, then memory is also, by implication, an extrapolated record of those underlying beliefs. It acts like a repository of the compiled beliefs that shape the reality in question, showing how they integrate to create the combined form. But if memory functions like an archive, how is it that its records can be altered, as happens in these two films?

Because memory, like anything else manifested through conscious creation, is a construct that arises from beliefs, there must also be beliefs in place allowing for an alteration capability. Many of us already use this ability yet probably aren't aware that we do so, suggesting that there must be other beliefs we more readily draw upon that trump its impact. For instance, many of us may remember a particular childhood event, like the first day of school, in one way at one point in our lives and in a totally different way at another. But did the event itself change or our memory of it? I believe both did; one set of beliefs was in place with the first recollection, and another was present subsequently, and in each case, the event that gave rise to it conformed to the beliefs shaping it, which, in turn, accounts for the difference in the memory record. Some would attribute an experience like this to faulty recall, a contention driven by the more widely held (and thus more potent) belief that one can't change the past. I believe, however, that an experience like this is more likely due to changed recall, based on whatever beliefs are in place at the time the recollection occurs. As with each consciously created manifestation, each recollection has its own validity; the only difference is that each arises from a different set of underlying beliefs.

Joel engages in practices like this as he strives to preserve his memories of Clementine. By shifting these recollections into locations not targeted for erasure, for example, he creates totally new memories of events that now incorporate the relocated recollections. And by doing so, he simultaneously alters the realities on which those recollections are based. Such changes allow him to see things about himself differently; alterations to past perceptions about his self-image make it possible for him to rewrite the beliefs he holds about himself that fuel those impressions. These are changes that he can employ in his present and, as I'm sure he would hope, carry forward into his future.

The implications of practices like this are significant, most notably the possibility of being able to rewrite the past. Many of us heavily buy into the belief that such a notion is impossible, yet the preceding examples illustrate, even if in only minor ways, that it can be done if we allow it. The example involving supposedly faulty recall noted earlier, in fact, shows we already do it, even if we're not aware of it. But if we were to employ the rewriting concept consciously, the ramifications could be tremendous. Letting go of painful, useless memories by changing them could benefit us greatly in both our present and our future, as long as we choose to do so. And should we not opt for that, we must ask ourselves why we're not; after all, if we're unwilling to let go of something totally, like a memory, then we must not want to let go of it at all.

In the alternative, even if we don't rewrite our memories, we can always choose to shift our focus of them. Joel does this as well, opting to zero in on his positive recollections of Clementine instead of the negative ones. It's a refocusing that, in the end, I'm sure he's glad he's chosen to do, too.

"Eternal Sunshine" is an unusual film in many ways, beginning with its casting choices of Carrey and Winslet, both of whom play against type in these roles. That decision paid off handsomely in the selection of Winslet, who deservedly earned Oscar and Golden Globe nominations for her portrayal of the kooky Clementine, but it worked less effectively in Carrey's case, despite a Globe nod for his performance. His character's demeanor is too restrained for Carrey's style, and he comes across as always being on edge, as if he's perpetually stifling the urge to break out and be outrageous.

The picture's visual style is unconventional as well. Much of it works brilliantly, particularly in the previously noted deconstruction sequences and in its seamless blending of actions going on in the real world and in Joel's memory. The film's script, an Oscar winner and Globe nominee, is witty, intelligent, and imaginative, although at times a little too conscious of its own quirkiness. Still, the elements all combine for an entertaining mix, especially for those times when you're in the mood for something different. In all, the movie picked up one Oscar on two nominations and four Globe nods but no statues.

A fresh start can work wonders in one's life, especially when we have taken deliberate steps to realize it. The results could even be . . . memorable.

## Color My World

**"Pleasantville"**
*Year of Release: 1998*
*Principal Cast: Tobey Maguire, Reese Witherspoon, William H. Macy,*
*· Joan Allen, Jeff Daniels, J.T. Walsh, Don Knotts, Jane Kaczmarek,*
*Marley Shelton*
*Director: Gary Ross*
*Screenplay: Gary Ross*

In a world saddled with the burdens of global warming, runaway crime, cutthroat economics, disease, and emotional disconnectedness, the stress of it all can take its toll. Those feeling overwhelmed by such anxieties may long for a simpler time, when life was carefree, right and wrong were as readily distinguishable as black and white, and the biggest dilemmas involved issues like what to make for dinner. But does the nostalgia for a reality like that really live up to its billing? That's what a brother and sister get to find out when they pay a visit to "Pleasantville."

Teenage twin siblings David (Tobey Maguire) and Jennifer (Reese Witherspoon) lock horns over the family television set.

Jennifer wants to watch a concert with her boyfriend, while David wants to watch a marathon of episodes of his favorite TV show, *Pleasantville*, a black-and-white 1950s sitcom in the tradition of such programs as *Father Knows Best* and *Leave It to Beaver*. Their squabble results in the remote control being damaged, essentially making the TV unwatchable. But help arrives with the unexpected appearance of a mysterious TV repairman (Don Knotts), who delivers a new remote, one with a little more kick that he promises David and Jennifer will make them feel like they're part of the show.

How prophetic his words prove to be. No sooner do they switch on the new remote than they're miraculously transported into the world of *Pleasantville*. The show's protagonists, George and Betty Parker (William H. Macy, Joan Allen), even see David and Jennifer as their characters' children, Bud and Mary Sue. Jennifer, needless to say, is livid, and David isn't exactly thrilled, either (though the prospect of getting to explore a world he has long fantasized about holds a certain appeal). He promises Jennifer he'll figure out a way to get them back home, but he impresses upon her the need to stay in character until then to avoid unduly disrupting the reality of *Pleasantville*, changes to which might prevent them from returning to their own existence.

Fitting in isn't easy, however. Jennifer, the free-spirited modern teen that she is, has trouble adjusting as Mary Sue; the vamp wannabee rails against the restrictions she's forced to endure as her geeky 1950s goody-two-shoes counterpart. And even though David settles in reasonably well as Bud, thanks to his knowledge of *Pleasantville* episode plotlines, he's still David, bringing the sensibilities of his reality into a world where conditions and outlooks differ markedly, both chronologically (given the show's time frame) and logistically (given its setting as the make-believe world of a TV series).

Inadvertently (in David's case) and purposely (in Jennifer's), their actions exert influence on the reality of *Pleasantville*, and life begins to deviate from the routine in innumerable ways. Characters behave differently, engaging in new activities, some as simple as performing tasks in different sequences and others as dramatic as having orgasms. Everyday events, which have always unfolded as if scripted (which, technically, they are), take unanticipated turns. Never-before-seen spectacles, like fire and rain, occur. Unimagined objects, like double beds, appear. Even an awareness of an outside world arises in the residents' consciousness. But the most radical change of all takes place with the sudden emergence of a totally foreign phenomenon—color.

Clearly, Pandora's box has been pried wide open, with a new reality quickly superseding the existing one. Some residents, mostly those for whom color has become skin deep, relish the changes and the liberation they allow. But for those who wish to preserve the predictable status quo, these transformations represent a threat to the way of life they've always known and believed in (and we all know what beliefs do). So to squelch the metamorphosis before it goes any further, the preservationists, led by the town's ultra-conservative mayor (J.T. Walsh), launch a campaign to maintain the world they have always seen as black and white, literally and figuratively. They draft a dogmatic platform to state their contentions. But, in pursuing their agenda, the preservationists' actions at times turn ugly, engaging them in behavior that makes the very name of their community an oxymoron. And to think all the fuss arises simply from the appearance of a little color in their lives.

"Pleasantville" is an excellent primer in demonstrating how beliefs create reality. Its use of an alternate existence to drive home this point is highly effective, too, for both characters and viewers alike. It shows, for example, how the scripted beliefs held in the minds of the characters in this TV show world result in the manifestation of some of its peculiar little quirks, such as bathrooms without toilets and a fire department that doesn't know how to fight fires. Because such materializations would never appear in any of the plotlines of a typical 1950s sitcom, beliefs necessitating them never cross the minds of the characters, which is why they're physically absent in this reality.

Such examples pointedly illustrate what happens when limiting beliefs are allowed to hold sway. But those are just a few isolated instances. Students in geography class, for instance, study only the map of their town, unable to imagine anything outside its confines. The owner of the local diner, Mr. Johnson (Jeff Daniels), can't envision how to handle alterations in his work routine without his trusty soda jerk, Bud, telling him what to do when schedules don't go according to plan. And when Mary Sue explains to her mother what sex is, Betty is so bewildered by the concept that all she can say is that it's something she knows her husband would never do.

The gradual formation of new beliefs results in the gradual appearance of changes in the surrounding reality. This is evidenced by the ongoing emergence of color in the film. The appearance of the new hues takes place in piecemeal fashion, with some elements appearing in color and some in black and white within the same scene, looking like one of Ted Turner's movie colorization projects in mid-completion. This very clever and skillfully handled photographic technique speaks volumes in illustrating this concept while providing viewers with an array of intriguing visuals.

Even though David and Jennifer effectively pass themselves off as Bud and Mary Sue, they have a fundamentally different outlook on the nature of existence, based on the prevailing assumptions in the realm from which they come. But then this makes it possible for them to introduce *Pleasantville* residents to broader spectrums of probabilities than they ever imagined. They help the locals unlock their potential by enabling them to formulate beliefs never before dreamed of. It's as if they're undercover ambassadors of a superior intelligence supplying advanced knowledge to lesser beings.

At the same time, David and Jennifer's interaction with the inhabitants of this sitcom world allows them to grow in ways they never envisioned, either, providing them with skills and capabilities that will serve them well in their future endeavors. David's experience in particular is significant, for it shatters his idealized notion about life in this seemingly idyllic world. It may represent a simpler way of life, but then it does so because such simplicity is governed by a more limited pool of operating beliefs in the first place. When David gets to compare the range of available opportunities of his own reality against those of *Pleasantville*, it's no contest to see where there are more options to choose from, a point that's driven home to him with great poignancy. Given the stresses of everyday life in David's world, it may be tempting for him to want to escape into a reality in which the grass is greener, but that's a little difficult when the grass of that refuge isn't even green to begin with.

The preservationists' reactions to the changes in their reality are full of parables, mirroring back to us, as viewers, allegories about developments that have often been resisted in our own world. Our own culture's reluctance to embrace various social movements of the past half century is less than subtly reflected once the backlash campaign begins. Women's rights, for example, are contested in mild-mannered but indignant tirades by husbands complaining about their wives not having dinner ready when they get home from work. Similarly, racial equality symbolically comes under attack when reactionary shopkeepers clinging to the disappearing black-and-white way of life blatantly post hostile "no coloreds" warnings on their storefronts. But, as is often the case when a genie is let loose from its bottle, the chances of returning it there grow progressively slimmer with each passing moment, just as they do in *Pleasantville*.

"Pleasantville" is a thoroughly enjoyable picture, far more substantive than the piece of fluff some of its marketing portrayed it to be. Its strengths are many, most notably in such technical areas as cinematography, art direction, and costumes. But it also shines in its intelligent script, its excellent performances, and its moving Randy Newman score. The picture received three Oscar nominations, for art direction, costumes, and music.

As tempting as it is to romanticize the simplicity enabled by seeing life in black and white, it also seriously limits our choices. Adding even a little color can work wonders, enlightening us to possibilities we might not be able to perceive or appreciate otherwise. It supplies vibrancy and brilliance the other option doesn't afford. And, if nothing else, it makes for an existence that is truly more palette-able.

# Double Feature: Respites for the World-Weary

### "Local Hero"
*Year of Release: 1983*
*Principal Cast: Peter Riegert, Burt Lancaster, Fulton Mackay, Denis Lawson, Jennifer Black, Peter Capaldi, Jenny Seagrove, Christopher Rozycki, Norman Chancer, John Jackson, Christopher Asante*
*Director: Bill Forsyth*
*Screenplay: Bill Forsyth*

"Enchanted April"
*Year of Release: 1992*
*Principal Cast: Josie Lawrence, Miranda Richardson, Joan Plowright,*
*Polly Walker, Alfred Molina, Jim Broadbent, Michael Kitchen*
*Director: Mike Newell*
*Book: Elizabeth von Arnim*
*Screenplay: Peter Barnes*

Escaping the vestiges of everyday life, especially when they weigh heavily on us (whether we're even aware of that), is often the best medicine for mending world-weary souls. And if we consciously create an escape into a world in which magic and wonder rule the day, the cure is that much more effective. That's the remedy put to use in two charming little films about adventures in worlds far away yet ever so close, "Local Hero" and "Enchanted April."

"Local Hero" tells the story of "Mac" MacIntyre (Peter Riegert), a high-powered acquisitions executive for a Houston-based oil company. He regularly arranges deals, generally by Telex, to acquire land and other assets to support the firm's operations, primarily in third world countries. But when he's called upon to make a huge acquisition in Scotland—an entire town and its adjacent bay—he's assigned by his supervisor, Cal (John Jackson), to handle the task in person. Mac is reluctant to go, believing he can sew up the deal in an afternoon over the phone. However, because the orders for this assignment come directly from the big boss, Mr. Happer (Burt Lancaster), the company's tenacious though somewhat eccentric CEO, Cal says there's nothing he can do. He further explains that this deal is different from those Mac typically handles, that on-site negotiations are necessary because "we're dealing with people like ourselves." And so Mac begrudgingly embarks on his journey, unaware that he's setting off on a trip that will change him in ways he can't imagine.

Life in the quaint, slow-paced Scottish coastal hamlet of Furness is far removed from what Mac is accustomed to. He initially goes about his task as if he were still in the button-down corporate world of Houston. Aiding him are a local accountant, Gordon Urquhardt (Denis Lawson), and a local representative from his own company, Danny Oldsen (Peter Capaldi). However, because the acquisition of an entire town is a deal that takes a while to complete, and because he has so much capable assistance at his disposal, Mac has plenty of downtime, allowing him to get to know the locale and its people. His cool, businesslike demeanor gradually melts as he's seduced by his beautiful and magical surroundings. In fact, as the acquisition nears its culmination, Mac begins to have reservations about seeing it through, knowing that its completion will mark an end to this very special way of life.

The locals, meanwhile, being the wily Scots that they are, want to see the deal close because of the piles of cash they'll each receive for their properties. Their wishes thus compound Mac's dilemma, filling him with mixed feelings about what he can—or should—do. However, deciding how to proceed may end up being a moot point. Once the negotiations involve the intervention of Mr. Happer and the shrewd maneuvering of the resident beachcomber, Ben (Fulton Mackay), an eccentric comparable in stature to his newly arrived Yank counterpart, matters are out of Mac's hands. He can only wait to see what happens to the deal he was once so passionate about and to the town he has so grown to love.

In "Enchanted April," four city dwellers seek to get away from the drudgery of life in post–World War I London. Lotty (Josie Lawrence) and Rose (Miranda Richardson), a pair of middle-aged, upper-middle-class housewives, are passing acquaintances from the same church. Desperate for a reprieve from London's bleak weather and her even bleaker marriage to Mellersh (Alfred Molina), an unfeeling, overbearing businessman, Lotty asks Rose to join her in a month's rental of a castle on the Italian coast near Portofino, an opportunity they both just happen to spot in a London newspaper ad. Realizing that she, too, could use a break from her routine and from her husband Frederick (Jim Broadbent), a philanderer with a penchant for living out the escapades he chronicles in the tawdry novels he writes under a pseudonym, Rose agrees to Lotty's proposal.

To defray the costs of their holiday, Lotty and Rose seek the company of two companions, both of whom look to escape their own woes: Mrs. Fisher (Joan Plowright), a prim and proper matron prone to fits of melancholy and regular dispensations of curt tongue-lashings; and Lady Caroline (Polly Walker), a beautiful, wealthy, slightly rebellious young heiress who is the object of many a man's attention but who wants to be appreciated for more than her looks and money. And so with their itineraries set and the keys to the kingdom in hand, as supplied by the property's kindly owner, London businessman George Briggs (Michael Kitchen), the foursome sets off on the adventure of a lifetime.

Once in Italy, life takes on a charm all its own. The beauty of the seacoast and the splendor of the landscape, with its flourishing flower gardens and magical oleander tree, are rejuvenating. The vacationers' worries dissolve, and abilities they never knew they possessed awaken, such as a strong intuitive sense. What's more, as these casual acquaintances come to know one another better, they also discover distant personal connections they didn't know existed. Their synchronous presence together on this trip is obviously no accident.

Given how much they're enjoying themselves, Lotty and Rose decide to share their bliss by inviting their husbands to join them, which they eventually do. Mellersh and Frederick savor the mood of the moment as much as their wives do, which works wonders for their marriages. Even Mr. Briggs pops in for a surprise visit, further adding to the delight. Together, this unlikely group of travelers creates an April that is indeed enchanted.

In both of these pictures, we see characters who have done superb jobs in creating marvelous and much-needed respites for themselves. There's nothing especially profound or philosophically significant in that—just basic conscious creation, done well. But what makes their manifestations so special is the sense of wonder with which they've imbued them. Scotland and Italy are real places, to be sure, but the personal versions of them that they've created are almost surreal, alternate realities unto themselves emerging out of the ranges of "probable Scotlands" or "probable Italys."

The sheer beauty of these locales alone makes them stand out as almost otherworldly (at least considering from whence those visiting these places came), but their charm is punctuated by elements that make them unique. Furness, for example, is home to a cast of colorful characters, including a parish minister originally from Africa who's on a mission to Scotland (Christopher Asante), a Soviet fisherman who loves vacationing in democracy and singing country-and-western songs (Christopher Rozycki), and even a modern-day mermaid of sorts (Jenny Seagrove). The recurring appearances of these and other eccentrics are sources of running jokes that make their presence—and Mac's time in Furness—that much more delightful.

Synchronicity also significantly adds to the travelers' enjoyment of their experiences, as happens routinely in "Enchanted
April." The characters certainly find their creations to be most
satisfying when all the pieces fall into place as projected, but when
unexpected synchronicities occur that heighten their adventures
in unanticipated ways, the readings on the pleasure scale go off
the register. Although this happens in both pictures, its impact is
felt especially strongly in "Local Hero," for whereas the characters
in "Enchanted April" knew they needed vacations, Mac wasn't
aware of it until he was ensconced in the magic of the Scottish
highlands. How magnificent for him!

Both films are joys to watch, especially for those looking to
get away from it all, even if only vicariously. "Local Hero" is
full of the eccentric quirkiness and good humor that characterize many of director Bill Forsyth's movies. His signature knack
for taking the happenstance of everyday life and making it stand
out as special and distinct is unmistakable in this picture, and he
gets his laughs with warmth and imagination, never stooping to
cynicism or mean-spiritedness. The picture's gorgeous cinematography, emotive Mark Knopfler musical score, and thoroughly
enjoyable performances complete this pleasing travel package. In
fact, about the only thing I disliked in this film was an annoying
and largely pointless story line involving Happer and his therapist
(Norman Chancer); whatever this sequence was meant to add, it
failed miserably.

"Enchanted April," by comparison, is a gentler, slightly more
serious film but with all the same warmth and magic. It might be
tempting to classify this movie as a chick flick, but I believe that
would be selling it short, for its metaphysical overtones give it a
hefty measure of substance. Its production values are excellent
across the board, as are its performances, which earned Golden
Globe Awards for Richardson and Plowright (who also received an
Oscar nod). The film received additional Academy Award nominations for its costumes and adapted screenplay and a Globe nod for
best comedy picture. This picture is presently available only in VHS
format, but a DVD version is said to be in production.

Conscious creation isn't always a means for fulfilling lofty
philosophical ideas; sometimes it's a practice that can be used for
just creating a good rest, even when we're not aware we need

it. These pictures give us two excellent examples of how to set up personalized sanctuaries in little worlds all our own. I can practically smell the flowers already . . .

## Bonus Features

"Waking Life": So what exactly are dreams anyway? That's the central question posed in this inventively animated collection of vignettes exploring different interpretations of what dreams might be, as well as some of the unique experiences to be had during them. Colorful, flamboyant, and thought-provoking. (2001; Richard Linklater, director and screenplay)

"Who Framed Roger Rabbit": In a fantasy version of 1940s Hollywood in which real live humans and animated characters ("toons") coexist naturally (if not always harmoniously), cartoon icon Roger Rabbit is wrongfully framed for murder. To solve the crime and clear his name, Roger hires a private investigator. There's just one catch—while the P.I. needs the work, he holds a major grudge against toons, creating an uneasy yet often comical alliance with his new client. Great fun and special effects, with a cavalcade of cameos by classic cartoon characters from Disney and Warner Bros., among others. Who says realities don't overlap? (1988; Bob Hoskins, Joanna Cassidy, Christopher Lloyd, Charles Fleischer [voice of Roger Rabbit], Kathleen Turner [voice of Jessica Rabbit]; Robert Zemeckis, director; Gary K. Wolf, book; Jeffrey Price and Peter S. Seaman, screenplay; three Oscar wins on six nominations, a special achievement Oscar for animation direction; two Golden Globe nominations)

"The Lake House": Lovers separated across time alter their individual realities in hopes of finding one another in the same existence, their only point of contact being a magical mailbox on the property of a beautiful lake house. A chick flick with substance and beautiful cinematography. (2006; Sandra Bullock, Keanu Reeves, Shohreh Aghdashloo, Ebon Moss-Bachrach, Willeke van Ammelrooy, Christopher Plummer, Lynn Collins; Alejandro Agresti, director; Eun Jeong-Kim and Ji-na Yeo, story source; David Auburn, screenplay)

# 11

---

# The Joy and Power of Creation

## *Living Life in Fulfillment*

What hath God wrought!
*Samuel F.B. Morse*

Taped to my home computer monitor is one of the most inspiring sayings I know: "The greatest joy is in creation." For a conscious creator, such is the exuberant essence of the philosophy and its practice. And what is the wellspring of these pearls of wisdom? A fortune cookie from my neighborhood Chinese restaurant. All of which goes to show that one never knows where one's most profound sources of inspiration will come from.

Conscious creation works much like that; creative ideas pop up, seemingly out of nowhere, and blossom into marvelous manifestations. Sometimes the results are so impressive that they leave us stunned, speechless, or overwhelmed with emotion. Such was apparently the case with Samuel F.B. Morse with the first long-distance test of the telegraph in 1844. He was said to have been so deeply moved at the success of his invention that he chose the biblical quote above[1] as the first words to be sent over the wires, a gesture intended to express his awe and gratitude that God had chosen him to be the one to reveal this creation to the world. Of course, had Morse been an avowed conscious creation practitioner, the quote might have been worded a little differently, perhaps something like "What hath God *and I* wrought!" or "What hath *we* wrought!" but that's beside the point. What's

330 | GET THE PICTURE

important is that his choice of sentiment aptly reflects the zeal that successful creation can evoke. It's also an enthusiastic validation of the wisdom of my fortune cookie.

The passion to create would appear to be our birthright. Evidence of this can be found throughout contemporary conscious creation texts, as well as in ancient religious scriptures, such as the Bible, wherein it is said that we are made in God's image and that God's greatest act was to create. From that, it would seem only logical that we are destined to follow in our divine predecessor's footsteps. Indeed, this notion is taken a step even further in a passage from the *Corpus Hermeticum*, an ancient text on alchemy, conscious creation's elder esoteric cousin, as cited by Dennis William Hauck in his comprehensive alchemy text, *The Emerald Tablet*: "If then you do not make yourself equal to God, you cannot apprehend God; for like is known by like. . . . But if you shut up your soul in your body, and abase yourself, and say 'I know nothing, I can do nothing; I am afraid of earth and sea, I cannot mount to heaven; I know not what I was, nor what I shall be,' *then what have you to do with God?*"[2]

Put another way, if we were not meant to be creators in our own right, a mirror of that from which we came, then what would be the point of our existence? To serve as a source of amusement for some distant, capricious, unknowable supreme being? To mark time until the next incarnation (if there is one)? To see how many toys we can accumulate in our allotted time on this planet? None of these options has ever seemed like a viable or satisfying answer to me, so I would have to go with my belief that our purpose for being is to at least approximate the principal creative practices of our divine progenitor.

There is tremendous potential inherent in the act of creation. By performing creative acts, we merge the power of our thoughts with the power of All That Is to bring into being that which we believe and desire. The implications of that are truly staggering. When we look at all of the ways in which we actually use that ability, and combine it with all of the ways we actually *could* use it, the notion becomes almost mind-boggling. By saying this, I'm talking about more than simply painting portraits, writing novels, or producing other tangible examples of creativity; I'm talking about the creation of *every facet* of one's existence, the entire canvas of life upon which our reality is expressed.

This, needless to say, illustrates why it's so important to understand how conscious creation works so that we can make the best use of it in our lives, both individually and collectively. I would certainly never pretend to have all the answers about this practice, but I'd like to think the concepts I've outlined in this book present a basic approach for showing how the process works, with the profiled films offering ample and appropriate illustration. Beginning with an understanding of the magical approach and how our perceptions color our view of the world, and then building upon those ideas with an awareness of our innate powers of choice and the ability to effect change, along with the courage to carry through on our convictions and make use of our knowledge of belief evolution, universal connectedness, special personal capabilities, and alternate realities, we arrive at where we are now—an appreciation of how all these facets combine and integrate into a collective whole, one that's intended to express and celebrate the sought-after objective of this process, the realization of the joy and power of creation.

★　　★　　★

If I were to sum up the essence of the joy and power of creation, I'd do so in two words—value fulfillment, a concept discussed sporadically in several previous chapters. It's a notion Jane Roberts and Seth deemed so important that they devoted a two-volume work to it, titled *Dreams, "Evolution," and Value Fulfillment.*[3] In a nutshell, they define it as follows: "In physical reality, . . . life is the name of the game—and the game is based upon value fulfillment. That means simply that each form of life seeks toward the fulfillment and unfolding of all of the capabilities that it senses within its living framework, knowing that in that individual fulfillment each other species of life is also benefited."[4]

Conscious creation allows us both to discover what our value fulfillment is and then to carry it out. By becoming aware of our purpose through the examination of our beliefs, and then by drawing upon our personal resources, in conjunction with those of the Universe of which we are a part, we have the means to transform our values into fulfilled manifestations. It's the very essence of living up to our potential for the benefit of ourselves and those with whom we share this reality.

This is not to suggest that we're each meant to become personified pinnacles of altruism (though I'm sure we could use all the help we can get in that area these days). Rather, it's meant that we each become the best *true* selves we can be. So if that means your value fulfillment is to be a file clerk, then become the best damned file clerk you can be. Similarly, if you're meant to be a songwriter, then compose to the best of your abilities. Your value fulfillment may even take a form as simple as being the best friend to others that you know how to be; if so, then be that friend. No matter what your value fulfillment is, go forth and become it. In the end, remember that success in any of these endeavors is measured by what you put into it, not by arbitrary external standards of achievement; as long as you're truthfully doing the best you can to live up to your particular purpose, that's what really counts.

There are so many films featuring characters joyfully being themselves as a means to manifest their value fulfillment that it's impossible to present them all here. Whether the expression of value fulfillment involves engaging in unabashed eccentricity, as in "You Can't Take It with You" (1938); or the inexplicable compulsion to build a baseball field in one's backyard, as in "Field of Dreams" (1989); or the drive of a Latino teenager to break into the world of rock 'n roll, as in "La Bamba" (1987); or the dreams of a single mother seeking success as a stand-up comedian, as in "This Is My Life" (1992); or the burning desire of a go-getter businessman to build a new kind of car, as in "Tucker: The Man and His Dream" (1988); or the joy of a young chess master seeking to play his game in the spirit of genuine sportsmanship, as in "Searching for Bobby Fischer" (1993); or the supreme confidence of a chubby teen looking to make a name for herself as a dancer and as an unlikely civil rights activist on a 1960s TV show, as in "Hairspray" (1988); or an actress looking to be true to herself both on- and offstage, as in "Being Julia" (2004), there are innumerable avenues to give life to this concept and countless movies portraying it for the big screen.

With no intended slight to the pictures just listed, this chapter's entries provide some of the best cinematic expressions of value fulfillment. They depict characters who truly live up to the nature of the concept, reveling in the joy and power of creation, as Jane Roberts and Seth wrote about in the following: "Your spirit joined itself with flesh, and in flesh, to experience a world of incredible richness, to help create a dimension of reality of colors and of form. Your spirit was born in flesh to enrich a marvelous area of sense awareness, to feel energy made into corporeal form. You are here to use, enjoy, and express yourself through the body. You are here to aid in the great expansion of consciousness. You are not here to cry about the miseries of the human condition, but to change them when you find them not to your liking through the joy, strength, and vitality that is within you; to create the spirit as faithfully and as beautifully as you can in flesh."[5]

What hath God wrought, indeed.

## Life Is a State of Mind

"Being There"
*Year of Release: 1979*
*Principal Cast: Peter Sellers, Shirley MacLaine, Melvyn Douglas,*
*Jack Warden, Richard Dysart, David Clennon, Richard Basehart,*
*Fran Brill, Ruth Attaway, John Harkins, James Noble*
*Director: Hal Ashby*
*Book: Jerzy Kosinski*
*Screenplay: Jerzy Kosinski*

As conscious creation practitioners know so well, our beliefs form our reality. Consequently, it doesn't take much of a leap to vault to the next level and embrace the sentiment that life truly is a state of mind. The essence of this idea dovetails its forerunner and does so in a way that's more comprehensive and assimilated than its predecessor. It's a notion whose expression is played out on screen in numerous ways in the gentle comedy, "Being There."

Chance (Peter Sellers) is a simple-minded gardener who tends the grounds of a townhouse in a once-elegant but now-rundown section of Washington, D.C. Being the childlike soul that he is, Chance can neither read nor write, having learned virtually everything he knows about the world from watching television. His everyday needs are looked after by an elderly benefactor, Mr. Jennings, and his long-devoted housekeeper, Louise (Ruth Attaway), making it possible for Chance to spend all his time doing what he does best—working in the garden. While the exact relationship between Chance and his patron is never explained, it's suggested the old man must feel some responsibility for Chance's care since the dutiful gardener has lived his entire life within the confines of the townhouse, having never even ridden in a car.

This sheltered existence comes to an abrupt end, however, when the old man dies and leaves no provision in his will for Chance's well-being. Chance learns of this when the lawyers handling the estate, Thomas (David Clennon) and Sally (Fran Brill), inform him that, since no allowance has been made for him, he has no legal right to stay in the house and must therefore vacate the premises. Chance, understandably, is at a loss to fathom any of this, but he complies with the lawyers' instructions. And so, with nowhere to go, he is forced onto the streets of the capital, left to fend for himself for the first time in his life.

As chance (or is that Chance?) would have it, a minor accident fortuitously lands our hero in the company of a wealthy and influential Washington couple, Benjamin Rand (Melvyn Douglas), an ailing tycoon and kingmaker, and Eve (Shirley MacLaine), his socialite wife. They are quickly charmed by their unexpected visitor's ways. They're taken with his plainspoken folksiness, captivated by his simple, straightforward statements, which they routinely misinterpret as profound insights. They are so impressed with his seemingly special wisdom that they introduce him to an assortment of high rollers in the worlds of business, media, and politics, including the President (Jack Warden) and the Soviet ambassador (Richard Basehart). Practically overnight, the once-simple gardener rockets to national prominence.

On a personal level, Ben and Eve welcome Chance into their midst as a breath of fresh air. Ben, who's in the final debilitating stages of aplastic anemia, develops an inner peace in Chance's presence, shedding his fear of dying and taking tremendous comfort in his new friend's strength. Eve, meanwhile, sees Chance as a fountain of compassion, grateful for the heartfelt consolation he offers during this trying time.

Through all of this, however, no one realizes who Chance really is; the various players in this story only have pieces of the puzzle as to his identity, each having encountered Chance separately, in different contexts. In fact, the only one who appears able to connect the dots is Ben's doctor (Richard Dysart), and he can't bring himself to divulge his bubble-bursting discovery once he uncovers it, considering what Chance has done to lift his patient's spirits. But even the doctor's findings may not tell the whole story; no matter how thorough he believes his investigation was, the doctor may have erred in his conclusion as well. Ultimately, there may be much more to this walking enigma than the empirical evidence suggests or than anyone realizes (viewers included).

So, in light of that, one can't help but ask, "Who is this guy anyway?" That's not easy to answer, but, in many ways, he appears to be whatever others need or want him to be. Chance obliges those who cross his path by projecting back to them whatever beliefs they hold, thereby fulfilling their expectations. Those who need him to be a simple man, such as Louise, Thomas, and Sally, see him as such. Those who require him to be a source of wisdom and comfort, like Ben and Eve, perceive him that way. Those who want him to be a cryptic economic guru perched atop a pedestal of fiscal acumen view him accordingly. Even the doctor, who sees him as a mysterious but explicable phenomenon, gets his wish fulfilled. Indeed, Chance, like all the other elements that go into making up these characters' realities, is a reflection of their beliefs, thereby showing how each of their individual lives really is its own existence, its own physically manifested state of mind.

Chance accomplishes this by engaging in a radically profound application of conscious creation, namely, that of using the process to simply be himself. In his case, his true nature is to be different things to different people. As strange as that may sound, that's who he *is*, and he effortlessly lives out the value fulfillment necessary to make that possible. Ben even senses this quality about him, complimenting Chance on his remarkable ability to be perfectly natural.

Being ourselves is probably one of the trickiest undertakings for conscious creators to attempt, for, as much as we aspire to the idea in theory, we instead tend to focus our thoughts more along the lines of exploring particular probabilities and achieving designated outcomes. We often believe we must formulate intents that come dressed up in specific packages, adorned with the trappings of distinct avenues of expression, all destined for the manifestation of identifiable results. (It certainly takes some of the mystery out of things, now doesn't it?) But what if we could simplify all that by putting forth the belief that just being ourselves is the desired outcome? That could save us considerable anguish and hand-wringing in discovering our true selves and the value fulfillment that we're meant to live out.

Chance succeeds at this by drawing upon one of the simplest but most powerful statements ever made in the prolific collaboration between Jane Roberts and Seth: "The present is the point of power."[6] It's quite a state of mind for living one's life. And by living in the moment, focusing his creative powers in the present, Chance draws to him whatever he needs to get by at that time. He doesn't get hung up on what may have happened in the past or what might happen in the future; he simply lives in his present. Again, as Jane Roberts and Seth wrote, "All of your physical, mental and spiritual abilities are focused together, then, in the brilliant concentration of 'present' experience. You are not at the mercy of the past, or of previous convictions, unless you <u>believe</u> that you are."[7] In the end, such thinking allows Chance to just be himself, whatever that self may be in any given moment.

This approach works to Chance's advantage, for it allows him to evolve as necessary along with everything else in his reality, embodying the idea that Jane Roberts and Seth so frequently noted that each of us is in a constant state of becoming. It also feeds his value fulfillment, living up to the concept's core meaning by benefiting Chance and everyone around him: "Value fulfillment means that each individual, each entity, of whatever nature, spontaneously, automatically seeks those conditions that are suited to its own fulfillment, and to the fulfillment of others."[8]

"Being There" is an utterly charming picture, perhaps one of the most underrated pieces of cinema of the past thirty years. Keep a box of tissues handy as you watch it; you'll need it to wipe away the tears, be they from laughter, sadness, or awe.

Sellers gives the performance of his career as Chance, playing the savant-like gardener with a Chaplinesque appeal and the deadpan vocal intonation of Stan Laurel, a portrayal that won him a Golden Globe Award and an Oscar nomination. Douglas turns in an equally fine performance as the once-robust but now-vulnerable power broker, a role that earned him awards at both the Oscars and the Globes. The remainder of the cast provides capable support, their reactions of gullibility, guile, or embarrassment entirely believable, depending on their relationships to the protagonist.

Given Chance's preoccupation with television, the film prominently features broadcast clips as part of the narrative. Snippets of commercials, cartoons, movies, and other programming appear throughout, their substance subtly but effectively reinforcing the main action taking place on screen, usually through splendidly dry wit. (Don't be surprised if you find yourself snickering when you think you probably shouldn't be.)

The picture is superbly written by Jerzy Kosinski, who adapted the screenplay from his own novel, an effort that earned him a Golden Globe nod. The choice of the palatial Biltmore estate as the location for filming the aristocratic Rands at home is a fitting and beautiful backdrop, and the movie's soundtrack, dominated by the wispy, lilting Gnossiennes of Erik Satie, is the perfect background music for this delightfully airy tale. Pulling it all together is the expert direction of Hal Ashby, who produced some of his best work on this picture. In all, the film received one Oscar on two nominations (far short of what it deserved) and two Globes on six nominations. It was also a Palme D'Or contender at the Cannes Film Festival.

Throughout our lives, we all have moments when we wonder why we're here. We search high and low for answers, for truths that we hope will point the way for us. But in doing so, we often spin our wheels, never finding what we're searching for. Maybe we should instead just look to the moment we're in at the time, soaking up the present and seeing where our state of mind is at that point. If we do that in complete sincerity and openness, we just might see where our lives truly are.

**Extra Credits:** Living life in the moment, and making that the basis for one's state of mind, is the focus of another film profiling a character with a simple approach to life, "Forrest Gump." The picture tells the story of a young Southern man who seems to have a number of breaks going against him but who also makes the most out of living by simply being himself, rising to surprising levels of notoriety and creating a happy and fulfilled existence for himself. Although some of it admittedly plays like a live-action version of *Peabody's Improbable History*, the movie is full of gentle humor and a knockout performance by Tom Hanks in the role of the title character. (1994; Tom Hanks [Oscar and Golden Globe winner], Robin Wright, Gary Sinise, Mykelti Williamson, Sally Field; Robert Zemeckis, director [Oscar and Golden Globe winner]; Winston Groom, book; Eric Roth, screenplay [Oscar winner]; six Oscar wins, including best picture, on thirteen nominations; three Golden Globe wins, including best dramatic picture, on seven nominations)

# Finding Happiness by Finding Oneself

"It's a Wonderful Life"
*Year of Release: 1946*
*Principal Cast: James Stewart, Donna Reed, Lionel Barrymore,*
*Henry Travers, Thomas Mitchell, Beulah Bondi, Frank Faylen,*
*Ward Bond, Gloria Grahame, H.B. Warner, Frank Albertson,*
*Todd Karns, Samuel S. Hinds, William Edmunds, Sheldon Leonard*
*Director: Frank Capra*
*Story: Philip Van Doren Stern*
*Screenplay: Frances Goodrich, Albert Hackett, Frank Capra, Jo Swerling*

The search for happiness in life sometimes is stymied by a lot of overwrought, self-induced frustration. We think we want something that never materializes, causing us to brood mercilessly, all the while overlooking the real joy we've created that's right before our eyes. But if we're able to perceive things as they really are, we just might have a chance to discover true, unconditional happiness for ourselves. Such is the odyssey of the likable hero of the perennial Christmas classic, "It's a Wonderful Life."

This is another of those cinematic icons that's so entrenched in popular culture that it's hard to imagine anyone not knowing its fabled story line. But for the few who haven't had the good fortune to see it, here goes.

George Bailey (James Stewart) has big plans for his life. He wants to build things, travel the world, and make a name for himself. If nothing else, he wants to flee the confines of Bedford Falls, the "crummy little town" in Upstate New York where he grew up. But each time he tries to make his escape, something happens that locks him into staying put. For example, when his father (Samuel S. Hinds) suffers a stroke, George puts off his own plans to manage the affairs of the family business, the Bailey Building & Loan. And just when he thinks he can crawl out from under that responsibility, other setbacks arise that keep him from moving forward. Over time, his mounting sacrifices take their toll.

As if that weren't enough, George is forced into regularly matching wits with the town's curmudgeonly robber baron, Old Man Potter (Lionel Barrymore). He owns practically everything in Bedford Falls except the Building & Loan, a definite sore spot for the greedy old miser. He wiles away the hours counting his money and hatching schemes to take over the one business in town he can't seem to get his hands on, thanks in large part to George's intervention.

Of course, not everything goes against George. He courts and weds his adoring wife, Mary (Donna Reed), starts a family, and builds many long-lasting friendships with the citizens of Bedford Falls, mainly by making decent, affordable housing available to them through the Building & Loan.

But no matter how well George takes his misfortunes in stride, life seems to keep tossing curve balls his way. The worst of these comes one Christmas Eve morning, when he's suddenly thrown into a severe financial crisis that threatens to ruin him, his business, and his family, launching George into deep despair and anguished desperation. He even contemplates making the ultimate sacrifice so that a life insurance policy payout will save the day for his heirs. It's when that ominous prospect looms that the time comes for divine intervention, and it arrives in the form of a good-natured, though oft-befuddled cherubic soul named Clarence (Henry Travers), George's guardian angel.

Clarence has a vested stake in the outcome of George's ordeal, too. As a second-class angel in search of his wings, he must successfully guide George through his turmoil and restore his sense of hope to receive them. But how?

After Clarence succeeds in preventing George's suicide, George grouses over yet another set of failed plans, lamenting that he can't even kill himself properly. With his financial woes still unresolved, he sputters rhetorically that perhaps everyone he believes he's let down would be better off if he'd never been born. That statement gives Clarence the inspiration he needs to help show George the way out of his troubles. He then proceeds to give George a glimpse of what the lives of those he's touched would have been like if he hadn't been born. As George watches this dark alternate reality play out before him, one in which those he cares about suffer miserably in his absence, he comes to see the magnitude of his contributions to bettering their lives, which makes his current problems and his long-unrealized plans seem trivial by comparison. He realizes, as Clarence says to him with the utmost sincerity and compassion, "You see, George, you really had a wonderful life." George is thus reborn, his perspective renewed, his life reaffirmed. But as good as all that is, it's just the beginning. Things are about to get even better, in ways beyond anything he could possibly imagine.

From a tender age, George always had a good grasp of the nature of his value fulfillment. He was right on target in recognizing that he'd carry out big plans someday. Unfortunately, he doesn't acknowledge their manifestation when it happens. He's so hung up on envisioning the physical form his plans should take that he fails to recognize the materialization of their underlying intents when they come into being, and when his expectations of form aren't fulfilled, he's sorely disappointed. Yet his creations surely are big, if not in scope then at least in terms of impact.

For example, the countless Bedford Falls residents who have affordable housing because of George would be leading very different lives if it weren't for him, but he downplays his role in this. What's more, he even gets to live out his dream of being a builder through the homes he constructs. But he again discounts this, seeing the houses as small potatoes compared to the bridges and skyscrapers he'd much rather be building. Even from the standpoint of being a good, helpful friend, George fails to see the significance of his efforts, including in life-or-death situations. No matter how he tries to dismiss the influence of his contributions, George does more personally to enrich the lives of his peers than anything his so-called big projects ever could have.

What George needs to realize and appreciate what he's done is the metaphysical equivalent of a good stiff poke in the ribs, which is where Clarence comes in. Clarence helps lift the self-imposed fog that's obscured George's view of things, helping to give him vision about his visions, a clarity of perspective that has long been lacking. He helps George get out of his own way, to value the *meaningful* outcomes of his labors and not just the tangible ones. With such a clarified view, George can then see how his beliefs and value fulfillment have been realized. Their form may not be what he anticipated, but their impact lived up to the expectations he carried around with him since childhood. With a fresh perspective now in place, there's no telling what George could do next. He can revel in being himself and all the resplendent glory that goes along with that.

The payoffs to George for his newfound awareness are tremendous. Besides the satisfaction of knowing he accomplished what he set out to do (at least from an underlying intent standpoint), as well as the tangible and intangible rewards that come with that (which vastly exceed his expectations), he can take pride in having given life to his value fulfillment. George lives up to the nature of the concept in its strictest sense, too, for his actions benefit both him and others around him. What joy there is in creation like that! To see it manifest as abundantly as it does, and then to witness it benefit so many, is indeed a blessing.

Of course, an outcome like this is not unexpected when we're aligned with our value fulfillment, for life's true purpose is given realization. The degree of success that results from such an alignment is not surprising, either, for the support of the Universe is behind us when we're in line with our value fulfillment. As such films as "The Secret" (see chapter 3) show, the Universe gets behind those who follow their aspirations with gusto and sincerity. In George's case, that support takes the form of direct intervention, personified through the appearance of Clarence in his life. But no matter how divine assistance manifests itself, it's an integral characteristic of our Universe, as Jane Roberts and Seth wrote in *The Nature of the Psyche*: "Nature is luxurious and abundant in its expression. The greater reality from which nature springs is even more abundant, and within that multidimensional experience no individual is ignored, forgotten, lost or forsaken . . . You are a portion of All That Is; therefore the universe leans in <u>your</u> direction."[9]

It's hard to imagine anyone not liking this movie, a contemporary fable presented with warmth, emotion, hopefulness, and an overriding sense of compassion, magical in every respect. It seems like it should have been just the picture for battle-weary Americans to flock to in the wake of World War II. However, it received a tepid response when initially released, despite earning five Oscar nominations, including nods for best picture, best director, and Stewart's performance as lead actor. Amazingly, it went home empty-handed, and two of its strongest performances, those of Reed and Barrymore, were even overlooked as nominees. The only major recognition it received was a much-deserved Golden Globe Award for director Frank Capra.[10]

By finding ourselves, we find our happiness, as George discovers, albeit a little late but better than not at all. And that, as I'm sure we can all appreciate, truly has the makings for a wonderful life.

# Reach for the Stars

### "The Right Stuff"
*Year of Release: 1983*
*Principal Cast: Sam Shepard, Scott Glenn, Fred Ward, Ed Harris,*
*Charles Frank, Dennis Quaid, Lance Henriksen, Scott Paulin,*
*Barbara Hershey, Pamela Reed, Veronica Cartwright,*
*Mary Jo Deschanel, Kim Stanley, Jeff Goldblum, Harry Shearer,*
*David Clennon, Donald Moffat, Scott Wilson*
*Director: Philip Kaufman*
*Book: Tom Wolfe*
*Screenplay: Philip Kaufman*

From nearly the time we're born and all through our formative years, we're repeatedly prodded to strive to live up to our potential (that is, achieve our value fulfillment). Be it through avuncular advice, a favorite teacher's inspiration, graduation speech clichés, or even savvy Microsoft commercials, we're all heartened to reach for the stars. Beginning in the late 1940s, an intrepid group of seekers began such a quest in earnest—and quite literally. It was a journey that took a special breed of individuals, those with an elusively indefinable set of qualities that distinguished them from all others, those who had "the right stuff." And it is their story that is presented through the feature film bearing the same name.

"The Right Stuff," based on the best-selling book by Tom Wolfe, tells the heroic saga of American test pilots who flirted with, and eventually surpassed, the sound barrier and later went on to become the country's first astronauts. Beginning with the first faster-than-sound flights at Edwards Air Force Base in California's high desert, the movie then chronicles the lives of those who vied to join the space program. In doing so, the film looks at their stories from a variety of angles—the search for finding those who had what it took, the impact this adventure had on the individuals and their families, the quest for recognition of personal accomplishments, and the interaction between those who performed these daring feats and those who helped make them possible, both fiscally and scientifically. The result is a thoroughly involving story that engages viewers from start to finish (a pretty nifty trick for a picture that's nearly three and a half hours long—and hardly seems like it).

As for what constituted "the right stuff," it was the serendipitous mix of attributes and skills essential for successfully fulfilling the program's objectives. Those who had it were, among other things, part consummate professional, part barnstorming daredevil, part noble explorer, part technical expert, and part goodwill ambassador. Those possessing these qualities in the right combination became the first generation of Americans to travel into space, the Mercury 7 astronauts.

The movie focuses primarily on four of the spacemen, Alan Shepard (Scott Glenn), Gus Grissom (Fred Ward), John Glenn (Ed Harris), and Gordon Cooper (Dennis Quaid), the first three and the last, respectively, of the astronauts to embark on solo space flights. It simultaneously follows the story of Chuck Yeager (Sam Shepard), a peer of those in the Mercury program who was the unsung hero of the test pilot corps. Yeager was the courageous flyboy who broke the sound barrier in 1947 but who didn't receive accolades for his accomplishments at the time, an achievement kept secret for national security reasons; he was also passed over for the space program, being seen as too much of a maverick to fit the squeaky clean image NASA sought. Yet, despite the divergent paths these daredevils ultimately took, they had sincere mutual respect for one another, as well as sheer exuberance for the objectives they pursued. Those qualities play a large part in engendering the inspiration these characters evoke.

As the film shows, these flyboys certainly love what they do, and it's apparent in all the ways they go about it. Their beliefs create whatever they need to do the job and to have a good time doing it. Clearly, when one authentically lives out his value fulfillment, as these characters do, it shows. Their joy is particularly evident in the film's unmistakable sense of humor. Many sequences elicit responses ranging from mild chuckles to outright guffaws, but never becoming slapstick, juvenile, or obvious in doing so. Such humor aptly depicts the genuine fun that these characters had and that should be an integral part of the conscious creation process. After all, one of the most gratifying aspects of working magic is the sheer enjoyment that comes from participating in it. The envelope-pushing daredevils of this movie play that for all it's worth.

The primary benefit these characters reap from their conscious creation efforts is a tremendous outburst of confidence, a belief in themselves that they can accomplish whatever they set out to do, and that's certainly not lost on viewers. Watching them merrily go about their undertakings is inspiring, but in a genuine way, without being forced or resorting to cheap, schmaltzy sentimentality. They personify the upbeat, can-do attitude that characterized the space program's early days, a hopefulness that fueled the optimism of a whole generation of young Americans who believed passionately in the pursuit of the possible, in no matter what field of endeavor. The film's positive portrayal of a more innocent, more idealistic time, without falling prey to revisionist nostalgia or chest-beating propaganda, is certainly refreshing in troubled and cynical times. That was the case when the picture was initially released, and it's just as true today.

"The Right Stuff" is a wonderful picture. Philip Kaufman's masterful, well-paced direction fleshes out a great story that has a little bit of everything and something for everyone. The movie has a heroic bravado that's tremendously rousing without ever becoming corny, clichéd, cartoonish, or monodimensionally macho, all of which it easily could have been if left in the hands of a less skillful director. Rich character development infuses the excellent performances of everyone from the protagonists to the innumerable one-scene walk-ons, all of whom lend ample color and wit to the narrative. These strengths are further underscored by a knockout script, great special effects, and gallant original music by Bill Conti. The film deservedly captured four Oscars for original score, sound, sound effects editing, and film editing, as well as four additional nominations, including nods for Shepard's supporting performance and for best picture. It also earned a Golden Globe nomination for best dramatic picture.

The crew that put together this film—and the real-life characters whose stories provided fodder for it—are to be commended for their topflight contributions to cinema, aeronautics, space exploration, and the lore of conscious creation. They showed it well. They lived it well. They had the right stuff. And that's important, for that's what it truly takes to reach for the stars and to experience the joy and power of creation.

**Author's Notebook:** "The Right Stuff" holds a special place for me in the evolution of my conscious creation abilities. When I first saw it, at the time of its initial release, the movie helped nurture the germination of some recently sown metaphysical seeds that have been sprouting ever since.

In 1983, I was spearheading the launch (pun intended) of a new trade magazine, *Interior Landscape Industry*, a monthly journal for the indoor horticulture business. I was excited about the project, because I was living out my value fulfillment at the time. But I was also working alone and putting in extremely long hours, so much so that I had virtually no time for a social life, including on weekends. Even my primary mode of entertainment—the movies—was sacrificed during this start-up phase. As I plugged away, however, I was quickly getting burned out from not having any fun, not the best state of mind to operate under when trying to bring out the best in one's creativity.

Then one Saturday night, after a full day's work, two friends invited me to join them for a screening of this film. I really wanted to see it, but, with an encroaching deadline, I thought I needed to be responsible and keep working. I hemmed and hawed but finally relented, realizing I *really* needed a night's diversion to stay fresh.

When we got to the theater, we found a long box office line. (This was in the days before online ticket sales and the proliferation of neighborhood multiplexes.) We managed to get tickets, but, when we entered the theater, it was packed. I began to wonder whether leaving my work behind to watch a three-and-a-half-hour movie in a warm, crowded theater after a tiring day's toil was a good idea. How wrong I was.

I was engaged from start to finish, as was seemingly everyone else in the audience that night. People were actively involved in what they were watching, laughing heartily on cue and actually applauding at the end. When was the last time you remember *that* happening at a movie? We left the theater feeling significantly recharged, especially me.

I wasn't aware of the conscious creation message this movie delivered at that time, but I must have sensed something about it because I was able to throw myself back into my work with a vengeance. I went on to create some of the most stellar elements that went into the magazine's premiere issue. Some might want to chalk that up to simply having a night off at last, but I believe there was more to it than that—namely, the energizing influence of the film. It was infectious, igniting an outburst of creativity just when I needed it most. It helped show me my own sense of the joy and power of creation.

## When a Spiritual Existence Isn't Enough

"Wings of Desire"
*Year of Release: 1987*
*Principal Cast: Bruno Ganz, Otto Sander, Solveig Dommartin,*
*Curt Bois, Peter Falk*
*Director: Wim Wenders*
*Screenplay: Wim Wenders, Peter Handke*

Many followers of both New Age thought and traditional religion put their faith in the notion of slipping the bonds of physicality, transforming themselves into transcendent noncorporeal beings who become one with the Universe. They long for the time when they can ascend to a perceived higher plane of existence, one in which they shed their earthly skin for an experience that's nonphysical but appreciably more substantial than that of the secular realm, one in which they bask in the undifferentiated expanse of the cosmos. Sounds positively blissful, doesn't it? (I can practically hear those harp strings being plucked already.) But what if it isn't enough? Maybe the loss of distinctiveness, the eradication of one's readily identifiable character, the disappearance of sensual physicality, aren't everything they're said to be. The lure for experience of this world may be greater than any of us can possibly imagine. That's the prospect a discontented angel evaluates in the otherworldly fantasy, "Wings of Desire."

Damiel (Bruno Ganz) is fascinated by the human condition. As an angel, he has observed it through the eons in all its permutations. The operative word there, however, is *observed*. Direct, firsthand experience has eluded him. Accompanied by his companion Cassiel (Otto Sander), Damiel has watched the grand spectacle of humanity unfold across time, recording the details of it in an immortal journal for an eternal posterity. But as intriguing as bearing witness to all this has been, Damiel still longs to be more than a mere spectator.

Roaming about Berlin, his home throughout eternity, Damiel takes in all he sees of this divided city during the days not long before the fall of the Wall. He sees happiness. He sees loneliness. He sees love, worry, dissatisfaction, ennui, youthfulness, age—the whole range of human experience. He soaks up every detail and nuance of life there is to be had with a mixture of envy and sadness, jealous that he can't readily engage in everything mortals take for granted and sorrowful that they don't appreciate the one thing that they have that he most wants—the chance to be human in the truest sense of the word.

What Damiel needs to overcome this unrequited longing is a reason to commit to taking the plunge, to fall from the sky[11] and assume human form. He wanders the city in search of an incentive to become physical, and he finds it in the form of a lovely but lonely trapeze artist, Marion (Solveig Dommartin). Love, it seems, conquers all, even the barrier between the worlds.

Guiding Damiel in the ways of his newfound existence is actor Peter Falk, playing a fictionalized version of himself. Damiel encounters him while visiting a movie set, and after several such interactions, Falk, sensing Damiel's presence, begins speaking to him, even though he can't see his apparitional colleague. Once Damiel becomes physical, he visits Falk again, who confides that he can relate to Damiel's transition, having done it himself years earlier. Damiel is astonished by this revelation, but Falk assures him it's not uncommon—that many others in their shoes have done the same, seeking more out of being when a spiritual existence isn't enough.

Being physical appears to be a far more seductive proposition than most of us realize. But none of this should come as any surprise. We, as physical beings, are often equally intrigued by the abilities that spirits and other noncorporeal beings are said to possess, such as the abilities to float, pass through solid objects, or bilocate. So should it be any wonder that they'd be mesmerized by what we do that they can't? Things we completely take for granted are sources of amazement to those whose realities operate according to different principles.

Damiel cites endless examples of things he'd like to experience, such as seeing the color in another's eyes, feeling the ink of a newspaper page when it rubs off on one's fingers, even having a cup of coffee. We may find such aspects of life mundane, but those who can't experience them find them an endless source of fascination.

In seeking to become physical, Damiel engages in his own version of conscious creation. He longs to realize this goal, but, of course, he can't do so until he believes he can. And he can't believe he can until he has sufficient incentive (the proper value fulfillment) to do so, which comes in the form of his infatuation with Marion. When these elements at last come into play, he's able to make his transition, all of which suggests that conscious creation and value fulfillment are concepts whose principles transcend the laws of physical existence, that they operate across realities other than just our own, applying as much to angels as they do to mortals.

Berlin in the days before the collapse of the Wall is the perfect metaphorical setting for this story. As a casualty of Cold War ideology, this once-divided city came to epitomize the separation of East and West, capitalism and communism, even good and evil (depending on one's political orientation). But, even more than that, it also came to symbolize humanity's separation from itself, the deliberate division of our physical and nonphysical selves, our secular and spiritual beings, our heavenly and earthly natures.

Damiel's longing to be part of a world that he can almost touch but from which he also appears to be intentionally cut off is filled with both a hopeful yearning and a desolate sadness. His feelings not only reflect those experienced by Berliners at the time but also by many in the world at large today who feel detached and lonely, longing for connection to (or reconnection with) parts of themselves from which they have become woefully divided.

This setting also provides the perfect backdrop for exploring many big philosophical questions, such as those related to life and death and the nature of existence. Issues like these are explored from both earthly and heavenly viewpoints, simultaneously showing their disparate, separated qualities and their inherent interconnectedness. Such perspectives are addressed frequently in poetic voice-over soliloquies by Damiel, Cassiel, Marion, Falk, and an aging poet, Homer (Curt Bois).

One particularly intriguing concept that Damiel and Cassiel discuss is the eternal permanence of experience. Although some may think of experience as fleeting and meaningless, they note that, once something occurs, in no matter what realm of expression, it exists forever, recorded in the annals of the Universe. The notion that a probability's manifestation lives on in perpetuity, even if the one who brought it about is no longer around to personally recollect its materialization, is comforting to those who view existence as a pointless exercise in futility. The sheer expression of experience, no matter what it may be, obviously must have some value if the Universe is willing to go to all the effort of keeping a record of it for eternity.

Damiel's decision ultimately to seek physicality, to bring about the long-anticipated union of spirit and flesh, ironically presaged the fall of the Wall and the reunification of both Berlin and its German motherland. This bold move, taken of his own volition, provides an empowering example of what's possible when an individual (or a city or a country) decides to reconcile artificially separated elements. His actions serve as significant inspiration to those who are today searching for this same sort of harmony for themselves, provided they remember that the first step must always be theirs.

"Wings of Desire" is a hauntingly beautiful film, visual poetry at its finest. Its script is itself highly poetic, drawing heavily from the works of Rainer Maria Rilke. Its use of both black-and-white and color photography is especially intriguing in portraying the perspectives of angels and mortals, respectively, a reversal from what one might expect in light of traditional views of heaven and Earth. The picture was a Palme D'Or nominee at the Cannes Film Festival and was the winner of the competition's best director award for filmmaker Wim Wenders.

If any of us ever feel that physical existence isn't worth it, we should pause to consider Damiel's experience, how much he longs for what we have that he does not. And if that isn't enough to change our outlook, then we should look to the words of French theologian Pierre Teilhard de Chardin, who so eloquently stated that "We are not human beings having a spiritual experience. We are spiritual beings having a human experience."[12]

# As When the World Was New

### "Star Trek II: The Wrath of Khan"
*Year of Release: 1982*
*Principal Cast: William Shatner, Leonard Nimoy, DeForest Kelley,*
*James Doohan, Walter Koenig, George Takei, Nichelle Nichols,*
*Bibi Besch, Merritt Butrick, Paul Winfield, Kirstie Alley,*
*Ricardo Montalban, John Vargas*
*Director: Nicholas Meyer*
*Story Source: Gene Roddenberry (TV series creator)*
*Story: Harve Bennett, Jack B. Sowards*
*Screenplay: Jack B. Sowards*

There comes a time in almost everyone's life when we need a little revitalization. For many, this often arises in middle age, when it dawns on us that the years have piled up and that we're suddenly closer to the end than we are to the beginning. It's a time when we can begin to feel old and worn out, especially if we've lost sight of our value fulfillment, either through letting it slip away or never having found it to begin with. Some kind of spark is needed to get us back on track, just the kind that's sought in the sci-fi classic, "Star Trek II: The Wrath of Khan."

James T. Kirk (William Shatner), the longtime captain of the Starship Enterprise, is interminably bored now that he's been promoted to admiral, a position that's turned the galactic swash-buckler into a paper-pushing administrator. He seems resigned to a future of bureaucratic mediocrity, all the while wishing he were back gallivanting through the stars. His best friends try to be supportive, but they don't mince words when it comes to his decision to accept promotion. Dr. Leonard "Bones" McCoy (DeForest Kelley) accuses Kirk of hiding behind rules and regulations as a way to cover his dissatisfaction, while Captain Spock (Leonard Nimoy) appeals to his friend's sense of value fulfillment, saying that accepting promotion was a decision that goes against his first, best destiny—that of being a starship commander. And, as things would have it, Kirk soon gets an opportunity to heed their advice and take back his command, not to mention his power and his life.

While on a routine training mission to evaluate the performance of Spock's newest crop of cadets, an emergency arises that calls for Kirk to assume command. He unexpectedly becomes embroiled in battle with an old nemesis, Khan (Ricardo Montalban), a genetically engineered superman whom he exiled to a remote untamed planet fifteen years earlier. Having commandeered a starship of his own, Khan is now back to exact revenge on his old foe.

As the battle between Kirk and Khan unfolds, however, it quickly becomes a feud over more than just vengeance. They also vie for control of the technology associated with a scientific research program called Project Genesis. The Project's intent is to create life from lifelessness, rearranging particles at the molecular level to turn inanimate material into organic matter. By introducing this technology onto a barren planetary body, such as an uninhabited moon, a lifeless rock in space can be transformed into a living, breathing planet capable of supporting life. It's a technology that, like the biblical book after which it is named, brings the power of creation to bear in the most literal sense. Of course, if the technology were introduced someplace where life already existed, it would eradicate such life in favor of the new patterns it was programmed to generate. Creation, it would seem, can be quite the dual-edged sword.

On top of all this, Kirk must also wrestle with his unresolved feelings toward an old flame, Dr. Carol Marcus (Bibi Besch), the researcher who developed Project Genesis along with her son and fellow scientist David (Merritt Butrick), the love child from whom Kirk has long been estranged. It would thus appear the venerable admiral has a plate that's fuller than he's seen in a long time. But cheating death, saving the day, and getting the girl are all in a day's work for a natural-born hero like Kirk. This adventure gives him the catalyst he needs to rediscover his value fulfillment, shedding the middle-aged funk that's been devouring him and allowing him to feel young again, as Carol so aptly puts it, "as when the world was new."

The value fulfillment theme permeates this picture, affecting virtually every character in one way or another. For instance, when Kirk initially explains to Spock the nature of the emergency the ship is facing, he asks his longtime colleague how his crew of trainees will respond, to which his wise friend simply replies, "each according to his gifts." The impending crisis will thus give them all an opportunity to see how well they perform, to test the viability of their perceived value fulfillment. Those who rise to the occasion will discover their calling to serve as starship crew members; those who don't will recognize the need to pursue other vocations and courses of living.

After answering Kirk's question, Spock then engages in his own brand of value fulfillment by relinquishing command of the ship. Kirk initially declines his offer, but Spock reminds him that, as the superior officer aboard, he's obligated to take charge now that the ship is heading into active duty. Kirk tries to evade this responsibility by making it appear as though he's sparing Spock's feelings, but Spock, who comes from a planet whose culture eschews emotion and operates on the basis of logic, reminds his old friend that he has no ego to bruise, that surrendering control of the ship will not offend him. Spock thus practices his value fulfillment, first by knowing his proper place and then by prodding Kirk into performing his command duty, an action that would be in line with the value fulfillment he has been ducking ever since accepting promotion. Spock further emphasizes this point by concurring with Kirk's philosophical contention that "the needs of the many outweigh the needs of the few, or the one." This is a theme that comes up on more than one occasion in the film and, in many ways, echoes sentiments at the very heart of value fulfillment.[13]

Khan, vile though he may be, has his own important value fulfillment to live out. Were it not for him, Kirk would likely still be stuck behind his computer console. In addition, Khan draws into focus the debate over how to use the Project Genesis technology, be it for good or evil purposes. Without him, this issue might have never seen the light of day; worse yet, had he not raised the issue (and drawn Kirk into the debate), who knows how this technology might have been used?

Then there are the Drs. Marcus, who certainly give life to their value fulfillment in grand fashion. Their ambitious science project takes the notion of conscious creation to a whole new level with the manifestation of ecosystems on a planetary scale. The imagination and beliefs required to envision such a concept, let alone create the technology necessary to help bring it into being, are awe-inspiring indeed, dwarfing even the most elaborate plans that most of us will probably ever undertake. But the inspiration this project provides shows how it's not only possible, but also desirable, to dream large.

In the course of dreaming large, big issues are likely to surface, and that's very much the case in this film. All throughout, the characters regularly deliberate such themes as life and death, creation and destruction, good and evil—all the topics that make the essence of a worthy morality play. Although the outer space setting may not seem a likely venue for such musings, these issues are just as applicable there as they would be in any terrestrial locale, evidencing their inherent universality. Getting a little philosophy as part of the package only serves to heighten the value of this picture as one that's fun both to watch and to learn from.

"Star Trek II" is without a doubt the best film in this long-running theatrical series.[14] The story is a winner from start to finish, and its stellar writing lives up to its usual degree of excellence. The special effects, which were state of the art for the time, are a bit dated now, though still impressive. And its performances, while certainly not award caliber, were definitely a cut above any of the *Trek* offerings that preceded or followed it.

The joy and power of creation are celebrated in this movie with flair, style, and feeling. It reminds us of what's possible when we allow ourselves to draw upon the conscious creation process to bring into being what we imagine, envision, and desire. It truly shows us, as its famous signature tagline maintains, how to "boldly go where no one has gone before," in all its implications. In this particular adventure, that involves going to an entirely new world, one in which our dreams contribute to ushering in its creation just as much as any technology ever could.

Moreover, this picture's exploration into the concept of consciously creating the world is the exact opposite from where we began in this book with "Fat Man and Little Boy," a film wherein the protagonists actively worked at developing technology capable of destroying it. In that sense, then, this movie is the perfect counterpoint to where we started, the opposing cinematic bookend. Of course, there are other mirror-image parallels at work in these two pictures that are just as significant as well. For instance, just as Dr. Oppenheimer speculated about the beneficial uses of nuclear technology, as noted in this book's opening entry, this picture clearly illustrates the researchers' concerns over the use of their creation as a weapon to wipe out life where it already exists, a grotesque perversion of its intended purpose.

All of which ultimately brings us back once again to the idea of knowing what our intents are when we engage in conscious creation, for, as these two pictures so fittingly show, one creation can be used in multiple ways, depending on the beliefs behind it. That's significant, for as these films also show, the world—and our very existence—may depend on it. May we thus always have the wisdom to make the right choices, to see the joy and power of creation gloriously expressed in all its beauty, bounty, and splendor.

# Epilogue

## Inspiring the Multiplex of the Mind

You must be the change you wish to see in the world.
*Mahatma Gandhi*

When we engage in conscious creation, we partake in a process that brings into being what we envision for ourselves. Our hoped-for manifestations can take many forms, from the ideal job to the perfect mate to any number of material objects that fulfill our heart's desire. Certainly all are valid choices, especially when they help build a strong foundation for our well-being. But what if we already have most of what we want and need? What should we use the process for then?

I'd like to propose that we employ conscious creation for a daring, radical application: What if we were to use it to shoot the works and reach for the stars—to courageously draw upon it for changing the world? Now *that* would be an accomplishment. It's one that calls to mind the vision of legendary Chicago architect Daniel Burnham, who enthusiastically asserted that determined practitioners of his profession should "make no little plans."[1]

As daunting a task as that might sound, it needn't be. Think of it this way. If the conscious creation process works for small applications, like bringing you a parking space or an elevator when you need it, then what's to say it can't work in larger ways, too? The only limitation preventing that from happening would be the beliefs we put out. If we dream small, we'll reap small rewards. If we think big, we'll realize harvests of like magnitude. The process works in both instances, the only difference being the scope of what's sought, an attribute directly tied to the beliefs driving it in the first place. Granted, it may take a little time to build up the proficiency and confidence necessary to employ conscious creation intentionally for a goal as ambitious as this, but with familiarity and practice come progressively enhanced outcomes. Like a muscle, it grows stronger with use.

Perhaps the trickiest aspect in this is figuring out what we would want a changed world to be like. That's where the wisdom of Gandhi comes in. Being the change we want to see in the world is a brilliant insight, one of the most astute pieces of guidance we can draw upon for this endeavor. It's also a great starting point, one that's premised on the belief that changing ourselves makes it possible for the surrounding world to follow suit. If we dare to dream a notion so bold, there's no telling what wondrous creations might manifest as a result.

Some might contend that this proposition goes too far, even for conscious creation, that it's a wholly implausible scenario or amounts to little more than warm fuzzy rubbish. But think for a moment before you embrace that idea. I'm sure many who lived in the nineteenth century would have unhesitatingly scoffed at proposals for the transportation, medical, and information-processing technologies we now take for granted. Similarly, there are those who as recently as the 1980s would have asserted that the Cold War was something destined to drag on in perpetuity. At some point, however, giving up on old ways of seeing things—no matter how entrenched they are and no matter how officially sanctioned they may be—only makes sense.

★ ★ ★

In seeking a vision for how to change the world, one of the natural questions that arises is where to look for inspiration. Many metaphysical visionaries suggest in their writings and teachings that we look to ourselves first in initiating any kind of creative undertaking. Finding the value fulfillment that we need to bring forth the best of ourselves into the world is a process that generally begins at home, in the world of our own thoughts and beliefs. But if the answers there are elusive, then perhaps the next best place to look is to the arts, for they are a valuable source of ideas and encouragement, the very notions that we just might need to begin the process of changing the world.

The arts are a powerful stimulus to the imagination. The works of art that we ourselves create through the power of our beliefs could be vehicles that foreshadow the emergence of significant changes in the world, a fact science fiction fans know all too well, as evidenced, for example, by the prescience of *Star Trek* creator Gene Roddenberry. Many of the prototype technological gadgets that he envisioned for his pioneering television shows and movies have today manifested as elements of everyday life. Indeed, as Jane Roberts and Seth so aptly put it, "Men may react to future events by unconsciously translating them into art or motion pictures."[2] Roddenberry, for his part, did both.

I find the specific reference to motion pictures in the preceding quote particularly poignant, for, as I have attempted to show through this book, movies are an especially potent means for conveying meaningful ideas. Famed filmmaker Ingmar Bergman recognized this when he so thoughtfully noted, "No art passes our conscience in the way film does, [going] directly to our feelings, deep down into the dark rooms of our souls."[3] Once those flickering images find their way off the screen and into the heart of our consciousness, there's no telling what grand ideas they may spawn, brilliant conceptions whose manifestations break through from within and materialize resplendently into existence.

Radio, in its early days, was often referred to as "the theater of the mind," for it required its listeners to picture for themselves the actions that were being related to them through the spoken word alone. In many ways, radio was at that time merely the latest embodiment of the time-honored ritual of storytelling, a practice begun eons earlier through the tales told around the campfires of the ancients. Movies today continue that long-established tradition. We're fortunate to now have imagery to augment the narrative, providing even greater degrees of inspiration to our "multiplex of the mind," insights that we can use to shape the beliefs that shape our reality.

From that, then, it would appear that Muriel Rukeyser's observation that the Universe is made up of stories and not of atoms—the contention that led off this book—is correct after all. And, in the wake of such validation, I can only append that conclusion with the addition of the following:

Cut; print it.

# Endnotes

*Introduction* | *Coming Attractions*

1. Muriel Rukeyser, "The Speed of Darkness," part 9, lines 3–4 (1958).

2. An intriguing memoir of Jane Roberts can be found in *Speaking of Jane Roberts*, by Susan M. Watkins (Needham, MA: Moment Point Press, Inc., 2001). In addition, a movie about Roberts is in the works.

3. Ehryck F. Gilmore, *The Law of Attraction 101* (Chicago, IL: Eromlig Publishing, 2007), pp. 27–28.

4. Brent Marchant, "Seth and the Silver Screen—My 10 Favorite Films from a Sethian Perspective," *Reality Change* 11:2 (Seth Network International, Second Quarter 1997), pp. 10–18. *Reality Change* was a quarterly journal of Seth Network International, a now-dormant organization devoted to the discussion and dissemination of the works of Jane Roberts and Seth.

5. Oscar(s)® and Academy Award(s)® are registered trademarks of the Academy of Motion Picture Arts and Sciences.

6. Golden Globe(s)® is a registered trademark of the Hollywood Foreign Press Association.

7. Emmy(s)® is a registered trademark of the Academy of Television Arts & Sciences and the National Academy of Television Arts & Sciences.

*Chapter 1* | *It's Just What I Wanted—Sort of*

1. David Byrne and Brian Eno, "Once in a Lifetime" (Index Music/ Bleu Disque Music Co., Inc., 1980), recorded by the Talking Heads on *Remain in Light* (Sire Records Co., 1980).

2. Irini Rockwell, "Embodying Wisdom," *Parabola* 31:1 (Society for the Study of Myth and Tradition, Inc., Spring 2006): 70. Emphasis added.

3. Jane Roberts, *The Magical Approach* (San Rafael, CA: Amber-Allen Publishing/New World Library, 1995).

4. Sharon Franquemont, *You Already Know What to Do* (New York, NY: Tarcher/Putnam, 1999), p. 1. Emphasis in original.

5. I say "as portrayed in the film," because this movie, like all historical dramas, is a work of fiction based on actual people and events, not a strict historical narrative. (That may be particularly germane in this case; given the highly secretive nature of the Manhattan Project, the facts of this program might be elusive to come by, making depictions of what really happened conjectural at best.) Consequently, this film, like all others in the historical/biopic genre, takes dramatic license with the characters and their actions in various respects, and that should be borne in mind with any movies of this type presented in this book. The portrayal of the leads in this film is one such example. Though they reportedly had their differences, Groves and Oppenheimer were said to have had a relationship that was actually more cooperative than confrontative in nature. But for purposes of dramatics, this alternate take on the characters has been employed here. That portrayal, fictional though it may be, is what helps make this picture such a good candidate for illustrating some of the conscious creation concepts that are the focus of this chapter.

6. The film's assessments about Oak Ridge are likely exaggerations, at least for that time, but they do convey a clear sense about the path that the United States was about to embark upon militarily in years to come.

7. Bhagavad-Gita, 11:32. The exact wording of this verse is open to some debate. This particular wording, which is widely quoted in accounts about Oppenheimer's recollections of the bomb's first test blast, may have been his own paraphrasing of the passage, even though many have come to accept it as a literal translation. It closely parallels the wording used in other translations of the ancient text and appears to reflect the same general sentiment of the verse as used in those other translations. As with most scriptural documents, the wording used in different translations varies slightly from version to version, depending on word use at the time of translation and the individual translator's linguistic preferences (some versions substitute the word "shatterer" for "destroyer" in this passage, for example).

8. Bhagavad-Gita, 11:12. Because accounts conflict on which verse Oppenheimer actually thought of at the time of the test, neither is presented in the film.

9. Broadcast on CBS Radio, November 6, 1938.

10. When "Apocalypse Now" was released in 1979, it was one of the first major movies about Vietnam to hit the theaters. Two others, "Coming Home" and "The Deer Hunter," had preceded it in 1978, but they were unlike this film. The former was set almost entirely stateside and examined what happened to veterans upon their return; the latter focused primarily on a tight-knit group of friends from a small town and showed how the war changed them through sequences at home and abroad both before and after the war. "Apocalypse Now," by contrast, was the first major release focusing entirely on Vietnam from a war zone perspective. Given the unprecedented battlefront detail with which this war had been covered in the media at the time it was happening—the first-ever conflict to have news about it broadcast into living rooms all across America every night—there were many stories that arose from that coverage that came to characterize the Vietnam experience, indelibly etching themselves into the culture of the era and the mythos of the conflict. In making "Apocalypse Now," Coppola tried to encapsulate all of that experience into one finished package, hence the label "the ultimate Vietnam film."

11. *The Philadelphia Daily News*, 1977.

12. Lucius Annaeus Seneca (Seneca the Younger), *De Tranquillitate Animi*, § XVII, 10.

13. Bryan Ferry, "Dance Away" (E.G. Music, 1979), recorded by Roxy Music on *Manifesto* (Atco Records, 1979).

**Chapter 2** | *Perception Is Everything, Isn't It?*

1. Caroline Myss, *Energy Anatomy* (Boulder, CO: Sounds True, 1996).

2. Jane Roberts, *Adventures in Consciousness* (Needham, MA: Moment Point Press, Inc., 1999), p. 9.

3. Jane Roberts, *The Nature of Personal Reality* (San Rafael, CA: Amber-Allen Publishing/New World Library, 1994), p. 195 (Seth Session 641, February 19, 1973).

4. My apologies for any semblance of a soapbox approach here, but I believe this is important not just from the standpoint of current events but also from the vantage point of being conscientious, fully awake, fully participating conscious creators. To do less is to roll over and pull the covers over our heads. Still, I find it uncanny how many

of this movie's elements eerily parallel real-world events of recent years, particularly with regard to media coverage (or lack thereof) of the military and politics. (You're doing a heck of a job, guys.) In that sense, this film is a cautionary tale in the truest sense of the word, having presaged similar events years before they took place.

## Chapter 3 | Self-Actualized Cinema

1. Jean Houston, "Jump Time" (seminar, Chicago, IL, November 1999).

2. Matthew Gilbert, "Movies on a Mission," *Shift* 12 (Institute of Noetic Sciences, September–November 2006): 28–31.

3. Fritjof Capra, *The Tao of Physics* (Boston, MA: Shambhala Publications, Inc., 2000).

4. Nancy Ann Tappe, *Understanding Your Life Through Color* (Carlsbad, CA: Starling Publishers, 1982).

5. Lee Carroll and Jan Tober, *The Indigo Children* (Carlsbad, CA: Hay House, Inc., 1999), pp. 5, 236.

6. Pamela Oslie, *Life Colors* (Novato, CA: New World Library, 2000), pp. xiv, xv, xvii.

7. Lee Carroll and Jan Tober, *The Indigo Children* (Carlsbad, CA: Hay House, Inc., 1999), pp. 1–2.

8. Caroline Myss, *Energy Anatomy* (Boulder, CO: Sounds True, 1996).

9. Fritjof Capra, *The Tao of Physics* (Boston, MA: Shambhala Publications, Inc., 2000), p. 25.

## Chapter 4 | Igniting the Flame of Manifestation

1. George Bernard Shaw, *Maxims for Revolutionists: Reason* (1903).

2. www.saidwhat.co.uk/research/free_will_quotes.

3. Jane Roberts, *The Nature of Personal Reality* (San Rafael, CA: Amber-Allen Publishing/New World Library, 1994), p. 95 (Seth Session 625, November 1, 1972).

4. *Ibid.*, p. 401 (Seth Session 672, June 25, 1973). Emphasis in original.

5. *Ibid.*, p. 243 (Seth Session 648, March 14, 1973).

6. Pollock's nickname was bestowed upon him by *Time* magazine in 1956, though it's not used in the film.

7. For a more complete look specifically at the artist's paintings, see the following two documentaries: "Frida Kahlo" (1982) and "The Life and Times of Frida Kahlo" (2005).

**Chapter 5** | *Let's See What Happens When We Do This . . .*

1. Jane Roberts, *The Nature of Personal Reality* (San Rafael, CA: Amber-Allen Publishing/New World Library, 1994), p. 72 (Seth Session 621, October 16, 1972).
2. Gregg Braden, *The Lost Mode of Prayer* (Boulder, CO: Sounds True, 1999).
3. Jane Roberts, *The Nature of Personal Reality* (San Rafael, CA: Amber-Allen Publishing/New World Library, 1994), p. 276 (Seth Session 653, April 4, 1973). Emphasis in original.
4. Jane Roberts, *The Nature of the Psyche* (San Rafael, CA: Amber-Allen Publishing/New World Library, 1995), p. 190 (Seth Session 795, February 28, 1977).

**Chapter 6** | *Storming the Castle*

1. Jane Roberts, *The Nature of Personal Reality* (San Rafael, CA: Amber-Allen Publishing/New World Library, 1994), p. 159 (Seth Session 637, January 31, 1973). Emphasis added.
2. "Blade Runner" (1982).
3. President Franklin D. Roosevelt's first inaugural address, March 4, 1933.
4. Walt Kelly, *Pogo* comic strip (Manassas, VA: OGPI, Earth Day edition, 1971).
5. Marianne Williamson, *A Return to Love: Reflections on the Principles of* A Course in Miracles (New York, NY: HarperCollins, 1992), pp. 190–91.
6. Susan M. Watkins, *What a Coincidence!* (Needham, MA: Moment Point Press, 2005), p. 28. Emphasis in original.
7. *Ibid.*, p. 9.
8. Jane Roberts, *The Magical Approach* (San Rafael, CA: Amber-Allen Publishing/New World Library, 1995), p. 55 (Seth Session 5, August 20, 1980).

**Chapter 7** | *Road Trip!*

1. I do this, for example, whenever I attend metaphysics seminars. I consciously create journeys in which I *purposely* separate the experience of my everyday life from that of the conferences, allowing the teachings of the programs (and whatever personal insights I glean from them) to stand out in my mind more than they probably would have otherwise. I accomplish this in various ways, such as

attracting adventures to me on each end of my trips, making a point of only attending conferences that require some effort to travel to, generally going alone (even if I know others who will be present upon my arrival), and visiting locales that are unusual or off the beaten path.

2. "Over the Rainbow," written by Harold Arlen and E.Y. Harburg, has won many accolades besides its Academy Award. In 2001, for example, Judy Garland's movie rendition of this ever-hopeful composition topped the "Songs of the Century" list, a survey intended to identify the top 365 songs of the twentieth century, sponsored by the Recording Industry Association of America, the National Endowment for the Arts, Scholastic Inc., and AOL@School. It was also named the No. 1 entry on the American Film Institute's all-time Top 100 Songs list. Not bad for a song that was almost cut out of the film with which it has since become synonymous.

3. James Redfield, *The Secret of Shambhala* (New York, NY: Warner Books, 1999).

4. Olga Kharitidi, *Entering the Circle* (New York, NY: Harper-SanFrancisco, 1997).

5. Holy Bible, Luke 17:21.

6. The film's "Undiscovered Country" subtitle is a reference to a soliloquy from William Shakespeare's *Hamlet*, which is referenced repeatedly throughout the movie in both the dialogue and narrative. Ironically, Hamlet's allusions to the undiscovered country refer to death, a fate that befell legendary *Star Trek* creator Gene Roddenberry not long before this picture's release. The film's story line was also particularly poignant for die-hard *Trek* fans by filling a significant gap in the franchise's mythology. In the original TV series, the United Federation of Planets and the Klingon Empire were bitter enemies, but in the sequel TV series, *Star Trek: The Next Generation*, set eighty-five years in the future, the one-time foes had inexplicably become fast friends. That's where this picture comes in, providing the much needed missing back story. Interestingly, the parallels between this movie's story line and the end of the Cold War, which immediately preceded its release, are more than a little coincidental.

### Chapter 8 | Connecting the Dots

1. Albert Einstein, *Out of My Later Years* (1950), chapter 8, part 1.

2. The ten-episode series premiered on the BBC in 1978 and first aired in the United States on PBS in 1979. Two sequels, *Connections 2*

and *Connections 3*, were broadcast in 1994 and 1997, respectively, on TLC.

3. Jane Roberts, *The Nature of Personal Reality* (San Rafael, CA: Amber-Allen Publishing/New World Library, 1994), p. 95 (Seth Session 625, November 1, 1972).

4. Actually, the birthing of a widespread social movement from a simple idea is the subject of another film, Frank Capra's "Meet John Doe" (see the chapter 2 Bonus Features). The main difference between the movements in the two movies is that, in "Pay It Forward," it arises from a student's sincerity, while, in its predecessor, it grows unexpectedly from a newspaper's contrived publicity stunt. Both pictures show, however, that sometimes a good idea is a good idea, no matter how it arises, as long as the underlying intents supporting it are sound.

## Chapter 9 | *Exceeding Our Grasp*

1. http://www.famousquotes.com/show.php?_id=1041243.
2. http://www.famousquotes.com/show.php?_id=1003900.
3. Maureen Caudill, *Dreamland*, Internet radio interview, www.UnknownCountry.com, February 2007.
4. http://thinkexist.com/quotes/albert_einstein/.
5. Julia Cameron, *The Artist's Way* (New York, NY: Jeremy P. Tarcher/Putnam, 1992).
6. Natalie Goldberg, *Wild Mind* (New York, NY: Bantam Books, 1990).
7. Jane Roberts, *The Nature of Personal Reality* (San Rafael, CA: Amber-Allen Publishing/New World Library, 1994), p. 122 (Seth Session 631, December 18, 1972).
8. Jane Roberts, *The Magical Approach* (San Rafael, CA: Amber-Allen Publishing/New World Library, 1995), p. 89 (Seth Session 10, September 10, 1980).
9. Reconnective Healing® is an alternative healing technique developed by Dr. Eric Pearl that primarily involves working with the energy field immediately surrounding a patient's body rather than making direct contact with the body itself. I note it here partly because of its general similarity to such hands-on methods as reiki and massage therapy but also because of Pearl's fascination with the original film version of "Resurrection," which was a source of inspiration that contributed to his development of the technique, as noted in his book, *The Reconnection* (Carlsbad, CA: Hay House, Inc., 2001), pp. 36, 39–40. http://www.thereconnection.com.

10. Frederick S. Oliver (1866–1899) was perhaps the first to have channeled a work that was put into print. Through a process of automatic writing, he chronicled the teachings of an entity named Phylos, who claimed to have been incarnated on Earth during the time of Atlantis. This collaboration, which took place when Oliver was only eighteen, resulted in *A Dweller on Two Planets*, the first edition of which was released around the turn of the twentieth century (Borden Publishing, 1952).

11. Edgar Cayce (1877–1945), sometimes known as "the Sleeping Prophet of Virginia Beach," was world renowned for his ability to intuit information about others while in a trance state. He initially used his skills to focus on diagnosing the illnesses of those who couldn't be helped by conventional medicine, later expanding into such areas as reincarnation and prophecy. His explorations into altered states of consciousness, though somewhat controversial at the time, nevertheless led to the establishment of the Association for Research and Enlightenment, Inc.,® an organization devoted to continuing his work. http://www.edgarcayce.org.

12. Esther Hicks is the channeler of a group of spiritual teachers who go by the collective name Abraham. Their psychic collaboration has led to a number of books, co-authored by Hicks and her husband Jerry, such as *The Law of Attraction: The Basics of the Teachings of Abraham* (San Antonio, TX: Abraham-Hicks Publications, 2006). These works parallel and complement many of the teachings of Jane Roberts and Seth. http://www.abraham-hicks.com.

13. Sonaya Roman is the channeler of an entity named Orin. Their collaboration has led to a number of books, such as *Soul Love* (Tiburon, CA: H J Kramer Inc, 1997). As with the Abraham teachings, the Orin channelings parallel and complement many of the works of Jane Roberts and Seth. http://www.orindaben.com.

14. Jane Roberts, *Adventures in Consciousness* (Needham, MA: Moment Point Press, Inc., 1999).

## Chapter 10 | When One Reality Isn't Enough

1. Jane Roberts, *Seth, Dreams and Projections of Consciousness* (Manhasset, NY: New Awareness Network Inc., 1998), p. 214 (Seth Session 115, December 16, 1964).

2. Robert Moss, *Dream Gates* (Boulder, CO: Sounds True, 1997).

3. Jane Roberts, *Seth, Dreams and Projections of Consciousness* (Manhasset, NY: New Awareness Network Inc., 1998), p. 124 (Seth Session 19, January 17, 1964).

4. Chuang Tzu, *Zhuangzi*, Book XXIII, ¶ 7. Ursula K. Le Guin, author of the novel on which this film is based, used this quote as an epigraph at the start of one of its chapters. A paraphrased version of it is featured in the film and is imparted to George during a dream sequence with an extraterrestrial.

5. For the film's DVD release, the rights issue involving the Beatles song ("A Little Help from My Friends") was resolved by including a cover version of the piece.

## Chapter 11 | The Joy and Power of Creation

1. The wizard Balaam, Holy Bible, Numbers 23:23.

2. Dennis William Hauck, *The Emerald Tablet* (New York, NY: Penguin/Arkana, 1999), p. 283. Emphasis added.

3. Jane Roberts, *Dreams, "Evolution," and Value Fulfillment, Volume One* (San Rafael, CA: Amber-Allen Publishing, 1997); Jane Roberts, *Dreams, "Evolution," and Value Fulfillment, Volume Two* (San Rafael, CA: Amber-Allen Publishing, 1997).

4. *Ibid, Volume Two*, p. 316 (Seth Session 910, April 23, 1980).

5. Jane Roberts, *The Nature of Personal Reality* (San Rafael, CA: Amber-Allen Publishing/New World Library, 1994), pp. 26–27 (Seth Session 615, September 18, 1972).

6. *Ibid*, p. 295 (Seth Session 657, April 18, 1973).

7. *Ibid*, p. 296. Emphasis in original.

8. Jane Roberts, *Dreams, "Evolution," and Value Fulfillment, Volume Two* (San Rafael, CA: Amber-Allen Publishing, 1997), pp. 403–404 (Seth Session 922, October 13, 1980).

9. Jane Roberts, *The Nature of the Psyche* (San Rafael, CA: Amber-Allen Publishing, 1995), p. 220 (Seth Session 800, April 4, 1977). Emphasis in original. This quote, incidentally, served as the theme of the 2007 Colorado Seth Conference (http://ColoradoSethConference.com).

10. Thankfully, "It's a Wonderful Life" has since gone on to receive the recognition it richly deserves. It has earned numerous accolades in the years since its release, most notably the top ranking in the American Film Institute's "100 Years, 100 Cheers" salute to the most inspirational films of the previous century, presented in 2006.

11. Images of the sky are prevalent in and significant to this film, for they tie into its original German title, "Der Himmel über Berlin," which can be literally translated as either "The Sky over Berlin" or, more appropriately, "The Heaven over Berlin."

12. http://www.brainyquote.com/quotes/quotes/p/pierreteil60888.html.

13. In this film's sequel, "Star Trek III: The Search for Spock" (1984), this theme was materially reversed to be restated as "The needs of the one outweigh the needs of the many." Philosophical twists like this have been hallmarks of the *Star Trek* franchise since its inception. Such thoughtful elements have contributed significantly to its enduring popularity for over four decades.

14. This picture played a significant role in saving the day for the *Star Trek* franchise. After the original TV series was unceremoniously dumped by NBC in 1969 just three seasons into its self-proclaimed five-year mission, the franchise went on a ten-year hiatus. The original cast was then reunited in 1979 for a feature film, "Star Trek: The Motion Picture," an overlong, boring, talky affair that was often fittingly dubbed, "Star Trek: The Motionless Picture." The future of the franchise was thus riding on the success or failure of this second feature. Fortunately, it succeeded critically, artistically, and financially, giving an enthusiastic green light to a variety of future undertakings, including eight more feature films and four spin-off TV series.

## Epilogue | Inspiring the Multiplex of the Mind

1. Henry H. Saylor, "Make No Little Plans," *Journal of the American Institute of Architects* (March 1957), pp. 95–99.

2. Jane Roberts, *The Magical Approach* (San Rafael, CA: Amber-Allen Publishing/New World Library, 1995), p. 109 (Seth Session 13, September 24, 1980).

3. Ingmar Bergman, as quoted by John Berger in "Ev'ry Time We Say Goodbye," *Sight & Sound* (London: June 1991).

# Acknowledgments

## *Roll Credits!*

It is with profound thanks that I extend my sincere gratitude to those who have been so helpful in bringing this book into being:

To Lynda Dahl, Kat Newcomb, and the late Stan Ulkowski of Seth Network International, for graciously publishing the original magazine article that gave rise to this book.

To Susan M. Watkins, author of *What a Coincidence!*, and Mary Dillman, organizer of the "Seth Applied" conferences, for unwittingly providing the catalytic sparks that launched this project.

To my muse, Cathy Aldrich, for introducing me to the books of Jane Roberts and Seth. Who would have thought a passing comment could lead to so much!

To my many friends in the Chicago area and worldwide Seth communities, for their suggestions, film recommendations, and ongoing backing, particularly Cyndi Safstrom, Del Potos, Patt Timlin, Sue Seggeling, Mark Coman, Linda and Howard Kaufman, Steve Martin, Damon Ables, Dion Tillmon, Nancy Sciortino, Elena de la Peña, Jane Erie, and Nancy Walker.

To Lee Levin, for his astute legal guidance.

To Jill Norton Photography, for superb portrait work, and Kathryn Sky-Peck, for a beautiful cover design.

To Dodie Ownes, for her invaluable promotional assistance.

To my many friends and colleagues for their zealous encouragement and support, most notably Mike Dunghe, Linnaea Burkett, Karen Sanders, Patti Schuldenfrei, Gary Castine, John Chaffin, Laura Harrington, Susan McCormick, Lavelle Porter, Pervaiz Ladhani, Chuck Spady, Kevin Haynes, Barbara Blum, Rob Kruss, Tim Nelsen, Bubba Smith, Thom Juul, Mary Stainton, Geoffrey Scott, Walter Winston, Ronnie Kleber, Tommy Johns, John Mills, Jerry Adams, Carlos Barragan, Willy Gutierrez, Mostapa abd Sukor, Kevin Keys, Mike Evans Jr., Nick Palumbo, Kerry MacKenzie, Marla Hillery, Sue Zyrkowski, Laure West, Elena Lockhart, Kathy Germolec, and Yolanda Griffin.

And last, but by no means least, to everyone at Moment Point Press, and particularly to my publisher, Sue Ray, without whose vision, expertise, commitment, and confidence in me, none of this would have been possible.

I truly thank you all from the bottom of my heart.

# Index

## Actors, Directors, Movies, and Screenwriters

**Moment Point Press**
publisher of books that help us all
consciously create limitless lives
in a limitless world

*momentpoint.com*